Borderland Memories

In the 1980s, as China transitioned to the post-Mao era, a state-sponsored oral history project led to the publication of local, regional, and national histories. They took the form of written and transcribed personal testimonies of events that preceded the turmoil of both the Cultural Revolution and, in many cases, the Communist victory in 1949. Known as *wenshi ziliao*, these publications represent an intense process of historical memory production that has received little scholarly attention. Hitherto unexamined archival materials and oral histories reveal unresolved tensions in post–Cultural Revolution reconciliation and mobilization, informing negotiations between local elites and the state, and between Party and non-Party organizations. Taking the northeast Russia–Manchuria borderlands as a case study, Martin T. Fromm examines the creation of post-Mao identities, political mobilization, and knowledge production in China.

Martin T. Fromm is an assistant professor at Worcester State University. He is the editor of the academic journal *Currents in Teaching and Learning*.

T0381600

Cambridge Studies in the History of the People's Republic of China

Series Editors

Jeremy Brown, Jacob Eyferth, Daniel Leese, Michael Schoenhals

Cambridge Studies in the History of the People's Republic of China is a major series of ambitious works in the social, political, and cultural history of socialist China. Aided by a wealth of new sources, recent research pays close attention to regional differences, to perspectives from the social and geographical margins, and to the unintended consequences of Communist Party rule. Books in the series contribute to this historical reevaluation by presenting the most stimulating and rigorously researched works in the field to a broad audience. The series invites submissions from a variety of disciplines and approaches, based on written, material, or oral sources. Particularly welcome are those works that bridge the 1949 and 1978 divides, and those that seek to understand China in an international or global context.

Studies of the Weatherhead East Asian Institute, Columbia University

The Studies of the Weatherhead East Asian Institute of Columbia University were inaugurated in 1962 to bring to a wider public the results of significant new research on modern and contemporary East Asia.

A list of titles in this series can be found at the back of the book.

Borderland Memories

Searching for Historical Identity in Post-Mao China

Martin T. Fromm

Worcester State University

CAMBRIDGE
UNIVERSITY PRESS

CAMBRIDGE
UNIVERSITY PRESS

University Printing House, Cambridge CB2 8BS, United Kingdom

One Liberty Plaza, 20th Floor, New York, NY 10006, USA

477 Williamstown Road, Port Melbourne, VIC 3207, Australia

314-321, 3rd Floor, Plot 3, Splendor Forum, Jasola District Centre, New Delhi - 110025, India

103 Penang Road, #05-06/07, Visioncrest Commercial, Singapore 238467

Cambridge University Press is part of the University of Cambridge.

It furthers the University's mission by disseminating knowledge in the pursuit of education, learning and research at the highest international levels of excellence.

www.cambridge.org
Information on this title: www.cambridge.org/9781108469289
DOI: 10.1017/9781108571784

First published 2019
First paperback edition 2022

A catalogue record for this publication is available from the British Library

Library of Congress Cataloging in Publication data
Names: Fromm, Martin T., 1974– author.
Title: Borderland memories : searching for historical identity in post-Mao China / Martin T. Fromm.
Description: Cambridge ; New York, NY : Cambridge University Press, [2019] | Series: Cambridge studies in the history of the People's Republic of China | Includes bibliographical references and index.
Identifiers: LCCN 2018056574 | ISBN 9781108475921 (alk. paper)
Subjects: LCSH: China – History – 1976–2002 – Historiography. | China – History – 1976–2002 – Sources. | China – History – 1949–1976 – Historiography. | China – History – 1949–1976 – Sources. | Borderlands – China – Historiography. | Borderlands – Soviet Union – Historiography. | Nationalism and historiography – China. | Nationalism and collective memory – China.
Classification: LCC DS779.19 .F76 2019 | DDC 951.05/8072–dc23
LC record available at https://lccn.loc.gov/2018056574

ISBN 978-1-108-47592-1 Hardback
ISBN 978-1-108-46928-9 Paperback

This book is dedicated to my lovely wife, Minjin Fromm. I can't wait to see what's on the next page of our blessed life together.

Contents

Acknowledgments   *page* x

Introduction   1

1 Reconfiguring Cultural Production in the Post-Mao
   Transition   20

2 Borderland Ambiguities in Narratives of Modernization and
   Liberation   45

3 Relocating the Nation outside the Nation: Forging a
   Borderland-Centered Nationalist Discourse   75

4 The "Historical Science" of *Wenshi Ziliao*   110

5 Affective Community and Historical Rehabilitation:
   "Widely Making Friends" to Resecure Political Loyalty   154

6 Mobilizing a "Patriotic United Front"   200

7 Local, Regional, and National Dynamics of *Wenshi Ziliao*
   Production   223

   Conclusion   255

References   261
Index   280

Acknowledgments

I am deeply indebted to the mentorship, collaboration, friendship, and generosity of others without whom this book could not have come into fruition. The research for this book began during my years of graduate study at Columbia University, and I owe tremendous gratitude to my primary advisor, Eugenia Lean, who guided and supported me through the many challenging phases of this project with incredible wisdom and patience. With sagely mentorship, transformational discernment, and unwavering commitment, Professor Lean guided and saw me through numerous successive versions of the manuscript. In the process, she has not only played a pivotal role in the development of this book, but has also taught me in a profound way what it means to be a truly dedicated mentor.

Several other individuals also played important mentoring roles during the formative period of research. Adam McKeown, whose pioneering work in global history has helped to reshape the field, taught me to look beyond national boundaries and encouraged me to put borders, borderlands, and frontiers at the center of history. I also benefited from Joseph Tse-Hei Lee's brilliant ability to identify and articulate the core essence hidden in the tangled-up words of earlier drafts and his generous, compassionate commitment to building scholarly community. Dorothy Ko gave me inspiring advice and encouragement about forging ahead with oral history and memory at a pivotal transitional moment in my research. The original impetus for this study came from Madeleine Zelin, whom I burdened with many muddled drafts in the early stages of the project and who was gracious about giving her advisees the freedom to explore topics ranging far from her own.

The research in China that was crucial to the formation of this book relied on the expansive generosity and warm, family-like friendship of Dan Ben-Canaan. He and his wife, Yisha Liang, hosted me on multiple occasions in Harbin, which because of them became a second home for me. Dan Ben-Canaan has devoted the past fifteen years of his life to making Harbin a hospitable place for scholars from around the world, and I am indeed fortunate that he extended that gracious hospitality to

me. In addition to generously hosting me, he and Yisha Liang did everything within their power to make resources accessible to me, to connect
me to other scholars and stakeholders in my field, and to introduce me to
talented students in his program, including Chen Chen and Ivy Chi, who
provided important research assistance.

The archival research for this book would not have been possible without the courageous determination and fiery resolve of my intrepid colla-
borator Chen Chen. With a fierce commitment, assiduous diligence, and
unshakable boldness, she undertook the arduous labor of collecting
essential documents from county, city, and provincial-level archives in
Heilongjiang. There were times during our trip along China's northeast
border when I gave up hope of finding the valuable materials we were
pursuing, but it was Chen Chen who refused to give up and through her
perseverance found a way to access the sought-after documents and to
fulfill our research mission.

Several other individuals deserve special thanks for their encouragement and assistance in accessing resources in China. During my last
research trip for the book in the summer of 2015, Youping Wang went
to great lengths to make personal connections on my behalf with archive
personnel and to arrange interviews with prominent local historians and
members of the Heilongjiang branch of the People's Political
Consultative Conference. In the course of my interactions and conversations with Mr. Wang, I was moved by his love for and devotion to the
people, history, and culture of Heilongjiang Province. I also greatly
appreciate the kindness of Xiuming Wu and his colleagues at the Local
Historical Materials section of the Heilongjiang Provincial Library, who
created a friendly and relaxed research environment for me that summer.
During an earlier research trip, Xiaoping Ma at the Liaoning provincial
branch of the Chinese Academy of Social Sciences generously hosted me
and patiently assisted me with all aspects of my living and research
conditions, truly going out of her way and experiencing great inconve-
nience on my behalf. During the long, frigid winter, the warm friendship
of Rongquan Yu at the Liaoning Provincial Library made the library feel
like a second home and made my initial foray into the library's vast
collection of *wenshi ziliao* a delightful experience.

I have benefited at every turn from the critical insights and feedback of
colleagues and friends. During my Mellon Teaching Postdoctoral
Fellowship at Wheaton College (MA), John Bézis-Selfa and Gen Liang
provided me with wise mentorship. Professor Bézis-Selfa opened me up
to more sophisticated conceptual understandings of borderlands and
pushed me to pursue this theme more deeply. His commitment to cultivating and enriching all aspects of his junior colleagues' academic

experience, and his devotion to rejuvenating and renewing the social and cultural mission of academia in general and the historian as scholar-educator in particular, are an inspiration for me. I benefited immensely from Professor Liang's extraordinary dedication to academic rigor and excellence. His grounding of powerful concepts in examination of human interactions and networks taught me the importance of highlighting the detailed fabric of the human experience and set a high standard of research practices to which I have aspired. Fabio Lanza was exceptionally generous with his time and devoted extraordinary intellectual energy to providing critical insights and detailed feedback that have been transformative in the book's revisions and conceptual reframing. Beyond being personally indebted to him for the guidance that he gave me, I am also humbled by his passionate and courageous commitment to infusing social consciousness, moral integrity, and vibrant community into the scholarly enterprise. In my ongoing years at Worcester State University, I have cherished the rich and supportive collegial environment within and beyond my department. I owe particular gratitude to Tona Hangen, whose tireless dedication to cultivating and celebrating the gifts and talents of her colleagues and her embodiment of the scholar-educator ideals have given me continually renewed encouragement and hope through the tenure-track years of book writing and revisions.

I am appreciative of the community of scholars whose collaborative spirit gave me encouragement at all stages of the research and writing journey. Joseph Tse-Hei Lee, Lida Nedilsky, Siu-Keung Cheung, Lu Zhang, Victor Seow, and Mark Elliott organized stimulating symposia and conference panels. I am also grateful for the helpful feedback that James Flath, Thomas Looser, and HoFung Hung shared with me as discussants at various Association of Asian Studies annual conferences. It was a memorable joy collaborating with June Hee Kwon, Benno Weiner, Sandrine Catris, and Dasa Mortensen in putting together exciting panels.

The institutions and organizations that sponsored these scholarly venues for presenting and sharing my research include the Association of Asian Studies, the University of Virginia Jefferson Scholars Foundation, Hong Kong Shue Yan University, Harvard University, and the University of Antwerp.

Generous funding for this project came in the form of grants and fellowships from a number of institutional sources. These included a China and Inner Asia Council Small Grant Award funded by the Association of Asian Studies and the Chiang Ching-kuo Foundation; a Sasakawa Young Leaders Fellowship sponsored by Columbia University's Weatherhead East Asian Institute; the Whiting

Foundation's Whiting Dissertation Writing Fellowship; and a Fulbright IIE Fellowship for Dissertation Research with host institution support from the Chinese Academy of Social Sciences.

I am grateful for the anonymous reviewers' painstakingly thorough and constructive comments, and also for the expert and steady editorial hands through which the manuscript passed at every stage of the review and publication process. Eugenia Lean and Kenneth Ross Yelsey were steadfast in their belief in the manuscript and patiently guided the book through successive rounds of review, pushing and encouraging me to make the necessary revisions. The manuscript then advanced into the capable hands of Cambridge University Press Senior Commissioning Editor Lucy Rhymer, who oversaw with diligent care the final stages of the review process. Cambridge University Press Editorial Assistant Lisa Carter, Senior Content Manager Ian McIver, and Integra Project Manager Sunantha Ramamoorthy guided me expertly through each step of post-review production. I also thank Ami Naramor for her highly detailed and thorough attention to copyediting the manuscript.

I want to express my love and affection for my family, including my brother, Christian Fromm, whose courage and truth-seeking spirit I have always admired, and my mother, Sharon Fromm, who always supported my academic pursuits with unconditional love. I am thankful to Bradley Hanna for his kindness, generosity, and delightful conversations. My father-in-law Yong-Cheol Kim's story of overcoming hardship and fearlessly bringing his family to and building an academic career in America is a moving example for me, and my mother-in-law Hyung-Soon Kim's profound wisdom and loving-kindness are a blessing to everyone around her. They both welcomed me into their home and family with generous and open arms from the moment I met them. I write this in loving memory of my father, Hans Fromm, whose dedication to research and scholarship in the medical field was a deep source of inspiration for my own academic endeavors. Finally, I dedicate this book to my lovely wife, Minjin Fromm, whose boundless and tender love and friendship endow with deep meaning and joy every day of our blessed life together.

Introduction

In the early 1980s, in the town of Heihe on China's northeast border with the Soviet Union in what was formerly northern Manchuria (*Bei Man*), a teacher, editor, and local Party official named Liu Banghou unearthed documents containing transcribed interviews that had been hidden away for more than a decade during the political turmoil of the Cultural Revolution. Fifteen years earlier, the Heilongjiang provincial government had sent a group of researchers to the Heihe vicinity to seek out and interview elderly residents who had migrated to the area before 1900 from "China Proper" (mostly from Shandong and Hebei Provinces). Specifically, they targeted individuals whose destinations had included Blagoveshchensk, the city directly across the river from Heihe on the Russian side, and an area just to the east of Blagoveshchensk formerly known as the "Sixty-Four Villages East of the River" (*jiangdong liushisi tun*) that had long been a source of dispute between the two countries. Conducted in the midst of heightening border tensions between China and Russia, the investigation culminated in a published report released later that year that utilized selected excerpts from the testimonies to corroborate Chinese territorial claims to a contested area along the Amur River, and also to stir up anti-Russian nationalist sentiments through highlighting historical memories of previous Russian imperialist aggression.

The subsequent decade of the Cultural Revolution suspended this state-orchestrated oral history project, but in the early 1980s, the provincial branch of a Party-affiliated institution called the People's Political Consultative Conference (*Zhongguo renmin zhengzhi xieshang huiyi*), hereafter referred to as the PPCC, revived this investigation as part of a larger nationwide project of historical memory production known as the *wenshi ziliao*, translated literally as "cultural and historical materials." Once again, this time on a much broader scale, teams of interviewers consisting of a mix of Party cadres, researchers, and retired non-Party representatives from various sectors of society – including finance, commerce,

1

education, and culture – combed villages and towns throughout the region collecting memories from eyewitness survivors of various historical events that the Party deemed significant. In this context, Liu, who had participated in the earlier stage of interviews, revisited the testimonies within a radically changed regional and national context of cross-border commerce in which Chinese cities along the border reenvisioned themselves as "dragon wings" expanding northward. The bloodstained memories of borderland migration that resurfaced through Liu's work of compilation and editing bore new and conflicting meanings for a society undergoing market liberalization and political reconsolidation. Did memories of Chinese migration to this region in the early twentieth century tell a story of national humiliation to foreign aggression, of triumphal Chinese economic expansion, or of the formation of a culturally hybridized borderland society?

The competing meanings latent in memories of migration to China's northeast borderland were central to the larger post-Mao historical memory project of which Liu Banghou's work was a part. The production of history and historical memory, a vital legitimizing task of the nation-state, took on particular significance during China's post-Mao transition, in the wake of the Cultural Revolution's destruction of not only the institutional infrastructure but also the historical identity of the Party. For this reason, the post-Mao regime mobilized its subjects to produce historical artifacts in the form of written and orally transcribed memories; compiled, edited, and framed these narratives in a way that could be incorporated into new Party-approved local, regional, and national histories; and systematically published and circulated these *wenshi ziliao* accounts for various educational, ideological, cultural, and political purposes. To accomplish this, county, city, and provincial branches of the PPCC, which consisted of an eclectic amalgamation of organizations and individuals of non-Party as well as Party affiliation, mobilized teams of investigators to seek out, collect, and edit personal testimonies regarding firsthand experiences of events that had taken place before the Cultural Revolution, with particular attention to the pre-1949 period, that were deemed relevant for constructing new post-Mao identities.

The *wenshi ziliao* project did not take place under the auspices of institutions traditionally associated with historical work, such as the local gazetteer office, the Party history institutes, or academic research institutions. Instead, the PPCC oversaw this endeavor. At first sight, this was a strange choice. Founded as a multiparty organization attempting to bring the Chinese Communist Party (CCP) and the Guomindang (GMD) together as a coalition government, the PPCC had evolved after 1949 into an institution that mediated and brokered communications between officials and representatives from various political parties and social organizations who were inducted as PPCC members. To co-opt members of these organizations into supporting the new regime and to ensure that the Party kept close tabs on what was happening at the local level, county and provincial branches of the PPCC organized ideological study sessions, invited PPCC members to make policy recommendations, and mobilized teams to conduct inspections of economic and social conditions in surrounding villages and towns.[1]

In 1959, as chair of the national PPCC, Zhou Enlai called for the collection of firsthand "cultural and historical materials" pertaining to the pre-1949 period to be added to the list of the organization's tasks. Prompted by the traumatic aftermath of the Anti-Rightist Campaign against intellectuals and the ongoing disaster of the Great Leap Forward, the PPCC's involvement in the collection of historical memories from individuals outside the Party had distinct political objectives. These included bringing about healing and reconciliation through inviting people to tell their stories about travails they had endured in the past, constructing an authentic narrative based in firsthand testimonies that would remind people of the Party's liberatory role in history, and rebuilding a broader-based "united front" of support for the Party by including different perspectives in the official historical narrative.

Cut short by the Cultural Revolution, the *wenshi ziliao* found fertile ground for revival in the crisis of socialist legitimacy that faced the post-Mao transitional leadership in the late 1970s and early 1980s. Torn apart by the ideological battlefields of the preceding decade, PPCCs were gradually reconstituted, and by the early 1980s, all provincial and most county branches had formed offices and committees specially designated for *wenshi ziliao* work. In spite of scarce resources and low budgets, teams of local researchers, interviewers, editors, and writers set out to collect information and to interview surviving witnesses about events and people they deemed historically significant.

For decades, scholars have mined the published *wenshi ziliao* materials for their detailed firsthand accounts of and perspectives on social conditions in China during the first half of the twentieth century. This is the first study to use archival materials to examine systematically the processes, politics, and debates behind the mobilization, production, circulation, and publication of *wenshi ziliao*. Neither fabricated state propaganda nor authentic historical records, the *wenshi ziliao* constituted a highly nuanced and localized process where concepts and practices of

---

[1] The PPCC's roles and activities are explained in more depth in subsequent chapters, especially in Chapters 1 and 5.

seeking historical truths converged with post-Mao transitional political and cultural strategies and identities.

The northeast borderland, situated at once outside of, on the margin, and at the center of the Chinese nation, was of particular significance in the *wenshi ziliao* production and writing of history during the 1980s. As Manchu homeland separated from China proper; as the site of competing visions of multiethnic Russian colonialism, Japanese pan-Asian empire, and Qing frontier expansion; and as the intersecting zone of intense cross-border movements of different ethnic groups at the interstices of shifting colonial and national boundaries, the region's complicated past identities presented risky but fertile ground for experimenting with and reconciling different ideas about the nation, the Party, and the relationship between Communist revolution, nationalism, and market reform. The region's more recent formative place in the People's Republic of China's (PRC) military, political, and industrial development, and more specifically the PPCC's establishment as a mediating institution, made the project of producing historical narratives about this place especially meaningful for the Party. In the case of *wenshi ziliao* and the northeast borderland, therefore, the margin was indeed the center.

Political Mobilization through *Wenshi Ziliao*: The United Front and Mass Line Revisited

In the context of post-Mao China, scholars have directed attention to the flexible institutions and processes alternately described as "consultative authoritarianism," "guerrilla-style politics," and "decentralized authoritarianism," arguing that these characteristics have contributed to the political resilience of the Party through times of crisis and transition.[2] In both economic and cultural spheres, this flexibility favored local experimentation and initiative within certain prescribed limits, encouraging local actors to appropriate national Party agendas and ideology to champion the celebration and commemoration of local histories. The *wenshi ziliao* was in many respects a model case of this flexibility, experimentation, and resilience at work. The continuous tension between devolution of initiative to the local level and top-down integrative

---

[2] Baogang He and Stig Thøgersen, "Giving the People a Voice? Experiments with Consultative Authoritarian Institutions in China," *Journal of Contemporary China* 19.66 (2010): 675–692; Sebastian Heilmann and Elizabeth J. Perry, "Embracing Uncertainty: Guerrilla Policy Style and Adaptive Governance in China," in Heilmann and Perry, eds., *Mao's Invisible Hand: The Political Foundations of Adaptive Governance in China* (Cambridge, MA: Harvard University Press, 2011), 1–29, at 4, 7–8; Chenggang Xu, "The Fundamental Institutions of China's Reforms and Development," *Journal of Economic Literature* 49.4 (Dec. 2011): 1076–1151.

measures lent *wenshi ziliao* participants a structured space in which to reimagine who they were historically. Indeed, the integrative push from above reinforced regional particularity, as PPCC members collaborated across county and provincial lines to revive pre-1949 concepts of northern Manchurian and northeastern regional identity.

In doing so, they drew deeply on pre-Mao and Maoist approaches to mobilization and the construction of social and political "truth." The flexibility in the Party's oversight of cultural projects during the 1980s speaks to what Sebastian Heilmann and Elizabeth Perry have referred to as an underlying continuity in Maoist "guerrilla-style" politics marked by "a process of ceaseless change, tension management, continual experimentation, and ad-hoc adjustment" and by "decentralized initiative within the framework of centralized political authority."[3] In the 1940s and 1950s, key components of this flexible framework had been the United Front (*tongyi zhanxian*), the mass line (*qunzhong luxian*), and investigative research (*diaocha yanjiu*). Originating in the 1920s with the so-called First United Front brokered by the Soviet Union–backed Comintern between the CCP and the GMD, by the 1940s, the Communist Party had established a more comprehensive and coherent United Front strategy that involved reaching out to and making connections with a broad array of economic, social, and cultural elites such as business managers/entrepreneurs, intellectuals, scientists, and artists. This alliance with non-Party elites was an important instrument in the Communist Party's "war of position" to alienate and isolate the Nationalist regime.[4]

After 1949, the Party continued to use this United Front alliance as a mechanism for mobilizing broad-based support for socialist policies, carrying out what Lyman Van Slyke calls a "bridge function" connecting the Party to other social groups and interests, and providing the Party with administrative, managerial, and scientific expertise.[5] The PPCC, which established branches at the local and regional levels after 1955, was the institution that embodied and mobilized the United Front (and continues to do so to this day). This United Front strategy that the Party adopted was, to use Antonio Gramsci's terminology, a means by which the CCP could subsume narrow particularist interests within a broader

---

[3] Heilmann and Perry, "Embracing Uncertainty," 4, 7–8.

[4] Gerry Groot, *Managing Transitions: The Chinese Communist Party, United Front Work, Corporatism, and Hegemony* (New York, NY: Routledge, 2004): 5.

[5] Eddy U, "Dangerous Privilege: The United Front and the Rectification Campaign of the Early Mao Years," *China Journal*, no. 68 (July 2012): 35–39; Lyman Van Slyke, *Enemies and Friends: The United Front in Chinese Communist History* (Stanford, CA: Stanford University Press, 1967): 215, cited in Eddy U, "Dangerous Privilege," 35–39.

national ideology, "gain the consent of other classes and social forces through creating and maintaining a system of alliances by means of political and ideological struggle," and thereby achieve hegemonic rather than merely coercive control of society.[6] As recent scholarship has shown, the success of the United Front as a political strategy lay in "the rapid rise of a 'culture of accommodation' with CCP rule within elite populations because of their 'profound concerns about personal careers and family trajectories,'" "'hopes for political and material rewards,'" and the psychological comfort and confidence they derived from the Party's warm invitation to participate as a privileged group in the construction of a new socialist society.[7] The United Front was not implemented consistently across the Maoist period, with notable breakdowns being the 1955 "Campaign to Wipe Out Hidden Counterrevolutionaries," the 1957 Anti-Rightist Campaign, and the Cultural Revolution, and even in the most robust periods of alliance building, United Front elites were subjected to continual criticism, self-criticism, and reeducation.[8] Drawing on Jack Goldstone's ideas, Gerry Groot observes that "it is precisely at times of crisis, as states seek to maintain or regain the political initiative, or even collapse, that the role of ideology is most important in influencing action," which, he suggests, helps to explain the CCP's focus on and revival of United Front work at "critical junctures . . . between 1945 and winning power and after many subsequent crises."[9]

The *wenshi ziliao* emerged for the first time in 1959 as an attempt to revive the United Front alliance and reconciliation through historical memory production at a moment when the Party was facing its gravest political crisis yet in the aftermath of the Anti-Rightist Campaign and as the disastrous consequences of the Great Leap Forward were starting to become apparent. A much lengthier and more dramatic breakdown of the United Front followed shortly thereafter before the project made extensive headway. Following the Cultural Revolution, the resumption of the *wenshi ziliao* marked another critical juncture of ideological and political crisis when the Party once again turned to the United Front and the PPCC as an important mechanism and institution for achieving its aims

---

[6] Roger Simon, *Gramsci's Political Thought: An Introduction* (London: Lawrence and Wishart, 1982): 22, cited in Groot, *Managing Transitions*, 3–4.
[7] Jeremy Brown and Paul Pickowicz, "The Early Years of the People's Republic of China: An Introduction," in Brown and Pickowicz, eds., *Dilemmas of Victory: The Early Years of the People's Republic of China* (Cambridge, MA: Harvard University Press, 2007): 10, cited in Eddy U, "Dangerous Privilege," 35; Eddy U, "Dangerous Privilege," 34–35.
[8] Eddy U, "Dangerous Privilege," 41–46.
[9] Jack A. Goldstone, "Ideology, Cultural Frameworks, and the Process of Revolution," *Theory and Society* 20.4 (1991): 405–454, cited and discussed in Groot, *Managing Transitions*, 5.

of political reconciliation and reconsolidation for the purpose of unified Party-led development. Once again elites were drawn toward the regime with psychological and material benefits and privileges, which inspired at least some to participate in the project, and once again this privilege was mixed with criticism, self-criticism, and thought reform. Though not nearly as extreme as the reversals and breakdowns that had punctuated the previous decades, 1980s United Front practice as embodied in the *wenshi ziliao* continued to manifest inconsistencies, with organizers and editors regarding United Front elites with varying degrees of enthusiasm and suspicion. As with earlier periods, the Party's United Front strategy embedded in the *wenshi ziliao* was aimed at subsuming narrow local and class interests within an integrative national interest. The Party used nationalist discourse to frame its leadership in national terms that would make it hard for groups to legitimately go against the Party's ideology and leadership.

Alongside these important continuities, *wenshi ziliao* in the 1980s reflect a significant change from the Maoist period in the political dynamics of United Front work. Politically and ideologically fractured at the end of the Cultural Revolution, the Party turned to the *wenshi ziliao* with an urgent need to bring about healing and reconciliation through conceptualizing changes and evolutions across historical time. Whereas in the 1940s and 1950s the Party had incorporated United Front elites into its singular revolutionary agenda and teleology that drew a clear line between revolutionary "new society" and pre-revolutionary "old society," *wenshi ziliao* organizers in the 1980s drew up a more complicated mapping of the past that accommodated both change and continuity across the 1949 and Communist divides. This more complicated understanding of the past was conditioned not only by post–Cultural Revolution trauma and rupture but also by the Dengist leadership's effort to reconcile communism with market reforms. The relatively decentralized nature of *wenshi ziliao* implementation, informed by a broader set of post-Mao strategies to encourage local economic and cultural initiative and experimentation, added still more complexity and diversity to *wenshi ziliao* processes of reconstructing the past. In this context, *wenshi ziliao* became not simply an important mechanism for the Party's incorporation, absorption, and transformation of non-Party interests, but also created a more flexible and heterogeneous space for local non-Party elites to articulate their identities and interests more assertively and creatively, to redefine revolution and nationalism in borderland-centered terms, and to celebrate their past lives and achievements in the pre-1949 period.

Along with the United Front, the mass line was another aspect of Maoist social mobilization that became adapted with significant change and variation in post-Mao *wenshi ziliao* practice. As Aminda Smith discusses, the mass line involved a back-and-forth "from the people to the people" approach to "thought reform" and ideology construction that attempted to reconcile social heterogeneity with political unity, and democratic pluralism with Party control.[10] This central feature of Maoist social mobilization, though never explicitly mentioned in the 1980s, had a clear influence on *wenshi ziliao* organizers and editors who approached the production of historical materials as a process of seeking out raw materials "from the people" (in this case mostly "united front" local elites rather than the "masses"), "processing" them using the Party's ideological framework, and then delivering back "to the people" a final product that was reframed and "polished" according to this framework.

More broadly, the *wenshi ziliao* continued the long and fraught relationship between instrumental rationality and affective sentiment and emotion that had informed China's twentieth-century modernization project. Indeed, as Eugenia Lean has shown, rationality was never divorced from affective politics in the processes of modernization in China.[11] The integration of empirical investigation with political mobilization as central principles of *wenshi ziliao* drew in particular on a rich tradition of Mao-era investigative research methods. During the communist period, Mao's investigative research approach to knowledge production brought the fusion of rationality and affective sentiment to a new level that put locally based, empirical, fact-finding research in the service of mass social and political mobilization.

While these elements of the mass line and investigative research methods were clearly present in the *wenshi ziliao*, the deep post–Cultural Revolution political and ideological crisis of the early 1980s generated some peculiarities in how *wenshi ziliao* participants employed and adapted these Maoist principles. Unlike the victorious Party confident in its ability to transform and liberate society through unleashing class struggle in the 1950s, *wenshi ziliao* cadres in the 1980s were deeply ambivalent about social mobilization. Acutely aware of the traumatic chaos and divisions sown by Cultural Revolution excesses and the need to regain the trust of local economic and cultural elites, organizers and editors focused their energies on blurring class distinctions, fostering reconciliation and unity rather than unleashing class struggle, and cultivating a complex, multifaceted view of historical identities that obscured the moral truth boundaries between preliberation

[10] Aminda M. Smith, *Thought Reform and China's Dangerous Classes: Reeducation, Resistance, and the People* (Lanham, MD: Rowman and Littlefield, 2012); see especially chapter 3.
[11] Eugenia Lean, *Public Passions: The Trial of Shi Jianqiao and the Rise of Popular Sympathy in Republican China* (Berkeley and Los Angeles, CA: University of California Press, 2007).

(pre-1949) and postliberation. In a break from the *suku* (speaking bitterness) and *yiku sitian* (recalling bitterness and reflecting on sweetness) communist traditions of contrasting the bitterness of the "old society" with the "sweetness" of life under communism that Uradyn Bulag and others have documented, *wenshi ziliao* compilers produced a syncretic vision of history that reconciled tradition with revolution.[12]

While variation in unity had always been a central part of the mass line, in 1980s *wenshi ziliao*, the emphasis on reconciliation and the significant room for participants' localized expression and appropriation of different historical narratives and perspectives meant that, in practice, editors accommodated a great deal of ideological variation and heterogeneity. At the same time, the *wenshi ziliao* also constituted a much more constrained approach to the mobilization of sentiment that reveals the post-Mao transitional state's fundamental ambivalence about the relationship between political mobilization, personal and local historical memories, and Party control. Indicative of this ambivalence was the half-open, half-closed approach to producing and circulating historical memories that both drew upon and diverged from the Maoist investigative research method of integrating empirical investigation with social mobilization. *Wenshi ziliao* cadres' adoption of the hybrid *neibu/gongkai* (internal/open) circulation framework and their selective recruitment of local elites provided a controlled environment of political mobilization. Organizers of the project were both dedicated to and wary of the materials they produced, trying to maximize their social impact while limiting the potentially disruptive influence of their unintended and excess meanings.

Recreating the Historical Landscape of the Northeast Borderland

Here the context of the northeast borderland of Heilongjiang and what was formerly known as northern Manchuria played an important role. *Wenshi ziliao* approaches to reconstructing the historical landscape of "northern Manchuria" shed light on the significance of the northeast borderland in relation to the post-Mao party-state's nation-rebuilding project. Borderland scholars have envisioned the borderland as an open-ended process of movement, transgression, and circulation that resists, subverts, and displaces linear nation-state-centered historical narratives and reveals the limits of state control.[13] At the same time, state expansion

---

[12] Uradyn E. Bulag, "Can the Subalterns Not Speak? On the Regime of Oral History in Socialist China," *Inner Asia* 12.1 (2010): 95–111.

[13] See, for instance, Pekka Hämäläinen and Samuel Truett, "On Borderlands," *Journal of American History* 98.2 (Sept. 2011): 338–361.

did not necessarily diminish but rather shaped the emergence and persistence of these borderland dynamics.[14] The dynamic, fluid, and transgressive features of borderlands expose the limitations of state power, are an unintended consequence of state projects of expansion and consolidation, and highlight tensions in society that contribute to shaping state policies, laws, and governance approaches.[15]

The *wenshi ziliao* reveals a somewhat different relationship between borderland dynamics and nation-state building. In 1980s China, the post-Mao state sought out and actively recreated the messy historical landscape of the northeast borderland to make room for, experiment with, and meld together a new post-Mao identity. It provided a flexible space for asserting local and regional voices and identities while reaffirming party-state national integration. The Chinese state, through its sponsorship of *wenshi ziliao*, contributed to the production and recreation of the borderland as a discursive strategy for constructing a new post-Mao paradigm that would reconcile different ideologies and political and social interests. From this perspective, the borderland was "kept alive" in the historical imagination by the state as a strategy of political reconciliation, providing a flexible tableau that could reconcile nationalist United Front, international market liberalization, and socialist revolution components of the Party's reform agenda and legitimacy claims.

This multilayered Party initiative to revive borderland memories, even and especially those that distinguished it culturally from other parts of China, was in marked contrast with *wenshi ziliao* projects happening at the same time in the Uighur and Tibetan northwest and southwest borderlands of China. Unlike the clear and present dangers of ethnic separatism that complicated historical memory projects in the Uighur and Tibetan borderlands of the southwest and northwest, in the northeast borderland, *wenshi ziliao* organizers viewed the historical reimagining of the borderland in its messy and open-ended complexity as a discursive opportunity to bring about political, social, and cultural healing and reconciliation. Ethnicity in the northwest and southwest borderlands was a sensitive issue that threatened not just Party legitimacy but also Chinese control of the region and required careful obscuring of Chinese colonialist

---

[14] Charles Patterson Giersch, "Afterword: Why Kham? Why Borderlands? Coordinating New Research Programs for Asia," *Cross-Currents: East Asian History and Culture Review* (Honolulu, Hawaii), no. 19 (2016): 202–213; Eric Tagliacozzo, *Secret Trades, Porous Borders: Smuggling and States along a Southeast Asian Frontier, 1865–1915* (New Haven, CT: Yale University Press, reprint edition, 2009).

[15] Regarding the latter point especially, see Gloria Anzaldua, *Borderlands/La Frontera: The New Mestiza* (San Francisco, CA: Aunt Lute Books, 2012), 4th edition.

violence, particularly in reference to moments of rebellion like 1958.[16] In Heilongjiang there was no such dire threat. Manchu, Banner, and Han Chinese identities had long been mixed together in Manchuria during the Qing period, and the subsequent Chinese, Russian, and Japanese regimes further weakened the political potency of Manchuness.[17] Far less of a threat were the other indigenous ethnic minority groups like the Oroqens, Dagurs, and Solons who inhabited the Amur and Ussuri river basins. The only other significant threat to Chinese claims in the region, Russian and Japanese occupations, had ceased to exist by the end of the first half of the twentieth century. Moreover, whereas the Chinese state was implicated in colonial violence in the northwest and southwest borderlands, in the northeast, the Party could associate the borderland with foreign Russian and Japanese aggression and Chinese victimization and resistance.

In this context, complex and multifaceted accounts of the political, cultural, and ethnic history of the borderland were not only permissible, but encouraged as a way to generate a multilayered historical narrative that could accommodate and reconcile different facets of post-Mao reform ideology. *Wenshi ziliao* writers alternately celebrated and denigrated Russian influences, depending on the individual and local perspective, and both attitudes could be folded into broader narratives of anti-imperialism and internationally oriented market reform. Meanwhile, similar to the two-pronged state effort described by Thomas Mullaney to reclassify ethnic minorities in Yunnan as Chinese and as "Achang, Bai, Lisu, Wa, Yi, Zhuang, and so forth," in the northeast borderland, local *wenshi ziliao* committees had a two-pronged approach to representing ethnic minorities: one was to enclose them in the nationalist Chinese narrative of anti-Japanese resistance, and the other was to portray them as an exotic cultural other to highlight the region's distinctiveness from other parts of China and even other regions within the northeast.[18]

In this process, the memory-space of northern Manchuria was, to draw on Henri Lefebvre's vast corpus of ideas, a dynamic and shifting site of identity production in which local actors' memory work was in negotiation

[16] Benno Weiner, "State Commemoration of Tibetan Anti-State Resistance in Qinghai's *Wenshi Ziliao*: Rebellion in Three Frames." Paper presented at Association of Asian Studies Conference, Toronto, March 18, 2017; Sandrine Catris, "Searching for the Elusive Past: The Production of Historical Narratives in Post-Mao Xinjiang." Paper presented at Association of Asian Studies Conference, Toronto, March 18, 2017.

[17] Dan Shao, *Remote Homeland, Recovered Borderland: Manchus, Manchoukuo, and Manchuria, 1907–1985* (Honolulu, HI: University of Hawaii Press, 2011).

[18] Thomas Mullaney, *Coming to Terms with the Nation: Ethnic Classification in Modern China* (Berkeley and Los Angeles, CA: University of California Press, 2011): 11.

and contestation with the state's efforts to impose control.[19] In the case of the *wenshi ziliao*, the Chinese party-state was not a homogenizing force that found resistance in local everyday practice. Rather, the state actively contributed to mobilizing diverse memory practices in an effort to create a messy and complex space within which multiple ideologies, historical perspectives, and social interests could be accommodated, rearranged, and ultimately reconciled to each other.

Seeking Truths from Facts

Reconstructing the historical landscape of the northeast involved a continuous and diverse process of interpreting and reinterpreting the iconic slogan of "seeking truth from facts" (*shishi qiushi*). This concept at the core of post-Mao ideology had a long history in China and had evolved as a vehicle for reordering society in response to social and political change, in some cases traumatic change. During the Ming–Qing transition, intellectuals turned to seeking truth in the form of evidential learning (*kaozheng*) as a way ultimately to cope with and make sense of the fall of the Ming and the Manchu conquest. During the early twentieth century, responding to the crisis of colonial modernity and seeking to put China on equal footing with the Western powers, Chinese elites organized a social survey movement that reinterpreted seeking truth from facts as an empirical fact-collecting mission geared toward building a rational, efficient modern state.[20] Mao's subsequent investigative research approach to seeking truth from facts integrated empirical investigation and fact collecting with social and political mobilization.

During the post-Mao transition, seeking truth from facts was once again put in the service of state building and political mobilization through providing a rational intellectual framework integrating historical narrative, empirical research, and ideological production. As in the social survey movement, *wenshi ziliao* organizers' pursuit of a systematic scientific method was in part a strategy for proving to the international community, particularly overseas Chinese whose loyalties they were seeking to obtain, that China was capable of conforming to the logic of international law, diplomacy, and market transactions. At the same time, the dynamics of *wenshi ziliao* conceptualization and implementation reveal

[19] See Henri Lefebvre, *The Production of Space* (Oxford: Blackwell, 1991). Cited in Fabio Lanza, *Behind the Gate: Inventing Students in Beijing* (New York, NY: Columbia University Press, 2010): 6–7.

[20] Tong Lam, *A Passion for Facts: Social Surveys and the Construction of the Chinese Nation-State, 1900–1949* (Berkeley and Los Angeles, CA: University of California Press, 2011).

that theorists at the national level, provincial organizers, and local editors were continuously reinterpreting and reinventing the concept of seeking truth from facts to fit their agendas. Seeking truth provided a flexible tool with which actors at the local, regional, and national levels could intervene in and articulate their concerns about the project of reconciling diversity of local "truths" with integrative political consolidation.

Wenshi Ziliao Truths and Reconciliation

The *wenshi ziliao* "truth-seeking" project took place at a time when a new global wave of transitional justice and truth and reconciliation was beginning to emerge in societies undergoing democratic transition, first in Latin America and then extending to the postcommunist and postapartheid regimes in Eastern Europe and South Africa. Like these truth and reconciliation commissions, the *wenshi ziliao* pursued restorative (focusing on reconciliation and reintegration) rather than retributive justice and privileged personal testimonies as a basis for getting at historical truth and justifying compensation to victims of past mistreatment and persecution.[21] A significant difference in the *wenshi ziliao* approach was rooted in the political context in which the project was carried out. In contrast with the more clear-cut regime transition that took place in other contexts like that of South Africa, in China, the CCP was overseeing its own reinvention. As a result, the Party overseeing the reconciliation project and the perpetrator of the crimes that had made reconciliation necessary were in fact one and the same. In this situation, the victims (i.e., the local elites who were mobilized to participate in the *wenshi ziliao*) could not directly talk about their victim experience in the Cultural Revolution but could only refer to earlier events, and thus truth and reconciliation was approached in a way that elided the real source of victimization.

In addition, an important reason that the Party was able to play the role of overseeing truth and reconciliation in spite of its past perpetration of violence lies in the complex positioning of the Party during the Cultural Revolution. In addition to United Front elites, Party cadres themselves were victimized. Indeed, temporarily pushed aside from Party leadership after the Great Leap Forward debacle and increasingly viewing the Party as a new oppressive class hierarchy, Mao had as one of his objectives in initiating the Cultural Revolution to shake up and upend the Party

---

[21] While *wenshi ziliao* organizers and editors did not make explicit reference to Latin America or South Africa, a comparative consideration of these international trends and contexts sheds light on the broader conceptual implications and significance of post-Mao approaches to truth, reconciliation, and restorative justice.

apparatus. As a result, even within the Party itself the lines between Enemy and People and between perpetrator and victim were obscured. In this chaotic context, it was generally impossible and politically inexpedient to draw a clear distinction between victim and perpetrator. As a result, while truth commissions such as South Africa's Truth and Reconciliation Commission drew a clear line between perpetrator and victim, *wenshi ziliao* editors' approach to truth and reconciliation was to blur these boundaries and to characterize people and historical events in terms of their multiple and complex dimensions.

In this context of regime transition under one Party's continuous control, *wenshi ziliao* editors integrated what Gil Eyal has referred to as processes of individuation and embeddedness.[22] Driven by the entangled imperatives of continuity with and departure from the Maoist period, the Party had an ambivalent mandate to mobilize the release of different perspectives (individuation) while trying to contain, control, and re-embed these narratives within an integrative national framework. Given that discussion of the Cultural Revolution and criticism of the CCP were off limits, it is reasonable to argue that the extent of individuation was quite limited. Nevertheless, individuation was an integral part of the *wenshi ziliao*'s healing process that was seen as necessary to regain the trust and loyalty of local elites. This dimension of *wenshi ziliao* also informed editors' ambivalence about individual voice and personal narrative and subjectivity as authentic expressions of the past. Leaders of the project emphasized the critical importance of firsthand personal accounts, yet in practice and theory, they also saw it as imperative to reframe, re-embed, and even challenge as ideologically inappropriate the personal narratives they encountered.

The *wenshi ziliao* approach to healing and reconciliation is also worth examining in the context of the relationship between the party-state and local elites and intellectuals during the PRC period, as well as in relation to other post-Mao approaches to transitional justice. Concerning the former, the Party had regarded local elites and intellectuals with ambivalence and mistrust during the Maoist years. United Front accommodation of this group as potential allies to be embraced by the Party – as in the Hundred Flowers Movement – alternated with Anti-Rightist Campaigns beginning with the Yenan Rectification Campaign that subjected them to physical labor and reeducation. In spite of the policy of rehabilitating members of this group after the Cultural Revolution, the *wenshi ziliao* nevertheless shared with the Maoist regime an ambivalent attitude toward

---

[22] Gil Eyal, "Identity and Trauma: Two Forms of the Will to Memory," *History & Memory* 16.1 (2004): 5–36.

local elites. While using redemptive historical accounts to reach out to these individuals, seeking to win their loyalty and support, *wenshi ziliao* organizers kept them in suspense about their acceptance by the Party and demanded their show of loyalty through acts of physical endurance and suffering in the process of collecting materials for the project. From this perspective, the marked shift that Alexander Day observes in discourses on the peasant, which he describes as a shift toward a conservative view of the peasant that fit in with market reform priorities, did not quite happen in regard to local elites, at least not in the context of the *wenshi ziliao*.[23] Instead, overseers of the project dealt with members of this group in a way that integrated tactics of coercive reeducation and conciliatory embrace.

The *wenshi ziliao* was not the only truth and healing project or state-sponsored approach to transitional justice undertaken during the post-Mao transition. From the outset, the most visible spectacle of transitional justice was the trial of the Gang of Four. The *wenshi ziliao* constituted a markedly different approach to transitional justice than that employed in the trial.[24] Unlike the trial's focus on retribution, its clear delineation of the perpetrators and their crimes, and the public visibility of the trial as a national spectacle, *wenshi ziliao* organizers pursued a restorative approach to justice that highlighted multifaceted complexity rather than clear lines of innocence and guilt. Fearful of exposing the Party's involvement in past crimes of political persecution, PPCC officials oversaw a project that was at once much more expansive and far-reaching in scope than the trial and at the same time much more ambivalently handled and restricted in regard to public visibility and access.

Meanwhile, in contrast with the more spontaneous outpouring of post-trauma expression in the so-called scar literature and other post-trauma memoirs and literature, the *wenshi ziliao* avoided any direct reference to the Cultural Revolution or other Maoist persecutions. The *wenshi ziliao* project dealt with the Cultural Revolution and the scars of the "lost generation" indirectly by attempting to salvage the "rubble" of history in the wake of the physical and epistemic violence of the Maoist campaigns. But rather than reveal the catastrophic realities of this violence in a dangerous flash of repressed memories, to use Walter Benjamin's imagery, *wenshi ziliao* organizers elided these realities and used the salvaging

---

[23] Alexander F. Day, *The Peasant in Postsocialist China: History, Politics, and Capitalism* (Cambridge: Cambridge University Press, 2013).

[24] For details on the trial, see Alexander C. Cook, *The Cultural Revolution on Trial: Mao and the Gang of Four* (Studies of the Weatherhead East Asian Institute, Columbia University) (Cambridge: Cambridge University Press, 2016).

of a more open-ended and complex history of the borderland as a space for negotiating truth and reconciliation.[25]

Sources

This study is the first to look at the policy discussions, interviewing and mobilization strategies, editorial processes, and circulation practices that were behind the production and publication of *wenshi ziliao*. The following chapters employ analysis of primary sources that can be classified into three categories: first, official PPCC and *wenshi ziliao* committee reports, correspondences, and transcribed speeches obtained from county, city, and provincial archives; second, retrospective personal reflections by former *wenshi ziliao* participants regarding their role as editors and interviewers in the 1980s; and third, the published *wenshi ziliao* accounts themselves.

The official reports, correspondences, and speeches, which comprise the core composition of my source materials, provide a lens onto the internal agendas, motivations, and tensions that informed the decisions and actions of local and regional organizers, editors, and interviewers in the process of producing *wenshi ziliao*. These documents are revealing of the complex relationships between participants at different levels of the PPCC organization, the subtle discursive strategies they used to appropriate the project in different ways, and their varied perspectives on the connection between political ideology and historical truth.

These internal documents were obtained from the provincial-level archives of Heilongjiang and the city-level archives of Harbin, Fujin, Tongjiang, Fuyuan, and Raohe. These archives, selected in part for their geographical and historical significance and in part for the availability of materials, have certain characteristics that have informed the issues discussed in these chapters. The histories of Fujin as a key juncture of commerce and migration along the Songhua River, Tongjiang and Raohe as areas of Hezhe settlement where the indigenous group was of notable interest to *wenshi ziliao* cadres, Fuyuan and Raohe as direct points along the Russian border, Harbin as the Russian colonized center of "northern Manchuria," along with the broader regional concerns at the provincial level, present a cross-range of northeast borderland contexts and regionalities as they shaped the *wenshi ziliao* project.

Wenshi ziliao participants' later personal reflections on these processes comprise the second category of sources used in this study. Given the

---

[25] Walter Benjamin, "Theses on the Philosophy of History," in Hannah Arendt, ed. Harry Zohn, trans. *Illuminations* (New York, NY: Schocken, 1969).

potential complications that come with evaluating accounts produced in a later political context, I have approached my analysis of these personal recollections with critical scrutiny and consideration of discrepancies between these and the earlier official documents. For the most part, however, my findings indicate that the evidence and views expressed in the retrospective accounts are consistent with and corroborate those articulated in the contemporary official sources.

As for the third category of sources, the published *wenshi ziliao* accounts constitute the actual final product of the collecting, interviewing, and editing stages of production. While the internal reports and personal reflections indicate the expressed intentions, beliefs, and ideologies of the *wenshi ziliao* participants, the published articles comprise what they ultimately produced and approved for publication and distribution. A close look at the contents and structure of these accounts sheds light on the subtle ways in which local participants used the personal life narrative format of the *wenshi ziliao* to appropriate, integrate, and subvert official party ideologies.

Scope and Limitations

Using the lens of historical memory production in the northeast borderland during the 1980s, this study examines the post-Mao transition as it unfolded through local, regional, and national processes of political reintegration, reconciliation, and mobilization. Reflecting on the interlayered individual and institutional strategies of recruiting and interviewing informants, collecting and editing historical "truths," and circulating materials within and beyond Party channels, this book explores how *wenshi ziliao* participants innovatively mediated between Party and borderland-centered projects of producing the past.

The geographic focus of this study is the northeast borderland region of Heilongjiang Province located within what was formerly known as northern Manchuria during the period of Russian and Japanese spheres of influence. It does not include the eastern and southern parts of Manchuria in Jilin and Liaoning Provinces, and therefore the analysis that follows cannot be generalized for Manchuria or the Northeast (*Dongbei*) or the "Three Northeast Provinces" (*Dongbei sansheng*) as a whole. For the sake of brevity, I at times use the term "Northeast" to refer specifically to the northeast borderland area under examination here. Moreover, multiple layers of regionality appear in the pages that follow, whether they be centered locally on the originally Russian-built city of Harbin, the river commercial city of Fujin, and the border towns of Fuyuan, Raohe, and Heihe, or more broadly on the northeast borderland,

Heilongjiang Province, and the three provinces of the Northeast as regional identifiers. *Wenshi ziliao* participants were continuously engaging with these multiple levels of regionality, which could therefore only be understood in relation to each other.

Within this geographic scope, the *wenshi ziliao* officials, organizers, and editors who appear in these chapters conceive of the region's history through certain ethnic lenses. The main protagonist of history, as they present it, is Han Chinese, and the main antagonist is Japanese imperialism. Russians appear on the scene in an ambiguous way in narratives of anticolonial resistance, revolutionary liberation, exoticized nostalgia, and economic modernization. The indigenous populations of the northeast borderland, in particular the Hezhe, make a more marginal appearance in editors' efforts to reconcile borderland and Party-centered discourses of ethnic particularity and United Front nationalism. Largely omitted from these *wenshi ziliao* discussions are other ethnic groups, in particular Manchus and Koreans, who played a major role in Manchuria's history. This can perhaps partly be explained by geography, with concentrations of Manchu and Korean populations in the southern and eastern regions of Manchuria, respectively. But there likely is a political factor involved in this omission, namely the construction of a Han Chinese-centered narrative of the northeast borderland's history. Whether one or both of these factors are at play here, there is much more to be explored in regard to these ethnic dimensions, particularly in the southern and eastern parts of Manchuria, than is possible within the scope of this study.

Chapter 1 situates the *wenshi ziliao* more broadly within the context of post-Mao cultural production in the 1980s. Chapters 2 and 3 examine more closely how *wenshi ziliao* informants, writers, and editors creatively navigated, appropriated, and reconciled tensions in the party-state's socialist, market reform, and nationalist discourses through engaging with and reinterpreting the historical landscape of the northeast borderland. Rethinking the iconic slogan of "seeking truth from facts" was a key component of these endeavors, as Chapter 4 details. In addition to truth seeking, Chapter 5 discusses how *wenshi ziliao* organizers invoked the rhetoric of affective community to bring about political healing and to reintegrate alienated scientists, intellectuals, and entrepreneurs. This concern about binding non-Party members to the Party apparatus informed the relationship between *wenshi ziliao* production and social mobilization, an issue discussed in Chapter 6. As Chapter 7 shows, *wenshi ziliao* also involved a systematic mobilization of state agencies, social organizations, and village collectives in the collection and writing of historical materials. The process of reconstructing the past went hand in hand with the reintegration of local political, social, and economic structures, demanding that they both cooperate efficiently and specialize in certain areas that together would constitute a unified system.

In this book's closing remarks, the Conclusion discusses the longer-term implications and significance of this project in light of recent developments in contemporary China. Given the trends toward nationalism and neoliberal authoritarianism since the 1980s, what legacies and lessons might the *wenshi ziliao* approach to reconciliation and accommodation have to offer China's present and future?

1 Reconfiguring Cultural Production in the Post-Mao Transition

Experiments in Mobilization and Consolidation

In the aftermath of the Cultural Revolution, the successors to Mao were faced with a party-state apparatus in disarray, economic collapse, and an invalidated ideology. Disavowing the ideological excesses associated with the Gang of Four, the new leadership under Deng approached the challenges of the new era by pursuing a two-pronged path of economic liberalization and political consolidation. To restore administrative cohesion and rational efficiency, policy makers attempted to professionalize the bureaucracy by emphasizing education and expertise rather than ideology as the criteria for selection and promotion to government positions. As a result of a general administrative reform in 1982, by the mid-1980s the average age of leading cadres in the State Council went down by five years to 56.6, and the percentage of State Council department heads with a university education went up by 27.5% to 71%.[1] The Party exercised control over this process through requiring the approval of Party committees at every level; placing management of the selection process in the Party's organization, United Front, and propaganda departments; and inserting small Party core groups into consultative organizations such as the PPCC and the People's Congress. In addition, while ideology officially took a back seat, the Party leadership envisioned cadres who would be "revolutionary, younger, specialized, and more highly educated." Defined in terms of the "four basic principles" of "adherence to Marxist principles, communist virtues, [the] socialist line, and Party leadership," "revolutionary integrity" continued to be an important criterion for entry into official organizations.[2]

While advocating for rational and objective procedures of personnel recruitment, Party leaders continued to seek ways to mobilize various social groups to support and demonstrate loyalty to the Party. At times

[1] John B. Burns, "Civil Service Reform in Contemporary China," *Australian Journal of Chinese Affairs*, no. 18 (July 1987): 48.
[2] Ibid., 62–63.

these mobilization strategies were highly visible, such as in the case of the "Democracy Wall" street demonstrations in 1978–1979. These instances of what Elizabeth Perry calls "controlled mobilization" frequently exceeded the limits prescribed by the Party and required "demobilization" measures that involved violent suppression.[3] This pattern of mobilization and demobilization was not new to the post-Mao regime. Since at least the early 1940s, Mao had periodically invited individuals and organizations outside the Party to participate in the political process and even to criticize Party policies in an attempt to expand mass support, defeat opposing factions, and bypass the bureaucracy.[4] Given this history, the early post-Mao regime had clearly not resolved the dilemma of balancing extra-Party participation and mobilization with exclusive Party control.

But these sporadic campaigns were not the only way that the Party sought expanded social participation and initiative. As described earlier, the cultivation of United Front alliances with non-Party economic, political, and cultural elites had been a key strategy for securing the support of individuals with extensive social connections and influence, expand Party control of society without relying on coercion, and mobilize these individuals' expertise and social capital for achieving the goals of socialist development. After a series of breakdowns and revivals in the 1950s and 1960s, the Party went about the task of rebuilding the United Front in the early 1980s on a more expansive, flexible, and accommodating scale as a way to reconcile political fractures and social alienation at the end of the Cultural Revolution and to reestablish Party legitimacy and hegemonic control at the local, regional, and national levels.

Adopting what Heilmann and Perry refer to as a "guerrilla style of politics" inherited from revolutionary and early PRC days, the post-Mao leadership regarded "policy making as a process of ceaseless change, tension management, continual experimentation, and ad-hoc adjustment."[5] Chen Yun's flexible principle of "feeling the stones while crossing the river," which Deng Xiaoping adopted, was grounded in a political process of integrating decentralized initiative with centralized political authority. Politically, "input institutions" like "letters-and-visits departments, people's congresses, administrative litigation, [and] mass media" fostered an environment of "'accountability,' 'transparency,' and 'popular participation' at the local level" that made the Party appear more

---

[3] Elizabeth Perry, "Studying Chinese Politics: Farewell to Revolution?" *China Journal*, no. 57 (Jan. 2007): 1–22.

[4] Gregor Benton, "Dissent and the Chinese Communists before and since the Post-Mao Reforms" (Special Issue *Dissent before and since Post-Mao Reforms*), *International Journal of China Studies* 1.2 (October 2010): 311–329.

[5] Heilmann and Perry, "Embracing Uncertainty," 4.

in tune with local conditions and social needs.[6] Economically, this system of "regionally decentralized authoritarianism," as Chenggang Xu describes it, made room for regional experimentation with market reforms in an incremental, case-by-case manner under central Party guidance.[7] The policy of supporting localized innovation at "experimental points," disseminating "model experiences" to other regions, and then incorporating these successful local initiatives into national policy served as an effective mechanism for mobilizing broad-based innovation at the local level while preserving the central Party's ultimate policy-making authority.[8] Further contributing to this flexible mode of governance were informal practices by individuals and social groups who capitalized on political ambiguities to enact changes in subtle ways without coming into conflict with rigid institutional and ideological requirements. As Kellee Tsai notes, local actors like private entrepreneurs used "coping strategies" such as registering their businesses as collectively owned to secure the Party's legitimation of "red capitalists," paving the way to more formalized reforms and the inclusion of this group as Party members.[9]

Ideological Malleability and Multiplicity

This malleable style of governance also informed the development of a post-Mao ideology. With Maoist communism discredited by the Cultural Revolution, the new Party leadership encouraged a more open and critical evaluation of Chinese culture and institutions. While conservative reaction to market reforms sporadically took center stage at moments like the Anti-Spiritual Pollution Campaign in 1983, liberal reformers with backing from Deng generally held the commanding position in shaping policy and ideology. Nevertheless, the ambiguities in the official discourse of socialist "material and spiritual civilization" enabled Deng and the reformist leadership to reconcile the Party's socialist identity with market liberalization. The two concepts of material civilization and spiritual civilization both made room for multiple meanings and interpretations that could accommodate different points of view and agendas along the entire political spectrum. Retaining and reappropriating elements of the Maoist lexicon in slogans like "five stresses, four goods

---

[6] Ibid.
[7] Chenggang Xu, "The Fundamental Institutions of China's Reforms and Development"; C. X. George Wei, "Mao's Legacy Revisited: Its Lasting Impact on China and Post-Mao Era Reform," *Asian Politics & Policy* 3.1 (Jan. 2011): 3–27.
[8] Sebastian Heilmann, "From Local Experiments to National Policy: The Origins of China's Distinctive Policy Process," *China Journal*, no. 59 (Jan. 2008): 1–30.
[9] Kellee Tsai, "Adaptive Informal Institutions and Endogenous Institutional Change in China," *World Politics* 59.1 (Oct. 2006): 116–141.

and three loves," "study Lei Feng," and "service to the people," Deng used the concept of "material civilization" to articulate market reforms in socialist terms. Similarly, "spiritual civilization" could encompass a wide range of meanings including socialist class determinism, traditional morality, patriotic duty, and Western-style modernity.[10]

While debates ensued about how to define these concepts, such as in the 1982 "Zhao Yiya Incident" dispute over the relative importance of "culture" and "class," this multivalent ambiguity allowed for a broad inclusiveness of political and social voices without undermining the basic tenets and legitimacy of the post-Mao reform agenda. The Party incorporated the spiritual civilization idea into the revised PRC constitution of 1982 as a "duty of the state" in Article Four and as "love of the motherland, of the people, of labor, of science, and of socialism" in Article Twenty-Four, and the Party disseminated the discourse at the provincial and local levels through the media, schools, work units, and Party and state organs.[11] Researchers in state-run academic institutions developed intellectual frameworks for conceptualizing these ideological principles at a more fundamental and universal human level. Representative of these philosophical innovations was the theory of "subjective content (zhuguan cengmian), objective structure (keguan jiegou) and the historical process of subject-object unification" proposed by Li Zehou, a senior researcher at the philosophy institute of the Chinese Academy of Social Sciences. His attempt to reconcile moral and spiritual subjectivity with objective material and social structure by arguing that they were interrelated processes formed the philosophical basis and justification for the "two civilizations" discourse.[12] Like the state's ideology, this intellectual discourse wove together competing visions of society and the role of the individual vis-à-vis the state that accommodated diverse interpretations and perspectives.

"Correctly Guide Public Opinion": Localization and Diversification of State-Sponsored Cultural Production

These characteristics of flexibility, ambiguity, and multiplicity factored into the processes of state-sponsored cultural production at the local, regional, and national levels. Alongside their efforts to construct and disseminate a politically accommodating ideology, Party leaders attempted to heal the

[10] Nicholas Dynon, "'Four Civilizations' and the Evolution of Post-Mao Socialist Ideology," *China Journal*, no. 60 (July 2008): 83–109.
[11] Ibid.
[12] Lin Min, "The Search for Modernity: Chinese Intellectual Discourse and Society, 1978–88 – The Case of Li Zehou," *China Quarterly*, no. 132 (Dec. 1992): 969–998.

cultural scars inflicted by the Cultural Revolution through the encouragement of local cultural and historical restoration initiatives. Particularly in
borderland regions where history, culture, and ethnicity were politically
sensitive issues, the Party sought to rekindle support from marginalized
groups by lending implicit approval to projects aimed at rebuilding local
identities and managed by local cadres with close ties to the communities
they represented.[13] These projects, largely financed at the grassroots level,
provided a mechanism for the state to sponsor healing and reconciliation
processes at the ground level with minimal investment of central funds and
political will. Similar economic and political motivations drove the restructuring and localized proliferation of the media, including newspapers,
magazines, radio stations, and TV stations, that was intended to reinvigo-
rate the central Party's image and message. Reorganized into a four-tier
structure of county, prefectural, provincial, and national levels, newspapers
multiplied at the rate of one new title every one and a half days while the
number of TV stations shot up, especially at the county level, from 47 in
1982 to 366 in 1987.[14]

Tying the output of news and entertainment to regional conditions and
market demand, Party leaders attempted to transmit their social and
political views in a diversified, locally attuned manner that would appear
more authentic and be more compelling to viewers. The functions of
these media outlets also diversified. As Zhang Xiaoling observes, "[the
media's] primary function ... shifted radically away from serving merely
politics to a combination of promoting a market economy, public relations for the Party, information and knowledge sharing, and making
commercial profits. Another equally important new role taken up by the
media was to act as the channels through which the party-state reinvented
and reconnected itself with the people."[15] Throughout the decade tensions emerged between central Party control of the message and localized
diversity and popular appeal, as manifested in the political controversies
surrounding programming such as the TV documentary *Heshang* that
exposed deep ideological rifts within the Party.[16] While central leaders
viewed local media outlets as channels for disseminating Party policy and
ideology so that the Party could "correctly guide public opinion," local

[13] Hildegard Diemberger, "Life Histories of Forgotten Heroes? Transgression of
Boundaries and the Reconstruction of Tibet in the Post-Mao Era." *Inner Asia* 12.1
(2010): 113–125.
[14] Zhang Xiaoling, *The Transformation of Political Communication in China: From Propaganda
to Hegemony* (Series on Contemporary China, vol. 29) (Singapore: World Scientific
Publishing Company, 2011), 39–42.
[15] Ibid., 42–43.
[16] Shu-Yun Ma, "The Role of Power Struggle and Economic Changes in the 'Heshang
Phenomenon' in China," *Modern Asian Studies* 30.1 (Feb. 1996): 29–50.

media practices increasingly produced their own content and programs that were profitable and appealed to the concerns and desires of local audiences.[17]

The localization and diversification of cultural production was a tension-laden process: the party-state sought to elicit the enthusiastic support and participation of social groups outside the Party while risking the marginalization of the Party from the narratives that were produced. In regard to other research-based endeavors, policy makers similarly struggled with finding the right balance between innovative experimentation and political control. This was manifested in evolving ideas about which kinds of social science articles belonged in the restricted category of "internal circulation" (*neibu faxing*) among state agencies and which were eligible for open circulation (*gongkai faxing*) to the general public. In 1983–1984, for instance, three-fourths of the 150–200 new articles written about the Soviet Union in the fields of sociology, politics, and economics were classified as *neibu*.[18] Underlying this pervasiveness of the *neibu* designation were complex political and economic factors, including fear of exposing divisions within the Party, the desire to create a politically safe space for discussing new perspectives, and the economic incentive of minimizing publication costs.[19] The *neibu/gongkai* issue had implications for cadres' views of the relationship between cultural production and social mobilization, and by extension the Party organization's relationship to other social groups.

"Integrating Theory and Data": Post-Mao Projects of Reconstructing the Past

An important part of this cultural production centered on the construction and reconstruction of historical memories. Over the course of the decade, historians revised their conceptualization of historical methodology incrementally, first from "using theory to lead data" to "integrating theory and data" in the first half of the decade, and then again in 1988 to "derive theories from data" to further de-emphasize political ideology.[20] The "seeking truth from facts" premise that individuals should be evaluated within their historical context rather than simplistically judged as either positive or negative provided a philosophical justification for the

---

[17] Zhang Xiaoling, *Transformation of Political Communication in China*, 42–44.

[18] Gilbert Rozman, "China's Soviet Watchers in the 1980s: A New Era of Scholarship," *World Politics* 37.4 (July 1985): 435–474.

[19] Ibid.

[20] Alisa Jones, "Policy and History Curriculum Reform in Post-Mao China," *International Journal of Educational Research* 37 (2002): 545–566.

rehabilitation of certain "counterrevolutionaries" as patriotic figures. Individuals whose historical records had been either ignored or maligned during the Cultural Revolution reemerged in the 1980s in commemorative exhibits, memorials, memoirs, biographies, and TV dramas that reevaluated their achievements and service to the nation. Guomindang commanders who lost their lives during the Second Sino–Japanese War, for instance, were now venerated as national martyrs fighting alongside the CCP as a common united front.[21] Entrepreneurs who had managed businesses in the pre-1937 period reappeared in academic journals and literature as models for post-Mao management reform, downplaying economic exploitation and highlighting their dedication to maximizing market efficiency, instituting welfare policies for workers, making technological improvements, and serving the company and nation selflessly.[22] Even figures from ancient history associated with Chinese tradition, such as Confucius and Qu Yuan, underwent a historical revival that was driven by a post–Cultural Revolution desire to restore continuity with the past, both modern and ancient.[23] Along with the reevaluation of individuals in the past, post-Mao historians also redefined Communist terminology to provide theoretical justification for reforms. Concepts such as "feudal despotism," "dialectical materialism," and "seeking truth from facts" took on new connotations that placed the Party's sponsorship of market-oriented transformation in a positive light.[24]

To guide and regulate this process, the post-Mao state sponsored a number of memory initiatives including museums, memorials, gazetteers, textbooks, and oral history projects. The reopening of established museums and the building of new ones like the Memorial Hall of the People's War of Resistance against Japan, the Nanjing Massacre Memorial Hall, and the Yuhuatai Martyrs Memorial Park marked a systematic effort to "re-institutionalize memory of the past" and to fill in the ideological vacuum with a nationalist historiography that served to

---

[21] Arthur Waldron, "China's New Remembering of World War II: The Case of Zhang Zizhong" (Special Issue *War in Modern China*), *Modern Asian Studies* 30.4 (Oct. 1996): 945–978.

[22] Tim Wright, "'The Spiritual Heritage of Chinese Capitalism': Recent Trends in the Historiography of Chinese Enterprise Management," in Jonathan Unger, ed., *Using the Past to Serve the Present: Historiography and Politics in Contemporary China* (New York, NY: Routledge, 1993), 205–238.

[23] Ralph Croizier, "Qu Yuan and the Artists: Ancient Symbols and Modern Politics in the Post-Mao Era," in Jonathan Unger, ed., *Using the Past to Serve the Present: Historiography and Politics in Contemporary China* (New York, NY: Routledge, 1993), 124–150.

[24] Lawrence Sullivan, "The Controversy over 'Feudal Despotism': Politics and Historiography in China, 1978–82," in Jonathan Unger, ed., *Using the Past to Serve the Present: Historiography and Politics in Contemporary China* (New York, NY: Routledge, 1993), 174–204.

"'verify' history and to extol such moral virtues as patriotism and self-sacrifice."[25] The new museum exhibits represented an expansive Chinese nation, including former opponents of the Communist Party and overseas Chinese communities, united against foreign imperialism.[26]

Similar values infused the People's Education Press editors' comprehensive revision of school textbooks, replacing class division with national unity and ethnic harmony as the central themes running through history. In regard to relations between Han and ethnic minorities like the Jurchens and Manchus, for instance, the editors now referred to them as "brothers," supplanted the terms "invasion" and "class contradiction" with "internal struggle" to describe conflicts between them, and incorporated non-Han heroes into the historical narrative.[27] The new textbooks also shifted their focus away from the agricultural laborer and proletarian worker "masses" to educated and entrepreneurial individuals who had formerly been maligned as "collaborators" and "capitalist roaders."[28] As in other areas of cultural production, education planners worked within a structure that balanced centralized uniformity overseen by the Ministry of Education (renamed the State Education Commission) with localized input from regional education bureaus and other agencies.[29] The content that was developed reflected these structural dynamics, highlighting local figures as national heroes. At the same time, influenced by the trend toward professionalism and rational objectivity, the Ministry of Education established, appointed, and supervised Inspection Committees composed of expert historians and educators to evaluate and approve revisions in the history curriculum.[30] These reforms lent an objective credibility to the state's historical revision agenda, opening spaces for local and "expert" input contained within central guidelines and control.

Along with reforming the history curriculum, the post-Mao state revived the long-established tradition of county and provincial gazetteer writing. Systematically produced and rigidly formulaic in style, the gazetteers constituted an organized initiative of the state to extend its official version of history to the local and regional levels. These government-

[25] Kirk Denton, *Exhibiting the Past: Historical Memory and the Politics of Museums in Postsocialist China* (Honolulu, HI: University of Hawaii Press, 2014), 20–21.
[26] Rana Mitter, "Behind the Scenes at the Museum: Nationalism, History and Memory in the Beijing War of Resistance Museum, 1987–1997," *China Quarterly* 161 (Mar. 2000): 279–293.
[27] Nimrod Baranovitch, "Others No More: The Changing Representation of Non-Han Peoples in Chinese History Textbooks, 1951–2003," *Journal of Asian Studies* 69.1 (Feb. 2010): 85–122.
[28] Jones, "Policy and History Curriculum Reform in Post-Mao China."   [29] Ibid.
[30] Ibid.

authorized works gave scant, vague coverage to controversial and embarrassing topics for the Party such as the Great Leap Forward disaster, more fleshed-out histories of which were relegated to private and unofficial memoirs and literature.[31]

In contrast with the mechanical formalism of gazetteer writing, firsthand testimonial oral histories, sponsored in many cases by local and regional officials, offered more personally compelling versions of the past. Influenced both by the domestic context of post–Cultural Revolution reflectiveness and by the international East Asian context of World War Two testimonials in Japan and nationalist oral history projects in Taiwan, these localized initiatives introduced a more socially inclusive narrative of China's anti-imperialist and wartime past.[32] In some cases, local officials and elites appropriated the officially recognized category of *huiyi lu* (record of memories) to put forward historical narratives that were at variance with the Party-centered orthodox discourse.[33] The boundaries between oral history and literature blurred in the spontaneous outpouring of "scar literature," "in memoriam literature," and popularized oral history series featured in literary journals that adapted the earlier Maoist genre of oral histories of factories and laborers to the post-Mao market reform context.[34] Compared with the more formal modalities of history in museums, history textbooks, and gazetteers, these forms of memory allowed for greater diversity and nuance of perspective along with the appearance of authenticity and unfiltered transparency. As such, they addressed in a more compelling way what Wang Ban has described as "a rupture in the collectively shared sense of time, a lack of consensus ensuring the figuration of past, present, and future ... a serious problem in the understanding of the past and its connection to the current reality as a living, continuous history."[35]

During the early post-Mao period, therefore, the party-state attempted to reconsolidate its organizational integrity and political authority through

---

[31] Felix Wemheuer, "Dealing with Responsibility for the Great Leap Famine in the People's Republic of China," *China Quarterly* 201 (Mar. 2010): 176–194.

[32] Aaron William Moore, "The Problem of Changing Language Communities: Veterans and Memory Writing in China, Taiwan, and Japan" (Suppl. *China in World War II, 1937–1945: Experience, Memory, and Legacy*), *Modern Asian Studies* 45.2 (Mar. 2011): 399–429.

[33] Paul G. Pickowicz, "Memories of Revolution and Collectivization in China: The Unauthorized Reminiscences of a Rural Intellectual," in Rubie S. Watson, ed., *Memory, History, and Opposition under State Socialism* (Santa Fe, NM: School of American Research Press, 1994), 127–148.

[34] Geremie Barmé, "History for the Masses," in Jonathan Unger, ed., *Using the Past to Serve the Present: Historiography and Politics in Contemporary China* (New York, NY: Routledge, 1993), 260–286.

[35] Wang Ban, *Illuminations from the Past: Trauma, Memory, and History in Modern Cinema* (Stanford, CA: Stanford University Press, 2004), 6.

a delicate balancing act that involved nationally sponsored localization of cultural production and expression. Informal personal memories sprouting from the ground up fed into, informed the contours of, and pushed the boundaries of official Party discourse. The organizers of various cultural projects, in the decisions they made about choosing collaboration partners, identifying their target audience, and selecting subjects to memorialize, wrestled with the question of how to redefine the relationship between Party insiders and social groups outside the Party. Different cultural sites and genres also posed different opportunities and limitations for social and political healing and reconciliation, ranging from relatively rigid formalistic structures that heavy-handedly imposed official standards on one extreme to loosely organized informal mediums that provided compelling yet risky outlets for conveying the Party's message.

"Inspect, Consult, and Reeducate": Evolution of the People's Political Consultative Conference

The PPCC as an institution had its roots in the negotiations between the CCP and the GMD at the end of World War Two. On February 2, 1945, Zhou Enlai of the CCP and Wang Shijie representing the GMD met to lay the groundwork for a political consultation meeting regarding the formation of a coalition government. A year later, on January 10, 1946, the PPCC (sometimes referred to as the "old PPCC") held its first meeting to draft resolutions for electing a new government committee based on principles of multiparty shared democratic governance. Among the parties participating in these proceedings was the Democratic National League (DNL), which attempted to maintain its integrity as an independent third party. However, in June, negotiations broke down and fighting began; on November 15, the GMD unilaterally convened a People's Congress, and soon thereafter the DNL, formally declared illegal by the new GMD-headed government, forged an alliance with the CCP. Thus closed the first brief chapter in the PPCC's development as an attempt to transcend ideological and political difference under an inclusive umbrella of multiparty consultation.

As the tide began to turn in favor of the CCP, in October 1947, Mao called for constructing a new united front joining "workers, peasants, soldiers, intellectuals, and merchants; all people's organizations; all democratic parties; and all minorities, overseas Chinese and other patriots."[36] Nearly a year later, on August 1, 1948, Mao invited representatives of these

[36] Lin Shangli, *Zhongguo gongchandang yu renmin zhengxie (The Chinese Communist Party and the People's Political Consultative Conference)* (Shanghai: Dongfang chuban zhongxin, 2011), 23–24.

various parties, both within China and overseas, to join the CCP in convening a new meeting of the PPCC to establish a people's congress and coalition government. In March of the following year, the PPCC system of multiparty coalition under the mantle of CCP leadership became formalized and parties like the DNL completed the transition from independent entity to full absorption within the Communist Party-led framework. By 1949, the CCP leadership had transformed the PPCC from a primarily mediating body for building pluralistic coalition between opposing parties to an organization actively engaged in the project of politically transforming its subjects and reconfiguring the boundaries that defined who belonged within the category of the "people." At the first meeting of the national PPCC on September 1, 1949, Zhou Enlai distinguished between "the people" (*renmin*) as workers, peasants, and members of the "capitalist and feudal" classes who had been "reeducated" and "awakened," and "citizens" (*guomin*) who were stripped of the rights of "the people" until they had undergone the required reeducation.[37]

The newly reorganized national PPCC also attempted to reconcile tensions that had been at the heart of CCP identity since the 1930s. These conflicting priorities included anti-imperialist nationalism versus internal class struggle, national economic development versus championing the rights of one class against another, unified "democratic centralist" party leadership versus pluralistic "united front" coalition-style politics, and, finally, competing conceptions of the Communist regime's identity in relation to the world outside of China. The PPCC's national "common program" (*gongtong zhangling*) encapsulated these priorities. The first of its four general guiding principles subsumes the first two of these tensions, first by conjoining the nationalist objectives of "anti-imperialism" and "ending imperialist countries' rights in China" with the socialist imperative of "anti-feudalism" and transferring land into farmers' hands, and then by grouping together the economic development goal of "industrializing China" with the Communist struggle to overthrow "bureaucratic capitalism." The second and third principles attend to the search for a way to integrate and reconcile the priorities of "democratic centralism" (principle two), which emphasizes vertical hierarchical lines of control emanating from the Party's central leadership, and a "united front" (principle three), which stresses horizontal lines of equal status between

---

[37] For discussion of the Party's construction of a united front coalition during this period, see Eddy U, "Dangerous Privilege," 35–39; Lin Shangli, *The Chinese Communist Party and the People's Political Consultative Conference*, 28. Though his focus is on the 1980s, Yan Xiaojun also briefly notes the PPCC's early evolution in "Regime Inclusion and the Resilience of Authoritarianism: The Local People's Political Consultative Conference in Post-Mao Chinese Politics," *China Journal*, no. 66 (July 2011): 58.

various "democratic parties and organizations." The fourth principle, stating the goal of "integrating nationalism with internationalism," reflects a concern going back to the earliest days of the Chinese Communist Party as it sought to reinvent and nativize an ideology imported from abroad.[38]

During the initial years of political consolidation between 1949 and 1954, the PPCC, besides drafting broad ideological guidelines for the new regime, presided over the major policy-making functions until the National People's Congress (NPC) took over this formal political role in 1954. After the NPC's formation, the CCP leadership redefined the PPCC's role from one of mediating the establishment of a national coalition government to one of maintaining the integrity and unity of the new regime through overseeing a coalition of political and social groups under the mantle of CCP control.[39] In his statement outlining the redefined purpose of the PPCC, Zhou Enlai laid out the following as its primary objectives: to assist government organs, mobilize energies of society, and resolve conflicts in society like class tensions; to connect with the people and communicate to relevant bureaus the people's sentiment and the PPCC's recommendations; to bring about cooperation between various groups and parties; and to carry out study and ideological reeducation, directed especially toward intellectuals.[40] From these principles one can see that the party leadership reconceived of the PPCC as an instrument for continually adjusting the relationship between the CCP and other social and political groups.

Zhou Enlai's mandate for the PPCC reflected the perceived need for an intermediary institution that would translate central Party policies into a language accessible and acceptable to a broader array of social groups, assess the broader political climate beyond the walls of the formal party-state apparatus to measure the degree of resistance or acceptance that policy directives would encounter, and extend mechanisms of state enforcement and coercion like ideological reeducation in a way that appeared neutral and removed from formal state authority. To this end, Zhou Enlai envisioned a combination of mechanisms for facilitating the maintenance of a stable and secure Party-led political environment. These ranged from the empathetic, conciliatory strategy of opening up channels for hearing various groups' concerns and grievances, and making policy recommendations to the relevant government bureaus in accordance with these

---

[38] Ibid., 29–30.
[39] Brantly Womack, "Modernization and Democratic Reform in China," *Journal of Asian Studies* 43.3 (May 1984): 430–433.
[40] Ibid., 44–45.

concerns, to more coercive mechanism of control such as reeducation study sessions.

The PPCC committees swung into action in 1954 on all of these fronts as the campaigns to expropriate and collectivize private capital and enterprises intensified. Targeting owners of private commercial and industrial firms, a number of whom were already PPCC members, meetings were held to convey and interpret the new policies in a way that would assuage their fears while mobilizing their support for the campaigns through reeducative study sessions and mutual and self-criticism reports. By 1956, during the short-lived Hundred Flowers campaign to promote "mutual coexistence and mutual supervision" among various "democratic" parties and groups, the PPCC's approach to interpreting and enforcing government policy began to take on a pattern that would continue through the post-Mao period: sending down inspecting teams to assess on-the-ground conditions and the degree to which those conditions conformed with policy directives, relaying reports and recommendations to the relevant government bureaus based on the teams' findings, and then reinforcing policy guidelines through study programs.

Aiding in its capacity to mobilize inspection, consultation, and reeducation committees was the formalized establishment of PPCC branches at city and county as well as provincial levels throughout the country by the mid-1950s, paralleling the structure of the administrative and party apparatus. With this structure in place, starting in 1955 PPCC committees at all levels mobilized inspections twice a year. At the same time, reflecting the importance of ideological reeducation in their activities, PPCC branches played an active role in the establishment of socialist schools from the central socialist academy in Beijing to schools at the local level, including reeducation centers for business owners.[41]

While playing an integral role in the central party-state's efforts in political consolidation, the PPCC's inclusion of individuals and groups representing diverse political and socioeconomic backgrounds also made it susceptible to attack during periods of heightened radicalism and campaign fervor. In late 1957, as the Anti-Rightist Campaign aimed mostly at intellectuals swung into high gear, 10.7% of the national PPCC committee (78 out of its 729 members at the time) were labeled rightists. The movement paralyzed PPCC operations for two years. In the wake of the collective trauma and dislocation of these mass persecutions, and with Party leaders' growing awareness of a dangerous disconnect

---

[41] James R. Townsend, *Political Participation in Communist China* (Berkeley and Los Angeles, CA: University of California Press, 1969): 145–150; Lin Shangli, *The Chinese Communist Party and the People's Political Consultative Conference*, 64–65.

between Great Leap Forward policy directives and local realities, Zhou Enlai turned again to the PPCC and its role as an instrument of political reconciliation and reintegration in 1959. Enticing alienated groups, particularly intellectuals, back into the political fold, the PPCC held sessions at all levels with the slogan "no pulling of hair, no wearing of caps, no beating of sticks," attempting to create a welcoming, healing atmosphere within which to reenergize a diverse base of support for the Party.[42]

In the midst of the unraveling crisis that threatened to undermine the legitimacy of the CCP for the first time in its decade of rule, Zhou Enlai added a new dimension to the PPCC's role, one that could bolster the young regime's shaken frame with a solid foundation in history. In 1959, as director of the national PPCC, he introduced the "historical and literary materials" (wenshi ziliao) project. Applying the "inspect, consult, and reeducate" model of the PPCC to the area of historical investigation, the wenshi ziliao involved the mobilization of teams of interviewers throughout the country to elicit life stories and firsthand testimonies covering pre-1949 events deemed historically significant. Editors, sometimes serving concurrently as interviewers, and, in some cases, editors of their own narratives, compiled and organized these accounts into wenshi ziliao publications with limited internal circulation.

This historical memory project complemented other aspects of the PPCC's efforts to bring about political consolidation, healing, and reconciliation in the aftermath of collective trauma, to resecure central party-state authority at the local and regional levels, and to redefine the Party in relation to class, nation, and transnational ethnicity. However, the operations of the PPCC came to a halt in 1966 with the onset of the Cultural Revolution before significant progress was made in producing the wenshi ziliao. Zhou Enlai again experimented with wenshi ziliao in the mid-1970s on a small scale by restoring some of the functions of the national-level PPCC and inviting former members of the "United Front" to write accounts of pre-1949 events that could be used as historical evidence against ultra-leftist factions in the Party. However, it was not until after Deng's consolidation of power in 1978 that the project resumed in an official and organized fashion.

In the post–Cultural Revolution atmosphere of political, moral, and ideological crisis in the early 1980s, the Party turned to the PPCC and wenshi ziliao as instruments once again of healing, reconciliation, and political reconsolidation, but did so in a much more systematic, extensive,

---

[42] Lin Shangli, *The Chinese Communist Party and the People's Political Consultative Conference*, 64–65.

and sustained way.[43] Compared to the more restricted scope of initiative at the national and provincial levels of the PPCC and the heavier focus on political and military content in the earlier stage of historical production, the post-Mao *wenshi ziliao* involved more localized processes of production and addressed a diversified range of societal and cultural issues.

The structure and social composition of its committees and personnel reflected the PPCC's search for continuity and self-perpetuation as an institution across the Cultural Revolution divide. In spite of the infusion of new blood into its ranks and the expanded representation of certain categories of people, a remarkable degree of structural continuity characterized the PPCC's transition from the early 1960s to the early 1980s. While official rhetoric emphasized a shift in the Party's priorities toward the areas of science and technology, commercial enterprise, and opening to the outside world, the actual composition of PPCC committees pointed to a sustained effort to preserve and perpetuate pre–Cultural Revolution institutional norms.

After 1978, the PPCC at all levels underwent an expansion in personnel, with an increase in members' education level, a somewhat higher ratio of women to men, and a modest rise in the percentage of personnel with scientific expertise and overseas connections. In the mid-1980s, PPCC committees saw an across-the-board generational shift from the elderly pre-1966 contingent, many of whom were dead, dying, or ill, to a somewhat younger group that consisted in part of educated, middle-aged individuals. *Wenshi ziliao* subcommittees structured the writing and editing process partly along generational lines, with middle-aged editors working alongside elderly writers with a wealth of historical knowledge and informants with prerevolutionary experience.[44] This cross-generational dynamic among PPCC personnel was compatible with the broader aims of the *wenshi ziliao* in reconciling historical change and continuity.

The age shift accompanied changes in other areas of representation. While the PPCC had always focused its attention on the more educated sector of the population, with only a small fraction at or below the primary school level, the average level of education rose further by the mid-1980s as secondary level education became the base requirement for entry.

---

[43] For an overview of the PPCC's political and social functions during the post-Mao period, see Yan Xiaojun, "Regime Inclusion and the Resilience of Authoritarianism: The Local People's Political Consultative Conference in Post-Mao Chinese Politics," *China Journal*, no. 66 (July 2011): 53–75.

[44] Liu Feilin, "Wenshi gongzuo de sanshinian jiyi" ("Thirty Years' Reflections on Literary and Historical Work"), in *Heilongjiang wenshi ziliao*, vol. 41 (Heilongjiang renmin chubanshe, 2010): 359–366.

The ratio of women to men rose by about 5%, along with a similar percentage increase in the number of experts in science and technology. Party membership grew overall, with a somewhat higher rate of growth at the local level (with some city committees reaching 40%) compared with a more modest growth at the provincial level. Representation of the commercial and entrepreneurial sector varied between cities. Business managers held around 10% of PPCC positions in the mid-1980s, while the Jilin PPCC for unclear reasons saw a decline in that category from a peak of around 10% in 1955 to only 2–3% by the mid-1980s. It is possible that the reintegration of intellectuals and experts in science and technology-related various fields, in the context of the Four Modernizations campaign, was a more pressing and politically sensitive priority for the PPCC. Other categories remained stable, including only a 1% increase in the overseas Chinese contingent in spite of the more internationalist-leaning rhetoric.[45]

The PPCC came out of the Cultural Revolution, therefore, altered somewhat in accordance with the priorities of post-Mao reform yet largely conforming to the pre-1966 model in terms of both organizational structure and social composition. Among the classes of people represented on PPCC committees both before and after the Cultural Revolution, farmers and workers constituted a small minority (about 5%) while the categories of science and technology, the humanities, medicine, and commerce and industry occupied more than half of all the positions. Other categories included women's federation members, ethnic minority and religious leaders, leaders of other so-called democratic parties including the China Democratic League, Chinese returned from overseas, and "special invitees." Between the PPCC's establishment in the northeast in the mid-1950s and its reconstitution in the early 1980s, very little change occurred at either the city/county level or the provincial level in social composition and distribution of members across these sectors, even as the committees underwent a steady expansion in size.[46] Moreover, many of the members

---

[45] Ma Kaiyin, "Wo yu Haerbin shi zhengxie bansheng yuan" ("Half of My Life with the Harbin City PPCC"), in *Heilongjiang wenshi ziliao*, vol. 41 (Heilongjiang renmin chubanshe, 2010): 304–321; " Jilin shi zhengxie zuzhi jigou" ("Organizational Structure of the Jilin City PPCC"), in *Jilin shizhi (Jilin City Gazetteer)* (Jilin shi zhengxie weiyuanhui, 1997): 78–92; Jiamusi difangzhi bianzuan weiyuanhui, "Zhengxie zuzhi"("PPCC Organization"), in *Jiamusi shizhi (Jiamusi City Gazetteer)*, vol. 2 (Zhonghua shuju, 1996): 1319–1334; Youhao District Government, Youhao Lumber Bureau, *Shizhi ziliao huibian (Historical Gazetteer Compilation)* (Yichun: Youhao District Gazetteer Committee, 1986–1987): 182–185; *Zhengxie weiyuan shouce (Handbook for PPCC Personnel)* (Zhengxie heilongjiangsheng weiyuanhui bangongting, 2008): 163–167.

[46] See, for instance, "Organizational Structure of the Jilin City PPCC," 78–92.

during the earlier phase were reinstalled at the end of the Cultural Revolution.

Besides the social composition of its committee, the PPCC's initial approach to restoring the *wenshi ziliao* also reflected a search for continuity. Beginning in 1979 at the national level, and then extending to the local PPCC offices by the early 1980s, *wenshi ziliao* committees unearthed materials collected in the early 1960s but then abandoned and locked away in dusty bins over the subsequent decade. In her later reflections, Shen Meijuan describes her reunion with her father at the national *wenshi ziliao* office following his release from prison. Her role at the time was to assist in recopying, inspecting, and verifying the dates and source information of these unearthed documents, and she recalls the poor condition of these materials, in some cases barely legible.[47] The discourse of salvaging and imminent loss, therefore, referred not only to elderly surviving individuals but also to paper remnants and record traces from the earlier phase of memory production. The *wenshi ziliao* work of the early 1980s thus provided an avenue for bypassing the "lost decade" and constructing a narrative of unbroken continuity for the *wenshi ziliao* project itself. The PPCC created a self-legitimizing history of itself, and by extension the Party, as a constant entity sustained through time.

"New Things Always Come Out of Old Roots": Handling Contradictions and the Search for Continuity

One of the central crises that the Communist Party faced a decade after the founding of the PRC was one of historical identity. The *wenshi ziliao* initiative to salvage the past entailed a balance between preserving a continuous thread of historical development and defining the new against the old. These competing imperatives underlay the Party leadership's attempt to establish its historical legacy through tracing the Party's lineage along a continuous line through history while constantly affirming its socialist legitimacy in terms of breaking away from the past.

The question of its relationship to the past was a dilemma for the Party that had troubled the organization since its founding in Shanghai in 1921. Defined by an ideology rooted in Western Europe and relying on the material and political assistance of the Soviet Comintern, the Party struggled in its early years to develop an agenda grounded in the social and cultural realities of China. Did its revolutionary vision draw from

---

[47] Shen Meijuan, "Shen Zui funü yu quanguo zhengxie" ("National PPCC and Shen Zui Father and Daughter"), in *Wenshi ziliao xuanji*, vol. 154 (Zhongguo wenshi chubanshe, 2009): 70–86, at 75.

a glorious historical tradition of peasant revolution (as Mao claimed), was it the product of an international, universal stage of historical development emanating from the Soviet Union (as Li Dazhao declared in 1918), or did the Communist movement involve the superimposition of another country's history of urban industrial class formation onto China's primarily rural peasant conditions? Over the course of the 1930s and 1940s, from the Jiangxi Soviet through the Long March to the CCP's decade-long experimentation with moderate socialist policies and anti-Japanese nationalism, the CCP evolved from a constituency of urbanized intellectuals based in the semi-colonial enclaves of Shanghai and Canton to a rural grassroots movement.

The success of the Party in mobilizing mass support and defeating the GMD to oversee national reunification in 1949 appeared to close the book on the question of historical identity. Not only had Communism emerged victorious as a Chinese national ideology, but more importantly, the CCP had created a new historical tradition. The Long March, tracing a curved trajectory around the outer circumference of China proper, became the symbol of the Party's forging of a new identity tied to China's social and historical landscape.

However, after a decade in power, this identity became increasingly contested. Following Mao's May 1 pronouncement in 1949 reaffirming the Party's leadership of a broad-based coalition of parties and interests, successive political campaigns in the 1950s aimed at intellectuals and individuals with overseas and capitalist connections split apart that coalition and the "united front" that it represented. Mao attempted to address the increasing fissures within the political landscape in his statement on "handling contradictions." In this statement, he espoused the view that the Party was capable of working out and reconciling conflicting views and disagreements among various parties and groups, what he called "internal contradictions among the people," in a way that would enhance the Party's quality of governance. This principle, embedded in the PPCC's approach to building a united front, informed the Hundred Flowers movement in the early part of 1957 that encouraged intellectuals to weigh in with critical views on Party policy. This heady vision of the Party's capacity to represent and incorporate a broad range of interests and organizations degenerated rapidly later that year, however, as mounting criticism and demands ignited a stark reversal in policy from broad-based inclusiveness to a terror campaign of ideological struggle. Exacerbating these tensions, in 1959, it was already becoming apparent that the Great Leap Forward campaign to industrialize the countryside was spiraling into disaster, as the political pressures exerted on the party-state's command economy placed massive strains on agricultural production. The Party began to find itself doubly alienated both from intellectuals and other members of the "united front" and from the rural population of peasants that had been its primary base of support. Faced with this crisis of unprecedented proportions, between 1959 and 1961, some members of the Party leadership, including Zhou Enlai, turned toward a policy of retrenchment, beginning in 1959 with scaling back production targets. By the time the Ninth Plenum of the CCP's Central Committee met in January 1961, a return to the more gradualist approach to socialist transformation that had informed the initial period of the PRC, including a return to limited privatization, was in full force.[48]

Amidst recent and ongoing political and economic crises, during the period from 1959 to 1961, the Party turned inward and backward, switching gears from forward-oriented momentum to reverse intro-spection and self-reflection. While in the economic domain this took the form of a slowdown and eventual rollback of Great Leap Forward communalization and rural industrialization, in the cultural realm this involved a turn toward history as a source of reevaluating and recon-solidating the Party's position. In this context, "salvaging history" became a key part of the PPCC's role. Zhou Enlai, in his position as chair of the national PPCC committee, announced in 1959 the estab-lishment of the *wenshi ziliao* project at a gathering of PPCC members sixty years of age and older. In this announcement, he designated the parameters of *wenshi ziliao* historical examination as the period between 1898, the year of the first abortive attempt to comprehen-sively reform the Qing monarchy, and the founding of the PRC in 1949. He characterized this fifty-year period with a combined empha-sis on change and continuity. After referring to these years as marking great social change, he insisted that "new things always grow out of the foundation of old things. Everything, from the most backward to the most advanced, must be recorded. We must courageously expose things in the distant past so that later generations will be aware of the old roots and history will not be cut off."[49] Zhou's exhortations suggest the *wenshi ziliao*'s intended role, at a moment of upheaval and crisis, of providing a sense of historical continuity that preserved and to some extent redeemed the pre-Communist past while uphold-ing the Party's historical identity as the agent and culmination of progress and advancement.

---

[48] Townsend, *Political Participation in Communist China*, 99.

[49] Zhang Pingfu et al., *Renmin zhengxie gailun* (*General Discussion of PPCC*). Beijing United Front Teaching Materials (Beijing: Zhongyang bianyi chubanshe, 2008): 241. See also Luke S. K. Kwong, "Oral History in China: A Preliminary Review," *Oral History Review* 20.1/2 (Apr. 1, 1992): 23–50.

A central aspect of this initiative involved the amnesty of high-level political and economic "criminals," many of whom had occupied important positions in the Nationalist (GMD) government, on the condition that they write personal recollections of the "dark days" prior to Communist "liberation." Zhou Enlai professed that the amnesty of these "counterrevolutionaries" would serve an important symbolic purpose for the Party both domestically and abroad. Commenting on the significance of the memoir of the last emperor, Pu Yi, he emphasized the account's intended purpose of laying bare the old (pre-1949) society's darkness. "What you wrote has value," he said in a meeting with Pu Yi. "It is a mirror on the old society; [the memoir] basically has to declare war against the old society, exposing it to its core."[50] One former cadre in the national *wenshi ziliao* office described her introduction to the *wenshi ziliao* as a middle school girl after the national PPCC inducted her father as one of these amnestied "criminals" in 1962. During a meeting of amnestied individuals with Zhou Enlai and other officials in 1961, Zhou instructed them to expose all the "counterrevolutionary" activities in which they had participated that had impeded the Party's development and had killed revolutionaries. In this way, he informed them, their *wenshi ziliao* biographical and autobiographical accounts could serve as "negative-model education" to inspire appreciation of the Party's heroic efforts and struggles.[51] Pu Yi himself became the embodiment of this attempt to elide the present crisis by redirecting attention to the pre-Communist "bad old days." Guo Chunhua, who took over day-to-day responsibilities for the Heilongjiang *wenshi ziliao* committee, worked alongside Pu Yi when the latter was assigned to the northeast regional branch of the national *wenshi ziliao* committee. His recollections suggest that Pu Yi played a prominent symbolic role in showcasing the CCP's historical contributions to both domestic and foreign audiences, informing those who interviewed him that the old Pu Yi was gone and that he had begun a new life thanks to the Party.[52]

The symbolic value of these autobiographical narratives by former enemies of the Party lay, therefore, in directing attention away from the

[50] In regard to reflections on his interviews with Pu Yi, see Zhang Tong, "Zhou enlai yu PPCC wenshi ziliao gongzuo" ("Zhou Enlai and the PPCC's *Wenshi Ziliao* Work"), *Shihai cunzhen (Gems of Culture and History)* no. 2 (2009): 18. The publication that emerged out of this project in which Pu Yi was compelled to participate was entitled *Wo de qian bansheng (The Early Half of My Life)* (Xianggang: Wen tong shu dian, 1964), and has been translated into English: W. J. F. Jenner, *From Emperor to Citizen: The Autobiography of Aisin-Gioro Pu Yi* (Oxford: Oxford University Press, 1987).
[51] Shen Meijuan, "National PPCC and Shen Zui Father and Daughter."
[52] Guo Chunhua, "Nanwang de huiyi" ("Indelible Memories"), in Heilongjiang sheng zhengxie lianyihui, *Wo yu zhengxie* (Internal circulation, 2002): 292–299.

current crisis by highlighting just how bad social conditions had been prior to the revolution, and in the process placing a longue durée emphasis on the Party's emancipatory historical role. The former vice-chair of the national *wenshi ziliao* committee, Du Jianshi, himself a former military advisor to the Nationalist government, recalled this early stage of *wenshi ziliao* production during a 1986 interview with an editor of the project in its post-Mao revived form. In this transcribed interview he expressed his ambivalence about the environment in which these accounts emerged and the "factual errors" that he believed resulted from the political agendas driving their production:

At that time the *wenshi ziliao* work was really energized: they were willing to write for Zhou Enlai, and there were many accounts submitted and many eyewitnesses still alive who could cooperate in examining the drafts. Over 1,000 accounts were submitted each month.

But there were two problems: one was that many accounts had falsities, not on purpose, but were influenced by leftism. The CCP had difficulty talking about Guomindang-related affairs. Another problem was that in order to talk about oneself in the pre-liberation Guomindang, one had to talk about how reactionary one was and curse oneself back then, and then show how quickly one transformed into a proper revolutionary after liberation. This just wasn't truthful.[53]

Du Jianshi, himself speaking from the new post-Mao reformist perspective, articulated the tension within the project between the twin agendas of making room for diverse voices in order to heal the mistrust created by the Party's backlash against the Hundred Flowers protests, and containing and mobilizing that very diversity for constructing a triumphant Party-affirming historical narrative.

To this end, the PPCC organized the production of memoirs into various committees according to their members' political backgrounds. Alongside the amnestied "counterrevolutionaries," Party cadres and People's Liberation Army officers met in a separate section to narrate in heroic terms their participation in revolutionary events leading up to liberation.[54] The purpose was to gather a broad spectrum of life histories from these groups with sharply conflicting political backgrounds and to harmonize them into a unified overall framework of linear progress from old to new, from dark feudalism to the bright new Communist order. Zhou Enlai confirmed the role of such autobiographical accounts as symbolic and microcosmic reflections of this overall historical trajectory

---

[53] Chen Min, "Wo yu wenshi gongzuo – fang du jianshi" ("My Part in the Work on *Wenshi* Materials – My Interview with Du Jianshi"), *Liaowang*, no. 13 (1986).

[54] Xu Chengbei, "Wenshi san ti" ("Three Points Regarding *Wenshi* Materials"), *Beijing guancha (Beijing Observation)*, no. 8 (2000).

when he announced his own plan, though never realized, to record his own dark feudal family past from which he had emerged.[55]

This attempt to mobilize historical consciousness in order to balance the prerogatives of unbroken continuity and revolutionary change became subjected to increasing ideological pressures from leftist politics during the period between 1962 and 1965 leading up to the Cultural Revolution. Incited by Mao's speech in 1962 reinjecting class struggle into the political atmosphere, rejecting the more conservative retrenchment approach, subsequent struggles against the director of the United Front Bureau were a reminder of the PPCC's vulnerability to accusations of "counterrevolutionary" activities. PPCC committees devoted more time to struggle sessions, while *wenshi ziliao* committees came under pressure to designate class struggle as the key framework for the accounts they produced.[56] The outward appearance and rhetoric of class struggle at times provided little more than window dressing disguising more pressing regional agendas. In Heilongjiang, faced with the prospect of military conflict with Russia along their northern border, regional *wenshi ziliao* committees couched their historical investigations in terms of class differentiation while mobilizing the testimonies that they collected in the service of ethnic nationalism.

By 1966, however, the outbreak of the Cultural Revolution paralyzed PPCC operations entirely. The project of salvaging the past, carried out under the guidelines of opening up about one's personal history to serve as "reverse model" education, had become a dangerous enterprise, coming back to haunt *wenshi ziliao* writers and editors as evidence of "counterrevolutionary" crimes. Shen Meijuan, who had assisted her father with editing *wenshi ziliao* materials, recalled the display of one of his biographical pieces on a *dazibao* big character poster denouncing his work as feudal propaganda, after which he was imprisoned for five years.[57] The subsequent decade threw out Zhou Enlai's approach to constructing a longue durée historical identity for the party, and activists attacked any associations with the prerevolutionary past, the "four olds," as refuse to be discarded. This uprooting of the Chinese people from their past and the unhinging of the party-state apparatus from its historical foundations proved unsustainable culturally and psychologically, and by 1978, with Deng's ascent to power, the Party leadership once again looked to the past for a way to reconsolidate political legitimacy and reinvent its identity.

On September 24, 1983, in his closing speech for the fourth national *wenshi ziliao* work conference, Yang Chengwu, vice-chair of the national

[55] Zhang Tong, "Zhou Enlai and the PPCC's *Wenshi Ziliao* Work."
[56] Lin Shangli, *The Chinese Communist Party and the People's Political Consultative Conference*, 64–66.
[57] Shen Meijuan, "National PPCC and Shen Zui Father and Daughter," 73–74.

PPCC, defined the nationalist purpose of the *wenshi ziliao* in terms of restoring a historical continuity that had been lost in the Cultural Revolution. He invoked Zhou Enlai's assertion, mentioned earlier in this chapter, about new things always coming from old roots and the urgency of preventing the next generation from being cut off from history. He went on to conclude that these words imply nationalist thought.[58] One of the questions, then, was how to determine what qualified as history. Deng Yingchao, speaking to the same audience as chair of the national PPCC, emphasized the need to salvage historical memories about the pre-1949 Republican period, lamenting that many young and middle-aged people were ignorant about events that had occurred sixty to seventy years in the past.[59] Yang Chengwu in turn called for a broad inclusiveness of topics extending beyond military and politics to include culture/education, science/technology, commerce/economy, etc.[60] City- and county-level committees likewise inscribed these new principles for selecting materials in their guidelines to the *wenshi ziliao* collection staff. The Harbin city PPCC sent letters to these individuals twice, in February and December 1982, explaining that the materials they collected should "have a united front characteristic" and should include "matters relating to politics, military, economy, commerce, culture, education, science/ technology, ethnicity, religion, overseas Chinese, everyday life, and any other firsthand accounts reflecting changes that society underwent during the period between the 1898 reforms and the Cultural Revolution."[61]

Conclusion

In the early 1980s, the Party leadership undertook an array of ambitious cultural projects, including the construction of museums and memorials, the revival of local gazetteers, and the sponsorship of oral history

---

[58] Yang Chengwu, "Zai di sici quanguo wenshi ziliao gongzuo huiyi shang bimuhui de jianghua" ("Speech at the Closing Ceremony of the Fourth National *Wenshi Ziliao* Work Conference") (Sept. 24, 1983), *Haerbin zhengxie* (*Harbin PPCC*), no. 3 (no. 13 overall) (1984) (Special Issue of the First [Harbin City] *Wenshi Ziliao* Work Conference) (Heilongjiang Provincial Archive): 21.

[59] Haerbin shi zhengxie weiyuanhui mishuchu, "Deng yingchao tongzhi zai quanguo zhengxie disici quanguo wenshi ziliao gongzuo huiyi shang de jianghua" ("Comrade Deng Yingchao's Speech at the National PPCC's Fourth National *Wenshi Ziliao* Work Conference") (Sept. 24, 1983), *Haerbin shi zhengxie* (*Harbin PPCC*), no. 3 (no. 13 over- all) (Jan. 8, 1984) (Recorded and organized without the speaker's inspection.) (Special Issue of the First [Harbin City] *Wenshi Ziliao* Work Conference): 8–9.

[60] Yang Chengwu, "Speech at the Closing Ceremony of the Fourth National *Wenshi Ziliao* Work Conference," 19–21.

[61] *Haerbin shizhi* (*Harbin City Gazetteer*). Haerbin shi difangzhi bianzuan weiyuanhui (1993): 199–200.

initiatives, to bring about healing and reintegration after the Cultural Revolution. This constituted a monumental and sustained effort by the Party to produce a new national historical consciousness based in centrally guided, locally driven initiatives. With its origins located in an earlier moment of political crisis, the *wenshi ziliao* was a key part of this endeavor to resecure the Party's legitimacy in the popular historical imagination.

Several themes and tensions that run through the chapters of this book informed the methodology and significance of the *wenshi ziliao* as a vehicle for reimagining history. First is the theme of continuity and change in the approach to producing and criteria for defining historical "facts" and "truths." As is explored more deeply in Chapter 4, the policies regarding who would participate and what topics they would investigate reflect a continuation of the Maoist debate about how to reconcile "redness" with "expertise." In this regard, the PPCC continued to function as an ambivalent organization mediating between the Party's conceptions of itself as an expansive, United Front coalition and as unified Party regime. In the 1980s, however, paralleling developments in other cultural areas such as news and entertainment media, the PPCC's mediatory role proliferated to the local levels where, as we see in what follows, the Party's control was extended, diversified, and subtly appropriated and challenged.

This leads us to the second theme of centralized Party control and localization of initiative. As Heilmann, Perry, and others have shown, the post-Mao state adopted a flexible "guerrilla style" of governance that accommodated localized experimentation in economic and cultural matters. Through its allocation of investigatory, editing, and publishing responsibilities to county, city, and provincial *wenshi ziliao* committees across the country, the Party applied this approach to re-narrating the past. The result was an interpenetration of Party-centered nationalist narratives with extra-Party localized reinterpretations of the past and the revival of extra-national regional concepts.

A third theme, explored in more depth in Chapter 6, is ambivalence about social mobilization. The post-Mao state periodically asserted its control and adjusted social relations through campaigns of what Elizabeth Perry has called "controlled mobilization." The *wenshi ziliao* was a more sustained and less visible project of social mobilization in the service of producing history, or rather producing history in the service of social mobilization. However, unlike the previous Maoist campaigns of mass mobilization, the *wenshi ziliao* was a finely tuned, narrowly restricted approach to mobilization that involved a selective network of local elites and a semi-internal framework for publication and dissemination.

We now turn to a more detailed discussion of these issues as they informed specific local practices of *wenshi ziliao* in China's northeast borderland. As we see in the next chapter, the specific regional and historical context of northern Manchuria posed a particular set of problems and opportunities for the Party to reimagine the past and legitimize its post-Mao reform project.

2 Borderland Ambiguities in Narratives of Modernization and Liberation

Introduction

Wenshi ziliao officials and editors in Heilongjiang were faced with the task of overlaying the Party's reform agenda onto the historical landscape of the northeast borderland. One salient feature that defined the early twentieth-century history of the region was the heavy Russian colonial influence. This had to be taken into account, and the question for *wenshi ziliao* organizers and editors was how to reconcile this colonial past with the project's goals of creating a nationalist historical narrative. This chapter argues that one way in which editors addressed this problem was by juxtaposing stories celebrating the expansion of Chinese migrant enterprise into the region alongside accounts bemoaning Chinese victimization to Russian colonialism. They reappropriated the border's mixed history of cross-border migration, trade, and ethnic conflict as a discursive space for melding together cosmopolitan market liberalization and anti-foreign nationalist narratives that tied into post-Mao reform ideology.

Scholars have amply demonstrated the historical importance of borderlands in the history of migration, trade, ethnic conflict, and state expansion. The seventeenth- and eighteenth-century contexts of imperial expansion have been a focus of borderland scholarship, highlighting the borderland as a space where local indigenous actors far from imperial state centers could play off imperial powers against each other and thereby maintain a degree of regional power, autonomy, and freedom outside the scope of colonial control.[1] However, more recently, scholars like Pekka Hämäläinen and Samuel Truett have conceived of the borderland as not merely a transitional stage in inter-imperial power relations but also as a continuous phenomenon of instability, mobility, and resistance that unsettles and exposes the limitations of the homogenizing

---

[1] See Stephen Aron and Jeremy Adelman, "From Borderlands to Borders: Empires, Nation-States, and the Peoples in Between in North American History," *American Historical Review* 104 (June 1999): 814–841.

national state-building project.[2] Elaborating on this, Pat Giersch and a new generation of Asian borderland scholars have pointed to overlapping layers of local, regional, and imperial/national power in the borderlands, arguing in the context of Qing imperial expansion that the expansion and penetration of the state could and often did overlap with the expansion of powerful regional indigenous networks.[3] Others have shown that borderland economic transactions and ethnic relations were an unintended consequence of and an important influence on colonial and national state building.[4]

As in other contexts, the historical positioning of the northeast borderland beyond the scope of Chinese national state power was a potential dilemma for the post-Mao political reconsolidation effort. How could this extra-national space be reintegrated into a national and nationalist version of the past? *Wenshi ziliao* editors pursued several strategies to resolve this issue. One strategy was to highlight the role of Chinese migrant entrepreneurs in the region's economic development and to reframe their commercial transactions in nationalist terms by incorporating them into a broader narrative of anti-Russian resistance. A second related approach was to erase or downplay the Russian presence and to repopulate the region in the historical imagination solely with Chinese immigrants, thereby resignifying the northeast borderland as a space that had always been or was in an inexorable process of becoming Chinese. A third representational strategy was, in a certain sense, the opposite of the second: it involved highlighting Russian aggression and incursion while depicting Chinese residents as helpless victims. In practice, *wenshi ziliao* editors combined and integrated these strategies of reimagining the borderland as a Chinese national space.

Wenshi ziliao depictions of the region's colonial past in nationalist terms of Chinese rightful claims to the land and Chinese victimization to Russian aggression were not new to the 1980s and had appeared in the earlier stage of *wenshi ziliao* production in the early 1960s.[5] What *was* new was the emphasis on and celebration of migrant enterprise, entrepreneurial ventures, and other economic and cultural achievements as defining features of Chinese nationalist claims to the region. Whereas earlier

---

[2] Hämäläinen and Truett, "On Borderlands."
[3] Giersch, "Afterword: Why Kham? Why Borderlands?"
[4] See, for instance, Tagliacozzo, *Secret Trades, Porous Borders;* Kate Brown, *A Biography of No Place: From Ethnic Borderland to Soviet Heartland* (Cambridge, MA: Harvard University Press, 2003); Anzaldua, *Borderlands/La Frontera.*
[5] Given the short time frame and restrictive political environment in which it was implemented, *wenshi ziliao* were generally not finalized as complete accounts before 1966. The rare examples of *wenshi ziliao* content that I have found from the earlier period appeared in separate reports and not as *wenshi ziliao* publications.

accounts, such as the 1965 narration of Sino–Russian border conflict at the turn of the twentieth century, had interwoven elements of class struggle and nationalist resistance that highlighted the role of peasants, 1980s *wenshi ziliao* recast the successful migrant entrepreneur as a central character in the nationalist story of the northeast borderland.

With this in mind, we turn first to the story of how *wenshi ziliao* participants in the 1980s reconciled themes of nationalist continuity and socialist revolution in rewriting this borderland history. While touting continuity and comprehensiveness as critical principles of historical reconstruction, PPCC leaders also structured history in a way that conferred onto the Party the status of national liberator and subsumed the recent catastrophes beneath a longue durée perspective on the Party's historical role. They did this by organizing historical materials into the categories of "old society" (pre-1931), "Japanese occupation" (1931–1945), and "liberation" (post-1949) in such a way that history appeared to progress inevitably from dark oppression to CCP-led emancipation. Explaining the concept of historical change that underlay *wenshi ziliao* production, a report by the local PPCC of Fuyuan County describes the thought processes of the *wenshi ziliao* research committee's vice-chair, Zhang Jitai, as follows: "[He] experienced the three periods of old china, false Manchukuo, and new china, tasting the bitterness of the human experience. In the new society, particularly since the third meeting of the twelfth session of the [CCP's] Central Committee, the Party's enlightened policy inspired him to grasp his pen and describe and indict the corrupt politics and people's harsh conditions in the old society."[6] Eliding discontinuities within the Maoist period and between the Maoist and post-Mao periods, *wenshi ziliao* editors reconfigured history into three distinct stages that prioritized above everything else the events of Japanese imperialism and national consolidation.

This nationalist framework for organizing historical chronology offset and contained the messiness of political and ideological conflict that took place under Communist rule. This way of dividing history informed the kinds of questions that editors asked informants, incorporating within the questions themselves value-laden assumptions about historical periodization across the "liberation" divide. The following questions illustrate this:

[6] Zhengxie fuyuan xian weiyuanhui bangongshi, "Guanyu erjie erci huiyi de cailiao" ("Regarding the Materials of the Second Meeting of the Second Session of the Fuyuan County PPCC") (Mar. 15, 1985) (Fuyuan City Archives).

1) What was peasant life like after land reform? What role did those who joined the military and participated in fighting play in defeating GMD reactionaries? Give examples comparing people's living situation at that time to that during the nine years of false Manchukuo.
2) Explain the situation with the [postliberation] recovery of each occupation and industry in Fujin, and explain the development and change in industry, commerce, medicine/hygiene, education, etc. (including how many factories, the situation with production, main products, annual production, number of shops, their characteristics, main products they sold, annual sales, and income; how many hospitals, names of reputable doctors, medical fields; how many schools, how many teachers, provide a list of names of school principals, number of students, be clear about age).
3) Describe the position and role of the CCP from 1945–49 in democratic revolution in Fujin (including people and important decisions, etc.).[7]

These questions directed informants to frame their answers in terms of measuring the significant extent of progress that Party control had brought to society in contrast with the preliberation period. The highly detailed information that interviewers were hoping to glean was geared toward providing specific, persuasive evidence of the Party's role in ushering in improvements on a wide range of economic, social, and cultural fronts.

During the earlier phase of *wenshi ziliao* between 1959 and 1965, as Uradyn Bulag has shown, Zhou Enlai oversaw the production of two main genres of memoir, one written by former "reactionaries," the most famous being the last emperor, Pu Yi, and the other written by Party revolutionaries.[8] The former cast a dark shadow on the pre-1949 period, while the latter celebrated the Communist Party's glorious history of constructing a new, enlightened society. In the 1980s, however, the post-Mao reform agenda required redeeming the pre-1949 history as part of a continuous thread of national development and as a reference point for affirming the value of market reform. The Party faced a quandary of how to balance a nationalist narrative of continuous progress and heroism celebrating Chinese character with a Party liberation narrative relegating the preliberation period to the category of unredeemed feudal oppression. In an effort to resolve this, *wenshi ziliao* committees targeted a range of materials that contributed to the intertwined construction of both narratives. A general outline of contents for the pre-1945 period drafted by the Raohe County *wenshi ziliao* committee, for instance, is divided into

[7] Fujin xian zhengxie, "Qing lao tongzhi xie huiyilu cankao tigang" ("Reference Outline for Asking Old Comrades to Write Memoirs") (Aug. 8, 1981) (Fujin City Archives): 2–3.
[8] Bulag, "Can the Subalterns Not Speak?"

two sections on the Republican and Manchukuo periods, respectively. The section on the former lends emphasis to positive developments in agriculture, business, education, and medicine alongside negative accounts of banditry and opium, gambling and prostitution dens, while the section on Manchukuo emphasizes negative aspects of colonial oppression juxtaposed against positive recollections of anticolonial resistance and the Party's role in it.[9] For each of the two periods, the editors create a positive/negative binary that simultaneously promotes the Party liberation and nationalist versions of history. While Japanese colonial rule is the primary foil for a nationalist reconstruction of the period between 1931 and 1945, the approach to organizing collection of materials related to the pre-1931 "Republican" period presents social chaos and moral corruption as the main negatives against which progress in modernization is defined. *Wenshi ziliao* collectors along the northeast borderland thus articulated three distinctive historical features of the region: Chinese achievements in transforming the borderland economically and culturally; chaos, violence, and corruption endemic to the "wild" northeast frontier; and a unique experience of colonialism and anticolonial resistance.

Using these tropes, they attempted to weave together a narrative integrating an emphasis on modernization and development with a vindication of the Party's role as liberator of the society and the nation. While the negative representation of banditry contributed to the Party liberation narrative of preliberation social disorder, at other times *wenshi ziliao* editors portrayed banditry in a more positive light as an unofficial agent of the borderland's integration into the Chinese nation. Planning for work in the year 1986, the Heilongjiang *wenshi ziliao* office laid out the three "main special topics" that should be the focus of material collection: the Chinese Eastern Railroad (CER),[10] banditry, and land administrative development.[11] The order in which these topics are listed is telling of the historical narrative that editors were constructing, progressing from Russian railroad imperialism, embodied by the CER, to unofficial and official agents of Chinese national integration of the borderland, as represented by the movement of Chinese bandits and state officials into the

---

[9] "Raohe wenshi ziliao zhengji cankao tigang" ("Reference Outline for Collecting Raohe *Wenshi Ziliao*") (Materials of Raohe County PPCC's Second *Wenshi Ziliao* Work Conference) (1985) (Raohe County Archive).

[10] The CER was an extension of the Trans-Siberian Railroad that cut through Manchuria, overseen by Finance Minister Sergei Witte as an important instrument of Russian colonial expansion.

[11] Heilongjiang sheng zhengxie wenshi bangongshi, "1986 nian sheng zhengxie wenshi gongzuo jihua" ("Heilongjiang Provincial PPCC's Plans for *Wenshi Ziliao* Work in 1986") (Mar. 26, 1986) (Heilongjiang Provincial Archive).

region. *Wenshi ziliao* participants thus drew on the political and social ambiguities of the borderland and its ensemble of characters to address selectively different aspects of post-Mao ideology, reconciling narratives of liberation emphasizing the pre/post-1949 divide and of nationalist consolidation stressing continuity across the twentieth century.

In individual *wenshi ziliao* memoirs, former migrant entrepreneurs creatively engaged with these tensions in post-Mao discourse to construct their life narratives, drawing on and adapting symbolic images, literary conventions, and publicly circulating narratives.[12] In doing so, they brought to bear their own set of moral and emotional resources for interpreting historical events, drawing attention to inner conflicts and ambivalences and giving voice to psychological and moral dimensions of historical experience.[13] The construction of the self and subjectivity by even the marginalized illiterate individual operates in complex, socially embedded ways and reflects the interdependent workings of personal narration and political discourse.[14] The multiple dimensions of narrativity within the former migrants' life history accounts thus constitute a contested terrain where the individual intervened in and superimposed himself/herself onto the officially sanctioned discourse of History.

In the *wenshi ziliao* context, the flexible localization of memory production and the transitional open-endedness of discourse construction lent a certain space for informants and writers to retailor their life stories in creative ways. If, as Alena Pfoser has argued, memories are "always both

[12] As Ruth Behar shows in her in-depth analysis of the single life history of a poor woman in Mexico, even uneducated and socially marginalized individuals develop a complex cosmological framework built upon a repertoire of circulating stories through which to construct their own life histories, and the "storied selves" thus produced embody "the ambiguous double meaning of 'historias' as histories and stories." Ruth Behar, *Translated Woman: Crossing the Border with Esperanza's Story* (Boston, MA: Beacon Press, 2003). Discussed in Mary Jo Maynes, Jennifer Pierce, and Barbara Laslett, *Telling Stories: The Use of Personal Narratives in the Social Sciences and History* (Ithaca, NY: Cornell University Press, 2008), 75.
[13] As Gwyn Prins has pointed out, memories of distant but formative events in one's life such as childhood can reevoke moments in the past with a fresh intensity and vivid clarity that is irretrievable in its complex psychological and social dimensions through any other source. Gwyn Prins, "Oral History," in Peter Burke, ed., *New Perspectives on Historical Writing* (University Park, PA: Pennsylvania State University Press, 2001), 120–155.
[14] The contrast at a structural level between testimonies by Japanese World War Two survivors and former Chinese migrants to Manchuria highlights the significance of political context embedded within the very structure of life histories. Japanese wartime survivors, recalling their experiences in the context of a vacuum of public memory and official discourse on that period, created stories in terms of amorphous wanderings absent of any temporal closure, while Chinese migration testimonies superimposed their own life experiences in a clear progressive teleology onto an established PRC discourse of nationalist redemption. See Haruko Cook and Theodore Cook, *Japan at War: An Oral History* (New York, NY: New Press; Distributed by W. W. Norton, 1992): 12.

'embedded' and 'embodied,'" *wenshi ziliao* participants intervened in
history by negotiating between and interfusing "embeddedness" in the
national state discourses and "embodiment" of a "unique set of past
experiences" of the northeast borderland.[15] Former migrant entrepreneurs wove contradictory versions of history into the fabric of their
personal accounts, and they did so in a way that affirmed their lives as
stories of continuous progress and transformative redemption. In a *wenshi
ziliao* account that he wrote in Jiamusi, for instance, former migrant
entrepreneur Xing Jinghuan laid out the temporal structure of his life
history in a way that subtly navigated contradictions in the party-state's
historical identity. He presented the division of old from new, "feudal"
past from Communist liberation, in terms of his own personal development from inexperienced youth to seasoned adult. He writes, "I am
a seventy-eight-year old man of experience who had ventured through
the business world for twenty years in the old society, who at the age of
thirty-six happily met with liberation," depicting his twenty years of
business activities prior to 1949 as a youthful prelude to the transformative moment in his life of Communist liberation. In doing so, he employs
the temporal logic of the broader national narrative to structure his own
path toward economic success, yet the official temporal marker of 1949
does not appear. Instead, he refers to the founding of the Communist
state in terms of his own age, and, by extension, his formative stage of
personal growth.

The CCP's victory serves as a personal marker dividing Xing
Jinghuan's youth from his maturation into an experienced businessman.
The grand sweep of CCP history, and the official demarcation of history
into the dark old society and the bright new order, are circumscribed
within the life trajectory of the individual. The opening section of his
memoir, entitled "The hardships of venturing into commercial enterprise
in the old society,"[16] adapts the Communist discourse of collective suffering under the old regime to foreground his own attributes of courage
and determination in the early stages of his career. In this way, he
translates the public memory of past social injustices into a vehicle for
validating the individual's drive to get ahead in entrepreneurial pursuits.

This process of inscribing his personal history onto the state's official
historical timeline was not, however, without inherent tensions.
As discussed earlier in this volume, official narratives of twentieth-

---

[15] Alena Pfoser, "Between Russia and Estonia: Narratives of Place in a New Borderland,"
Nationalities Papers, Journal of Nationalism and Ethnicity 42.2 (2014): 269–285.

[16] Xing Jinghuan, "Wo congshi shangye liushi duo nian de jingli" ("My Over Sixty Years'
Experience with Commercial Enterprises"), *Jiamusi wenshi ziliao* (Jiamusi shi weiyuan
hui wenshi ziliao yanjiu weiyuan hui), 8 (1989): 80.

century history revealed a tension between two historiographical tendencies of the Party: to assert its legitimacy as liberator of China by defining the new order against the old society, and to define itself against the excesses of the Cultural Revolution by rehabilitating aspects of that "dark" past. There was a resurgence of interest in and a positive reevaluation of aspects of the Chinese past ranging from Confucius to GMD officials formerly regarded as the implacable enemy. Chinese historians during the 1980s reexamined the role of Chinese entrepreneurs during the early twentieth century in heroic terms as patriotic pioneers leading China in the path of economic modernization.

Xing Jinghuan skillfully maneuvered these tensions in the way that he structured his own life history, maintaining the temporal divide between old and new while valorizing his commercial activities in the pre-"liberation" period. While acknowledging the PRC's founding as a temporal marker, Xing Jinghuan portrayed the span of history as a continuous line from childhood to old age. According to this teleology, the "old society" appeared as a phase of cumulative business experience that served as the foundation for later commercial success. While paying lip service to the major events of Communist Party history, therefore, he was restructuring that history into a continuous trajectory in the individual's life progress from youth to seniority, and in the process reconfigured the "feudal old society" as a vigorous stage of youthful enterprising spirit integral to his lifelong course of personal development.

While writers reconstructing their own lives found subtle ways to reconcile problematic contradictions in post-Mao discourse, local PPCC officials and *wenshi ziliao* editors struggled to develop a conceptual framework for guiding the collection of materials that could overcome the tension between continuity-focused modernization and discontinuity-focused liberation narratives of history. At Raohe County's first *wenshi ziliao* work conference in 1984, the local PPCC chair, Zhang Zhenbang, delineated Raohe's twentieth-century past into three successive stages: a destructive, corrupt opium- and banditry-driven economy; Japanese oppression and anti-Japanese resistance during the Manchukuo period; and rapid agricultural and commercial development driven in part by the state-sponsored migration and mobilization of de-enlisted soldiers and sent-down youth after the founding of the PRC.[17] Zhang highlights the northeast borderland's special historical

---

[17] Raohe zhengxie bangongshi, "Gaoju aiguo zhuyi qizhi kaichuang woxian wenshi ziliao gongzuo de xin jumian – zhang zhenbang tongzhi zai raohe xian diyici wenshi ziliao gongzuo huiyi shang de jianghua" ("Raise High the Banner of Patriotism to Pioneer the New Phase of *Wenshi Ziliao* Work in Our County – Comrade Zhang Zhenbang's Speech at Raohe County's First *Wenshi Ziliao* Work Conference") (Mar. 7, 1984) (Raohe County Archive): 9–10.

character as a wild and unruly frontier, an intense site of Japanese occupation, and the inspiration for political and economic transformation and consolidation. In so doing, he sets his region apart historically while simultaneously fitting it into the Party-prescribed national liberation teleology.

At the same time, a detailed draft of the *"wenshi ziliao* reference outline for collecting materials," distributed at the same conference, tells a rather different story of a continuous process of the borderland's economic, cultural, and political development and integration across the 1949 divide. It begins in the late Qing period with attention to Raohe's administrative establishment by the imperial government as a county, and subsequent officials' efforts to encourage Chinese migrant settlement and cultivation of the land. It then proceeds to discuss the emergence of the opium industry, with primary emphasis given not to its destructiveness (though that is included as a factor), but rather to its productive role in spawning commercial enterprises and agricultural settlements that drove the county's development. Attention is also given to cultural developments in the form of schools, charitable associations, medical establishments, and temples. As might be expected, the section on the Manchukuo period focuses on aspects of Japanese oppressive rule and organized anti-Japanese resistance. Moving on to the "liberation war" and post-1949 PRC periods, while including references to socialist land reform and political campaigns, the overall focus is on the renewed project of economically developing and integrating the borderland through initiatives like the mobilization of soldiers and sent-down youth in the "Northern Wilderness" labor campaigns.[18]

While the two stories, one told by the PPCC leader in his speech and the other conveyed by the collection outline, do not overtly contradict one another, the difference in emphasis on either historical continuity or rupture across the 1949 divide is evident. In both cases, the authors place Raohe's distinctive historical identity as a borderland at the front and center. But whereas Zhang Zhenbang, in his position as leading party cadre, privileges the Party's role as liberator, the local *wenshi ziliao* editors who drafted the outline highlighted instead the continuous historical achievements and progress of their regional community irrespective of Party leadership.

Socialist Revolution and Market Liberalization in Redemptive Accounts of Migrant Enterprise

Former entrepreneurs, in their own *wenshi ziliao* recollections of relocation to the northeast from "China proper," juxtaposed the "Communist

---

[18] Raohe zhengxie bangongshi, "Wenshi ziliao zhengji cankao tigang (taolungao)" ("Discussion Draft of Reference Outline for Collecting *Wenshi Ziliao*") (Mar. 1984): 1–7.

liberation/feudal past" and "celebration of pre-1949 enterprise" discourses to create self-valorizing narratives of personal redemption and triumphal individualism. Wang Ruiyi's locally edited reminiscences of his past experiences as a gold mining speculator along the Amur River basin open with a formulaic description of feudal oppressiveness, official corruption, and foreign aggression in his hometown in Shandong Province.

> During the Guangxu years [1875–1908] the court was already very corrupt. There were many foreign missionaries in Shandong, and the foreigners went everywhere wreaking havoc and tyranny. Corrupt officials bribed and blackmailed, they governed people abusively, and villagers had a hard time getting by. There were many people in my family and it was hard making a living. So at age twelve I started laboring in the fields, and when I was eighteen I ventured east of the pass.

Wang opens the narrative with a clear reference to the standard PRC historical discourse on the dark pre-1949 past. This rhetorical strategy, though highlighting collective and personal hardships, casts a light of heroic determination on his migration to the northeast.

Along with lending official validity to personal hardship, Wang invoked the "oppressive old order" discourse to make sense of failures and destructive habits formed during his mining years. According to his account, soon after landing a job through his brother in Harbin, he signed on with recruiters for the Guandu Mining Company to work at its mines in Taiping Valley along the Amur River. These mines had come into existence as part of late Qing projects of frontier consolidation. Beginning in the 1880s, Li Hongzhang sponsored their development as part of a "Self-Strengthening" campaign to adopt Western techniques and to invest in a limited program of industrialization. In northern Manchuria, the object against which Li and his cohorts directed this initiative was the expanding Russian development of the area on the opposite bank of the river, and in particular a parallel system of Russian state-sponsored mines.

Qing officials visiting the region at the turn of the century regarded Chinese migrants circulating among the mines as an uncontrollable lot whose activities frequently disrupted orderly management of the mines.[19] At the same time, authorities supervising the mines anxiously promoted the recruitment of Chinese migrant labor both to generate official

---

[19] See Li Shutang, *Dongjiao jixing* (*Records of Travels along the Eastern Borderland*) (s.l.: s.n., 1899) and Cao Tingjie, *Eguo xiboli dongpian jiyao* (*Account of Russian Eastern Siberia*) (1885), reprinted in Shen Yunlong, comp., *Jindai zhongguo shiliao congkan xubian* (*Collection of Modern Chinese Historical Materials*), vol. 52 (Taibei xian, Yonghe zhen: Wenhai chubanshe, 1978).

revenues and to secure control over the border region.[20] With the excep-
tion of the years of Russian occupation between 1900 and 1906, the
mines operated according to a hybrid model of private management and
official supervision in which the Heilongjiang governor-general, the
Beijing government, and businessmen recruited from China proper
shared the profits from gold production. Within this context of overlapping political interests, the two adjacent mining sites of Guanyinshan
and Duluhe merged into the Guandu mining enterprise in 1913 in order
to resolve disputed boundaries of territorial jurisdiction and local revenue
extraction.

Over the ensuing decade the mines became reorganized into private
joint-stock enterprises, and in 1924, the Zhenyuan Company, founded by
Heilongjiang transportation officials in 1916 before going private in 1919,
assumed management of the Guandu mining site.[21] Regional officials
adapted their political leverage to assume the role of official-
entrepreneurs supervising the reconstituted mining companies. This evolution of the private investment/official supervision model structured the
proliferation during the 1910s and 1920s of commercial and land development companies through the collaboration of private investors and
regional officials. The larger of the enterprises used these political connections to assume control over vast amounts of land and to manipulate
local market prices for everyday goods, while establishing recruiting
offices in major cities throughout southern Manchuria and northern
China to supply cheap migrant labor.[22]

In recounting his experiences as a migrant laborer, Wang Ruiyi drew
upon the Communist narrative of class exploitation in pre-1949 society to
attach moral and political significance to his personal struggles:

During the Republican period gold miners at Taiping Valley were organized
under the system of manager supervision. In reality the manager was really the
labor boss. Food, clothing, housing, everything was under his control. Production
was mainly administered in sections, and when [the miners] handed over the
mined gold to the manager, it was valued according to internal pricing.

[20] The mixture of suspicion and desire with which Qing officials regarded Chinese migrants
was particularly evident in the clash between Qing and Russian authorities over claims to
mining privileges at the border settlement of Mohe. Chinese migrants, freely circulating
across both sides of the Heilong River, constituted a community with ambiguous political
loyalties on whom both states relied for their frontier consolidation projects. See
Liu Wenfeng, *Dongchui jixing* (*Travels to the Eastern Frontier*) (China: s.n., 1901): 16–20.
[21] Wan Fulin, Zhang Boying, and Li Yushu, *Heilongjiang zhigao* (*Heilongjiang Gazetteer*),
"Kuangchan" (Taibei xian, Yonghe zhen: Wen hai chu ban she, 1965, 1933).
[22] For more on these developments, see Tian Fang, *Zhongguo yimin shilue* (*History of
Chinese Migration*) (Beijing: Zhi shi chubanshe: Xinhua shudian, Beijing faxing suo
faxing, 1986).

I remember the manager at Beizhongka [mining site] was surnamed Shi. He allocated to a dozen or so of us a big section. Opening up and digging deep into the gorge, the work was really exhausting. But come autumn we still hadn't seen any gold, so it was all for nothing. And in the winter the manager didn't give unskilled workers any clothing, so most went away frozen.[23]

Wang articulates his failed mining efforts through identifying himself as a member of the exploited class of unskilled workers helplessly subject to the labor boss management's control. Using the Communist historical discourse as a reinterpretive lens, he resignifies personal failure as righteous victimization and liberates himself from responsibility for failed enterprise by emptying his past of social agency.

Wang uses a similar rhetorical tactic for representing his struggles with destructive addictions that were a commonplace feature of migrant mining communities. With the large influx of young men circulating between seasonal lumber and mining enterprises in northeastern Manchuria, gambling houses became profitable enterprises catering to their restless lifestyle and fortune-seeking desires. Though officially illegal, these became lucrative businesses for entrepreneurs colluding with local officials and generated supplementary income for the land development and mining companies. Travelers in the region during the 1920s and 1930s observed the integration of gambling into the migrants' seasonal labor cycles of productive earning and wasteful consumption. According to their reports, the migrants would alternate between making quick fortunes, gambling their earnings away, and scattering into throngs of bandits preying on unsuspecting travelers.[24]

Whereas contemporary observers had associated gambling with an endemic social pattern of migration in this region, after 1949 the problem of designating blame for "social ills" such as gambling and prostitution became a core concern of the PRC government. In defining its own vision of purifying the national body from social decay, the CCP collected stories of those who had engaged in these industries to demonstrate the

---

[23] Wang Ruiyi, "Taojin yu 'fuma' shenghuo" ("My Life as Gold Digger and 'Emperor's Son-in-Law'"), *Yichun wenshi ziliao* 1 (Yichun shi weiyuan hui wenshi ziliao yanjiu weiyuan hui, 1984): 147–148.

[24] Owen Lattimore, *Manchuria: Cradle of Conflict* (New York, NY: Macmillan Company, 1932; republished, New York: AMS Press, ca. 1975): 228. A Chinese official traveling through the region at the turn of the century also commented on the gambling habits associated with frontier enterprise, remarking that it was not uncommon for people to flee or even to lose their lives on account of gambling debts. Cao Tingjie, *Account of Russian Eastern Siberia*, 118. A similar gambling culture developed in other booming frontier mining towns such as those in California, where immigration laws exacerbated the lopsided gender and age ratio of Chinese immigrants. See Yong Chen, *Chinese San Francisco 1850–1943: A Trans-Pacific Community* (Stanford, CA: Stanford University Press, ca. 2000).

corrupt practices of the former regime while mobilizing expressions of the people's gratitude for their transformation by the new regime into morally renewed citizens. Former prostitutes, for instance, were rounded up and mobilized to "speak bitterness" by recounting harrowing tales of abuse, portraying themselves as innocent victims of past exploitation ripe for salvation and reeducation by the Party.[25] The subjects' historical agency and complex maneuverings for social mobility were thus reified in binary terms of exploiter/exploited in order to align state and subject in a smooth, seamless transition together as joint liberator and liberated. According to this schema, "liberation" would happen through the Party's active volition and the liberated subjects' passive receiving of the Party's instruction.

Wang utilized this discursive project to alter the meaning of his gambling addiction, redefining his active and at times self-destructive participation in the boom-and-bust cycle of frontier ventures as a politically sanctioned struggle against the forces of class exploitation.

As soon as the managers saw that a mining worker had money in his hands, they devised a nasty scheme. In those days the mining bureau's "treasure bureau" and "dominoes bureau"[26] were thriving. The labor bosses ran them all. I had never gambled before, and even after the gambling bureau had been in operation for a while I still didn't play. But the manager wouldn't let me keep my money in my pockets, and so he pulled me and pushed me into playing. He grabbed my hands and taught me, and within a few days I picked it up. Once I'd learned it I wanted to do it, once I started I couldn't stop, and once I'd become addicted I was bound to lose. In a short time I lost all of that gold. The whole year of tiring work was all for nothing.[27]

He coalesces all the managers into a monolithic entity and conceives of gambling itself as a manifestation of "bureau" authority, identifying the very word for gambling with a unit of managerial control. Stripping himself of agency, he describes the process of gambling as a negative inversion of political reeducation in which he lost control over his own hands.

Here the Communist narrative of class exploitation serves as a redemptive transcript that expiates Wang from responsibility for the losses that he incurred. In other parts of his account, however, he turns to the economic liberalization narrative celebrating pre-1949 economic development to celebrate his efforts to make a quick fortune. By alternating between and juxtaposing these two aspects of post-Mao

[25] See, for instance, Gail Hershatter, *Dangerous Pleasures: Prostitution and Modernity in Twentieth Century Shanghai* (Berkeley, CA: University of California Press, 1997).
[26] Names referring to gambling facilities.
[27] Wang Ruiyi, "My Life as Gold Digger and 'Emperor's Son-in-Law,'" 148–149.

discourse, Wang (and the editor organizing Wang's life history) inter-
fused images of the "exploited worker" and "swashbuckling entrepreneur" to create a redemptive personal narrative of bold migrant initiative
overcoming hardship. This rhetorical strategy becomes evident in his
description of the circumstances surrounding his temporary return to
Harbin from the gold mines:

> On my way to Harbin, there was also a little episode – I squatted in a "balizi" (prison)
> for two days. In the years of the Republic there were a lot of people who went to
> Heilongjiang escaping from famine and begging for food. When I was ready to get on
> a boat at Tongjiang, the harbor was full of people begging for small change. Though
> I say I "ran off" destitute at that time, in my pocketbook I still had a little gold and
> quite a bit of *dayang* cash. Whoever came to me for money was able to receive some in
> his hands. To some I gave one yuan, to some five jiao. Currency during the Republic
> was strong. It was only a little over a yuan to buy a sack of "Shuanghesheng" Golden
> Rooster-brand flour. The police got red-eyed [with envy] when they saw me holding
> out big amounts of money. At that time the "gray dogs" only made about ten bucks
> a month. Seeing that there's oil who wouldn't skim off of it? So they asked what did
> I do? I boastfully said: "My esteemed name is Wang Maoying, manager of Jinman
> Valley. What is this little money worth to me?" Once the "gray dogs" saw that there
> was a lot of oil on me, they put me behind bars for two days. They found someone
> from Jinman Valley who verified that I was indeed Labor Boss Wang, I gave them
> a little money, and they released me.[28]

An abrupt shift takes place from Wang's self-depiction as the exploited
worker to his sudden reappearance on the scene as the ostentatious labor
boss. To illustrate his wealth, he describes a scene in which he is casually
handing out generous amounts of cash into the extended hands of
a crowd of beggars. The mid-to-late 1920s was a period in which
waves of migration from northern China reached a crescendo.
Contemporary reports by journalists, sociologists, and famine relief
agencies described the programs coordinated among fellow local organizations in northern China, international famine relief agencies, regional and local government officials, and land development companies in
the northeast to relocate masses of refugees. These reports frequently
addressed complications arising from bureaucratic entanglements, lack
of sufficient coordination, and the migrants' inability to adapt to the new
conditions.[29]

[28] Ibid., 149–150.
[29] See Feng Hefa, *Zhongguo nongcun jingji lun: nongcun jingji lunwen xuanji* (*Selected Articles on the Chinese Rural Economy*) (Shanghai: Liming shudian, 1934): 340–350; Su Xinliu, "Lüping henan zhenzai hui huodong shimo" ("History of the Activities of the Henan-in-Beiping Disaster Relief Organization"), *Nandu xuetan* (Feb. 2004); Andrew J. Nathan, *History of the China International Relief Commission* (Cambridge, MA: East Asian Research Center, Harvard University, 1965).

Wang's portrayal of the starving refugees resonates with the PRC discourse on the Republican period as one of deprivation and hardship prior to liberation by the CCP. Rather than using this scene to comment on and testify to the period's stark social and economic conditions, however, he employs this imagery to define by contrast and draw attention to his own fast-earned wealth, swashbuckling generosity, and exuberance of spirit. He further delineates the scale of his fortune by alluding to Shuanghesheng, a successful business venture founded by Zhang Tingge, a migrant hailing from Wang's native region. The *wenshi ziliao* project in Heilongjiang devoted extensive biographical accounts to this prominent businessman's legacy as part of the post-Mao concern with discovering a new history of the development of capitalism with Chinese characteristics. In addition to valorizing Zhang Tingge's personal rise to successful entrepreneurship, the publications extolled Zhang's managerial principles as a model for reforming contemporary managerial practices. Standing out incongruously from the surrounding narrative of material deprivation, Wang Ruiyi's reference to the "Golden Rooster brand" resembles an advertisement promoting this enterprise's products, and, by extension, situates his own life experience within the context of Chinese enterprising initiative. More importantly, his promotion of Shuanghesheng's products juxtaposed with the beggars' poverty pulls together two competing modes of post-Mao historical representation to craft an image of himself as a socially conscious entrepreneurial hero.

Individuals who contributed their memoirs to the *wenshi ziliao*, therefore, were quite adept at turning tensions in post-Mao discourse between condemnation and redemption of the pre-1949 social order into a productive framework for reconstructing their lives in terms of heroic redemption. As an alternative to making a choice between continuity and discontinuity, *wenshi ziliao* editors attempted to reconcile socialist and nonsocialist elements of post-Mao historiography by including them in the narrative in an undifferentiated way. In his illustration of what kinds of materials "reflect deeply the fundamental character of society," had "important realistic significance," and "can move and educate youth," the vice-chair of the Harbin *wenshi ziliao* research committee office, Li Xingchang, wrote that:

[A]s for ordinary events and people, one can write about them so long as they have a typical case significance and can represent particular characteristics of that time period. For example, the rise and fall of a feudalistic landlord family; the development of a factory, shop, or restaurant; the invention of a name-brand product; or the life experiences and hardships of every kind of person such as soldiers, shop employees, Daoists, sorcerers, Buddhist nuns, and prostitutes are all within the scope of collection.[30]

Instead of presenting them as diametrically opposed forces of history, Li refers to people from a broad cross-section of social classes simply as typical case studies representing multiple dimensions of historical reality. In doing so, editors like Li were rejecting rigid black-and-white ideological polarization in favor of a more subtle and inclusive approach that left the materials more open to multiple interpretations.

"Highlighting the Best of the Special Characteristics of United Front and Locality"

Further illustrating their efforts to reconcile the Party's socialist ideology with its market reform agenda, *wenshi ziliao* editors celebrated local, regional, and national identities as the defining features of liberation in a way that elided reference to class difference. This was part of a broader post-Mao cultural approach to repackaging the past, from museum exhibitions reframing Communist revolution in terms of continuous economic modernization to textbooks' downplaying class struggle as a feature of the Party-centered nationalist narrative.[31]

In the northeast context, by incorporating references to the Party within a broader sea of references to anti-Russian and anti-Japanese resistance, Chinese business successes, and international cultural vibrancy, *wenshi ziliao* editors implicitly redefined what the Communist Party's socialist ideology meant. A report drafted by the *wenshi ziliao* office of the Heilongjiang PPCC on October 10, 1980, addressed to the national *wenshi ziliao* office, reflected this orientation. Explaining the Heilongjiang committee's priorities in the upcoming years, the letter foregrounded anti-Japanese and anti-Russian patriotic resistance as the centerpiece of upcoming publications. Aspects of socialist revolution such as land reform were buried later in the document as secondary concerns.[32] Discussing their plans for editing the third and fourth volumes of Heilongjiang *wenshi ziliao*, the

---

[30] Li Xingchang, "Huiji houshi de guangrong shiye – mantan wenshi ziliao gongzuo" ("A Glorious Enterprise Benefiting Later Generations – Some Comments about *Wenshi Ziliao* Work"), in Haerbin shi zhengxie weiyuanhui mishuchu, *Haerbin zhengxie* (Harbin PPCC), no. 2 (no. 6 overall) (1983): 33–34.
[31] See, for instance, Denton, *Exhibiting the Past*, and Jones, "Policy and History Curriculum Reform in Post-Mao China."
[32] Heilongjiang sheng zhengxie wenshi ban, Untitled Report on *Wenshi Ziliao* by the Heilongjiang Provincial *Wenshi Ziliao* Office. Heilongjiang Provincial Archive document no. 56, record no. 1, vol. 195 (quanzong 56, mulu 1, juanhao 195) (hereafter abbreviated as Heilongjiang Provincial Archive 56:1:195) (Harbin: Heilongjiang sheng danganguan, Oct. 10, 1980).

provincial office staff identified four main topics that were to be covered. The first two were "anti-Japanese resistance" and "Manchukuo crimes," while the last two were developments in "economy and commerce" and "culture and arts." This summary includes no mention of socialism. Instead, the cadres present special regional characteristics of anti-imperialist nationalism and economic and cultural development as the key historical features, resonating with the new post-Mao priorities of political reconsolidation and economic modernization. Having identified these key historical subjects, the authors of the report conclude that the editors' primary goals are to "highlight the best of the special characteristics of united front and locality."[33]

Wenshi ziliao organizers subsumed Communist Party–related events within a broad and disparate range of historical topics highlighting nationalism and economic development. The manuscript drafts collected by the Harbin *wenshi ziliao* teams between 1982 and 1986 were evidence of this tendency. The specific topics that these manuscripts addressed included the following: the development of enterprises such as the Tongji company and the Tianxingfu flour mill along with celebrations of the lives of entrepreneurs and industrialists like Wu Baixiang and Zhang Tingge; cases of foreign, particularly Japanese, aggression such as the Harbin police bureau under Japanese occupation, the Japanese consulate in Harbin, and the Manchukuo army; examples of anti-foreign resistance from the anti-Japanese student movement to an entire volume commemorating the fortieth anniversary of the Japanese defeat; mass organizations such as the Democratic People's Youth League and the Harbin Progressive Women's League; Party heroes and martyrs such as Zhao Yiman; and events highlighting the city's international appeal like the birth of the Harbin annual international ice festival, the founding of an international newspaper, the educational contributions of Russian translator and former student in Japan Deng Jiemin, and the activities of a Chinese-American writer.[34]

Wenshi ziliao committees at the county level echoed this philosophy. Reporting in 1986, members of the Party section of the Fujin County PPCC similarly tied together commercial and cultural developments with anti-Japanese resistance as the noteworthy subjects for inclusion in the third volume of the county's *wenshi ziliao*. Assessing the significance of these materials, the authors of the report note that "this accurate historical record is meaningful for understanding the county's history,

---

[33] Heilongjiang sheng zhengxie wenshi bangongshi, "Heilongjiang Provincial PPCC's Plans for *Wenshi Ziliao* Work in 1986."
[34] Ibid., 200–204.

propagandizing the Party's united front policy, providing a model for enterprises' management experience, and educating the next generation."[35]

While highlighting themes of economic development and nationalist resistance, *wenshi ziliao* editors also re-invoked socialist concepts of collective justice, equality, and comradery using traditional values such as native place identity rather than class consciousness. The Harbin PPCC committee, for instance, seeking new channels of investment from overseas, highlighted the life history of industrialist Zhang Tingge in *wenshi ziliao* accounts that were circulated abroad and allegedly inspired one of Zhang's overseas relatives to revive his enterprises in Harbin. Representing private enterprise in humane rather than exploitative terms, these accounts emphasized native place sentiment as a centerpiece of Zhang Tingge's business philosophy. According to recollections included in the *wenshi ziliao*, he recruited his workers primarily from Ye and Huang Counties in Shandong, and "attitudes based on shared place origins gave the workers a feeling of intimacy with the boss. Reportedly Zhang Tingge employed men without suspicion and did not employ those he had doubts about . . . He never once fired anyone whom he had personally consented to enter Shuanghesheng business."[36]

Other *wenshi ziliao* accounts used the theme of fellow local ties to reevaluate private enterprise as a source of shared regional customs, pride, and prosperity. As one account described, before an employee made a return visit to his hometown, all of his coworkers would contribute a share of their earnings to send him off. "They would purchase some specialty gifts for that person so that people in his hometown would have the feeling that 'the people who venture northeast bring back a lot of stuff! They must be doing really well out there!' This would give that person a sense of pride."[37] As another *wenshi ziliao* account recorded, a saying in Leting echoed this sentiment with the catchy phrase that "the sons who stay at Yifahe do not descend from their donkeys when they see relatives."[38]

---

[35] Zhonggong zhengxie fujin xian dangzu, "Guanyu chuban 'fujin wenshi ziliao' di sanji de baogao" ("Report on the Publication of the Third Volume of 'Fujin *Wenshi Ziliao*'") (Documents of the Fujin County PPCC's Party Subcommittee, no. 5) (Nov. 24, 1986) (Fujin City Archives).

[36] Jin Zonglin, "Zhang tinge qiren qishi" ("Zhang Tingge, Who He Was and What He Did"), *Harbin wenshi ziliao* (Harbin shi weiyuan hui wenshi ziliao yanjiu weiyuan hui), 2 (1983): 34.

[37] Guo Zhaoyan and Zhang Xiaoyun, "Tieling deshenghao xingshuai shimo" ("The History of the Flourishing and Decline of Deshenghao Enterprise in Tieling"), *Liaoning wenshi ziliao 26* (Liaoning renmin chubanshe, 1989): 263.

[38] Liu Yiwang, "Jingdong liujia yu changchun yifahe" ("The Liu Clan of Jingdong and Yifahe of Changchun"), *Jilin wenshi ziliao* (Jilin sheng weiyuan hui wenshi ziliao yanjiu weiyuan hui) 15 (1987): 26.

Wenshi ziliao writers also used the theme of male comradery to high-light courageous entrepreneurial undertakings. In one account, the three cofounders of a flour mill in eastern Jilin set out individually from three adjacent counties in Shandong at ages ranging from seventeen to twenty-one years. "Along the way to the northeast they swore oaths of brother-hood loyalty to the bitter end. The three of them followed the Muling River eastward, traversing mountain ridges and crossing through valley gorgers, eating and sleeping out in the open the whole summer through as they moved along."[39] Similarly, industrialist Wu Baixiang recounted the humble fraternal origins of his commercial success in a memoir written in unpublished form in the 1920s and reprinted in the Harbin *wenshi ziliao*. "There were six of us, all staying at the inn with no money. All of us being dirt poor, we made a brotherhood pact between us." These poor compa-nions, Wu continues, shared everything equally, so that "when he had money I'd spend his, and when I had money he'd spend mine."[40] These accounts, by articulating the quest to make money in terms of fraternal egalitarianism, resonated with the Communist Party's attempt to recon-cile its socialist origins with market liberalization.

Pivoting toward nationalism, historical editors at the national level restructured modern history as an economic struggle between foreign imperialism and homegrown industries. Explaining the need for more emphasis on historical materials relating to the economy, a writer for the national PPCC, Rong Mengyuan, described his prescription for how *wenshi ziliao* editors should conduct research in this area:

On the economic front, we should address how, during the period since the Opium War, China industrialized, what role imperialism played in industrializa-tion, what part we [Chinese] played, what the relationship was between the two, how industries developed in each locality, and how each occupation developed. We should concretely research the Chinese economy according to each individual factory, occupation, and faction. Only in this way can problems be discussed clearly. In the past foreigners said China didn't have handicraft manufacturing workplaces. Did China have these or not? We must research this. Even more importantly, we should study materials on how imperialism penetrated the coun-tryside and controlled agriculture. We must have a planned approach to expand-ing collection.[41]

---

[39] Wang Chunsheng, "'Yuji huomo' de bianqian," *Jixi wenshi ziliao* 2 (Jixi shi wenshi ziliao weiyuanhui, 1986): 7.

[40] Wu Baixiang, "Wushi nian zishu" ("Recalling Fifty Years"), *Harbin wenshi ziliao* (Harbin shi weiyuan hui wenshi ziliao yanjiu weiyuan hui), 3 (1983): 32.

[41] Rong Mengyuan, "Mantan shiliao gongzuo" ("Commentary on Working with Historical Materials"), Qiqihaer shi zhengxie weiyuanhui wenshi ziliao yanjiu weiyuanhui, *Wenshi tongxun* (*Culture and History Newsletter*), no. 3 (no. 7 overall) (1984) (orig. from the National PPCC's *Wenshi tongxun*, no. 4 [1983]): 5.

Rong's nationalist vision for producing *wenshi ziliao* avoids any reference to socialist revolution, assessing twentieth-century history as a struggle not between social classes but between Chinese and foreign nationals. In doing so, he rehabilitates pre-1949 private enterprise as a positive aspect of nationalism. The focus on imperialism thus allows for dispensing with class struggle discourse by reconceiving of social and economic struggle in nationalist terms. At the same time, Rong's ambivalence about whether to locate the main propellant of economic change externally in foreign imperialism or internally in homegrown Chinese enterprise reflected a broader post-Mao conundrum about how to represent a past in which the Party did not play a major role. The competing priorities of finding historical precedent for market reform on one hand and reconceiving of the Communist Party as national liberator on the other informed these wavering tendencies in historical representation.

While at the national level Rong struggled with balancing these ideological priorities of the Party leadership, editors at the local and regional levels were much more prone to celebrate and magnify the achievements of former entrepreneurs as an assertion of local identity, assessing their contributions to society in nationalist terms of anti-imperialist struggle. One way that they did this was by housing articles celebrating the lives of former entrepreneurs within publications that also featured accounts of patriotic anti-foreign resistance. Summarizing the highlights of the first two volumes of Harbin *wenshi ziliao*, Niu Naiwen refers to accounts memorializing former entrepreneurs Wu Baixiang and Zhang Tingge together with references to other seemingly unrelated accounts of the 1929 Sino–Russian border conflict, the "Harbin electric streetcar workers' anti-Japanese strike," and Chinese boxer Ji Wanshan's challenge to a Russian strength giant.[42] By binding together these disparate articles under the theme of anti-imperialist nationalism, Niu and the compilers of these two volumes validate the historical and social credentials of private enterprise by presenting it as one integral component of a broader nationalist story.

Li Jianbai, who worked on Heilongjiang *wenshi ziliao*, reevaluated former commercial managers as valiant heroes in the struggle against foreign domination whose experiences provide both a testament to the superiority of Chinese national character and a lesson for post-Mao managerial reform. In his speech at the second provincial *wenshi ziliao* work

---

[42] Niu Naiwen, "Gaoju aiguo zhuyi qizhi kaichuang woshi wenshi ziliao gongzuo xin jumian" ("Raise High the Banner of Patriotism to Pioneer the New Phase of Our City's *Wenshi Ziliao* Work"), in Haerbin shi zhengxie weiyuanhui mishuchu, *Haerbin zhengxie* (*Harbin PPCC*), no. 3 (no. 13 overall) (1984) (Special Issue of [the First] Harbin City *Wenshi Ziliao* Work Conference): 56.

conference, he cited an account of the "Development of Chengji needle factory" as a reflection of the

> history of the Chinese national bourgeoisie's difficult development squeezed between internal troubles and external pressures. Under conditions of that time, this private enterprise competed with strong Japanese and German businesses to survive and develop. The primary reason for this [success] was that it made use of Chinese advantage to raise quality and keep down costs, and had much managerial experience. Some of this experience can be used as reference today.[43]

Rather than turning to the victimization narrative of Chinese humiliation to show how bad China's situation had been before Communist liberation, editors at the county and provincial levels highlighted their region's positive historical achievements while downplaying the Party's liberation role.

Retrospective accounts in local *wenshi ziliao* describe the colorful histories that some Chinese migrant enterprises had. According to one of these produced in Harbin, the creator of "Pockmarked Wang's" medical ointment, Wang Shusen, was the son of a former Qing imperial guard who had been part of a small, secrecy-bound circle that informally shared healing techniques for treating training-related injuries. Wang Shusen relocated to Harbin in the 1920s, where he refashioned his father's trade secrets "to invent a great ointment – 'Huguxiong ointment' – which specially cured all kinds of hypothermia and hypothermia-related sterility ... This cream was inexpensive, easy to apply and very effective, so whether they were sick or not people still put it on."[44] The pale moles on his face earned him and the product he sold the nickname Pockmarked Wang, and by the 1930s, his medicine was distributed "as far as Yili in Xinjiang and abroad to Japan, the Soviet Union, Mongolia, Southeast Asia and the United States." Other storeowners in Harbin tried to mimic his success using somewhat comical devices. While the sign over Wang's pharmacy read "The Real Old Pockmarked Wang's Medical Ointment Store," other storeowners displayed signs such as "The Real Pockmarked Wang's Medical Ointment Store," "This is really the Pockmarked Wang's Medical Ointment Store," and "The Real Fake Pockmarked Wang's Medical Ointment Store."

[43] Haerbin shi zhengxie weiyuanhui mishuchu, "Li jianbai tongzhi zai dierci quansheng wenshi ziliao gongzuo huiyi shang de jianghua" ("Comrade Li Jianbai's Speech at the Second Provincial *Wenshi Ziliao* Work Conference"), in *Haerbin shi zhengxie (Harbin PPCC)*, no. 3 (no. 13 overall) (Jan. 8, 1984) (Special Issue of [the First] Harbin City *Wenshi Ziliao* Work Conference): 38.
[44] Chen Zhankui and Chen Zhanyuan, "Chenshi zhenggu yuan de chuangjian he fazhan" ("The Founding and Development of Chen's Osteopathic Clinic"), *Harbin wenshiziliao* (Harbin shi weiyuan hui wenshi ziliao yanjiu weiyuan hui), vol. 5 (1984): 119.

Subsequently the street along which these businesses emerged came to be known as "Pockmarked Wang Road."[45]

Integrating Narratives of National Victimization and Regional Economic Expansion

Along with these colorful and amusing recollections, local editors found ways to organize survivor testimonies in ways that integrated nationalist victimization with celebrations of entrepreneurial achievement and commercial expansion. This is evident in editor Liu Banghou's compilation of testimonies by Chinese survivors of the Blagoveshchensk Massacre that had been collected in 1965. In his introductory statement, he conveys the article's main significance as lying in the exposure of the tragic violence and injustice wrought against the Chinese people:

> Hailanpao, Blagoveshchensk being the Russian name, is situated on the left bank of the Heilong River and on the right bank of the mouth of the Jingqili River, facing our country's border city, Heihe. Hailanpao is located in the long narrow area that originally was our country's Huanghe village near the bank of the Jingqili River and Meng Clan village near the bank of the Heilong River. These had been just across the Jingqili River from and mutually interacted with the Sixty-Four Villages East of the River.
>
> In 1856 the Czarist Russian fleet aggressively moved down the Heilong River and illegally established a sentry post at Hailanpao, calling it Ust-Zensk sentry post. The following year it was rebuilt as a Cossack town. In May 1858, to "celebrate" the signing of the unequal Sino–Russian Aigun Treaty, the Russian governor-general of eastern Siberia, Muraviev, renamed this place "Blagoveshchensk," meaning "Happy Tidings City," and secured the Czarist government's formal approval.
>
> Blagoveshchensk soon served as the political, economic, and military center of the Czarist Amur Province and became an important base for expansion and incursion into northeast China.[46]

Liu Banghou begins the introduction by positioning Blagoveshchensk and Heihe across the border from each other within the framework of contemporary Sino–Soviet geopolitical relations, an enduring legacy of the "unequal" treaties signed in 1860. He then immediately juxtaposes this current configuration with a detailed description of Blagoveshchensk's origins as an integral territory of China comprising a network of peaceful Chinese settlements interwoven with the "Sixty-Four Villages" as a natural

---

[45] Chen Kezheng and Pang Guowen, "Xiang you shengming de wangmazi gaoyao" ("The Celebrated Pockmarked Wang's Medical Ointment"), *Harbin wenshiziliao* (Harbin shi weiyuan hui wenshi ziliao yanjiu weiyuan hui), vol. 10 (1986): 118–120.

[46] Yin Xingwen, Jin Baichuan, and Liu Qingqi, "Hailanpao da tusha jianwen" ("Firsthand Accounts of the Blagoveshchensk Massacre"), *Heilongjiang wenshi ziliao* 12 (1984): 117–118.

part of the Chinese nation-body. His emphasis on the long-standing ties between Blagoveshchensk and the Sixty-Four Villages East of the River was reminiscent of 1930s Japanese researchers' claim that the two areas had in fact been one integrated network of Chinese settlements since at least the seventeenth century. Into this peaceful setting of Chinese settlements enters the Russian fleet as the violent aggressor violating the established community and transforming it into a site of military aggression from which to launch further imperialist expansion southward across the Heilong River deeper into China. The editor further identifies the city with China's subjection to Russian aggression by asserting that the name "Blagoveshchensk" itself, meaning "city of joyful announcement," alludes to and celebrates the signing of the unequal treaties.

Having constructed Blagoveshchensk as the violent product of and stage for the political, military, and economic facets of Russian incursion into China, the editor introduces the Chinese migrants onto the scene. "Owing to history and geography-related reasons, as well as due to the needs of Czarist Russian far eastern policy, large numbers of Chinese residents engaged in business, gold-mining, manual work, and all kinds of forced labor in Blagoveshchensk. The Chinese residents' strenuous labor provided the most important conditions for the survival of Russians in Blagoveshchensk."[47] Liu turns attention here to the more recent entrepreneurial migrants in Blagoveshchensk as the primary subject, even as he presents them in terms of passive exploitation. He explains their flocking in large numbers to this center of Russian imperialism in vague terms of unspecified "history and geography-related reasons" and in relation to the Russian state's policy of expansion in eastern Siberia. Through reducing his explanation to this vague reference to unspecified factors, the editor elided the many historical factors that complicated the relationship between Chinese migration and Russian presence in the region. In particular, the agency of the migrants themselves, the various economic and social incentives that drove them to make the journey to Blagoveshchensk, and the importance of household demands and local community networks are buried beneath the vague reference to "history and geography-related causes." The different enterprises in which these migrants engaged are presented as subject to the Russians' economic exploitation. The excesses of history spilling outside the boundaries of the bifurcated nationalist discourse of foreign imperialism and Chinese humiliation are thus contained, and the migrants' economic activities are emptied of any agency among the migrants themselves and presented instead in terms of their bitter subjection to Russian exploitation. This in

---

[47] Ibid.

turn the editor identifies as a foreshadowing of and as the historical conditions building up to the Blagoveshchensk massacre.

In July 1900, while enthusiastically making plans for and participating in the eight-nation combined army's invasion of our country's Beijing-Tianjin area, massacring the Boxer masses, Czarist Russia also amassed a one hundred seventy thousand-man army for invading China and led a six-prong invasion of our country's northeast. Of these the Russian army in Blagoveshchensk was an important element. In order to eliminate any threat from behind and to seize the riches of the peaceful Chinese residents, on July 17, Blagoveshchensk's Czarist Russian authorities single-handedly carried out the "great Blagoveshchensk massacre" that shocked the world. In several days' time, they massacred seven thousand unarmed Chinese residents.[48]

The massacre appears here as a culmination of an ongoing history of exploitation and humiliation suffered by the Chinese. By relating the massacre in Blagoveshchensk to the eight-nation military intervention in the Boxer Uprising that same year, the editor presents the incident as an integral part of the overall interconnected and unified narrative of Western imperialism besetting the Chinese nation as a whole. Liu Banghou's use of this framework tied into the post-Mao state's project of engineering a new post-Communist nationalism. The editor concludes by asserting that the personal recollections that follow encompassed a collective memory through which the traumatic suffering associated with the event in 1900 is kept vividly alive.

Regarding this inhuman act of brutal violence by Czarist Russia, decades later the people of the Heihe and Aihun region still have fresh memories, and their bitter regrets do not fade away ... Here, compiled and set in order, are the records of some of the elderly Heihe residents' recollections. As of today these elderly men have already passed away, and the living materials that they have left behind for people are truly precious.[49]

The rhetorical power of such a nationalist discourse depends not on moving beyond a perceived past of traumatic suffering, but rather on constantly recreating and revivifying past events of shared collective suffering as a lens for constructing national solidarity in the present. The editor of this state-sponsored oral history project retrospectively framed the previously compiled personal narratives as a living medium for the transmission, validation, and preservation over time of this collective discourse of pre-1949 national humiliation and degradation from which the Communist Party led by Mao Zedong had emancipated China.

In contrast with the editor's representation of the city as embodying Russian imperialist aggression expanding menacingly south across the

[48] Ibid.   [49] Ibid.

Heilong River, the survivor testimonies describe Blagoveshchensk as the stage for Chinese entrepreneurs' energetic expansion northward. The recollections included in these *wenshi ziliao* push the Russian presence to the margins and populate the remembered landscape with a wide assortment of Chinese shops and industries. Ironically, it is the center of Russian military expansion as defined by the editor that informant Yin Xingwen resignifies as the symbol of Chinese economic vitality. Whereas the editor associates the city with the displacement of original Chinese settlements by Russian aggression, Yin conceives of Blagoveshchensk as a space in the process of rapidly becoming Chinese through the inexorable force of migrants' entrepreneurial spirit. In addition, Yin draws particular attention to the dominant economic presence of enterprises affiliated with his region of origin. In doing so, he presented his own native place, and, by extension, his regional identity, as the model and exemplary embodiment of this Chinese entrepreneurial spirit. Instead of being an undifferentiated Chinese collectivity exploited by Russian imperialism, Yin's narrative represents Blagoveshchensk as the site where competing regional affiliations strove for economic dominance over one another, revealing the particularities of regional identity that drove Chinese migration while simultaneously serving as a medium through which to extol his own achievements. As Yin recalls,

At that time Blagoveshchensk was already really large, it had 13,000 or 14,000 people. There were a great many Chinese, some who went over to find work during the day and came back to this side of the river by ferry (by sled in the winter) in the evening.[50] Some of them lived in shop buildings in Blagoveshchensk, and many of them opened businesses there. With storefronts and houses, they brought their wives and children to live together in Blagoveshchensk ... Chinese owned all kinds of businesses, large and small, and no matter what size they all had storefronts. Taizi Street was the most energetic in Blagoveshchensk, and it was mostly businesses that Chinese had opened.[51]

Yin portrays the city as dominated by an energetic collective Chinese enterprising spirit. He begins by resignifying the Heilong River not as a border between rival nationals or the symbol of Russian violence, but rather as a peaceful, everyday channel of commerce through which the "Chinese" and "Russian" sides of the river became integrated into

---

[50] By the turn of the twentieth century, a steady flow of human and commercial traffic joined the towns of Blagoveshchensk and Heihe on both sides of the Amur River. Ferries transported the crowds regularly and many of the passengers commuted back and forth in the same day. This belied the river's designation by the Chinese officials as a political boundary.

[51] Yin Xingwen, Jin Baichuan, and Liu Qingqi, "Firsthand Accounts of the Blagoveshchensk Massacre," 118–119.

a single social space. Crossing the river comes to represent the spontaneous initiative of Chinese businessmen setting up their own enterprises
and successfully occupying and engaging in a bustling commercial environment. The Russians disappear from the scene, as he describes the
vitality of the urban landscape and the lively streets as occupied predominantly by a plethora of Chinese shops of all sizes.

Yin reframed the regional particularity of migration as an expression of
a Chinese commercial vitality dominating and driving the urban prosperity of Blagoveshchensk. He goes on to illustrate this commercial initiative
by listing as exemplary models three large enterprises according to their
regional origins. "The largest of these were three businesses: one was
Yonghezhan founded by a native of Ye county from Shandong province,
one was Huachangtai, a two-story building, founded by a Cantonese
native, and there was also Tongyongli founded by another native of
Shandong Ye county."[52] Chinese hailing from his own native place of
Ye in particular, he notes, run two of the three counties. Migrants like Yin
in the early twentieth century relied extensively on native place networks
for obtaining various social and economic resources including housing,
jobs, and capital for business investment. The majority of the Chinese
migrant enterprises in Manchuria during this period grew out of these
tightly knit but geographically extensive social networks, and relied on
fellow locals for capital from informally pooled funds based on mutual
trust and on a system of native-place traditional banks. Those who set up
their own enterprises or branches of businesses already established in
northern China reinforced this channel of localistic ties by recruiting
only from among the young natives of their home regions. The coastal
region of Shandong Province and villages in northeastern Hebei Province
in particular developed a Manchuria-centered commercial culture
according to which employment in such migrant enterprises became the
measure of success and a rite of initiation into manhood for youths living
in these areas. Ye County was one such region along the northern coast of
Shandong Peninsula with a long history of extensive commercial ties with
Manchuria across the Bohai Sea.

This expression of regionally defined commercial vitality paralleled
Yin's articulation of economic class particularities in relation to the
collective Chinese experience. In presenting a list of occupations and
enterprises, Yin reveals the vast disparities and exploitation of labor that
took place among the Chinese migrants in Blagoveshchensk. His intention, however, is clearly not to show the level of class contradictions
dividing the Chinese population. Rather, he ties together and reframes

[52] Ibid.

these disparate points along this socioeconomic spectrum as illustrative of the city's overall economic domination by the Chinese as a whole:

> These businesses all hired a large number of employees, with Huachangtai alone having more than a hundred. Aside from these, there were Chinese-owned restaurants, noodle houses, travel lodges, bathhouses, and small shops and street stalls everywhere. Chinese did all kinds of work, like carpenters, bricklayers, glass artisans, electrical engineers, masons, coolies ... even sofa contractors were all Chinese. Many of those who took care of the children, cooked meals, carried the water and delivered food for Russian households were also Chinese, and some of them were teenage youths.[53]

To demonstrate the success of Chinese migrant enterprises in the city, Yin refers to the exceptional scale of the exemplary enterprises noted earlier. Having illustrated the dominant economic position of these particular enterprises, he then goes on to list the wide range of trades in which Chinese engaged, from restaurants and lodges to small peddling stalls, from skilled craftsmen to coolie laborers. He extends this list to the various types of domestic service that Chinese migrants, including young boys, provided for Russian households. In the last reference to young boy servants, he was alluding to his own experience of working in the home of a German industrialist's family. In doing so, he ennobled his own humble experience of serving the German household by linking it to his celebration of Chinese dominance in all sectors of society in Blagoveshchensk.

Yin proceeds to turn on its head the editor's excoriation of Russian demand for labor and services. Rather than relating them to Russian expansionary ambitions, Yin portrays these demands as integral to an environment of profit and mobility available for any Chinese with the proper dose of entrepreneurial spirit. "Labor was in high demand in Blagoveshchensk, and it was pretty easy to make a living. Wielding an axe or cleaver one could make two strings of cash in a day, and food was inexpensive: one *jin* (around five hundred grams) of bread cost four cents and a meal, less than ten cents."[54] Alongside glorifying even the lowliest occupations as embodying the Chinese community's economic dominance and entrepreneurial spirit in the region, Yin describes the great demand for labor in Blagoveshchensk as creating a bountiful paradise of high wages for everyone regardless of the skill level.

Unlike the editor's portrayal of Blagoveshchensk as symbolizing the violent displacement of a long-standing Chinese community by the Russian state, Yin presents the Blagoveshchensk area as a dynamic space rapidly becoming integrated within a constellation of Chinese native place networks. In doing so, he sandwiches Russian state-sponsored urban

[53] Ibid.   [54] Ibid.

development within a larger narrative on Chinese commercial vitality and community integration dominating the local economic and social land-scape. Thus, Yin empties out the Russian presence in the city's development and resignifies the Russian expansion into the region as an expansive domain of opportunities for Chinese migrants to enrich and empower themselves. Immediately after talking about the economic opportunities for Chinese migrants, Yin describes in detail the large scale of Blagoveshchensk's urban infrastructure and industrial development:

> At that time there were four avenues going east to west and twelve going north to south in Blagoveshchensk. The east–west avenues extended over ten *li* (one *li* equivalent to five hundred meters or half a kilometer) and the north–south avenues were three-to-four *li* long. The avenues were very wide and there were few buildings along them. There was one ironworks factory, one match factory, three or four flourmills, and one alcohol distillery in Blagoveshchensk. The two largest businesses were the Russian-owned Qiulin Company and the German-owned Kong foreign enterprise.[55]

In particular, Yin notes the city's orderly grid of spacious avenues, and relates this to the presence of major factories and the two largest commercial establishments. Like these two businesses, the factories were predominantly Russian. Instead of pointing out their Russian ownership in the same way that he had identified the specific Chinese regional affiliations of the commercial enterprises in the previous section, Yin simply presents these foreign industrial units as a part of the city's economic landscape.

The markers of the Russian state's dominant presence in planning the city as an industrial and commercial center are once again emptied of their political significance and presented instead as a manifestation of the expansive arena of economic opportunities that the city offered. Whereas in the previous passage Yin filled the streets with Chinese traders and workers of all kinds hustling their wares, in his references to the Russian infrastructures he presents the streets and buildings as an empty urban space facilitating Chinese economic activities. Yin juxtaposes this depopulated urbanscape with the Chinese settlement immediately north of the city as densely filled with several hundred households and many thousands of individuals.

> Five *li* north of Blagoveshchensk city was the small north village, where all the residents were Chinese. Most were from Shandong and Hebei provinces, and there were also some from Henan and Guangdong. Every summer evening, relatives would find each other, some going south and others going north, and it did not seem like being in a foreign country. Little North Village had several

[55] Ibid.

hundred households, several thousand people, and Russians called it the new village.[56]

In contrast with the grandeur of the spatial and economic scale described in the preceding passage, "Little North Village" appears as the reembodiment and transplantation of the fabric of native Chinese village life. Unlike the wide, empty avenues of the Russian infrastructure, Yin describes this area in terms of the circulation of densely knit native place and kinship networks, and integrates Blagoveshchensk with the migrants' native hometowns as a single unitary social fabric. He confirms this impression by remarking that "it did not seem like being in a foreign country."

While resonating with an earlier stage of Chinese economic expansion in the region, this emptying out of the Russian state's presence also bears striking parallels to both Western and Japanese imperialist narrative techniques of deleting the colonial landscape and naturalizing it as an empty space for exploration, occupation, and domination. In the Japanese discourse on the colonization of Manchuria by Japanese farmers during the 1930s, the areas to be colonized were emptied of any Chinese inhabitants and represented as an empty space onto which to establish a new, organized administrative and societal model. But, according to David Tucker, there was an irreconcilable tension between the Japanese settlers' reliance on Chinese inhabitants for their economic livelihood and the Japanese colonialists' characterization of Manchuria as an empty frontier on which to transpose a utopia free from interference by other populations.[57] In a similar fashion, Yin retrospectively inverts this paradigm of the imperialist gaze by deleting the signs of Russian expansion in his mental landscape and situates his own personal experiences of seeking a livelihood in Blagoveshchensk within a triumphant narrative of Chinese enterprising initiative.

This account reveals that the mobilization of local and individual memories for the authentication of a homogenizing discourse of foreign aggression and victimization paradoxically created an official space on which to celebrate individual agency and entrepreneurial spirit, and to valorize a regional history of migrants' commercial vigor and expansiveness. Yet this paradox of historical meanings inscribed within the *wenshi ziliao* project served to reconcile rather than to undermine the state's simultaneous imperatives for sponsoring the memory production. The manner in

---

[56] Ibid.
[57] David Tucker, "City Planning without Cities: Order and Chaos in Utopian Manchukuo," in Mariko Tamanoi, ed., *Crossed Histories: Manchuria in the Age of Empire* (Honolulu, HI: Association for Asian Studies and University of Hawaii Press, 2005).

which contradictions were exposed in these accounts both reflected and enclosed the multiplicity of meanings inherent within the post-Mao state's pursuit of modernization. The editor-narrator mode of structuring the historical testimonies harmonized the political objective of constructing the nationalist narrative of foreign aggression and victimization to maintain national unity with the simultaneous effort to justify market reforms through a celebration of the achievements of Chinese commercial ventures across and beyond national borders. The agenda of promoting a homogenized national unity went hand in hand with an effort to mobilize and channel the energies unleashed by the resurgence of regional pride and identification.

Conclusion

The northeast borderland historical context of migration, colonialism, cross-border trade, and ethnic conflict provided a flexible tableau for reconciling aspects of post-Mao reform ideology.

Wenshi ziliao writers and editors intervened in this potentially problematic colonial and extra-national past to redefine Party socialism in nationalist and regionalist terms of the northeast borderland's becoming Chinese. This involved a collusion of informants with the editors and Party officials sponsoring the project, as former migrant entrepreneurs manipulated the flexible discursive landscape to weave together and make sense of their stories of personal life failures and successes. Seen from this perspective, the story of the northeast borderland as reappropriated past is integrally tied to the story of the reconfiguration of the post-Mao state. In the next chapter, we expand on this discussion by turning to the *wenshi ziliao* revival of the concept of "northern Manchuria" and the reconceptualization of the northeast borderland as central to the story of China's becoming a nation.

3   Relocating the Nation outside the Nation
Forging a Borderland-Centered Nationalist Discourse

Introduction

A central feature of *wenshi ziliao* reappropriations of northeast borderland history was the revival of the concept of "northern Manchuria." Referring to the region's characteristics of Russian colonial influence, particularly after the Russo–Japanese War carved out Russian and Japanese spheres of influence in the northern and southern parts of Manchuria, respectively, the name also designated a place relatively removed from the Chinese and Manchu political and cultural influence centered in southern Manchuria. The Qing government had from the outset countered the Russian threat by establishing military strongholds in the region, and by the turn of the twentieth century, the Qing state responded to a new phase of Russian expansion by promoting Chinese migration north, sponsoring land reclamation, and overseeing the administrative and commercial development of towns and cities. After the fall of the Qing, the Chinese warlord regime based in Shenyang continued to sponsor this program of frontier development, resulting in tensions with Russia that culminated in the Sino–Russian border conflict in 1929 that was fought largely over control of the CER railroad that Russia had built as an instrument of expansion into the region at the turn of the century.

In spite of these Manchu and Chinese ambitions, the region developed and maintained a distinctive identity apart from the rest of Manchuria as a zone of Russian influence and cultural mixing that included the emergence of a Sino–Russian pidgin dialect. The city that was most symbolic of Russia's ambitions in the region was Harbin, which had been built at the turn of the century as a key juncture along the CER that Russians were constructing, with imported Chinese labor, at the time. Russian Finance Minister Sergei Witte envisioned northern Manchuria as a destination for Russian settlers, including ethnic and religious minorities whose relocation to this region would bring the double benefit to Russia of easing ethnic tensions within Russia while helping to expand Russia's colonial possessions. The CER network of railroads that crisscrossed the region became a sphere of Russian military, economic, and cultural influence, much as the South Manchuria Railroad (SMR) did for Japan. At the same time, the railroad's construction and the development of towns along it stimulated waves of Chinese immigrants who settled down in the surrounding land. The far northern and eastern parts of the region along the borders developed a reputation as rough and wild frontiers where Russian and Chinese migrants engaged in speculative mining and opium ventures. These were also the home of indigenous nomadic groups whose living and hunting grounds increasingly ran up against Chinese and Russian agricultural and commercial development.

Given this historical context, the resurrection of "northern Manchuria" as a compelling regional identity had problematic implications from a Party-centered nationalist perspective. However, *wenshi ziliao* editors employed several strategies for reimagining this space in a way that dovetailed with post-Mao reform ideology. First, they reappropriated northern Manchuria's distinctive history as a vehicle for making a case for the region's unique role in the story of economic and cultural development and modernization. Second, they redefined the exteriority and marginality of this borderland from the Chinese nation as an asset for nationalism, arguing that it was precisely the region's liminality from and position outside of the nation that placed it on the forefront of nation building in the twentieth century. Third, they renarrated the history of the non-Han indigenous people in ways that melded together national integration and regional distinctiveness.

In utilizing these multiple strategies of historical representation, *wenshi ziliao* editors actively engaged with an interpretation of past northeast society and culture as messy, dynamic, and in flux. Challenging national narratives that exclude diversity and impose static homogeneity, borderland scholars Peter Perdue, Helen Siu, and Eric Tagliacozzo have called for historical approaches that "focus on multilayered, interactive processes."[1] Inspired by Henri Lefebvre's idea that spaces "interpenetrate one another," Pat Giersch writes that:

[W]e need to treat spatial boundaries as "porous" and investigate how political and social processes cross boundaries. In Lefebvre's well-known analogy, he addressed this approach by arguing that a modern house is experienced as a bounded space, but, in reality, it is "permeated from every direction by streams of energy which run in and out of it by every imaginable route: water, gas, electricity, telephone lines, radio and television signals, and so on. [The house's] image of immobility would then be replaced by an image of complex mobilities, a nexus of "in and out

[1] Peter C. Perdue, Helen F. Siu, and Eric Tagliacozzo, eds., *Asia Inside Out: Changing Times* (Cambridge, MA: Harvard University Press, 2015).

conduits" that reveal the house's solidity to be illusory, a constructed representation of space.[2]

Wenshi ziliao editors, situated as they were within the party-state apparatus, nevertheless adhered in many respects to this paradigm of political and social processes crossing porous boundaries rather than a static homogenizing narrative of bounded national space. In part, as we see in what follows, local participants were using this representational strategy of rearranging and reimagining space as a way to reassert northeast borderland identities distinctive from a homogenizing national narrative. Yet, in the case of the *wenshi ziliao*, this paradigm of dynamic fluidity did not undermine, but rather contributed to the post-Mao nation-state rebuilding project. Through the *wenshi ziliao*, the state mobilized and set in motion these articulations of space *as a transitional governance approach to* reorganizing political and social space. This approach relied on an interscalar, interlayered, and permeable conception of northeast borderland spaces to make room for and give expression to different local, regional, and national modernizing voices and agendas.

The *wenshi ziliao* revisiting of northern Manchuria was strikingly different from the politics of historical memory production in other Chinese borderlands, particularly in the northwest and southwest. In those regions, as Benno Weiner, Dasa Mortimer, and Sandrine Catris have shown, the powerful and imminent threat of Uighur and Tibetan separatism and the violent history of Chinese colonialism made historical recollections a dangerous venture and contributed to what Catris has called a "double burden" of needing to justify both Party and Chinese legitimacy.[3] Drawing on the imagery of Pekka Hämäläinen and Samuel Truett and referring to the complex interpenetration of Tibetan and Chinese state expansion through the first half of the twentieth century, Giersch argues that "for modern China today, greater Tibet, including Kham, is one place where the national narrative comes unraveled, as the evidence simply cannot support current Chinese historical claims in the region."[4] Moreover, owing to the native perception of the Communist revolution and Party control as a continuation and intensification of Chinese colonialism, *wenshi ziliao* writers in places like Qinghai (Amdo) had to carefully distinguish between backward and oppressive elements of Chinese society on one

---

[2] Giersch, "Afterword: Why Kham? Why Borderlands?" 204–205.

[3] Weiner, "State Commemoration of Tibetan Anti-State Resistance"; Dasa Mortimer, "*Wenshi Ziliao* Narratives of Anti-Communist Resistance in Northwest Yunnan." Paper presented at AAS Conference, Toronto, March 18, 2017; Catris, "Searching for the Elusive Past."

[4] Giersch, "Afterword: Why Kham? Why Borderlands?" 207.

hand and the liberatory role of the Party on the other.[5] In regard to reorientations of the indigenous people, *wenshi ziliao* writers had to reinforce opposition between the GMD and the CCP to rationalize anti-Chinese indigenous uprisings prior to 1949 as reactions against oppressive GMD policies rather than resistance to Chinese imperialism. For this reason, as Uradyn Bulag points out in regard to historical memories of Mongol uprisings in the Mongolian borderland, the CCP's post-Mao reconciliation with the GMD has further narrowed the scope of events deemed safe and acceptable to remember.[6] The ethnic issue also shaped *wenshi ziliao* decisions regarding what time periods to prioritize. In northwest Yunnan, for instance, as Mortimer emphasizes, *wenshi ziliao* editors focused on the early 1950s as a seminal moment of confrontation and reconciliation between the Party and ethnic elites.[7]

This crisis of indigenous ethnic resistance and competition for power was not a significant issue in the northeast borderland.[8] Instead of having to delicately maneuver around the issue of Chinese colonial violence, *wenshi ziliao* participants here could represent *all* Chinese in the region as victims of external Russian (before 1931) and Japanese colonial aggression. This theme of Chinese nationalist resistance and victimization made it much easier in the northeast to produce a broadly inclusive united front version of history. At the same time, with the easing of relations between China and Russia and the resumption of cross-border trade in the 1980s, editors could alternate between and combine narratives of anti-Russian imperialism and nostalgic reminiscences of Russian cultural influence as strategies for promoting nationalism alongside regional otherness. Where indigenous non-Han ethnicity did come into play, the common external threat of Russian colonialism made it easier to incorporate these people's history into the Chinese national narrative while tying ethnic difference to local distinctiveness.

This chapter begins by situating concepts of northern Manchuria in relation to post-Mao reevaluations of private enterprise and, more broadly, the reconfiguration of historical events in nationalist terms. These revisionist trends were important in shaping the narratives about northern Manchuria that *wenshi ziliao* informants and editors constructed.

---

[5] Weiner, "State Commemoration of Tibetan Anti-State Resistance."
[6] Bulag, "Can the Subalterns Not Speak?" 107–108.
[7] Mortimer, "*Wenshi Ziliao* Narratives of Anti-Communist Resistance."
[8] Note that in eastern Manchuria, in the Yanbian region bordering Korea, the influx of Korean immigrants did clash, violently at times, with Chinese expansion and was entangled with Japanese imperialist ambitions in the region. The ethnic history and historical memories in this region deserve more scholarly attention but are outside the geographical scope of this study.

Taking Off the Capitalist Cap: Rewriting Private Enterprise in Regional and Nationalist Histories

During the 1980s, social and economic organizations made a concerted effort to rewrite and rehabilitate the role of private enterprise in China's regional and national development. The revival of the geopolitical concept of northern Manchuria was integral to this project. Business organizations capitalized on the *wenshi ziliao* to redeem and justify private enterprise as a positive engine in modern China's historical development. Teaming up with PPCCs, local branches of these organizations established their own historical materials collection groups to prioritize the historical rehabilitation of former entrepreneurs for inclusion in *wenshi ziliao* publications. Beginning in 1981, for instance, the Harbin branches of the Industry and Commerce Federation and the Democratic National Construction Alliance merged to form their own historical materials collection team. Over the ensuing years they worked closely with the *wenshi ziliao* editors to produce articles on prominent former industrialists in Harbin such as Wu Baixiang and Zhang Tingge and the enterprises they established in the early twentieth century. Of these articles, one appeared in a special national *wenshi ziliao* publication devoted to former leaders in industry and commerce, two were featured in provincial *wenshi ziliao*, and three were included in a volume of Harbin's *wenshi ziliao*. The research team wrote a report summarizing its progress in celebrating this history of local economic achievement, emphasizing these materials' importance in bringing back to life the city's major industrial figures and the hardships they endured, while providing valuable "experiential reference for economic work today."

A central theme that emerged in this literature was the struggle of entrepreneurial migrants in Manchuria to set up shops and factories in the face of Russian and Japanese competition. This theme integrated the nationalist and market liberalization strands of post-Mao ideology. The stories of businessmen like Zhang Tingge, a Chinese migrant who had become one of the most prominent businessmen in Harbin by the 1920s, were told and retold in this light, as local historians adapting their ink to the new Party line began to redirect their focus on the "national bourgeoisie" as the positive agent of pre-1949 regional and national development.[9] While the most conspicuous of these were men like Zhang Tingge, local branches of the PPCC also turned to lesser-known but often locally prominent individuals whose life stories encapsulated

---

[9] Søren Clausen and Stig Thøgersen discuss the reassessment of Chinese capitalism in the northeast in their edited volume, *The Making of a Chinese City: History and Historiography in Harbin* (Armonk, NY: M. E. Sharpe, 1995).

this dimension of historical experience that until recently had been relegated to the status of "counterrevolutionary."

Wenshi ziliao editors utilized these accounts to bring to the fore local and regional identities. The Harbin *wenshi ziliao* research and collection team, with support from the Industry and Commerce Federation (ICF) and the Democratic National Construction Alliance (DNCA), drafted a report that tied the rehabilitation of former businesspeople to a celebration of Harbin's regional distinctiveness and significance. "Harbin is the economic center of northern Manchuria," the writer asserts, "so there are a lot of valuable materials on industry and commerce awaiting to be unearthed."[10] A discursive tension arises here: "northern Manchuria" as separate regional entity is problematic from the standpoint of nationalist consolidation, yet it serves to promote the post-Mao agenda of emphasizing economic modernization and market reform. It appears from this passage that the agenda of championing local economic development and regional pride has, in this instance, overridden concern with nationalism and subsuming the region to the nation-state's prerogatives.

The concept of northeast regionality that local editors voiced in their speeches and reports differed markedly from the emphasis on Shandong and Hebei native place identities that appeared in many of the *wenshi ziliao* accounts. Biographical and autobiographical memorializations of entrepreneurs, educators, military officers, and political figures who had relocated from China proper highlighted their hometown ties as instrumental to their success. *Wenshi ziliao* published in Harbin, for instance, included an account of an ironsmith from Zhangqiu named Kang Yefu whose family had been practicing the trade for generations. After reaching Harbin in 1922 at the age of forty, according to the narrative, he teamed up with two close friends from Zhangqiu to set up a business making and selling cooking knives. "Frequently carrying a sack with 'Kang of Zhangqiu, Shandong' inscribed on it and loaded with knives," he adapted this local and family heritage as an advertisement and certificate of authenticity for the items he peddled.[11]

Another account, published in the Sino–Russian border town of Jiamusi, illustrated this through recollections of the founding of the

---

[10] "Haerbin shi minjian gongshang lian shiliao xiaozu" ("Harbin City Democratic Construction and Industrial and Commercial Federation's Historical Materials Small Group"), in Haerbin shi zhengxie weiyuanhui mishuchu, *Haerbin zhengxie (Harbin PPCC)*, no. 3 (no. 13 overall) (1984) (Special Issue of [the First] Harbin City *Wenshi Ziliao* Work Conference): 71–74.

[11] Gao Ruzhang, "Mingpai chu zi zhen gongfu – 'sanshenglu' caidao de youlai yu fachan" ("Famous Brand Arises from True Diligence – The Origins and Development of the 'Sanshenglu' Kitchen Knife"), *Harbin wenshiziliao* (Harbin shi weiyuan hui wenshi ziliao yanjiu weiyuan hui), 12 (1987): 61, 63.

Fuzengqing assorted goods store by Qu Puchen in 1921. According to the narrative, Qu raised more than 10,000 Harbin *Dayang* dollars by appealing to fellow locals from Huang County who went on to serve as the company's board of trustees.[12] Harbin *wenshi ziliao* made a similar point regarding the establishment of the Tianfengyong enterprise in that city by Li Yunting, who migrated from Leting County in Hebei and started out with a small street-vending stall at the turn of the century. The scale of his enterprise, according to the account, underwent a dramatic transformation when fellow locals invested capital in the renovation of two buildings for a storefront business. This initiative allegedly enabled profits to surge by 1930, when the enterprise was employing more than ninety shop clerks.[13]

Unlike editors' articulation of the goals of *wenshi ziliao* in official reports, their actual work of editing articles constructed a concept of northeast regional identity as constituted by native place attachments to other regions of China, particularly Hebei and Shandong. This perspective lent a broader Chinese national significance to the region, integrating former Manchuria firmly within a Chinese sphere of migration and enterprise. At the same time, it reaffirmed the regional distinctiveness of former northern Manchuria in a different way. Rather than conceiving of the region as separate from the rest of China by virtue of its specific history of Russian colonial influence, the native place narrative defined the Northeast's distinctive character in terms of both its appeal to migrants as a land of opportunity and its accommodation and incorporation of numerous regional identities from other parts of China. The native place version, therefore, rendered the northeast as at once broadly Chinese and narrowly localistic, constructing a historical narrative of the region as a space where localism and nationalism could coexist.

The celebration of the lives of former industrialists and businesspeople as an expression of local, regional, and national identities was part of a broader PPCC effort to reincorporate into the local economy former private enterprise managers whose expertise was needed for the market reform transition. Interpreting at the local level the latter two organizations' "decision regarding assisting the party and government in the work of assigning and utilizing former industrialists," the Fujin PPCC formed a finance and commerce work group that convened discussion forums and undertook inspection visits to various work units. The sites of these

---

[12] Ye Jinghuan, "Qu puchen yu fuzengqing shangchang" ("Qu Puchen and Fuzengqing Market"), *Jiamusi wenshi ziliao* (Jiamusi shi weiyuan hui wenshi ziliao yanjiu weiyuan hui), 6 (1987): 61–62.
[13] Zhang Ziyu, "Jingying shanhai zahuo de tianfengyong" ("Tianfengyong Specializing in Wild-Harvested Products"), *Harbin wenshi ziliao*, 12 (1988): 106–107.

meetings and inspections included an agricultural equipment factory, a trading company, a pharmaceutical shop, a youth photo shop, a travel company, and the commerce department's youth employment office.

The resulting report drafted in 1981, entitled "an investigation into the current situation with assigning and utilizing former industrialists and businesspeople," extols the economic and social benefits of reintegrating these individuals into managerial positions. It focuses in particular on their role in increasing profitability and efficiency while training and employing a modernized workforce. The author illustrates these benefits with case studies of individuals, all of whom were PPCC members, whose reintegration reversed patterns of inefficiency and indebtedness. One of the PPCC vice-chairs, Zhang Minghe, for instance, is credited in the report with using his fifty years of factory management experience to make the indebted water heating fittings factory profitable again. He allegedly did this by "grasping market conditions to meet needs unmet by state-owned production" and through inspiring the employees with his work ethic, which included waking up at 3 o'clock in the morning each day and participating in factory labor in spite of his age. Another PPCC standing committee member, Wang Weixing, had a similar record of achievement in the bathhouse industry, cutting costs by cleaning bathrooms himself or having the workers clean dirty pipes.[14]

But while *wenshi ziliao* editors glorified former entrepreneurs historically as patriotic heroes and exemplars of effective enterprise management, in practice local PPCCs faced challenges in reversing the destructive impact of the Cultural Revolution and reconciling competing Party agendas and attitudes toward these individuals. On one hand, reports highlight these managers' expressions of gratitude toward the Party for reinstating them in their positions and redeeming their status in society. Zhang Minghe, for instance, allegedly claimed that his "small achievement" was the result of the Party's having put his heart at ease by "taking off his capitalist cap," while another supervisor in a department of the county trading company, Zhou Jimin, commented on his gratitude to the Party for extricating him from the "capitalist class," allowing him to focus on doing business without any other worries. Wang Weixing added that "the party transformed him from exploiter to laborer, making him a new person," and he wanted to return the Party's favor by devoting all his energy to enterprise management.[15]

---

[14] Fujin xian zhengxie, "Guanyu dui yuan gongshangyezhe anpai shiyong qingkuang de diaocha" ("Investigation Regarding the Assignment and Use of Former Participants in the Business and Industry Sectors") (Apr. 1, 1981) (Fujin City Archives): 1–4.
[15] Ibid., 1–4.

Alongside these glowing reports of winning hearts and minds, however, PPCC cadres acknowledge struggles they faced with the ongoing legacies of past political campaigns. To begin with, they reflect gloomily on the irreparable losses of human talent and expertise that cannot be salvaged. In Fujin, of the 270 individuals classified as "people in commerce and industry" in 1956, six had been "reformed" during the Maoist years and the remaining 264 were reclassified after the Party congress in 1978 as "three smalls" (small businesspeople, small peddlers, and small handcrafts workers), which transferred them from the exploitative to laboring class status. However, 92.6% of this cohort were dead or unable to work as of the drafting of this inspection report in 1981. Of the remaining 7.4%, a total of twenty people, eleven were already retired and only nine were actually employed. These included "a factory head, a manager, a chair of a railroad office, a chair of a shop bureau, and five who do regular jobs." The PPCC facilitated the recruitment of six of the retirees to establish collective enterprises, while the remaining five "are still at home idle."[16]

Besides the irreparable damages inflicted by past socialist movements, PPCC cadres pointed out inconsistencies between the restorative discourse of official Party policy and lingering "leftist" discriminatory practices that these managers faced in their everyday lives. One manifestation of this was their continuing marginalization to low positions with little executive responsibility. One example given in Fujin was the case of PPCC vice-chair Zhang Minghe, who, while ostensibly grateful to the Party, was in fact frustrated with being stuck in a minor water heating equipment subunit position in spite of his original founding leadership of the agricultural equipment factory. Similarly, the former manager of a cooperative hotel enterprise, Sun Changming, complained that his status had not improved since his demotion during the Cultural Revolution in spite of his "decades of experience in hotel management and his expertise as a chef" that apparently made his name well known throughout the province. His recent transfer yet again to a low position in a cafeteria was the last straw, inducing him to "just retire and return home."

Even in cases where rehabilitation took place on paper, in reality, these former managers found a wide discrepancy between policy and practice. To begin with, their work unit supervisors "still have a leftist mindset and look at them as 'capitalists,'" allegedly excluding them from significant responsibilities and not listening to their recommendations. In addition, they were unsatisfied with the compensation they received from the Party for the economic losses and political trauma they had experienced. In one

[16] Ibid., 1–2.

such case, a former hotel manager named Wang Jinsheng had been labeled "counterrevolutionary on account of historical problems," placed under surveillance for three years, stripped of his job, and sent down to the countryside. In 1979, he was restored to work and rehabilitated, but only given compensation of 150 yuan. He complained that this measly compensation did not even cover the travel expenses incurred from the 100 times he had visited the county government over the previous three years to deal with his political status.[17]

While incomplete or unsubstantial reintegration and rehabilitation was an issue, in some instances, the complaints had to do with a perception that the local government was ruthlessly exploiting them without regard for their age and health, alleging that "the work assigned to them is too heavy and they are moved around too frequently, negatively affecting their enthusiasm." One example cited in Fujin was a manager in the hospitality industry, Li Chenglin, who at the age of sixty-seven

led 32 youths to set up a restaurant in front of a railroad station. The restaurant was open for only three years before he was transferred to another restaurant that was in shambles. After he worked hard to turn it around in three months, leaders saw how effective he was and again transferred him to the youth headquarters. Now he has been moved yet again to Songjiang hotel which is losing money. So, wherever there is a problem he is sent there to resolve it.

This tendency, according to the author of the PPCC inspection report, "will destroy their health, let alone their enthusiasm."[18]

These reports indicate that *wenshi ziliao* editors' historical reintegration of industrialists and entrepreneurs was part of a broader PPCC project of rehabilitating former enterprise managers into the local economy. However, while the published accounts celebrate the lives of these individuals as local heroes and incorporate them seamlessly into the new post-Mao nationalist narrative, the actual implementation of restorative policies that the *wenshi ziliao* accounts historically justified was marred by irreparable losses, conflicting workplace practices and attitudes, unwillingness to prioritize compensation to make amends, and local governments' tendency to "overmobilize" them as exploitable resources.

"Raising High the Nationalist Banner": Redefining the Categories of "Enemy, Self, and Friend"

The reevaluation of private enterprise described earlier in this chapter was one aspect of a nationalist reinterpretation of modern history through

---

[17] Ibid., 6–7.   [18] Ibid., 7–8.

which the Party sought to forge a broader "united front" and suture the political and social divisions wrought by the Cultural Revolution. The extensive attention to commercial development at the expense of writing about socialist revolution may not have taken hold, at least at the local and regional levels in northeast China, until the mid-1980s. Anecdotal evidence from earlier reports drafted at the beginning of the decade show that while anti-imperialist nationalism was a priority from the start, celebration of private enterprise was not immediately as apparent. In 1980, for instance, the same provincial office that emphasized commerce in later reports described its main objective as collecting materials focused on two areas: the first was imperialism and anti-imperialist resistance, including "the Northeast Righteous and Brave Army, the Allied Anti-Japanese Army, anti-Russian resistance, and the CER"; the second was "revolutionary materials" including "land reform and the war for liberation."[19]

Clearly the decision to include materials on anti-imperialist struggle was more unanimous and less controversial during the initial years of political transition from the Cultural Revolution than introducing private enterprise as a positive agent of historical progress. Even as late as the mid-1980s, local PPCCs in counties along the border that had a late start to collecting *wenshi ziliao* focused almost exclusively on imperialism and revolution as their priority for the contents of their initial publications. According to a Tongjiang PPCC report in 1985, for instance, recollections about anti-Japanese struggles such as the "Shandong people's inn massacre" and "Japanese imperialist invaders' destruction of the Hezhe people," along with tributes to key events and people in the Communist Party's ascendency to power in Tongjiang, were the main features of the county's first volume of *wenshi ziliao* released earlier that year.[20]

While the historical rehabilitation of private enterprise had not yet entered the picture in these initial endeavors, editors were already manifesting an approach to collecting and editing *wenshi ziliao* that privileged national integration and political and social reconciliation over class struggle and division. One way that they accomplished this was by replacing class division with a negative/positive binary of imperialism and anti-imperialist resistance. This way of structuring the past lent a redemptive, heroic voice to individuals and groups left out of the socialist narrative. This repositioning of the categories of the "people" and the "enemy"

[19] Heilongjiang sheng zhengxie wenshi ban, Untitled report on *wenshi ziliao* by Heilongjiang provincial wenshi ziliao office (Oct. 10, 1980).
[20] Zhengxie tongjiang xian weiyuanhui bangongshi, "Duanxun" ("Brief Report"), *Tongjiang zhengxie* (*Tongjiang PPCC*), no. 14 (no. 109 overall) (Dec. 10, 1985) (Tongjiang City Archive).

reflected the post-Mao revival of the United Front on a more stable and sustained basis. However, compared to earlier Maoist-period renditions of the United Front that incorporated economic and cultural elites without disavowing the central importance of class struggle, this new way of structuring history more fundamentally transformed social classifications by completely subsuming the class issue beneath nationalist considerations. Referring to the "raising high the nationalist banner" principle that PPCC leaders called for at the national level, the Heilongjiang *wenshi ziliao* committee drafted a report in 1986 outlining the key aspects of history that fell under this banner. "Our province's *wenshi ziliao* work has from the start seized upon this characteristic and made the contents of invasion and anti-invasion resistance the primary thrust ... These include the 3 aspects of 'enemy, self, and friend,' and relate to the realms of politics, military, economy, science/education, ethnicity/nationalities, and society."[21]

Those who oversaw *wenshi ziliao* production regarded the selection of topics as a process that distilled and classified the entire range of historical phenomena into points along a spectrum of proximity to or distance from the national "self" as defined by the Party. Thus, while expanding the definition of national citizenship, the new paradigm reconfigured the Maoist socialist categories of "revolutionary" and "counterrevolutionary" as nationalist categories of "enemy, self, and friend" that could once again be applied to all elements of history. At the same time, they incorporated the Communist Party seamlessly into this nationalist history, depicting the Party as the leading force in the people's resistance against external and internal sources of exploitation and oppression.

To reconcile socialist and nationalist elements of history, local editors seamlessly mixed together accounts commemorating the revolutionary struggle with recollections of anti-imperialist nationalism, as was the case with the 1985 Tongjiang report. By organizing the materials in this way, editors reframed the socialist revolution in nationalist terms as an integral part of the ongoing struggle for national self-determination. In addition to reconceiving of it in nationalist terms, editors also resituated socialist revolution as an integral part of, rather than a sharp break from, a continuous longue durée history of Chinese civilization. Local *wenshi ziliao* committees purposefully compiled materials on twentieth-century Communist Party activities with accounts of ancient artifacts and remains of Ming- and early Qing-era towns exhumed in archaeological digs.

[21] Heilongjiang sheng zhengxie wenshi ban, "Wenshi ziliao shi huanqi renmen wei gongtong lixiang er fendou de jingshen shiliang" (*"Wenshi Ziliao* Is Spiritual Food That Inspires People to Struggle for Shared Ideals") (Nov. 1986) (Heilongjiang Provincial Archives 56:2:263): 1–2.

In 1983, for instance, the Qiqihar *wenshi ziliao* office described the contents of its most recent publication as including, among other things, the "history of revolutionary struggle, historical individuals, the history of Bukui [the old Ming-period name for Qiqihar], and artifacts from Longcheng [the early Qing name for Qiqihar]."[22] One of the participants in this project, Liu Feilin, later recalled being approached by the Qiqihar *wenshi ziliao* committee in 1981 for his expertise in the preservation of historical objects. His essays about old temples, mosques, and memorial tablets in the area were included in publications such as a book on the local history and place of Longjiang, and served as reference materials for a park's restoration of its Guandi temple.[23] While at other times editors referred to pre-1949 society in negative terms juxtaposed against post-1949 "liberation," the Qiqihar *wenshi ziliao* office's description of these contents depicted revolution as the culmination of an ongoing glorious historical narrative reaching back to ancient imperial times. The two approaches work together to represent the Communist Party as both a force of social liberation and an inheritor and preserver of a glorious national heritage.

The Return of "Northern Manchuria"

These nationalist and market reform-oriented frameworks accommodated the discursive recovery of certain historical features of the northeast borderland. In spite of its problematic implications for a unified Chinese nation, *wenshi ziliao* editors' revival of the historical concept of "northern Manchuria," with its colonial associations, served to promote distinctive regional claims to economic and cultural development that resonated with the state's "Four Modernizations." The post-Mao reemergence and even nostalgic celebrations of European and Russian colonial influences have been well documented by scholars in contexts such as Shanghai, the Sino–Vietnamese borderland, and Harbin.[24] These studies have generally traced this trend to the 1990s as a cultural manifestation of

---

[22] Qiqihaer shi zhengxie wenshiban, "'Qiqihar wenshi tongxun' chuban" ("Publication of 'Qiqihar *Wenshi* Report'") (1983) (Heilongjiang Provincial Archive 56:1:298).

[23] Liu Feilin, "Thirty Years' Reflections on Literary and Historical Work," 359–360.

[24] See Denton, *Exhibiting the Past*; Yukiko Koga, *Inheritance of Loss: China, Japan, and the Political Economy of Redemption after Empire* (Chicago, IL: University of Chicago Press, 2016); Koga, "'The Atmosphere of a Foreign Country': Harbin's Architectural Inheritance," in Anne Cronin and Kevin Hetherington, eds., *Consuming the Entrepreneurial City: Image, Memory, Spectacle* (New York, NY: Routledge, 2008): 221–254; Steven Pieragastini, "Circular Lines: The History and Memory of Imperial Railways in Sino–Vietnamese Borderlands." Paper presented for panel "Memory-Making and the Construction of Collective Memory across East Asia's Twentieth century" at AAS Conference, Toronto, March 18, 2017.

intensifying commercialization, international economic integration, and local initiatives to attract tourist revenue.

Undoubtedly, intensifying market forces did make these cultural expressions more visible and pervasive in the 1990s. However, starting in the previous decade, *wenshi ziliao* writers and editors in the northeast borderland made a systematic effort to meld nostalgic tributes to Russian colonial influence with nationalist narratives emphasizing the region's Chineseness and resistance to Russian imperialism. Contradictory from one perspective, these historical reimaginings accommodated local, regional, and national layers of post-Mao reform identity.

Participants in the memory project portrayed the region's separate past identity entangled with Russian colonialism in a mixed and even positive light rather than simply as a foil for Chinese nationalist resistance. In a 1984 conference report, Wang Mingkui, a member of the Heilongjiang *wenshi ziliao* committee, criticized the apparently common perception that the region "lies on the border, developed late, and doesn't have any significant events or people and nothing to write about":

From the start of the 20th century to the victory of anti-Japanese resistance, our province has been the place that all imperialist countries had to struggle over. Before and after 1900 there was the Czarist Russian chaos that everyone knows about, Russian imperialism invaded Heilongjiang territory, occupied land, plundered wealth, massacred people, built railroads, established banks, opened factories, drafted unequal treaties ... Every nationality in our province resisted Russian imperialism heroically and without giving in.[25]

Wang's history of the region's significance and development hinges on and begins with the history of Russian expansion and occupation. Indeed, the story of economic modernization, so central to the post-Mao reform narrative, is credited to Russian initiative. Chinese agency in this narrative appears only in the form of resistance to this dominant influence. The writer places Russian colonization of the region at the center of the story of national modernization while at the same time highlighting the story of Chinese struggle and resistance, simultaneously hardening and dissolving the boundary between Chinese national self and foreign other. In this way, Wang reappropriates the region's historical dismemberment from the nation and subjection to Russian control for the post-Mao narrative of economic modernization and anti-imperialist nationalism.

---

[25] Wang Mingkui, "Gaoju aiguo zhuyi qizhi kaichuang wosheng wenshi ziliao gongzuo xin jumian" ("Raise High the Banner of Patriotism in Pioneering the New Stage of *Wenshi Ziliao* Work in Our Province"), in Haerbin shi zhengxie weiyuanhui mishuchu, *Haerbin zhengxie* (*Harbin PPCC*), no. 3 (no. 13 overall) (Jan. 8, 1984) (Special Issue of [the First] Harbin City *Wenshi Ziliao* Work Conference): 51–52.

A similar tension between national integration and regional difference occurs in editors' reflections on *wenshi ziliao* relating to Harbin, a city that had been Russia's prized center of expansion into Manchuria during the first two decades of the twentieth century. Their rationale for why compiling *wenshi ziliao* about Harbin was an important venture fuses contradictory representations of Russian colonialism to construct a historical image of Harbin that both conforms to and stands apart from the nationalist narrative. In a report written in 1983, the vice-chair of Harbin's *wenshi ziliao* research committee, Li Xingchang, describes his view of what makes Harbin's history significant and distinctive. He begins with the usual reference to anti-Japanese struggles, but then goes on to emphasize commercial and industrial development, and more specifically the city's former status as political, military, economic, and cultural center of northern Manchuria.[26] The term "northern Manchuria" refers to the region under Russian domination during the early twentieth century between 1905, when the Russians were pushed out of southern Manchuria by the Japanese, and 1931, when Japan occupied the whole of Manchuria. By using this term, Li Xingchang was making a conscious decision to highlight the region's distinctiveness from the Chinese nation, and in so doing he privileges Harbin as a major political, economic, and cultural center in its own right, elevated from a status within the nation as merely a remote frontier locale. In this way, through juxtaposing references to anti-Japanese resistance and northern Manchurian identity, Li draws on competing historical narratives of the region, one situated within and the other situated outside the nation, to construct a uniquely significant position for Harbin both within and beyond the nation.

At the city's first *wenshi ziliao* work conference in 1984, Niu Naiwen gave a speech entitled "Raise high the banner of patriotism in opening a new stage of *wenshi ziliao* work." In this speech, he summarizes the main features that characterize Harbin in the pre-Communist period:

Harbin is the earliest place in China where imperialists built railroads. It was one of the places in the Far East that imperialists contended to capture. The buildings, industry and commerce, culture, and religions in the city all have an obvious colonial and semi-colonial special character. Harbin people have a glorious tradition of resisting imperialist invasion and oppression. Chinese workers at the CER's No. 36 workers' unit were the first workers in the country to be exposed to socialism. Harbin is among the first cities to have a workers' movement, it was the first city to build a radio broadcasting station, it had the most foreign consulates, and it was the city with the most eastern orthodox churches constructed. After WW1 it competed with Shanghai as the country's flour-processing center. The oil, alcohol, rice, wheat, iron, lumber, and leather industries developed rapidly.[27]

---

[26] Li Xingchang, "A Glorious Enterprise Benefiting Later Generations," 35.
[27] Niu Naiwen, "Raise High the Banner of Patriotism," 61–62.

In the statement, Niu combines and celebrates a hodgepodge of different elements, including Harbin's colonial legacies, anticolonial resistance, socialist awakening, international political and cultural influences, and economic development. No single element dominates the narrative. Instead, the speaker presents the oppositional developments of colonialism and anticolonial resistance, socialism and private industry, together as symbiotic elements that work in concert to construct a new vision of Harbin as nationalist and socialist with unique colonial and capitalist characteristics. In so doing, Niu engages, synthesizes, and reconciles problematic and contradictory historical themes in such a way that Harbin reemerges historically as an economically and culturally vibrant, diverse, and cosmopolitan city that was at the same time on the cutting edge of the socialist and nationalist movements. The theme of colonialism and its economic and cultural by-products supplies for his narrative the exotic allure of cultural otherness and the stamp of modernization, while, turned on its head as the object of resistance, it provides material for nationalist discourse.

The issue of how to represent Russian influence was particularly problematic when it posed contradictions between nationalism, socialism, and economic development. For former migrant entrepreneurs whose families' livelihood had depended on collaborations with Russian businesses and who had suffered losses on account of the 1917 Communist Revolution, writing about the pre-1949 period was a risky venture that required subtle narrative strategies for reconstructing what significance these events had in their past lives. As in Niu Naiwen's speech to the *wenshi ziliao* work conference, Xing Jinghuan presented his personal history of relocation to Harbin in a way that at once exposed, concealed, and resignified the impact of Russian expansion, trade, and revolution on his family's fortunes. Through this means, he succeeds in "objectively" reflecting on his past while attaching new meanings to historical events that align his narrative with post-Mao ideology.

Entrepreneurial engagement with Russian traders in Manchuria had been commonplace among Chinese migrants in the region whose remittances from these ventures buoyed up local economies in northern China. Official reports at the time commented on the economic devastation that villages in Shandong and Hebei suffered when the value of the Russian ruble plummeted in the wake of the 1917 Revolution.[28] Xing Jinghuan's family was one of the households that painfully felt this impact of the Communist Revolution. Xing reveals that his father's migration to

---

[28] China Maritime Customs, 1917. Cited in Thomas R. Gottschang and Diana Lary, *Swallows and Settlers: The Great Migration from North China to Manchuria* (Ann Arbor, MI: Ann Arbor Center for Chinese Studies, University of Michigan, ca. 2000): 91–92.

Manchuria set his family apart from other "middle peasants" in his hometown in northern China: "My family was somewhat better off. The reason was that my father 'charged through the pass,' and on Toudao Street in [the] Daowai district of Harbin at a big enterprise called Tianfengyuan he became a 'lower-hand manager' [assistant manager], and so was able to supplement the family's income."[29] He goes on to indicate that the company for which his father worked as an assistant manager had relied on business transactions with Russians, using the Russian ruble rather than the regional Chinese currency. Faced with the loss of his father's remittances, Xing Jinghuan had to abandon his childhood studies and join his father in Manchuria to assist his household in financial crisis. In 1923, according to his account, he relocated to Harbin, where his father, still languishing without a job, assigned him to work at the bottom rungs of business to supplement the family's income.

From a post-Mao ideological perspective, the economic dislocation caused by the 1917 Revolution and its impact on the migrant entrepreneur was problematic in its implications for the incompatibility between commercial enterprise and socialist revolution. While indirectly linking his family's economic crisis to revolutionary events in 1917, Xing does not explicitly describe the trauma of being uprooted from his hometown in terms of his father's declining business with the Russians. Instead, he uses narrative strategies to resignify and de-problematize his migration to Manchuria in the post-Mao political context by framing his personal suffering and traumatic dislocation as a measure of the oppressiveness of the "old social order." Deemphasizing the role of his family's embeddedness within and reliance on Russian commercial ties, Xing draws on the politically acceptable discourse of the "bad old days" of warlord violence and "feudal" marriage arrangements to lend credibility to his personal suffering. It is the devastation of military campaigns that he blames for his forced departure. Referring to warlord Wu Peifu's retreat in 1923 across the pass into Hebei from the northeast after his defeat to Zhang Zuolin in the Second Zhi-Feng War,[30] Xing describes how the retreating army

passed through my hometown. The fleeing soldiers spent two days and two nights plundering every village in their path, seizing all of their livestock, carriages and clothing ... In this time of chaotic fighting, I couldn't do any studying nor was

---

[29] Xing Jinghuan, "My Over Sixty Years' Experience with Commercial Enterprises," 80.

[30] A personal record of the events and personalities of the war from an officer's perspective can be found in Zhongyang yanjiuyuan jindaishi yanjiusuo, *Chi Yich'iao xiansheng fangwen jilu* (*Records of Interviews with Ji Yiqiao*) (Taipei, Taiwan: Academia Sinica, Institute of Modern History, 1964). "Zhi-Feng" refers respectively to Zhili, now known as Hebei Province in northern China, and Fengtian, the southeastern-most of the three provinces of Manchuria later renamed Liaoning Province.

there any work I could do, so the only way out was to leave my hometown behind and join my father in Harbin to do an apprenticeship.[31]

Here he employs images of military violence accompanying warlordism in northern China as a backdrop to heighten the sense of traumatic disorientation and personal upheaval that the boy-becoming-man was experiencing in his own life transition. The larger political and military events of the time serve as a mirror reflecting the individual's own turbulent personal growth and physical journey. In the process, Xing reconfigures the officially prescribed framework for understanding the war-torn circumstances in warlord China as a formative backdrop to a story of personal growth and mobility. Defining the migrant's traumatic passage from one life stage to another, he sets the devastation of the conflict against business opportunities in the northeast to articulate his transformative journey from helpless childhood to adult initiative.

In doing so, he attributes legitimate collective social meaning to his personal trials by situating it in relation to the Chinese "*laobaixing*" (ordinary people's) suffering under the oppressive old order. He reinforces this mediation of trauma through the PRC discourse of "the bad old days" by defining his suffering in terms of the traditional marriage arrangements to which he had been bound since infancy.

We heard that Wu Peifu wasn't about to give up and wanted to re-ignite the conflict. This filled everyone with dread, and so everyone who had a daughter tried to pressure the parents of the prospective husband to carry out the wedding arrangements as soon as possible, in order to avoid possible misfortune. The Qiu family, who had arranged when I was just a baby to marry their daughter to me, also insisted that we consummate the union prior to my departure.[32]

The issue of arranged marriage practices based on family or lineage ties had been central to debates on projects of modernization and nation building since the early twentieth century. During the May Fourth movement, intellectuals espoused the idea of free marriage as an expression of gender equality and individual independence that would be essential to mobilizing a nationally conscious citizenry liberated from the particularistic attachments and repressive shackles of the hierarchical Confucian social order. After "liberation," the PRC government reinforced this intertwining of gender relations and political transformation, promulgating the new Marriage Laws in the early 1950s and promoting the idea that "women hold up half the sky" as central to the mobilization of the masses for socialist construction, while regarding previous arranged marital

---

[31] Xing Jinghuan, "My Over Sixty Years' Experience with Commercial Enterprises," 81.
[32] Ibid.

practices as symbolic of the defeated feudal society. For Xing Jinghuan, this discourse of defining the "liberated" society against the shackles of past "feudal" marriage customs provided a means for lending political legitimacy and significance to the personal trauma of his own migration event.

When he does acknowledge the foreign presence and its relationship to his migration experience, he does so through images that reinforce the sense of traumatic rupture and disorientation that defined for him the personal meaning of relocation to Manchuria.

Going to Harbin as I did in 1925 was definitely no easy task. Taking the train it still took three days. I first followed the road from my home to Tangshan [in Hebei], and took the Jing–Feng railway line to Shenyang.[33] There I changed over to a train on the South Manchurian Railroad administered by the Japanese until I reached Changchun, and then I changed over again to a small train on the Chinese Eastern Railroad managed by the Russians, before I could finally get to Harbin. Imperialism carved up the area of the Three Eastern Provinces[34] into two halves, the southern half belonging to the Japanese and the northern half belonging to the Russians. And when I got off the train at Harbin and took a look around, Daoli and Nangang [districts] were the specially administered Russian residential areas, while the customs of the Songhua River was under British management. At that time for me to venture east of the pass, rationally speaking I was going from Hebei Province in China to Harbin in the northeast of China. But it felt as though I had arrived in a foreign concession area.[35]

The rapid expansion of railroad lines in Manchuria during the early twentieth century, sponsored by competing Chinese, Russian, and Japanese development initiatives, dramatically facilitated and accelerated Chinese migration into the region. The projects of "railroad imperialism" led to a rapid integration of communications and transportation that intensified the economic ties between Manchuria and northern China proper. Migrants who wished to make the journey could not only expect a much easier and safer passage compared with their previous reliance on roads subject to seasonal conditions and bandit depredations, but also

---

[33] This railroad developed as a collaborative venture between Qing officials and Western interests, the latter providing much of the capital in order to facilitate their investment in industrial ventures such as mining along the railway. The railroad's first segment from Tangshan to Tianjin was completed in 1888, China's second oldest railroad designed largely for the purpose of transporting coal from Tangshan to the treaty port. Opposition from conservative Qing officials delayed the railroad's extension westward to Beijing and eastward to Shenyang (then referred to as Fengtian) until its eventual completion in 1912.

[34] The Three Eastern Provinces refers to Liaoning (then also known as Fengtian, like its capital city), Jilin, and Heilongjiang Provinces, and thus collectively refers to Manchuria, or northeastern China after 1949.

[35] Xing Jinghuan, "My Over Sixty Years' Experience with Commercial Enterprises," 81.

met with economic incentives in the form of ticket subsidies offered by regional officials and railroad authorities eager to recruit migrant labor for various agricultural and industrial initiatives.[36] Russian officials' desire for cheap Chinese migrant labor paradoxically fueled their anxiety about the flood of Chinese who subsequently targeted the railroad as an instrument for achieving their own livelihood goals, reflected in the dual Russian discourses of a "Yellow Russia" built on cheap Chinese labor and the "Yellow Peril" of hordes of Chinese utilizing the CER to invade Russia.[37]

Xing recasts the railroad's significance, however, within the nationalist discourse of Chinese victimization to foreign aggression as an evocative expression of his traumatic life stage initiation into manhood. His recollections of the complications besieging his path of migration serve to reflect on a personal level the seemingly arbitrary political boundaries carving up Manchuria at the time. Simultaneously, through framing his journey in terms of this maze of contesting political jurisdictions, he reinforces the traumatic and disorienting thrust across life stages that migration signified for him.

Xing's use of anti-imperialist and "oppressive old order" discourses as the framework to make sense of his migration experience lends official legitimacy to his past sufferings while deflecting attention from the Communist Revolution's problematic role. However, his approach to handling the big elephant in the room is not omission and erasure but rather inversion, as illustrated in the following passage celebrating the "success" of the Revolution:

After arriving in Harbin I went to find my father, but he was already without anything to do and was staying idly at an old friend's brokerage firm. The large business Tianfengyuan where he had been working before, like a lot of big companies in Harbin, did business with Russians. In 1918 (the seventh year of the Republic), under the circumstances of the success of the Soviet Union's October Revolution, the currency formerly put into circulation by the Czarist government, the "jiangtie," sharply went down in value. Those big businesses in Harbin that had been accustomed to doing business with the Russians were obliterated by the

[36] See Walter C. Young, "Chinese Colonization in Manchuria," *Far Eastern Review* 24.6 (June 1928): 241–250; Lattimore, *Manchuria*, 212–214; Ronald Suleski, "Regional Development in Manchuria: Immigrant Laborers and Provincial Officials in the 1920s," *Modern China* 4.4 (Oct. 1978): 419–434.

[37] See, for instance, David Wolff, *To the Harbin Station: The Liberal Alternative in Russian Manchuria, 1898–1914* (Stanford, CA: Stanford University Press, 1999); Lewis H. Siegelbaum, "Another 'Yellow Peril': Chinese Migrants in the Russian Far East and the Russian Reaction before 1917," *Modern Asian Studies* 12.2 (1978): 307–330; Alexander Lukin, *The Bear Watches the Dragon: Russia's Perceptions of China and the Evolution of Russian–Chinese Relations since the Eighteenth Century* (Armonk, NY: M. E. Sharpe, 2003): 58–59.

"jiangtie." Many of them went bankrupt, and Tianfengyuan could not escape being one of them. From this my father lost his job.[38]

Xing's disposition toward the October Revolution appears oddly paradoxical. The Revolution, according to the author's positive assessment, was a success, yet under the circumstances of that success Chinese businesses collapsed and migrant families like Xing's suffered the consequences. Yet while making clear that the conditions of the revolution were the context for this regional economic disaster, he seamlessly moves from the "success" of the revolution to the lingering malignant impact of the old political economy. In a subtle turn of rhetoric, he exposes the role of the Communist Revolution in the economic downturn yet folds it into a narrative of the old order symbolized by the Czarist currency obliterating Chinese businesses.

Xing exposes the historical conditions driving migration yet does so by inverting their political meanings in a way that preserves the "bad old order/socialist liberation" teleology of Party historiography. This strategy of folding together competing historical narratives enables the author to create multiple layers of signification that accommodate both historical authenticity and post-Mao ideology. His representation of migrant enterprise through images of warlord violence, feudal marital practices, railroad and "jiangtie" imperialism, and, finally, socialist revolution resonate with the multiplicity of meanings and priorities of market liberalization, socialist liberation, and anti-imperialist nationalism imbricated in post-Mao ideology.

Retelling the Story of the Northeast Borderland: From "Beyond the Pass" to Nationalist Front Line

Alongside these subtle strategies for dealing with historical complexities and ambiguities, *wenshi ziliao* editors appropriated the nationalist turn in the Party's discourse to reconceive of the northeast borderland as the historical site of China's coming into being as a modern nation. The relationship between integrative and marginalizing discourses on borderlands has been explored by Bérénice Guyot-Réchard in the context of northeast India (Assam), where the state's response of relief intervention to a devastating earthquake in 1950 contributed simultaneously to national absorption of the region and a marginalizing discourse on Assam as unable to take care of itself.[39] In the case of the *wenshi ziliao*, local

---

[38] Xing Jinghuan, "My Over Sixty Years' Experience with Commercial Enterprises," 82.
[39] Bérénice Guyot-Réchard, "Reordering a Border Space: Relief, Rehabilitation, and Nation-Building in Northeastern India after the 1950 Assam Earthquake," *Modern Asian Studies* 49.4 (July 2015): 931–962.

officials and editors flipped the marginalizing discourse of the northeast borderland (as insignificant and not really an integral part of the nation) on its head by claiming that the region's remote marginality was precisely what made it integral to the nationalist project. They turned to reconstruction of borderland history as a compelling way to renarrate the CCP's history in terms of defending the nation's territorial integrity against foreign invasion. In a speech given at the first *wenshi ziliao* work conference in 1984 in Raohe, a county seat along the Ussuri River at the Sino–Russian border, Li Rongchun summed it up in this way:

> In the past 100 years our county, like the whole province, has deeply felt the incursions of Czarist Russian imperialism and Japanese imperialism. Added to this was the people's suffering at the hands of the old political system's exploitation. The broad masses and every sector of patriots staged all forms of resistance against imperialism and reactionary power.[40]

Imperialism has overtaken social revolution as the primary emphasis of the narrative, with the "old political system's exploitation" relegated to an addition rather than the centerpiece. Moreover, in addressing the pre-Communist order, the speaker refers to the "broad masses and every sector of patriots" rather than to a particular social class as the protagonist of revolution. This rhetoric, therefore, not only deemphasizes social revolution but also redefines it in classless nationalist terms.

The northeast region occupied a tenuous position in relation to the Chinese nation, only recently incorporated politically and at the front lines of Russian and Japanese expansion. According to local editors, this is precisely what made this history particularly relevant for the post-Mao narrative of anti-imperialist nationalist struggle that was emerging at this time. In 1984, in a speech given at a *wenshi ziliao* work conference in Raohe, Zhang Zhenbang summed up the historical characteristics that made Raohe's *wenshi ziliao* distinctive. He declared that:

> Everyone knows Raohe lies along the borderland and has a very important position geographically. It's been 75 years since the establishment of the county in 1909. For a long time the laboring masses have worked hard to open Raohe and make the borderland prosperous. Most importantly, people here have given their lives in the struggle against Russian and Japanese aggression to protect the completeness of China's national territory, to gain the nation's liberation, and produce many heroic historical poems to be sung and cried.[41]

---

[40] Raohe zhengxie bangongshi, "Li Rongchun tongzhi zai raohe xian diyici wenshi ziliao gongzuo huiyi shang de jianghua" ("Comrade Li Rongchun's Speech at Raohe County's First *Wenshi Ziliao* Work Conference) (Mar. 6, 1984) (Raohe County Archive): 2.

[41] Raohe zhengxie bangongshi, "Raise High the Banner of Patriotism," 3–4.

He portrays Raohe's history of Russian and Japanese colonial occupation as an ideal site for constructing the new borderland-centered nationalist discourse. Incorporating the Party into this narrative, he adds, "During the anti-Japanese resistance, the entire Northeast Allied Anti-Japanese Army had 11 divisions. Raohe was the place of origin and the main site of activity of the Seventh Division. At the same time, it was the site of the Raohe base county committee of the underground CCP, one of 4 underground CCP base county committees in the province, leading Raohe, Hulin, Baoqing, Fujin, Tongjiang, and other places in anti-Japanese organizing."[42] Zhang appropriated post-Mao nationalism to render his locality as the cutting edge and front line of China's coming into being as a nation and the Party's role in that process.

Wenshi ziliao committee reports celebrate the extensive lengths to which members of collection teams went to find and interview survivors of key events that highlighted this nationalist version of borderland history. In Raohe, one report especially highlights the contributions of three retired men, Xu Rilu, Na Jie, and An Linhai, who had backgrounds in Party united front organization, secondary school language education, and supply and marketing cooperative management, respectively. These men, according to the report, overcame illness and physical frailty to travel across long distances to Mishan, Jixi, Tangyuan, and other places to collect materials and conduct interviews with surviving participants in the 7th Division.[43] An Linhai, on the occasion of the Raohe PPCC's formal recognition of him as a model PPCC worker, gave a speech explaining his "love for *wenshi ziliao*" in terms of a locally flavored nationalism. He began his statement by broadly theorizing on the importance of local historical production to the nationalist project:

Some people think *wenshi ziliao* is dispensable, and without it cultivation and growing food will go on just the same. But this way of thinking is ignorant. Without historical records, a country and people is ignorant and backward. For many years under "leftist" influence, we ignored local history research and writing. This loss is irreparable. *Wenshi ziliao* work is an indispensable part of building spiritual civilization, it's a great enterprise that comforts ancestors and benefits descendants, and it carries forward the past and awakens the future. History is a mirror on reality. Not knowing history means not knowing love for country.[44]

Having defined true patriotism as a product of historical reconstruction, he goes on to couch this in terms of Raohe's particular historical experience.

---

[42] Ibid. [43] Ibid., 2–3.

[44] Raohe zhengxie bangongshi, "An linhai tongzhi zai zhengxie raohe dierjie xian weiyuan-hui" ("An Linhai's Speech to the Second Session of the Raohe PPCC") (Mar. 21, 1985) (Materials of Raohe County PPCC's Second *Wenshi Ziliao* Work Conference) (Raohe County Archive): 2–3.

"As for the history of the decade-long Japanese devils' rule of Raohe, it's not easy to clarify everything. Some materials are worth digging up. Who can say clearly how many Chinese were killed by the devils? While doing *wenshi ziliao*, I developed a sense of historical responsibility. When some things can't be clarified and written about, it's letting down dead martyrs."[45] An explains his alleged passion for collecting and editing *wenshi ziliao* as rooted in an urgent sense of historical responsibility to clarify and recognize Raohe locals' prominence in the nationalist narrative. At the same time, local editors like An Linhai, who had undergone political and economic hardship during the Maoist years, demonstrated to the Party their own nationalist credentials through their dedication to compiling these historical records.

In Fujin, *wenshi ziliao* interviewers posed questions that specifically directed elderly informants to provide detailed information about episodes of Russian and Japanese violence and oppression. These questions included:

1) When did Soviet planes come to Fujin?[46] What places did they bomb first? What day did the Soviet army enter Fujin? How many were there and who were the high officers? After the Soviet army entered Fujin, how many battles were fought? How many were wounded and killed? How long did the Soviet army occupy Fujin? Where was the location?
2) What day did the Japanese flee? What kind of brutalities happened during their retreat?[47]

These were the standard questions drafted by the *wenshi ziliao* committee that interviewers were expected to ask as prompts to extract desired information from their informants. The contents of the questionnaire integrate attention to factual detail with clear ideological assumptions that determine and prioritize the kinds of facts that elderly survivors were expected to remember. As we see in what follows, however, those who told and wrote down their stories did not necessarily abide by this rigid formula. Rather than remain confined to the official guidelines, they creatively manipulated and wove together multiple strands of post-Mao ideology to conform to their own versions of history.

The nationalist ant-imperialist sentiment was echoed at the provincial level, where the *wenshi ziliao* committee redefined the northeast border's modern history as embodying in microcosm the heroic struggles of national formation. "Heilongjiang is on the nation's border," a report

---

[45] Ibid., 3.
[46] This is a reference to the Sino–Soviet border war, commonly referred to in Chinese as the CER Incident, in 1929.
[47] Fujin xian zhengxie, "Reference Outline for Asking Old Comrades to Write Memoirs," 1.

from the Heilongjiang *wenshi ziliao* office issued in 1986 asserts, "where over the past 100 years it has been land under assault from imperialism. This region's modern history has a salient unique characteristic, which is people's liberation struggle from start to finish. Our province's sacrificial heroes wrote on this territory a very tragic and noble page [of history] – this page embodies as a miniature the entire nation's people's [history of] humiliation and heroic resistance."[48] The writer begins with an acknowledgment of the region's marginal position on the edge of the nation and under foreign occupation, but then redefines marginality as centrality by characterizing its history of dismemberment from the Chinese nation as a history of continuous "liberation struggle" and "heroic resistance." This narrative speaks to the historical concept of Manchuria as a unique geopolitical space outside of China proper, "beyond the pass," yet does so in a way that reclaims it as a uniquely Chinese space at the forefront of the nationalist resistance story.

To lend substance and depth to this claim, Heilongjiang editorial committees homed in on the CER's history as a special topic of investigation for illuminating in microcosm the region's prominent role in anti-imperialist resistance. Beginning in 1984, the provincial *wenshi ziliao* office distributed a "reference manual for collecting CER special topic materials" to local county and city PPCCs as well as various institutions involved in historical research throughout the province. Two years later, to evaluate and accelerate progress with the project, the provincial *wenshi ziliao* research committee invited seventeen experts and scholars from universities, gazetteer offices, and social science research departments to collaborate with *wenshi ziliao* committees in collecting, compiling, and editing materials on the CER, and to design a plan for how to organize the materials thematically. Accordingly, they drafted the following outline that lists the overarching topics for each of the ten volumes in the CER special topic series that they planned to publish:

1) The CER's construction.
2) Czarist Russia's use of the railroad to invade and steal from China.
3) Anti-Russian struggles waged by Chinese along the CER line.
4) The international struggle over the CER and the Chinese government's restoration of railroad rights.
5) Materials about the CER after the 1917 Revolution.
6) The CER after 1931.
7) Historical figures associated with the CER (two volumes).
8) CER major events.

---

[48] Heilongjiang sheng zhengxie wenshi ban, "*Wenshi Ziliao* Is Spiritual Food That Inspires People to Struggle for Shared Ideals," 1–2.

9) Translated documents about the CER.[49]

This plan for series publication utilizes the CER as a lens for dramatizing and structuring the history of Heilongjiang as a continuous struggle between foreign incursion and Chinese nationalism. The narrative sequence begins with Russia's arrival on the scene as a force of railroad imperialism, followed by the railroad's evolution into a site of Chinese resistance and eventually successful claims to sovereignty until Japan's occupation of Manchuria. The only item in the outline that refers to the socialist revolution is item number five, which resituates the communist movement historically as an integral part of a larger and more important story of anti-imperialist nationalism. At the same time, by drawing attention to the spread of communism along the CER railroad in the aftermath of the 1917 Revolution, the editors are implicitly making the claim that the northeast borderland had become "red" before the rest of "China proper," predating the founding of the CCP.

In this way, using the CER as a focal point, Heilongjiang *wenshi ziliao* participants turned the region's historical marginality in respect to the Chinese nation on its head, reimagining the northeast borderland as the seminal gateway in China's story of national construction and socialist revolution. Heilongjiang editors juxtaposed episodes of Russian and Japanese oppression with incidents of Chinese resistance as key points of *wenshi ziliao* collection. These include testimonies by survivors of the Blagoveshchensk and "64 Villages" Massacre of Chinese residents along the border by Russian officers in 1900, whose "blood and tear-stained grievances forcefully exposed Tsarist Russian invaders' criminal acts; accounts of the biological experiments carried out by Japanese Unit "731" that "exposed the savage nature of Japanese imperialism" and "made one's heart bleed"; and other "history that can't be forgotten" relating to the "fourteen years of tragedies" during the Manchukuo period of Japanese control, in which "over thirty survivors expressed grievances about Japanese fascism, of which 80% had never been released before." "It's hard to find this kind of material in other history books," the writer of the report declares, and "when one opens up *wenshi ziliao*, it is like inhabiting that tragic era, immersed in the humiliation of national disaster with the witness' blood and tear-stained grievances."[50]

Alongside these themes of suffering and tragedy, investigators sought out materials that evoked the glories and heroism of resistance efforts,

[49] "Zhongdonglu zhuanti shiliao xiezuo hui huiyi jiyao" ("Main Points from [the] Meeting of [the] Committee on CER Special Topic Historical Materials") (1986) (Heilongjiang Provincial Archives 56:2:263): 1–3.
[50] Heilongjiang sheng zhengxie wenshi ban "*Wenshi Ziliao* Is Spiritual Food That Inspires People to Struggle for Shared Ideals," 2–3.

ranging from an account of a late Qing official who had challenged Russian expansion at the turn of the twentieth century, as narrated by his daughter-in-law, to testimonies about the anti-Japanese exploits of the "Righteous and Brave Army" and the Northeast Allied Anti-Japanese Army as presented by relatives, friends, and surviving officers. The Qiqihar *wenshi ziliao* committee, for instance, devoted an entire volume to painstakingly unearthing obscure details, filling in gaps, and correcting historians' mistakes concerning a military incident known as the Jiangqiao campaign involving Ma Zhanshan that is generally considered the opening event of the resistance movement. The inclusion of such particulars as the exact site at which the battle took place (apparently the Nenjiang steel bridge, rather than a wooden bridge as previously thought, was blown up) demonstrated the text's primacy as the authoritative source on what actually happened. These projects directed national attention to the regional histories that they highlighted. In the case of the Qiqihar *wenshi ziliao*, other books dealing with the Mukden Incident and Japanese occupation reprinted whole or parts of this volume within their chapters, and the military journal of the Guangzhou military district sent a specialist to Qiqihar to obtain this material.[51]

In addition to these political and military dimensions, outlines of key subjects to be addressed in these *wenshi ziliao* publications included writers, industrialists, and people of Hezhe minority ethnicity who demonstrated patriotism.[52] In this way, the editors envisioned a progression of content from the portrayal of Chinese as victims of foreign aggression to the glorification of Chinese as agents of resistance. This redeemed the early twentieth-century history of colonization of Manchuria as a natural, inevitable evolution toward the formation of the modern nation.

But these nationalist impulses took multiple forms within the context of thawing relations with Russia in the 1980s, as Perestroika and post-Mao liberalization reforms worked together to revive trade and migration across the Amur River. City and county governments in the region opened their doors to international investment while reenvisioning themselves as "dragon wings" aggressively pushing northward across the border. In this context, *wenshi ziliao* revisited the history of Sino–Russian interactions in order to redefine the region in cosmopolitan terms while asserting Chinese economic and cultural dominance. In contrast with the condemnation of all things foreign during the Cultural Revolution, *wenshi ziliao* articles published in Heilongjiang celebrated cultural mixing in the

---

[51] Liu Feilin, "Thirty Years' Reflections on Literary and Historical Work," 362–363.
[52] Heilongjiang sheng zhengxie wenshi ban, "*Wenshi Ziliao* Is Spiritual Food That Inspires People to Struggle for Shared Ideals," 3–4.

borderland to highlight the region's distinctive culture. At the same time, they highlighted the Chinese character of cities on both sides of the border, depicting the region's economic development as a process of becoming Chinese. These two representations of the borderland's history reflected the entangled post-Mao tendencies of nationalist ideology, regional identities, and opening to the outside world.

An account describing the histories of Heihe and Blagoveshchensk on opposite sides of the Amur River exhibits both of these tendencies. Sino–Russian pidgin and its pervasive influence in the region, for instance, is the subject of detailed discussion in the narrative, which lists examples of pidgin used in everyday conversation. In the realm of the household, the author writes that:

[S]torage rooms (*cangfang* in Chinese) were called "*anbala*," iron-rimmed buckets (*tiepi shuitong*) were called "*wedaluo*" … iron-rimmed stoves (*tiepi huolu*) were called "*bielaqi*" … the small rooms of a house (*xiao gejian*) were called "*naomen* … " [As for clothing items,] formal felt hats (*zhan limao*) were called "*shiliangbake*" … short leather vests (*duanshenpishangyi*) were called "*pinjiake*," leather shoes (*pixie*) were called "*bajinke*." [In the area of food and drink,] "bread (*mianbao*) was called "*lieba*," … cold drinks were called "*gewasi*."

The list extends to mainstays of the Chinese culinary tradition like dumplings and fried potstickers that had distinctive names in the pidgin lexicon.[53] At the same time, the author describes the Russian border city of Blagoveshchensk as a Chinese economic and cultural space. Describing the traffic between Blagoveshchensk and Heihe on the Chinese side, he notes that a ferry costing fifteen cents each way carried passengers back and forth six times a day, three times in the morning and three times in the afternoon. "Since they freely went back and forth, there was a constant, uninterrupted flow of people to Blagoveshchensk and every day people streamed without pause by the small ticket-vending building next to the river." Much of this traffic, according to the author, consisted of Heihe residents partaking in afternoon and evening entertainment in the larger city on the Russian side.

Among the people crossing the river, besides small traders, there were those who visited family and friends, those with nothing to do just wandering around, those looking for short-time work; there were people doing all kinds of things. At that time Heihe didn't yet have cinema, so some people crossed the river just to see a film. Most of those crossing the river went and returned the same day, having

[53] Xu Shuqiu, "'Kai jiaotong' shiqi de (bu) shi, huashang, lü e qiaomin ji qita" ("Blagoveshchensk during the Period of 'Open Transportation,' Chinese Merchants, Chinese Residing in Russia, and Other Matters"), *Heihe wenshi ziliao – Lü e huaqiao shiliao xuan* (Zhengxie heilongjiang sheng heihe shi weiyuan hui wenshi ziliao yanjiu gongzuo weiyuan hui), 8 (1991): 82–83.

lunch on that (the Russian) side. Lunch (there) was really cheap. At Russian restaurants, to purchase a meal, one could get a serving just by handing over ten cents upon entering. This serving included a slice of black and white bread, a bowl of cabbage, potatoes, carrots, and beef soup. The service at Russian restaurants was simple, just one female attendant who watched over the guests from a very high wooden platform, and the food was economical and wholesome. This became an essential noontime diversion.

Entertainment aside, the article describes in detail the businesses run by Chinese migrants in the city.[54]

Other *wenshi ziliao* articles used accounts of Chinese entrepreneurs to merge cosmopolitan and ethnic nationalist conceptions of the borderland. These narratives link cross-border and international trade to the consolidation of Chinese economic dominance. One biography's description of the rise to local prominence of a trader from Shandong illustrates this connection. Having lived for a few years in the Soviet Union before settling in Heihe in 1921, he hauled kegs of arracks across the river to sell to Russian customers in exchange for gold. With the capital he accumulated, Bi founded a company that sold everyday items like cloth and dried white radish from Japan to gold mine workers in exchange for gold. "Mr. Sun, a gold-smelting worker at that time[,] recalled that during the peak season of buying gold, every ten or fifteen days they could carry at least one iron basin of gold dust across the Soviet border and convert it into gold bricks or strips. Then Cui Baochun and three others, armed, would take it to places like Shanghai to sell."[55] With the profits accrued from this business, he bought up sizable real estate in Heihe and became a major landlord. His oldest son, Bi Chengxian, during *wenshi ziliao* interviews pointed out his father's formerly extensive holdings:

This land from the east entrance of [the] Heihe newspaper office on Sandao [S]treet north to Erdao Street and west to this area all belonged to my father. There was another section of family homes extending from the former district industrial bureau on Xixing [R]oad west to the district transportation bureau, this section of red brick buildings on the south side of Sandao [S]treet, and this area on the south side that all belonged to my father. It ends at the north side of Erdao Street.[56]

The life story of this migrant entrepreneur celebrates an expansive, internationally oriented commercial culture that ultimately allows for the realization of Chinese economic and territorial claims.

In tension with this cosmopolitan approach to nationalist discourse was the anti-imperialist narrative that pitted the Chinese migrant against the

---

[54] Ibid., 78–79.
[55] Bian Ji, "Bi Fengzhi de gongxian" ("Bi Fengzhi's Contributions"), in ibid., 89–90.
[56] Ibid.

Russian state. Reflecting the uneasy balance between inwardly focused anti-foreign nationalism and outwardly oriented market liberalization in post-Mao philosophy, *wenshi ziliao* alternated between nostalgic cosmopolitanism and Russian aggression/Chinese resistance as frameworks for the relationship between Chinese migrant enterprise and the Russian presence in Manchuria. A popular theme in the aggression/resistance narrative was the anti-Russian exploits of miner-turned bandit Wang Lin, who sabotaged sections of the newly constructed CER railroad following the suppression of the Boxer Uprising. Biographical accounts of his life and the lives of those who joined him elide the economic incentives that had drawn migrants to railroad construction work, painting a picture of him as a nationalist and communist hero who used fellow local ties to organize Chinese railroad workers against their Russian exploiters.[57]

"Filling in Gaps in the Building of a Border Spiritual Civilization": Writing Ethnic Minorities into Local and Nationalist Narratives

Alongside these competing representations of colonial encounters, the question of how non-Han ethnic minorities in the northeast borderland fit into regional and national narratives was also a concern for *wenshi ziliao* organizers. Discussing the implications of the state's ethnic classification program in southwest China, Thomas Mullaney argues that "non-Han citizens in the post-Classification (post-1954) period have thus been the subject of two state-led programs of nationalization: one geared toward 'becoming Chinese,' and the other toward becoming Achang, Bai, Lisu, Wa, Yi, Zhuang, and so forth."[58] As we see in this section, *wenshi ziliao* cadres similarly carried out a dual project of demonstrating the Chineseness of the Hezhe ethnic minority through narratives of anti-Japanese resistance while at the same time presenting them as ethnically distinct from the Chinese. These dual modes of classification and representation were related to the broader concerns of the *wenshi ziliao* explored in this chapter of tying the region's marginality and difference to national integration.

---

[57] See, for instance, *Jiaohe wenshi ziliao*, vol. 1 (Zhongguo renmin zhengzhi xieshang huiyi jilin sheng jiaohe xian weiyuanhui wenshi ziliao yanjiu weiyuanhui, 1985): 38–41; *Huadian wenshi ziliao*, vol. 6 (Huadian shi weiyuan hui wenshi ziliao yanjiu weiyuan hui, 1992): 12–15; Wang Xiting, *Xiangma yingzhang zong siling: wang delin zhuan (Bandit, Regiment Head and Supreme Commander: A Biography of Wang Delin)* (Harbin: Heilongjiang renmin chubanshe, 1987): 35–40.

[58] Mullaney, *Coming to Terms with the Nation*, 11.

The Oroqen population in the Amur borderlands had steadily dropped since the nineteenth century due to the encroachment of Chinese agriculture and commerce. Chinese exploitative commercial practices, particularly the use of opium as an addictive commodity, combined with the denuding of the forests by farming and lumber industries, increasingly drew the population away from hunting and into economic dependency and indebtedness. After 1931, Japanese policies of concentrating and isolating the Oroqen people into camps and mobilizing Oroqen men into military units (*shanlin dui*) to spy on the Soviet Union and fight against the Chinese resistance further undermined Oroqens' independent livelihood and freedom of movement.[59] During the Maoist period, as in other ethnic borderlands, communism and communalization involved the negation of cultural difference, in this case, by forcing Oroqens into a sedentary agricultural lifestyle.[60]

In the 1980s, *wenshi ziliao* organizers sidestepped the issue of how Chinese settlement of the region had impacted the Oroqens and avoided the history of Oroqen military mobilization under Japanese colonialism. Instead, they alternated between incorporating them into the Chinese anti-imperialist narrative and highlighting and exoticizing their ethnic particularity as a regional cultural asset. Local investigators led historical preservation campaigns to supply evidence for an uninterrupted Chinese dominance in the region while celebrating non-Chinese ethnic characteristics. While commemorating anti-Japanese martyrs, county PPCC teams also undertook inspections of various relics and archaeological remains of old cities from the Ming period that corroborated historical materials detailing Chinese military and political expansion to northeastern Heilongjiang in earlier dynastic eras. These projects were closely tied together but involved cooperation with different government institutions – the PPCC collaborated with the civil administration department on the anti-Japanese martyrs project, while the culture department cooperated in overseeing restoration of the Ming city remains, which was characterized as "filling in gaps in the building of a border spiritual civilization."[61] The reason for the civil administration department's involvement in historical work was likely related to the issue of political

[59] Prasenjit Duara, *Sovereignty and Authenticity: Manchukuo and the East Asian Modern* (Lanham, MD: Rowman and Littlefield, 2003); Katsumi Nakao, "Japanese Colonial Policy and Anthropology in Manchuria," in Jan Van Bremen and Akitoshi Shimizu, eds., *Anthropology and Colonialism in Asia and Oceania* (Richmond, Surrey: Curzon, 1999).
[60] Duara, *Sovereignty and Authenticity*.
[61] Lü Mingyi, "Zhongguo renmin zhengzhi xieshang huiyi dier jie weiyuanhui changwu weiyuanhui gongzuo baogao" ("Work Report of the Standing Committee of the Second Session of the [Raohe] PPCC") (Mar. 17, 1985, at the second meeting of the Second Session of the Raohe PPCC) (Raohe County Archive): 11–12.

rehabilitation, since many of those who had been either directly or indirectly connected with these modern historical events had undergone persecution during the Cultural Revolution. For this reason, research on and commemoration of these people and events was not only a symbolic nationalist activity but also a practical affair of reincorporating and providing economic relief and compensation to alienated members of society whom the Party wished to re-embrace (as is discussed further). In contrast, the restoration of old city relics was a primarily symbolic event that had broader and more abstract political implications for complicating Chinese national claims to the region.

At the same time, the national PPCC issued guidelines to "collect and organize materials about nationalities in minority nationality areas" to "benefit nationalities uniting and national unification."[62] The Heilongjiang provincial office passed on these directives to the local level, in part by putting pressure on county PPCCs to produce materials pertaining to this topic. The Fuyuan PPCC, for instance, according to a 1988 report, "wrote three *wenshi ziliao* articles on the Hezhe specially requested by the provincial *wenshi ziliao* office."[63]

Local *wenshi ziliao* committees capitalized on these upper-level initiatives to accentuate the non-Han ethnic composition of the borderland, celebrating distinctive non-Chinese traditions and histories as a kind of cultural capital uniquely possessed by the region. In Tongjiang, one of the areas with the highest concentration of Hezhe residents, the *wenshi ziliao* office sent investigators to conduct interviews in Hezhe villages. They allegedly collected "200,000 characters of Hezhe *wenshi ziliao*" and published a "'Hezhe nationality special issue' that had 13 articles, over 100,000 characters." Connecting ethnic particularity to national unity, You Zhixian, a standing committee member on the Tongjiang PPCC, described these materials as "enriching China's storehouse of nationalities culture."[64]

Local historical investigators alternated between framing this ethnic diversity in broad nationalist terms and incorporating it within narratives

---

[62] "Guanyu zhengxie diwuci quanguo wenshi ziliao gongzuo huiyi de qingkuang he jingshen de huibao tigang" ("Outline of Report Regarding [the] Situation and Spirit of [the] PPCC's Fifth National *Wenshi Ziliao* Work Conference"): 6–8 (Heilongjiang Provincial Archive 56:2:263 [1987]).

[63] Zhengxie fuyuan xian weiyuanhui, "Jiaqiang dui zhengxie gongzuo de lingdao, chongfen fahui zhengxie zhineng zuoyong" ("Strengthen [the] Leadership of PPCC Work and Fully Realize the Functional Potential of the PPCC") (Oct. 1988) (Fuyuan City Archives): 8–9.

[64] You Zhixian, "Zhongguo renmin zhengzhi xieshang huiyi tongjiang xian dier jie weiyuanhui changwu weiyuanhui gongzuo baogao" ("Work Report of the Standing Committee of the Second Session of the Tongjiang County PPCC") (From the speech at the first meeting of the First Session of the Tongjiang City PPCC) (Mar. 29, 1987) (Tongjiang City Archive): 7.

of local particularity. On one side of this spectrum, editors in Tongjiang County referred to the collection and editing of materials concerning the Hezhe minority population squarely in the context of anti-imperialist nationalism and the ascendancy of the Party as a political force, emphasizing the history of Japanese oppression as a defining feature of modern Hezhe identity.[65] According to a Tongjiang *wenshi ziliao* study report, the county PPCC's vice-chair contributed to this effort by writing two articles entitled "Hezhe customs" and "Japanese oppression of Hezhe people and true records of Hezhe anti-Japanese resistance," one of which was submitted to the provincial *wenshi ziliao* office.[66] Through these articles, participants in the local *wenshi ziliao* project highlighted ethnic particularity as a distinctive feature of the region while simultaneously embedding that particularity within a unified nationalist experience.

The local PPCC of Raohe, another site of significant Hezhe settlement, approached the topic with a somewhat different emphasis. In his speech at a local *wenshi ziliao* work conference in 1985, the chair of Raohe's PPCC, Zhang Zhenbang, tied together colonialism and ethnic particularity as mutually reinforcing cultural features that set the northeast borderland apart from the rest of the Chinese nation. His description of foreign imperialism appears immediately before his reference to the local Hezhe population's distinctive history, customs, and language. In his descriptions of both, he asserts northern Heilongjiang's unique national significance by emphasizing features that set the region apart from the Chinese nation historically and culturally. But he goes further than this to link the Hezhe presence to the region's continuing importance in the eyes of its former colonial rulers. "The Hezhe are not only researched by our country, but also by the Soviet Union, Japan, and other countries. Besides Tongjiang, no other cities and counties have this treasure of materials on Hezhe."[67] Zhang draws a continuous line of foreign influence and interest in the region, implying that Raohe's particular cultural character remains the object of Russian and Japanese curiosity and investigation. Unlike the Tongjiang PPCC's attempt to fully incorporate the history of ethnic particularity within the nationalist narrative, Zhang ties together Raohe's ethnic and colonial histories as a way to amplify the county's

---

[65] Zhengxie tongjiang xian weiyuanhui bangongshi, "Duanxun."

[66] Zhengxie tongjiang xian weiyuanhui bangongshi, wenshi xuexi shi, "Wenshi ziliao zhengji gongzuo jianxun" ("Brief Report on Work of Collecting *Wenshi Ziliao*"), *Tongjiang zhengxie* (*Tongjiang PPCC*), no. 2 (no. 96 overall) (Feb. 10, 1985) (Tongjiang City Archive): 3–4.

[67] Zhang Zhenbang, "Zai aiguo zhuyu de qizhi xia, jiaqiang nuli xiezuo, wei kaichuang wenshi ziliao gongzuo er fendou" ("Struggle to Pioneer *Wenshi Ziliao* Work through Strengthening Diligent Cooperation under the Banner of Patriotism") (Office of the Raohe PPCC) (Materials of the County PPCC's Second *Wenshi Ziliao* Work Conference) (Aug. 6, 1985): 8.

cultural distinctiveness in relation to the rest of the nation. At the same time, he adds a local dimension to the provincial narrative highlighting Heilongjiang's unique contributions to the nation's rich cultural resources. He does so by championing Raohe's uncontested claims to a prized portion of these cultural resources, asserting that only one other county, Tongjiang, can boast such possessions.

At the provincial level, editorial committees attempted to reconcile the integrative and differentiating aspects of engaging with the histories of ethnic minorities in the region. The nature of the topics that they emphasized in *wenshi ziliao* collection outlines reflects this effort. In 1987, the provincial *wenshi ziliao* research committee drafted a "Heilongjiang *wenshi ziliao* collection outline on minority nationalities." It begins with a focus on collecting materials that incorporate these groups into the overarching narratives of socialist revolution and anticolonial nationalism. Key themes to be addressed include "reactionary ruling classes' economic exploitation and political oppression of minorities" and "struggles against Russia and Manchukuo and the Japanese by minorities in our province."[68] The drafters of the outline subsume the history of ethnic conflict along the borderland within the framework of class exploitation and imperialist oppression.

However, further along in the outline, the emphasis shifts toward a focus on special characteristics that differentiate ethnic minorities from the Han Chinese. The last two sections on customs and religion, in particular, accentuate distinctive social practices in "clothing, eating, housing . . . marriage and funeral customs; birthday, holiday, and ritual customs; taboos, worship, and primitive idolatry practices."[69] While condescendingly referring to some of these cultural traditions as "primitive," the editors also made room for celebrating local ethnic minority figures who commanded respect in their respective communities. In the last section on religion, for instance, they instructed researchers to collect "materials regarding famous figures of shamanism, Lamaism, and Islam, and their religious proselytizing."[70]

The content and structure of this document suggest that the editors used the separate categories of "political, economic, and military" on one hand and "cultural" on the other to reconcile nationally integrative and locally differentiating features and agendas of *wenshi ziliao*. By placing the former at the beginning and the latter at the end of the outline, they implicitly subordinated the local to the national, implying that the objective of national Party unity enclosed and preceded local claims to cultural

---

[68] Heilongjiang sheng zhengxie wenshi ziliao yanjiu gongzuo weiyuanhui, "Heilongjiang sheng shaoshu minzu wenshi ziliao zhengji tigang" ("Outline for Collection of Heilongjiang Provincial *Wenshi Ziliao* Materials about Ethnic Minorities") (1987) (Heilongjiang Provincial Archives).
[69] Ibid.   [70] Ibid.

distinctness. At the same time, without compromising central political directives, the outline accommodated and affirmed, to an extent, local ethnic minority heritage, traditions, and pride. Through these representational strategies, editors in the northeast realigned the borderland's ethnic and cultural particularity with the new regime's attempt to integrate economic internationalization, regional cultural diversity, and nationalist consolidation.

Conclusion

By reviving the regional concept of northern Manchuria, *wenshi ziliao* compilers reappropriated the history of Russian colonial influence in the region as part of a broader narrative of regional economic modernization and cultural uniqueness. This approach to reimagining the region's history subsumed it within the national story of Chinese modernization while providing a lens for editors to overlay that narrative with a historical consciousness of and pride in a distinctive northeast borderland identity. *Wenshi ziliao* editors also incorporated the Party into a borderland-centered nationalist narrative, reimagining the Party as central to the borderland story while reconceiving of the borderland as central to the Party's national narrative. Sidestepping the problematic history of Oroqens' encounters with Chinese expansion and Japanese colonialism, *wenshi ziliao* editors elided the historical positioning of the Oroqens in between rival Chinese, Russian, and Japanese colonizing projects. Instead of exposing Chinese commerce and settlement as one among several competing colonizing powers, editors reconceived of the Oroqens as culturally distinctive yet fully integrated into the Chinese nationalist narrative.

In the next chapter, we turn our attention to the *wenshi ziliao* approach to "seeking truth from facts," observing how *wenshi ziliao* officials, theorists, and editors reinterpreted this concept to reconcile empirical historical research with political ideology, provide theoretical justification for the rewriting of northeast borderland history, and negotiate between respect for the authenticity of firsthand accounts and a wary attitude toward ideologically suspect narratives.

Introduction

In his evaluation of the science and truth behind the 1954 Ethnic Classification Project in Yunnan, Thomas Mullaney notes that scholars had not paid much attention to the project, and if they did, they either dismissed it as "arbitrary" and "procrustean" or held it up as an impressive model of extensive, rigorous fieldwork that documented in detail everyday life and customs. He argues in his compelling study that it was neither of these: it was neither simply Communist pseudoscience nor scientific work separated from politics.[1] This statement could just as well have been written about the *wenshi ziliao*, which is only now beginning to receive scholarly attention, and which similarly has either been viewed dismissively as state propaganda or taken literally as authentic historical truth. In reality, as this chapter shows, the *wenshi ziliao* was neither: it was a project where scientific historical concepts and methods intersected with locally, regionally, and nationally mediated politics to produce new post-Mao historical identities.

During the early period of the Communist Party and the PRC, the question of how to reconcile "redness" with "expertise" was a problem not only for the organization of the party-state bureaucracy and the training of bureaucrats, but also for the Party's approach to the work and training of historians. As Huaiyin Li discusses, the professionalization and "disciplinizing" of the historical field in the early to mid-1950s brought back hierarchy and professional standards into academia, underscored by continuity in the composition of senior professors from the pre-1949 period. Li notes that the Great Leap Forward and the mid-1960s radicalization of historiography entailed a reversal of this disciplinizing tendency, which younger junior historians used to

---

[1] Mullaney, *Coming to Terms with the Nation*, 3.

expand their authority and status as revolutionary relative to their "bourgeois" senior colleagues.[2]

The *wenshi ziliao* marked a return to this earlier trend of professionalization and disciplinization of history. At the same time, *wenshi ziliao* organizers tied scientific professionalism and systematic disciplinarity to political mobilization and to using history to serve the Party's agenda. In this way, the *wenshi ziliao* was an attempt to resolve the Party's historical challenge of reconciling its competing priorities of conforming to Western-style modernization and upholding its revolutionary tradition.

The reimagining of the northeast borderland historical landscape involved and required a conceptual reinterpretation of "seeking truth from facts." While most commonly associated with Deng Xiaoping and the post-Mao turn toward a more rational and scientific inquiry-based approach to governance and reform, the term in fact had historical roots going back to the Ming–Qing transition. Qing-period intellectuals organized the "evidential learning" (*kaozheng*) movement, a philological search for textual authenticity, to secure firm links with the Confucian past in the face of the Manchu invasion. A lack of rigorous evidence-based scholarship was blamed for contributing to the fall of the Ming dynasty. In the early twentieth century, local and regional elites again turned to truth seeking as a response to traumatic foreign impact. The social survey movement, as Tong Lam describes, entailed local elite initiatives to collect social facts and conduct empirical investigations of on-the-ground social conditions. The goals of these endeavors were to create the basis for a systematic, rational approach to state governance and to refute Western imperialist claims that China lacked the credentials of a modern nation rooted in the mobilization of scientific facts.[3]

While adopting an empirical scientific methodology, intellectuals in the 1920s and 1930s envisioned fact collecting as an integrative process of gathering information about the population and transforming and educating that population in how to become national citizens.[4] As Gloria Davies has pointed out, early twentieth-century Chinese intellectuals like Yan Fu and Liang Qichao endowed the Western-influenced values of empirical rationality and scientific precision with a pedagogical purpose of prescribing an ideal moral and political community.[5] As Eugenia Lean

[2] Huaiyin Li, *Reinventing Modern China: Imagination and Authenticity in Chinese Historical Writing* (Honolulu, HI: University of Hawaii Press, 2012), 19–23.
[3] Tong Lam, *A Passion for Facts.*   [4] Ibid.
[5] Gloria Davies, "Knowing How to Be: The Dangers of Putting (Chinese) Thought into Action," in Leigh Jenco, ed., *Chinese Thought as Global Theory: Diversifying Knowledge Production in the Social Sciences and Humanities* (Albany, NY: State University of New York Press, 2016), 29–54.

and Julia Strauss have argued, the GMD's modernization project wedded scientific technical training and objective rationality to affective sentiment and political mobilization.[6]

Mao adapted this politically motivated concept of factual precision and empirical research to his "mass line" and "investigative research" approaches to collecting and "processing" social facts. As Aminda Smith and Mark Selden have described, the mass line constituted an attempt to "mediate and resolve the antagonisms" between "strong, elite leadership" and "voluntary mass participation" through a "from the people, to the people" process of collecting social and historical facts from the people, reframing them in a "concentrated and systematic" form along the lines of Party ideology, and then delivering these facts in their ideologically repackaged form back to the masses "until all members of the People came to understand and accept them as their own."[7] Mao's concept of investigative research adhered to these basic principles of the mass line. As Ping-Chun Hsiung demonstrates, Mao used several principles of investigative research to integrate empirical precision with mass political mobilization and the political disciplining of intellectuals. These principles included the requirements that researchers eat, live, and work together with the informants ("three principles of togetherness"), that they immerse themselves in a local site for an extended period of time ("getting down from the horse to take a closer look at the petals"), and that they recognize the generalizability of case studies ("dissecting a sparrow"). Strenuous physical labor and hardship were an integral part of the investigative process for the researchers. While interacting closely with their local informants, investigators relied on the Party apparatus for the selection of team members, development of research objectives, and choice of local sites to investigate.[8]

These requirements point to several underlying features of the investigative research approach to truth seeking: first, Mao conceived of expertise and empirical accuracy on one hand and the participation and mobilization of ordinary people on the other as mutually reinforcing. Second, by imposing physical hardship on the investigators, the Communist state used the fact-collecting mission as an instrument for politically disciplining the intellectual elites. Third, investigative research provided a framework for

[6] Lean, *Public Passions*; Julia Strauss, "Morality, Coercion and State Building by Campaign in the Early PRC: Regime Consolidation and After, 1949–1956," *China Quarterly*, no. 188 (Dec. 2006) (Special Issue: History of the PRC [1949–1976]): 891–912.

[7] Smith, *Thought Reform and China's Dangerous Classes*, 99–100; Mark Selden, *China in Revolution: The Yenan Way Revisited* (Armonk, NY: M. E. Sharpe, 1995), 243.

[8] Ping-Chun Hsiung, "Pursuing Qualitative Research from the Global South: 'Investigative Research' during China's 'Great Leap Forward' (1958–62)," *Forum: Qualitative Social Research* 16.3 (2015).

integrating a localized participatory process of knowledge production with centralized Party control.

The *wenshi ziliao* approach to "seeking truth from facts" drew on these earlier models. Like the social survey movement, the *wenshi ziliao* was in part a response to international pressures. Social survey activists were facing the challenge of colonial modernity and attempting to prove China's equal status as a modern rational state. In the context of post-Mao China's reintegration into the international community, *wenshi ziliao* organizers used the scientific, empirical logic of the project to prove to the international community, especially overseas Chinese, that China would now conform to the rational logic of the global market and would follow scientific procedures for obtaining factual knowledge. Unlike the earlier movement's conscious engagement with and borrowing from Western concepts and methods, however, *wenshi ziliao* theorists staunchly opposed what they called Western "objectivist" thinking and instead firmly implanted themselves in Maoist terminology.

The emphasis in *wenshi ziliao* guidelines on integrating scientific empiricism and the collection of social facts with political ideology (and social mobilization, as we see in Chapters 5 and 6) and circumscribing localized knowledge production within the national Party framework were highly reminiscent of the Maoist mass line and investigative research model. However, the Cultural Revolution's political and ideological excesses, factional turmoil, and intra-Party conflict that blurred the lines between the categories of "People" and "Enemy" required a post-trauma period of social and political consolidation and reconciliation. *Wenshi ziliao* editors turned away from earlier mass line objectives of creating hard and fast truth claims and emphasized instead multifaceted complexity and characterized diverse avenues and expressions of historical truth as equally valid. In contrast with the use of the mass line by Party cadres in the 1950s to induce a popular reimagining of history in terms of a clear dichotomy between an oppressive old society before Communism and the liberated new society, *wenshi ziliao* editors in the 1980s sought political reconciliation by obscuring the moral boundary between the pre-Communist and Communist eras and emphasizing constructive continuities across the 1949 divide. In addition, whereas in the 1950s, the mass line reflected a Party that was confident in its truth claims and its ability to connect with, awaken, and reeducate the people, in the post-Mao transition crisis, the Party wavered in reaching a judgment about where the lines between truth and falsity, right and wrong, should be drawn. In this context, the *wenshi ziliao* served as a safe experimental space where multiple truths and differing historical perspectives on certain issues could be expressed and allowed to coexist. This ambivalence about and conciliatory accommodation of diverse truth claims made PPCC officials wary about the social mobilization aspect of *wenshi ziliao*, an issue explored in Chapter 6.

Unlike the investigative research method of sending down teams of investigators to local sites, the *wenshi ziliao* devolved much of the historical collection, writing, editing, and publication process to the county and city levels. This more decentralized structure allowed for greater agency in reinterpreting "seeking truth from facts" to suit different agendas. *Wenshi ziliao* editors capitalized on this flexibility to assert local "truths" about how liberation happened and who the heroic figures were that displaced the Party-centered narrative. To do this, they creatively reappropriated and redefined key Maoist concepts like dialectical and historical materialism in ways that accommodated a more multifaceted, inclusive, and locally centered history of the northeast borderland.

At the same time, local editors were by no means in agreement about what constituted historical truth, and debates about the ideological significance of certain historical events, such as the contested nationalist and socialist implications of the Sino–Russian border war of 1929, pulled editors into sometimes protective and sometimes combative attitudes toward their informants. The open-ended ambiguity in aspects of post-Mao ideology such as the "Two Civilizations" discourse added to the diversity of truth-defining strategies and gave *wenshi ziliao* writers a multivalent discursive space for making sense of and articulating their personal life truths.

This flexible interpretive process brings to mind insights that scholars have had about the relationship between the meanings attached to abstract theories on one hand and the local cultural contexts in which these ideas develop and through which they move on the other. Lydia Liu's "translingual practices," Naoki Sakai's "excess" of translation, Charles Taylor's attention to the cultural self-reflexivity of theoretical knowledge, and Wang Hui's look at how Chinese concepts like *shehui zhuyi* (socialism) evolve within certain "life-worlds" all point to how theories and concepts are never fixed universal entities.[9] Rather, they

---

[9] Lydia H. Liu, *Translingual Practice: Literature, National Culture, and Translated Modernity – China, 1900–1937* (Stanford, CA: Stanford University Press, 1995); Naoki Sakai, "Introduction," in Naoki Sakai and Yukiko Hanawa, eds., *Traces I: Spectres of the West and Politics of Translation* (Hong Kong: Hong Kong University Press, 2002), v–xiii; Wang Hui, *Wang Hui zi xuan ji (Selected Writings of Wang Hui)* (Guilin: Guangxi shifan daxue chubanshe, 1997), translated in Viren Murthy, "Modernity against Modernity: Wang Hui's Critical History of Chinese Thought," *Modern Intellectual History* 3.1 (April 2006): 137–165; Charles Taylor, "Social Theory As Practice," *Philosophical Papers* 2 (1985): 98, cited in Leigh Jenco, ed., *Chinese Thought as Global Theory: Diversifying Knowledge Production in the Social Sciences and Humanities* (Albany, NY: State University of New York Press, 2016), 4–5, 7–8.

are always in flux and in a process of continual reformation and reformulation as they interact with local cultural contexts.

The *wenshi ziliao* is an illustration of this dynamic process of meaning making across the local, regional, and national levels of history production. The excess of interpretation of socialist concepts built in a dynamic flexibility that was essential to the post-Mao project of healing the nation and restoring Party credibility after the Cultural Revolution, even as it also always threatened to subvert that very project.

From "Redness" and "Expertise" to "Quality Control"

Rebuilding a nationalist "united front" was a tricky endeavor that required delicately balancing Party control with accommodation of non-Party, and even anti-Party, elements in history. On an organizational level, to reduce the interference of holdovers from the Cultural Revolution and to confer scientific legitimacy to the history-writing process, PPCC and Party leaders placed a stronger emphasis on education and expertise as criteria for membership in the PPCC. Their attempt to reconcile professionalism with ideological concerns informed the requirement that *wenshi ziliao* team members be both "red" and "expert." Owing to transfer and new recruitment of personnel, by the late 1980s, 66% of PPCC members in Fujin had university degrees.[10] This was of particular concern in the process of selecting qualified individuals to edit materials.

However, in the eyes of the Party officials overseeing this process, professional and political qualifications were inseparable. Leaders attending the fourth national *wenshi ziliao* conference instructed PPCCs at all levels to "create specialized teams fully committed to *wenshi ziliao* work that are both red and expert."[11] Elaborating a bit on this at the first Harbin *wenshi ziliao* work conference in 1984, Wang Mingkui argued that "the science of *wenshi ziliao* requires that full-time cadres have a certain level of historical knowledge and literary skill, understand united front theory and policy, and are familiar with social trends. They should also have a certain editing level. But at this time among the team of *wenshi ziliao* full-time cadres in our province, not a few have low political quality and low professional level. Getting work done is very difficult."[12] To raise the quality of personnel, he recommended inviting experts in "historical knowledge and vocational knowledge to raise vocational ability";

---

[10] Guan Chengzheng, "Zhongguo renmin zhengzhi xieshang huiyi fujin shi diyi jie weiyuanhui changwu weiyuanhui gongzuo baogao" ("Work Report of the First Session of the Fujin City PPCC's Standing Committee") (Delivered on Mar. 14, 1989, at the Second Meeting of the First Session of the Fujin City PPCC) (Fujin City Archive): 4–6.
[11] Wang Mingkui, "Raise High the Banner of Patriotism," 53–54.   [12] Ibid.

"promptly transmit the national PPCC's directives on *wenshi ziliao* and united front theory and policy to raise political quality"; and "organize self-study on dialectical materialism and historical materialism, modern and contemporary history, and linguistic and literary knowledge."[13]

While past political campaigns during the Maoist years had pitted administrative and academic "expertise" against political and ideological "redness," PPCC cadres in the 1980s attempted to fuse the two categories into one combined label of "quality." The assumption was that given the proper implementation of "quality control," *wenshi ziliao* personnel would by definition be both professionally competent and politically reliable. This assumption informed the ambitious strategy of infusing *wenshi ziliao* "experts" into every locality and sector of society. At Raohe's second *wenshi ziliao* work conference, Zhang Zhenbang instructed that "every sector and township should assign one to two people to do long-term *wenshi ziliao* work. To ensure that they understand clearly the policies on *wenshi ziliao* work, don't lightly transfer them [to another post]. If personnel assignments are very tight, at least assign one to two part-time *wenshi ziliao* work personnel. These people need to report to the *wenshi ziliao* office to register and establish frequent contact."[14] While emphasizing expertise in areas of historical knowledge, local PPCC leaders were equally concerned about maximizing the scale of social and institutional mobilization for producing *wenshi ziliao*. In this way, dual organizational principles of selective professionalization and mass mobilization drove historical production.

Selecting, Refining, and Extracting: The "Science" of "Getting Beyond the Surface to the Core Substance"

Wenshi ziliao cadres also attempted to resolve the tension between Party control and accommodation on a conceptual level. They did this by redefining what it meant to "preserve truth and seek truth from facts" as a "historical science" that encompassed both objective fact-checking to determine historical accuracy and ideologically driven interpretation of historical significance. Writing at the request of the national PPCC about this issue, modern historical materials editor Rong Mengyuan theorized about what "seeking truth from facts" really meant in the context of researching, writing, and editing. He devotes a great deal of attention to the importance of discriminating between authentic and forged documents and evaluating carefully the accuracy of historical details presented in firsthand accounts. He urges researchers to expend real effort and time

---

[13] Ibid.   [14] Zhang Zhenbang, "Struggle to Pioneer *Wenshi Ziliao* Work," 17–18.

rigorously assessing the factual validity of each source. To illustrate this, he describes a pre-*wenshi ziliao* example of the extensive lengths to which historian Fan Wenlan went in the early 1950s to verify and corroborate the native place origins of a Boxer contingent that fought a battle with the Qing army in Hebei. Cross-referencing a written account of this battle that referred to the Boxers' place of origin as "Sichuan" with the oral testimonies of firsthand witnesses, Fan was able to ascertain that "Sichuan" was in fact a misspelling of a county in Hebei.[15]

In other cases, Rong advises researchers to preserve and include multiple versions and perspectives of a given event when it is not possible to determine conclusively which is most accurate. He argues that inconsistencies in how events are remembered are particularly evident in specialized volumes that feature multiple viewpoints on the same historical incident. He gives an example of "the recently published 'First-hand records of the Battle of Huaihai,'" "in which all [the articles] are former GMD commanders' recollections ... with each describing the battle in general and in its various stages." In this case, he points out, "[i]f there are points of difference and commonality in descriptions of event, place, time, people, etc., it is quite apparent. It's imperative to distinguish what is accurate, and the editor must expend a lot of effort. If after the utmost effort the truth still can't be discerned, then just let multiple perspectives co-exist."[16]

He conceives of the researcher's purpose and methodology in terms of objective empirical assessment of the historical materials' veracity and accuracy, and explicitly warns editors not to subject *wenshi ziliao* accounts to any subjective or ideological bias:

Historical materials are objective. Do not casually extract, remove or revise anything based on subjective views. Starting with collecting, one must stick to the principle of seeking truth from facts. One must never use any method to make anyone write recollections based on one's own agendas. Once materials are in hand, conduct research using seeking truth from facts. Do not selectively extract words or passages to obtain a certain meaning without regard to the contents of the whole narrative or draw out meaning that is not there, and especially don't fabricate things with no evidential support. After doing research, in accordance with seeking truth from facts, compile into a book the portions that are accurate and send it along to the history research department and other departments for their reference.

Rong asserts that this attention to objective evaluative rigor is essential to making *wenshi ziliao* "persuasive to people."[17]

[15] Rong Mengyuan, "Commentary on Working with Historical Materials," 7.
[16] Ibid., 8–9.   [17] Ibid., 9.

However, he describes this process as only the first stage of "historical science," which entails not only obtaining and evaluating the accuracy of materials but also knowing how to properly use them and evaluate their place and significance within the broader logic and pattern of historical "progress." This is where he reimposes Communist ideological principles, namely dialectical and historical materialism, as the overarching lens for determining whether and how informants' recollections were historically significant and worthy of inclusion in final publication. Quoting from Mao, he writes that editors must "rely on objective existing reality, carefully and with precision collect materials, and under the guidance of general Marxist–Leninist ideology derive from these materials the correct conclusion." Following a standard Communist teleology on the evolution of historical writing in China, he criticizes as lacking true scientific caliber both early Confucian-style histories that concealed negative truths about the "feudal" elite and "objectivism" introduced from the West that emphasized only the historical materials themselves and "did not grasp that history follows a certain logic." In contrast, he asserts that "Marx's scientific dialectical materialist and historical materialist approach to studying history finally grasped that history follows a certain logic, just like other sciences, and that one can use this logic to study the past and foresee the future. Thus historical studies finally reached the level of historical science."[18]

Rong's concept of "seeking truth from facts" and "historical science" thus reconciles the competing principles of empirical heterogeneity and ideological conformity by reenvisioning them as two interrelated stages of the research process. This allows for what he characterizes as the "refinement" of raw materials and "getting beyond the surface to the core substance," which he interprets as the extraction of politically appropriate meanings from the texts. The examples that he provides indicate that he viewed this refinement process as a way to construct a historical narrative based equally in nationalism and revolution. For instance, he advocated getting rid of "unrefined" materials that addressed whether Hong Xiuquan grew a beard, arguing that they did not deal with the real issue of the Taiping leader's revolutionary activities. Alongside this example of refining materials to highlight revolution, he turns to another example of "unrefined materials" dealing with Jiang Jieshi's blood lineage to criticize Cultural Revolution practices of using family histories to accuse individuals of counterrevolutionary crimes. As justification, he argues that doing research according to the principle of dialectical and historical materialism deals exclusively with the actions of the individual.[19]

---

[18] Ibid., 1–2.   [19] Ibid., 7.

In this way, Rong utilizes the "refinement" concept as a vehicle for incorporating a broader, nationalist united front into the Party's historical narrative. He finds similar application for the idea of "getting beyond the surface to the core substance," offering two case examples that balance nationalist and socialist priorities in historical interpretation. In his first example, he identifies the core substance of anti-imperialist nationalism that underlies superstitious accounts about Red Lanterns flying to Japan to take back money that China had paid as reparations at the end of the Sino–Japanese war. On the other hand, in his second example, he gives priority to socialist ideology, targeting Hu Shi's advocacy of an objective approach to evaluating historical and literary documents as a "surface phenomenon." "The core substance," he argues, "is that [Hu Shi] was opposing Marxism, was vilifying our studies, and was claiming that utilizing Marxism is having one's nose pulled by Marx."[20]

Through this process of refining and extracting the core substance from materials, Rong was weaving a delicate balance in the Party's project of reconstructing history between its claims to historical authenticity based in rigorous empirical research and its need to impose a guiding framework of political and ideological control. His interpretation of "seeking truth from facts" essentially applies the principle of democratic centralism to the *wenshi ziliao* process of producing history, accommodating a wide variety of sources and perspectives as "raw materials" that are then subject to processing, refinement, and extraction of the core substance in accordance with ideological imperatives.

Redefining "Seeking Truth from Facts" and "Dialectical Materialism"

Compared to this historian's relatively clear-cut distinction between the empirical and ideological dimensions of historical production, PPCC leaders at the local, regional, and national levels who oversaw *wenshi ziliao* work tended to blur this distinction, redeploying socialist concepts and terminology such as "leftism," "rightism," and "dialectical and historical materialism" in ways that meshed with principles of objective empirical analysis. At the national level, PPCC officials collaborated with other Party leaders, including the directors of the Propaganda and United Front bureaus, to reconceive of the historian's project of "seeking truth from facts" as integral to the political projects of spearheading patriotic education and generating "united front" support for the Party. A summary report on the fifth national conference on *wenshi ziliao* held

[20] Ibid., 7–8.

in Beijing in 1986, which included participation by representatives from the provincial-level PPCCs, commented that the "principle to follow is raising high the nationalist banner and seeking truth from facts ... The underlying task is to cultivate a socialist citizenry with ideals, morals, culture, and discipline; and elevate the mindset, moral quality, and scientific cultural quality of the whole Chinese people." More specifically, the stated objective was to "overcome 'leftist' influence; create an open, relaxed, harmonious atmosphere for academic discussion; and integrate politics with science." "By objectively evaluating and describing historical events and people," the report continues, "*wenshi ziliao* have a wide educational impact on society, thus advancing development and strengthening the patriotic united front."[21]

Thus, while Rong's analysis from a scholarly perspective carefully parsed out the empirical and ideological elements of historical production, PPCC officials articulated the scientific principle of empirical analysis as an integral dimension of the political processes of constructing a new post-Mao citizenry. In northern Heilongjiang, the heads of local PPCCs elaborated on these ideas and incorporated them into their projects of reinterpreting and redeeming northeast borderland history. Like their national and provincial counterparts, local PPCC cadres seamlessly melded together open-ended historical inquiry with political control. In the Fujin County PPCC work report that he drafted, Cao Mingren, vice-chair of the PPCC and chair of its study committee, recommended that editors "respect historical facts, write whatever happened, and however much there is write that much. *Wenshi ziliao* committees must study politics, study tasks, and study relevant central directives. In the work process they must study, continually reflect on experience, advance work, collect materials, get rid of the coarse and keep the valuable, and produce a final product."[22]

Regarding *wenshi ziliao* as a part of the PPCC's political study activities, Cao describes editors' work as a kind of dialectical process. Beginning with unfiltered recording of historical materials, the editor is expected to undergo continual political training and instruction that lead ultimately to the refinement and processing of the materials into an acceptable product. In this way, Cao envisions the process of writing and editing as

[21] "Outline of Report Regarding [the] Situation and Spirit of [the] PPCC's Fifth National *Wenshi Ziliao* Work Conference," 5–8.

[22] Cao Mingren, "Zhongguo renmin zhengzhi xieshang huiyi fujin xian diliu jie weiyuanhui changwu weiyuanhui gongzuo baogao" ("Work Report of the Sixth Session of the Fujin County PPCC's Standing Committee") (Delivered on Mar. 21, 1983, at the Third Meeting of the Sixth Session of the Fujin County PPCC) (Fujin City Archives): 9–10.

emblematic of political study in general, evolving from "unrefined" thought to fully indoctrinated, "refined" political consciousness.

From this perspective, Cao implies an analogy between historical "facts" and the raw materials of political thought that need to be systematically processed into historical "truth" analogous to Party-approved political consciousness. Zhang Zhenbang, PPCC chair in Raohe, utilized Maoist and Marxist terminology to lend socialist legitimacy to the more inclusive revisionist historical writing that he was overseeing. In his speech at the county's first *wenshi ziliao* work conference, he redefined "leftism" and "rightism" as failures to present historical people and events in a transparent and factual manner:

[We must] continue to eliminate "leftist" thought poison and at the same time be attentive to resolving rightist thought influence. "Leftist" thought mainly takes the form of fear of words being released and being confrontational, fear of "reversing the verdict of monsters," fear of "bearing historical responsibility," fear of "erecting monuments and producing heroic tales on behalf of reactionaries," fear of "being criticized for having faulty thought," "fear" of "hurting future generations," etc. As long as these fears remain, it's hard to take up the pen and write straightforwardly. Rightist influence is mainly manifested in finding the opportunity to beautify oneself and denigrate others; and the failure to take up the pen to expose the shady side of relatives, seniors, old friends and old colleagues.[23]

Eschewing any mention of class struggle and socialist revolution, Zhang recasts ideological deviations to the left or right as amounting to the same fundamental inability to write about events in the past as they actually occurred and about people in the past as they actually were. Rather than defining these political labels in terms of the conflict between socialist and capitalist worldviews, he reappropriates these terms to define and measure the balance between inclusivity and Party control.

Linking this reconceptualization of leftist and rightist tendencies to the political goals of *wenshi ziliao*, Zhang Zhenbang observed that "the process of mobilizing people to write *wenshi ziliao* is also a process by which we undertake meticulous political thought work." This involved, on one hand, the inclusive anti-"leftist" effort by PPCC cadres to "widely make friends, speak from the heart, gain trust, and help them understand the importance and significance of writing materials" and to "cause them to eliminate hesitation and lingering distrust." At the same time, Zhang emphasized the "need to raise their thought awakening to a high level of patriotism, making it clear that writing *wenshi ziliao* is their own noble

---

[23] Raohe zhengxie bangongshi, "Raise High the Banner of Patriotism," 7–8.

historical responsibility and an opportunity for them to contribute to the four modernizations."[24] Thus, the Raohe PPCC leader invoked the "seeking truth from facts" principle to resecure the political loyalties of people who had been alienated from the Party, sending them a mixed message of liberal accommodation on one hand and renewed demands and criteria of political loyalty under the new regime on the other.

While PPCC cadres deployed socialist terminology to recalibrate the Party's relationship with society, individuals who contributed their life stories to the *wenshi ziliao* reappropriated Maoist concepts to redeem aspects of their past that did not fit neatly into the Party's previous socialist ideology. This was particularly true of former entrepreneurs whose families' economic backgrounds earned them disrepute during the Cultural Revolution. The post-Mao proclivity to reinvent meanings for Maoist categories provided a rhetorical arsenal for former entrepreneurs like Xing Jinghuan, who melded together the vocabularies of local clan identity and socialist class to lend personal, local, and national significance to his family origins. The acknowledgment of local hierarchies based on kinship ties had run counter to the Maoist objective of tearing down particularistic clan and localistic loyalties in favor of Party-directed mass mobilization. Following the Cultural Revolution, however, the dethroning of mass political ideology and socialist ideals led to a revived celebration of regional identity and local particularism, a trend Xing echoed in order to assign historical significance to his own family's social position.

At the same time, in sync with the post-Mao state's attempt to reverse Maoist economic policies using the Maoist language of class categories, Xing employed the language of socialist classification to associate his family's background with pioneering economic initiative. Using this label not only situated his family background in a positive light within the evolving politics of "socialism with Chinese characteristics," but also served as a device for foreshadowing his own rise to entrepreneurial fortune. He writes that:

I was born in 1910 (the second year of the Qing emperor Xuantong's reign). My birthplace was in Luan County in Hebei Province, and my family lived in the Xing clan village of Hongjilin seventy *li* southwest of the county seat. It was a middle peasant household.[25]

He begins this profile of his family background by situating it temporally according to the modern calendar as well as the dynastic system that would have framed his understanding of time in his youth. Alongside

---

[24] Ibid., 8.   [25] Ibid.

this doubled temporal marker, Xing refers to his family both in universal socialist terms and in local particularistic terms that privilege family lineage as the central marker of identity. It had been common practice traditionally to name villages after the most powerful clans residing in them. During the nineteenth and early twentieth centuries, Chinese migrants brought this practice with them from northern China to Manchuria, where the names of numerous settlements reflected the dominant presence of particular migrant clans.[26]

At the same time, he juxtaposes this throwback to clan-centered local identity with the use of Maoist categories of socioeconomic classification. The "middle peasant" class, on account of its ownership of property and accumulation of private assets, had been viewed with some suspicion by the Maoist regime and held an inferior status within the Communist social hierarchy to the poor peasants and landless laborers. During the early phases of land reform, "middle peasants" were generally spared abuse as the more prominent landlords became the favored targets of the "speaking bitterness" campaigns, but as time wore on and the campaigns intensified, members of the "middle peasant" category became objects of public criticism.[27] After 1978, the reformist government under Deng Xiaoping's leadership, in its effort to stage the early phases of decollectivization and private initiative in the countryside, rehabilitated the status of the "middle peasants" and redeemed their role as the pioneers transforming agricultural productivity through household enterprise.[28]

---

[26] For observations on this practice in China proper, see Arthur Henderson Smith, *Village Life in China: A Study in Sociology* (New York, NY, and Chicago, IL: F. H. Revell Company, 1889); Martin Yang, *A Chinese Village: Taitou, Shantung Province* (New York, NY: Columbia University Press, 1945). In regard to the extension of this practice to the northeast, see James Reardon-Anderson, *Reluctant Pioneers: China's Expansion Northward, 1644–1937* (Stanford, CA: Stanford University Press, 2005), 133; Gottschang and Lary, *Swallows and Settlers*, 71.

[27] The official policy regarding "middle peasants" was an ambivalent one. During the early 1950s, economists discussed the advantages of the "middle peasant" class for agricultural development and even reflected on the possibility of "middle-peasantrification." Their voices, however, were drowned out in the radicalization of land reforms later in the decade. Li Boyong, "Tudi gaige hou nongcun jieji bianhua de quxiang" ("The Trend of Changes in the Rural Classes after Land Reform"), *Zhonggong dangshi yanjiu (Studies of CCP History)*, no. 1 (1989): 45–47. Cited in Yan Yunxiang, "The Impact of Rural Reform on Social and Economic Classification in a Chinese Village," *Australian Journal of Chinese Affairs*, no. 27 (Jan. 1992): 1–23. See also Jonathan Unger, "The Class System in Rural China: A Case Study," in James L. Watson, ed., *Class and Social Stratification in Post-Revolution China* (London: University of London and Contemporary China Institute, Joint Committee on Contemporary China, 1984).

[28] See Yan Yunxiang, "The Impact of Rural Reform on Social and Economic Classification in a Chinese Village."

Fusing this revisionist official representation of the "middle peasant" with the public narrative of collective suffering before Communist liberation, Xing deployed post-Mao social categories as a vehicle for dramatizing the hardships that he had to overcome and setting up the narrative of the entrepreneur-hero who pulled himself up by his bootstraps. Referring to family conditions during his youth, he recalled that "there were too many people and too little land in Luan County, and so the middle peasant household worked diligently and frugally all day long and yet was unable to eat anything but porridge."[29] His description befits early twentieth-century official reports on overpopulated, unproductive land and a seemingly endless series of famines in northern China that reached their most devastating scale during the late 1920s, to which both international and region-based famine relief agencies responded with massive projects of relocating famine refugees to the land-rich areas of the northeast. Drawing on these firsthand historical reports, scholarship has acknowledged ecological constraints as significant factors, in combination with warlord military conflict and civil disorder, pushing people to migrate to Manchuria. At the same time, Xing's description resonates with official discourse after the Cultural Revolution that repudiated Maoist revolutionary ideals concerning the infinite capacity of mass mobilization, and instead explained China's backwardness and its failure to modernize in terms of a surplus of population.[30] He was engaging here with multiple levels of truth and discourse to package his entrepreneurial history as a story of personal will overcoming hardship.

Alongside these personal narrative strategies, officials overseeing the *wenshi ziliao* aimed their redefinition of socialist terminology at rationalizing a more expansive and accommodating vision of a patriotic united front. They did this by reinterpreting the meaning of Marxist "dialectical materialism and historical materialism" as, in Zhang Zhenbang's words, "comprehensively analyzing each historical event, person, and issue within its historical conditions." Rather than the original Marxist focus on dialectical class struggle as the engine of historical change, the new emphasis in discourse on dialectical and historical materialism was on acknowledging historical complexity and multifaceted development.

---

[29] Xing Jinghuan, "My Over Sixty Years' Experience with Commercial Enterprises," 80.

[30] The post-Mao discourse on population surplus, as Ann Anagnost discusses, became associated with a perceived need to raise the "quality" (*suzhi*) of the population as a priority anterior to any discussion of political reform. Embedded in this concern was a latent fear of "chaos" (*luan*), and an implicit justification for social control by a strong centralized state. Ann Anagnost, "A Surfeit of Bodies: Population and the Rationality of the State in Post-Mao China," in Faye D. Ginsburg and Rayna Rapp, eds., *Conceiving the New World Order: The Global Politics of Reproduction* (Berkeley, CA: University of California Press, 1995), 22–41.

In reflecting on what a dialectical and historical materialist approach to analyzing history meant in practice, Zhang explained that his county, Raohe, "has experienced enormous changes in society; all kinds of revolutionary and anti-revolutionary political forces evolved, all kinds of political figures emerged, and the situation is extremely complex and varied. In investigating these historical issues, we need to do concrete analysis, refine and preserve accurate [analysis], and strongly avoid idealism." He went on to say that historical figures all have two sides and need to be analyzed accordingly.[31] While making reference to "revolutionary and anti-revolutionary" forces, his redefinition of dialectical materialism emphasizes instead the complex dimensions of history that allow for a broader accommodation of different social actors within the Party-ordained nationalist historiography.

In a seminal speech that she delivered to the fourth national *wenshi ziliao* conference in 1983, Deng Yingchao, chair of the national PPCC, similarly called for paying attention to different sides of each event and person in history, avoiding "subjective idealism." She asserts that: "Objective things always have two sides. Seeking truth from facts requires looking at each thing and each issue comprehensively. When researching, one can't with bias throw out anything and emphasize one side at the expense of another." She goes on to argue that "dialectical materialism and historical materialism" require that researchers and editors

look at each person and thing historically and comprehensively, and not just evaluate based on one salient aspect. The same goes with historical events. We should write and evaluate things from a historical perspective and not subjective idealism. If we use the dialectical materialism perspective to look at and write and edit materials, then the quality of materials will rise, they will have scientific quality, persuasive force, and will have beneficial and enlightening impact on people.[32]

Leaders at both the local and national levels, in this case Zhang Zhenbang and Deng Yingchao, raised the issue of "seeking truth from facts" in the context of addressing the need for a nationalist Party line that would bring all social actors together in united purpose. Deng preceded her statement on dialectical materialism with the exhortation "to have a clear goal when editing *wenshi ziliao* and inspecting collected drafts, which is raising high the flag of nationalism, and to see whether materials collected and published are beneficial to nationalism, to our country, our people, and the next generation. With a clear goal, it is easier to have

---

[31] Raohe zhengxie bangongshi, "Raise High the Banner of Patriotism," 8.
[32] Haerbin shi zhengxie weiyuanhui mishuchu, "Comrade Deng Yingchao's Speech at the National PPCC's Fourth National *Wenshi Ziliao* Work Conference," 8–9.

a united thought in choosing materials, and disagreements can be resolved." She sympathizes with those who see an incompatibility between unifying nationalist ideology and multifaceted analysis as principles of historical research, acknowledging that "you say seeking truth from facts isn't easy; this is true." But, she argues, "[s]eeking truth from facts helps the reader to derive benefits, become aware of and understand an issue, increase his knowledge, and this elevates patriotic thought and feeling."[33]

At the same time, once again balancing inclusivity and accommodation with Party control, Zhang differentiated the historical materialist approach from that of giving equal attention to all historical evidence, which he refers to as "objectivism." Instead, he states, "[w]e need to use dialectical materialism to select from complex, winding historical developments those events, people, and issues that have important historical value and to write about them."[34] With this redefinition of dialectical and historical materialism, PPCC leaders participated in creating an ideological middle ground for mobilizing a broader array of social forces historically while conferring to the Party a continuing lever of political control.

The PPCC leaders delicately balanced unity and homogeneity with diversity and heterogeneity through intermeshing nationalism and "seeking truth from facts" as principles of *wenshi ziliao* work. They also used this way of structuring their narratives to clarify and establish clear guidelines for what kind of "truth" researchers should be seeking. By foregrounding the section on "seeking truth from facts" with the message about the nationalist purpose of *wenshi ziliao*, PPCC cadres were laying out a framework for what kinds of "facts" merited attention and what kinds of "truths" could be included as legitimate history.

However, while national-level PPCC leaders like Deng Yingchao presented that framework in broad and somewhat abstract terms, their local-tier counterparts along the northeast borderland like Zhang Zhenbang worked hard rhetorically to redefine marginality as precisely what made the borderland central to the nationalist narrative. In his narrative, Zhang preceded his discussion of "seeking truth from facts" with an explanation in concrete local terms of Raohe's credentials as a key site in the nationalist historiography. From this standpoint he framed the conversation about "seeking truth from facts" in a way that put evidence-based historical inquiry in the

---

[33] Ibid.   [34] Raohe zhengxie bangongshi, "Raise High the Banner of Patriotism," 8–9.

service of building a persuasive nationalist narrative of the northeast borderland.

"Three Musts, Four Don'ts, and Three Gives": Editorial Strategies at the Local Level

While the leading PPCC cadres blended ideology with empirical historical inquiry to build their local and nationalist versions of "seeking truth from facts," the people who carried out the everyday work of *wenshi ziliao* were less interested in abstract ideological concepts and more concerned with how to reconcile multiplicity and unity in practice. At the provincial level, editors struggled to process and coalesce the diverse materials coming in from various cities and counties. One of the common slogans in *wenshi ziliao* circles during the 1980s was "systematization and specialization." This referred to the goal of taking a systematic approach to compiling materials on specific topics rather than haphazardly collecting scattered items that were unrelated to or in disagreement with one other. One of the main objectives driving this approach was to achieve centralized control over the entire process, from the point of conception of "key point" topics to the end product of the publication. From this perspective, provincial-level editors saw themselves as overseeing a messy assortment of local projects that somehow needed to be brought together as a unified and cohesive whole.

While leading PPCC officials utilized "seeking truth from facts" to reconcile historical revisionism with socialist ideology, editors at the provincial level reinterpreted the concept to resolve the tension between mobilizing diverse social forces and constructing a single unified narrative that suppressed conflicting versions of history. Adapting the "seeking truth from facts" framework, they explained this objective of obtaining systematic unity as the search for an ultimate truth that transcended individual and local agendas. Members of the Heilongjiang provincial *wenshi ziliao* committee fretted about the conflicting accounts and perspectives that undermined their efforts to establish a single consistent narrative. Referring to episodes in the life of Ma Zhanshan, a military commander who led a struggle against the Japanese, the editors complain that "all materials written by Ma's relatives and trusted friends exaggerate their praise and overlook his flaws, while his enemies all do the opposite."[35] To make matters worse, owing to shortage of staff and resources, editors were relying on "outside help" that could result in "writing in a scattered way, [such

---

[35] Heilongjiang sheng zhengxie wenshi ban, "Kaizhan da xiezuo, gaohao zhuantihua" ("Cooperate Greatly and Thoroughly Specialize") (Aug. 19, 1985) (Heilongjiang Provincial Archives 56:1:290): 5.

that] not only will different sections conflict with each other and not go together, but also there will be the flaw of different viewpoints on issues and different ways of writing. This results in the volume falling apart and not being integrated, giving people the sense of fragments thrown together."[36] To resolve this issue and to ensure that all the published articles convey a coherent and consistent message, the authors of this report recommend establishing "one team working well together that forms the main force, using outside help only as a supplement." Only then, they argue, can *wenshi ziliao* work result in the "integration of all the parts and sections," "comprehensively accounting for people, times, places and details," and "adhering to one main line."[37]

At the local level, some of the editors eschewed ideology in favor of objective factual truth as the penultimate goal of research and writing. Members of a small committee in Harbin collecting materials on local industry and commerce exemplified this outlook. Describing the process by which they ensured the historical accuracy of their article on a former industrialist, they emphasized the lengths to which they went to cross-reference different sources. "We used recollections of people in the know in Harbin and some materials for reference to create an initial draft. But later when we heard that there was another person in the know in Shandong, we immediately sent someone there to understand the situation better and cross-reference information. We filled in a portion of content, extracted some stuff that was not accurate, and thereby made the materials more reliable and more valuable."[38] Along with fact-checking, the editors on the committee insist that authenticity of authorial expression takes precedence over political correctness, asserting, "we are attentive to the writer/narrator's [original] style and tone, trying best to avoid argumentation and to focus on description ... [Editing] requires only reflecting facts and not emphasizing good or hiding the bad; absolutely avoid 'using theory to shape history.'"[39]

Perhaps freed from the political exposure and pressure that directors of the PPCC faced, and more invested in the day-to-day process of collecting and analyzing sources, editors demanded of themselves and their colleagues a principled devotion to getting the facts right and avoiding both subjective and ideological bias. Li Xingchang, the vice-chair of the Harbin *wenshi ziliao* research committee office, argued that the "basic principle of collecting *wenshi ziliao* is factually reflecting the original character of historical events." To put this into practice in research and

---

[36] Ibid., 6.   [37] Ibid., 5–6.
[38] "Harbin City Democratic Construction and Industrial and Commercial Federation's Historical Materials Small Group," *Haerbin zhengxie*, no. 3 (no. 13 overall), 73.
[39] Ibid.

writing, he recommends "three musts, four don'ts, and three gives." Participants "must truthfully, concretely, and boldly write. This requires the writer to break through thought hesitation and describe events truthfully according to their original character, not flattering or denigrating, not enhancing, not protecting, and doing their best to write concretely."[40]

What Zhang Zhenbang framed in ideological terms of "leftism" and "rightism" Li Xingchang describes here in plain language of direct, unadulterated truth seeking. He removes the concept of dialectical and historical materialism from consideration altogether, arguing that the *wenshi ziliao* process "does not demand the use of historical materialism in writing materials" and that the writer "should not on account of present requirements add or subtract anything." That means, he contends, that writers "don't need to analyze, theorize, evaluate, or criticize," and he encourages them to simply "write the truth, write down what one saw, and not be afraid to write something different from what others are writing, because the substance of things is complex, each person's experience and memory has limits, and there is subjective bias and unfactual elements in one's writing that is unavoidable." For this reason, he "encourages competing views" and asserts that it is important to "preserve multiple perspectives and tolerate multiple views when the truth of something is temporarily unclear."[41] Leaving out ideology entirely, he articulates all considerations in terms of the individual's firsthand observations as offering different sides of a complex and messy reality. In the category of "don'ts," he insists that "the writer be protected from bearing political and legal responsibility for exposing certain historical realities."

Whereas the PPCC leadership was primarily interested in navigating the complex political and ideological terrain of negotiating and balancing different kinds of historical truth, editors were more concerned with protecting writers (including, presumably, themselves) from political liability and scrutiny for what they wrote. Moreover, he demands that the PPCC "give the writer compensation for each article, give him help, and give him respect." Focusing on institutional obligations to the individual rather than the other way around, Li insists that the PPCC respect the writer's wishes "in cases where the writer demands secrecy, demands that [the article] not be publicly released, or when released demands that his real name not be used, etc."[42] At the level of the editorial board, therefore, participants appropriated the discourse of "seeking truth from facts" to protect their own interests and exempt them from any political repercussions for recording events and people as they saw fit. Whereas PPCC leaders and theorists at the national level were primarily concerned

---

[40] Li Xingchang, "A Glorious Enterprise Benefiting Later Generations," 32–33.
[41] Ibid., 34–35.   [42] Ibid., 32–33.

with establishing an effective procedure for obtaining the necessary materials to construct a persuasive narrative, local editors focused more attention on the writers themselves as vulnerable individuals who required special consideration and protection.

Yet not all local editors subscribed to this concern with protecting informants' freedom of expression and removing political considerations from the writing process. Some of those who reported on their participation in compiling materials saw ideology as very much an integral part of the writing process. However, unlike their superiors in the PPCC leadership who utilized and reworked abstract political terminology as general guiding principles for structuring history, these individuals viewed politics and ideology on the micro level as a constant struggle between editorial accuracy and informants' personal agendas. From their standpoint, cross-referencing sources and corroborating information was the editor's response to informants' projects of integrating history with ideology on their own terms. This was particularly problematic in cases where consensus was lacking about the historical significance of the topic under investigation.

One such topic was the so-called CER Incident, which broke out in 1929 along the northeast Manchurian borderland between the Soviet Union and regional Chinese forces under the command of Zhang Xueliang. It marked the culmination of contesting claims to control over the CER. Following the overthrow of the czarist regime, the newly established Soviet government renounced international imperialism as the global manifestation of bourgeois capitalist hegemony from which colonized countries such as China would, in the same manner as the proletariat, liberate themselves. This declaration included a renunciation of czarist claims to institutions in Manchuria such as the CER. In reality, however, after the conclusion of the civil war and the final defeat of "White Russian" forces in the early 1920s, the Soviet Union increasingly sparred with regional Chinese authorities to re-exert pressure on and control over the management affairs of the CER.

Zhang Xueliang's opposition to this reassertion of Czarist imperialist claims was compounded by his hostility to Communism, and he found in Jiang Jieshi's Nationalist government a virulently anti-Communist ally. The CER became the site of these mutually reinforcing tensions as Soviet influence fostered the spread of Communist organizations and sympathies among both Russian and Chinese railroad workers. In 1929, Zhang Xueliang's order to break into the Soviet consulate in Harbin, ostensibly to seize evidence of Soviet plans for disseminating Communist ideology, sparked all-out military conflict.[43]

---

[43] For a detailed summary of the CER Incident and its contested political significance, see Clausen and Thøgersen, *The Making of a Chinese City*.

Zhang Xueliang and Jiang Jieshi's goal to establish territorial sovereignty while eradicating Communism was in contradiction with the nascent CCP's vision of the Soviet Union as the vanguard of an international communist movement that would sweep through China and uproot Zhang Xueliang's warlord regime. At the same time, Feng Yuxiang, a warlord from northern China who a few years earlier had defected from the Zhili (Hebei Province) military clique, had taken part of his military staff to the Soviet Union for training in the hopes of staging a Soviet-backed invasion and reentry into Chinese warlord politics. In the process, many Chinese associated with Feng Yuxiang were redeployed along the border with Manchuria, where they fought alongside Soviet forces in the CER Incident and, in some cases, became involved in Communist propaganda activities.

This complex interplay of agendas that informed the 1929 regional conflict was reenvisioned during the post-Mao period in the context of a de-emphasis on Communist ideology and a burgeoning pride in national and regional identities. Along with the posthumous rehabilitation of historical figures ranging from Confucius to former GMD military and political leaders, the resurfacing of regional identities fostered a commemorative effort to salvage a unique Chinese history of the northeast from the dominant narrative of Russian and Japanese imperialism. Amidst these developments the image of Zhang Xueliang underwent a transformation. His instrumental role in forcing Jiang Jieshi to accept the terms of a Second United Front with the Communist Party in the 1936 Xian Incident had always set him apart from other warlords as a somewhat enlightened figure in the Communist Party's historical judgment. With the post-Mao reforms, a growing interest emerged in the life stories of both Zhang Xueliang and his staunchly anti-Communist father, Zhang Zuolin, with less attention directed to their relationship to the Communist Party and more emphasis given to their respective achievements in Chinese regional and national state-building efforts in the face of encroaching foreign powers. Zhang Xueliang's life story in particular was eulogized for his contributions to the northeast region's cultural development prior to Japan's occupation of Manchuria in 1931.

Zhang Xueliang's handling of the CER Incident presented a more contentious subject of investigation. Unlike the Xian Incident, where the objectives of nationalism and socialism appeared to go hand in hand, the CER border war posed a more ambiguous and fractured terrain where the defense of the Chinese nation's territorial integrity against foreign encroachment appeared to be incompatible with the CCP's support of the Soviet Union as its natural ally in the international socialist struggle. In the mid-1980s, local historians in the northeast sparred with one another over the historical significance of the event, as it became a site of debate over the relative importance of nation and socialist revolution. In 1984, historian Zhang Tong opened up this debate with an article in *Harbin History and Gazetteer* (*Harbin shizhi*) in which he reassessed the Soviet Union's approach toward the CER in the years leading up to the conflict as a "step backward" toward pre-1917 Russian imperialist policies. The article implicitly championed Zhang Xueliang's response as a patriotic act of defending the nation's territorial sovereignty while de-emphasizing the role of socialist ideology. The following year, historian Lü Lingui responded in the same publication by quoting and reaffirming the resolution of the CCP's Central Committee on July 12, 1929, that called for "defending the Soviet Union against imminent imperialist attack." He argued that the Soviet Union's assertive approach toward the CER had been a positive development against "reactionary and imperialist" opposition, that CER workers benefited from its policies, and, moreover, that "the true cause of the CER Incident is by no means the Soviet Union; the incident was caused by imperialism and the counter-revolutionary policy of the Guomindang."[44]

Zhang Fushan, a *wenshi ziliao* editor in Harbin, discussed his problems with editing personal recollections of the CER Incident. His stance on these materials is illustrative of the political challenges that editors faced in dealing with materials produced by individuals who had their own controversial interpretation of historical events:

Recently I read a school history, and I collected and compiled some recollections by schoolmates. One of them recalled a student movement during the 1929 CER incident. There were students from Pingyong University in Shenyang who were riled up by the GMD warlord gov't to go to Harbin to demonstrate against the SU. The [writer] referred to this event as a patriotic student movement. In reality the so-called "CER incident" was a reactionary anti-SU, anti-communist event stirred up in Harbin by imperialist-controlled GMD warlordism, and this was a reactionary student movement. Calling the CER incident a patriotic event would be confusing historical truth and falsity. This is a very serious issue. So, we who do *wenshi ziliao* work need to expand our understanding and accumulate more historical knowledge.[45]

---

[44] Zhang Tong, "Ershi niandai shouhui zhongdong tielu bufen liquan shi shulue" ("A Brief Historical Account of the Partial Recovery of Rights on the CER"), *Haerbin shizhi* (*Harbin History and Gazetteer*), no. 1 (1984): 23–32; Lü Lingui, "Zhongdong shijian fasheng qianhou de lishi qingkuang ji qi genyuan" ("On the Historical Circumstances and Causes of the CER Incident"), *Haerbin shizhi* (*Harbin History and Gazetteer*), no. 2 (1985): 44–53, cited in Søren Clausen and Stig Thøgersen, eds., *The Making of a Chinese City: History and Historiography in Harbin* (Armonk, NY: M. E. Sharpe, 1995).

[45] Zhang Fushan, "Tantan cunzhen qiushi" ("Some Observations about Preserving Authenticity and Seeking Truth"), in Haerbin shi zhengxie weiyuanhui mishuchu, *Haerbin zhengxie* (*Harbin PPCC*), no. 3 (no. 13 overall) (1984) (Special Issue of the First [Harbin City] *Wenshi Ziliao* Work Conference): 78–80.

As seen earlier, at the time Zhang wrote this report, local historians in the northeast were vigorously debating the significance of the CER Incident, disagreeing as to whether to assess the event in socialist terms as anti-Communist reactionary or in nationalist terms as anti-imperialist. Zhang Fushan was clearly siding with the socialist camp in his criticism of the author's evaluation of the anti-Soviet student movement as "patriotic." But he does so not by referring to abstract concepts like "dialectical and historical materialism," but rather by treating this as an instance of "confusing historical truth and falsity" and as a reminder of the need for the editor to arm himself with "more historical knowledge."

From "Confusing Historical Truth and Falsity" to Navigating Historical Truths to Redeem the Past

While these ideological disagreements at times disrupted the relationship between informants/writers and editors, in other cases, individuals who wrote down their recollections found subtle ways to bridge the ideological divide through their employment of subtle narrative devices. Rather than making a clear and definitive political statement about historical events like the CER Incident, they capitalized on the indeterminate multiplicity of political discourses on the past to resolve tensions and draw redeeming qualities from within their own experiences. As the foregoing discussion indicates, recollections of the CER Incident exposed a vulnerable point in the post-Mao official historiography at which nationalist and socialist priorities clashed. In his reminiscences about relocating to the town of Fujin, which Soviet forces attacked during the CER Incident, Xing Jinghuan translated the unresolved debate among Chinese historians about the ideological implications of the event into a set of rhetorical resources for ascribing meaning to a personal crisis in his entrepreneurial career. In contrast with the acrimonious debates and rigidly compartmentalized treatment of the conflict in official documents, Xing folded together competing historical representations as a means for making sense of disjunctures in his personal life and for constructing a heroic narrative of the entrepreneur overcoming obstacles.

Xing recalled his firsthand observations of the war in Fujin, where he had begun working at an assorted goods enterprise several years after arriving in Manchuria. This town had been part of a dynamic cross-border economic zone in which the Russian and Chinese sides of the political border were interwoven through commercial exchange. Situated on the lower Songhua River delta straddling the Russian border and lying directly across the river from Khabarovsk, Fujin had grown out of commerce with its Russian neighbors. Many of the major enterprises that constituted the economic core of this burgeoning frontier town were founded in the decade after the 1917 Revolution by Chinese migrants who had previously settled in cities in Russian eastern Siberia like Vladivostok and Khabarovsk. Following the Revolution, they escaped the ensuing chaos and brought the commercial relationships they had developed there to areas along the western (Chinese) side of the Ussuri River. There, they took advantage of their strategic location to pursue a profitable trade in goods transported from Harbin and Shenyang along the Songhua River to the crisis-ridden Russian settlements on the other side of the border.[46]

The outbreak of military conflict temporarily disrupted this trade and was indirectly responsible for a humiliating episode in Xing's career. In his recollections he manipulates the ideological fault lines running through the event in post-Mao historiography to reevaluate the event's significance in his personal life, restaging the conflict as a vehicle for defining the challenges he had to overcome before becoming a successful entrepreneur. He describes the conflict's unfolding as follows:

In the fall of 1929 (the eighteenth year of the Republic), the "CER Incident" broke out. The Soviet navy sailed from the upper Songhua River across Sanjiangkou, while the Chinese navy prepared for battle. There was fierce fighting. One afternoon a plane appeared in the sky and circled overhead. People assumed it was a Chinese plane, but a short time later it dropped two bombs. This threw all the town residents into panic, and all the businesses closed their shops. That evening people took advantage of the chaos to loot and set fires, and along the southern part of Zhongda Street numerous shops were burnt down and looted. The next day the Chinese fleet retreated from Sanjiangkou, and the Soviet warships advanced toward and fired on the city, hitting [the] Jinchang flourmill. Manager Wang of [the] Shuangfagong business led us twenty or so employees to escape for refuge to Jixian for the time being.

Later we heard accurate information that the Soviet army had not entered the city, but had only opened the flour mill's storage to hand out two sacks of flour to every poor resident and had not harmed any other businesses. So, Wang led us back to Fujin city. The river was about to freeze over at that time, so the Soviet navy withdrew, but the businesses were still too afraid to re-open their shops and resume business. Just then I received a telegram from my family back in Hebei asking me to go back for a visit. The next spring when I returned to Fujin,

---

[46] Vlademir Zatsepine discusses the fluid movement and commercial exchange along the Songhua River across the Wusuli River border in *Beyond the Amur: Frontier Encounters Between China and Russia, 1850–1930*. Vancouver: UBC Press, 2017. A local history produced within the *wenshi ziliao* project highlights the role in the town's commercial development after 1917 of Chinese migrants who had formerly settled east of the river. Zhang Jitai, "Biancheng maoyi de yanbian – fuyuan xian jiefang qian de shangye xiao shi" ("The Evolution of Border Town Trade – A Short History of Commerce in Fuyuan County Prior to 1949"), *Jiamusi wenshi ziliao* (Jiamusi shi weiyuan hui wenshi ziliao yanjiu weiyuan hui), 6 (1986): 115.

Shuangfagong had made the decision that anyone who left the business during the conflict would not be rehired. This was the first time I experienced the feeling of losing my job.[47]

In contrast with the polarized ideological debates waged by local historians over the conflict's political significance, Xing processes and weaves together these contradictions in his personal remembrance of the event. He navigates the fault lines of the ideological terrain not by concealing them or leaving out sensitive details, but rather by structuring and containing the opposing priorities of nation and socialist revolution within a unified framework. This enables him to come to terms with the conflicted feelings of personal ambivalence, guilt, and shame that the event evoked in his own life. By containing the tension between nation and socialist revolution, he resolves the personal contradictions between family attachment, independent manliness, and business duty that the war represented for him.

Xing refers to the border conflict according to the official name designated for it, the "CER Incident." The name itself harbors an ambiguity, similar to that of the 1989 "Tiananmen Incident," implying the unresolved nature of its political implications. Unlike such loaded terms as the "Blagoveshchensk Massacre," the vague name leaves open different interpretations of who the actors were, who is to blame, and what its political significance and ramifications are. Xing initially describes the Russians as the aggressors, charging down the river against the Chinese fleet and staging a violent assault on the city that climaxes with the attack on the Jinchang flour mill. In opposition to this threat, he refers to the "Chinese navy," superimposing the idea of a unified Chinese political entity onto Zhang Xueliang's fragmented and regionally autonomous authority. The people of the town gaze up in forlorn hope for the "Chinese plane" to protect them, only to discover their mistake when the bombs fall.

This scene of hapless Chinese victimization to foreign aggression, however, begins to splinter away as Xing's account continues. To begin with, the Russian warships appear not to be the only aggressors. Xing depicts the town residents themselves, after the initial gaze in search of the Chinese plane, as aiding and abetting in the destruction under the cover of chaos and darkness. His depiction of the scene quickly evolves from one of hapless victimization to one of self-inflicted harm based on greed and opportunism. The boundary between self and other, friend and foe, national self and foreign other, dissolves as economic class, and the division between haves and have-nots takes over. It is in this context

[47] Xing Jinghuan, "My Over Sixty Years' Experience with Commercial Enterprises," 83.

that Xing relates the "accurate information" that the Soviet army in fact had not come to occupy the city or commit any further acts of aggression, but suddenly metamorphoses into the heroic socialist liberator of the oppressed underclass. The Jinchang flour mill, initially depicted as part of the scene of Chinese victimization to Soviet aggression, becomes recast as a site of economic redistribution from the exploitative capitalist owners to the ordinary town residents.

Through weaving together these contradictions in official representations of the border war, Xing reconciles another set of personal issues with which he associates the event. These issues were tied to competing tendencies in the management of Chinese commercial enterprises in Manchuria of privileging native place identities yet demanding that young employees temporarily sever their ties to relatives back home. Fellow local ties did not only shape the patterns of recruitment from certain areas of northern China but also imposed strict disciplinary requirements and social expectations on young employees. These included the standard rule that each newcomer stay at the worksite in Manchuria for three uninterrupted years, resisting the longing or temptation to return home even for the traditional family reunion during the spring festival.[48] While shared native place ties fostered a family-like corporate environment, it was the willingness to resist emotional ties to one's family and hometown that determined the individual's level of loyalty to the business. According to Xing's account, the company at which he had worked in Fujin applied this concept to the outbreak of the war as a measure of the employees' loyalty to the business. Xing's violation of this contract on account of the CER Incident implied an irreconcilable contradiction between filial attachment and entrepreneurial responsibility and labeled him as a failure.

Xing's narrative of the conflict constitutes an effort on his part to overcome this apparent contradiction and to provide evidence demonstrating that he had in fact fulfilled both roles of filial son and dutiful employee. He describes in detail the harrowing sequence of events that transpired over the course of the conflict in order to underscore that he had witnessed and endured the truly dangerous period of the war with his business comrades. Only after the Soviet warships had retreated and calm was restored, according to the sequence of events as he narrates them, does he receive the telegram from his family asking him to return for a visit. In opposition to the implied judgment rendered by the business that had laid him off, the implication that he makes here is that his home visit in no way constituted a retreat from danger or abandonment of the

---

[48] See, for instance, Liu Wenfeng, *Travels to the Eastern Frontier*, 45.

business amidst the chaos of the fighting. Moreover, he draws on the "socialist revolution" narrative of the Soviet Union as the people's liberator to underscore that the conflict, concerning which he had been accused by the company of fleeing for the safety of his home, had in fact turned out not really to be a conflict after all. The fear of the supposed aggressors had been proven unfounded by the "accurate information" concerning the Soviets' role as liberators.

The political divisiveness of the CER Incident in post-Mao official discourse ironically provided Xing with the narrative resources for constructing a redemptive history of his own past. Alternating between nationalist and socialist versions of the event enabled him to recast past humiliation and conflicting loyalties as heroic struggle.

Problematic Informants and Activist Editors

While Xing's self-redemption relied on a subtle interfusion of political discourses, some editors complained about the tendency of informants to exaggerate and falsely ascribe political luster to certain historical events and people. Zhang Fushan provides several examples to illustrate this memory problem, including an interview with a former CER railroad worker that he conducted while writing about the history of Chinese workers' conditions along the CER during the period of czarist Russian management. In the context of describing the hardships they endured owing to foreign exploitation, the interviewee recalled how a worker named Chen Guangyuan had been killed in a work-related incident. But Zhang, apparently not convinced of the accuracy of this statement, checked CER records in the provincial archive and found that the incident had in fact taken place in 1926 after the railroad had come under joint Sino–Soviet control. "To add this to the ledger of the old czarist emperor's [wrongdoings]," he reflects," would not be historically accurate."[49] Ideologically, Zhang was on the same page as the interviewee. However, his editorial agenda of aligning fact-based inquiry with ideological correctness runs up against the informant's attempt to amplify his life story's resonance with the socialist-nationalist narrative of workers' exploitation by foreign imperialism.

In addition to skepticism about the truthfulness of interviewees' oral accounts, Zhang was also critical of writers' proclivity to exaggerate the revolutionary significance of certain events in which they had participated or with which they had special familiarity. He recalls a "comrade" who

[49] Zhang Fushan, "Some Observations about Preserving Authenticity and Seeking Truth," 78–80.

wrote a hagiographic article on a patriotic local student demonstration's leadership by a former middle school student who was also an underground Communist Party worker. Once again, Zhang intervened and, through cross-referencing sources, found evidence that this student had in fact not yet joined the Communist Party at the time of this event.[50] Zhang, therefore, saw himself as an agent of ascertaining and upholding both ideological and factual truth. Rather than the two-stage process of empirical research and "dialectical and historical materialist" interpretation that Rong Mengyuan theorized, Zhang Fushan saw both as an integrated process that required constant vigilance in respect to informants' hidden agendas.

Zhang does not emphasize writers' rights to free expression, neither does he encourage them with the idea that whatever they write will not be subject to political judgment. Instead, Zhang approaches the writer as an ideological problem and a potential threat that requires, on the part of the editor, extensive background political and historical training to resolve and overcome. Other local editors also struggled to ensure that historical content would not spill outside of the Party-approved version of the past. To this end, they actively guided and structured their informants' narratives. Speaking at a *wenshi ziliao* work conference in Harbin in 1984, a member of the city's editorial team, Tong Zhenyu, recalled his approach to interviewing Li Yichun, former commander of the GMD military's Jilin division. He begins by noting that "what they [referring to informants like Li] recall happened a long time ago and it's hard for them to remember things accurately just like that. Also, we know nothing about their experiences. Based on my experience, to do a good job collecting *wenshi ziliao* requires first of all strengthening my own studies." He starts, therefore, from the presumption that the informant does not necessarily recall events accurately, a reasonable observation about the faulty nature of personal memory.

In this context, however, the emphasis on memory's limitations justifies the editor's activist role in providing corrective guidance at each step of the narrative process. To do so, Tong prepared for the interview by brushing up on his "study [of] twentieth century history; Party history and philosophy; and political and economic theories," the primary goal being to "have fairly accurate guiding thought and establish the dialectical materialism perspective on history." Supplementing this broad ideological framework for historical analysis in general with specific applications of this ideology to the area of history experienced by the informant, he "systematically studied and put in order the whole [historical] process

[50] Ibid.

from the late Qing's establishment of the Northeast military academy to its takeover by Zhang Zuolin." "In this way," he concluded, "we not only helped Li remember more historical facts, but also I could more easily discern truth from falsity."[51] The editor came to the interview, therefore, armed with an authoritative version of historical events that he presented to the informant as a template and corrective measure to which any accurate rendition of what happened needed to conform. This approach enabled editors to compile stories that appeared to be representative of a diverse "united front" spectrum of society yet uniformly contributed to an overarching Party-approved version of the past.

In this way, local editors varied in their approach to the politics of historical production. While some viewed their role as advocates of an open-ended empirical process free from political constraints and protective of individuals' freedom of expression, others were political activists who approached the editing process and the encounter with the informant as a highly politicized and ideologically laden venture. Still others took a more middle ground in which they regarded their sources' reliability as limited by the inaccuracies of memory, justifying the interviewer's active intervention in the process of constructing historical truth.

Editors occupied an ambiguous position within the power complex of the party-state apparatus. Invested with the task of constructing and verifying historical truth, they held the keys to determining what and whose historical memories would become official history. At the same time, this role frequently put them in the uncomfortable position of interviewing and critically editing the writing of senior officials and Party cadres, which created for them the dilemma of whether to appease their superiors out of political expediency or risk reprisal in an effort to obtain the objective truth. Indeed, a number of reports mention that, when the *wenshi ziliao* were resumed in the early 1980s, the first to write down their recollections were those who occupied the top leadership positions in the PPCCs and other organizations. Zhang Fushan lamented that "[s]ome [interviewers] perhaps ignore facts in order to please the interviewee" and was particularly concerned about the often asymmetric relationship between editor and informant:

When interviewing and compiling materials, sometimes we meet this kind of problem: what a leader mentions or recalls will always be viewed as reliable. This is also not appropriate. When writing and compiling *wenshi ziliao*, we must

---

[51] Tong Zhenyu, "Wo shi zenyang zhengji wenshi ziliao de" ("How I Collected *Wenshi Ziliao*"), Haerbin shi zhengxie weiyuanhui mishuchu, *Haerbin zhengxie* (*Harbin PPCC*), no. 3 (no. 13 overall) (1984) (Special Issue of the First [Harbin City] *Wenshi Ziliao* Work Conference): 75–77.

not evaluate the accuracy of materials based on how high or low a person's position is. Everyone has limited memory and will make mistakes or be confused. The higher the position of the person submitting materials, the more likely it is that the materials are important. It's therefore even more incumbent upon the compiler to repeatedly corroborate [information].[52]

Zhang's advice on how to deal with materials submitted by senior officials indicates a dilemma about truth and power that lay at the heart of *wenshi ziliao* production. Those who edited the materials were tasked with the responsibility of melding detached scholarly analysis with obedience to political directives. In the process, they encountered two opposite challenges in dealing with informants: first, protecting and reassuring those whose memories of Cultural Revolution persecution were still fresh, and, second, boldly intervening to prevent those currently in seats of power from imposing their version of the past.

"Seeking Truth from Facts" and Local Identity Projects

Alongside the issue of power relations between interviewer and interviewee, editors also interpreted "seeking truth from facts" as a resolution to the tension between local economic and cultural incentives and political expediency. Driven by the desire to confer national and international prestige and recognition on their hometowns, researchers drew up plans to dig up materials about famous local historical figures. Occasionally, however, these pursuits ran up against ideological problems. In Hulan County, the *wenshi ziliao* committee was particularly interested in uncovering more information about the life of well-known writer Xiao Hong, who became famous for her nostalgic though somber literary depiction of her hometown under Japanese occupation in the 1930s. Local researchers expressed excitement about the international attention that Xiao Hong's fame brought to Hulan, but were concerned about the lack of any concerted effort to capitalize on it. "Xiao Hong is a famous young writer internationally and in the past few years scholars have come from within China and abroad to Hulan to see her home and understand her youth activities. But since much time has elapsed and not many who are still alive knew her, her family life and activities are not clearly understood. Some came excited and left disappointed, not finding what they hoped to find . . . We were

---

[52] Zhang Fushan, "Some Observations about Preserving Authenticity and Seeking Truth," 78–80.

determined to overcome difficulties and find a way to rescue materials on Xiao Hong that could be rescued."[53]

Their desire to place Hulan on the cultural map and satisfy visitors' curiosity about their local celebrity drove them to mobilize Party institutions in the search for informants. "For example," recalled the researcher who reported on this project, "we heard that her third aunt was still alive but we didn't know her whereabouts. We took advantage of the county Party holding propaganda committee meetings in each commune to do inspection visits ... Finally we found her 93-year old aunt in the Xiying production brigade of Mengjia commune. She was blind but still had pretty clear memory and was pretty clear in the head."[54]

However, a problem soon arose, which was that her version of several events in Xiao Hong's life (their report does not specify what these events were) conflicted with the official narrative. Since the aunt died shortly after their taped interview, they were not able to ask her follow-up questions to verify what she had said. This, according to the researcher, "caused hesitation in thought and created three fears. One fear was of disturbing the distinction between truth and falsity; the second fear was of having one's 'pigtail pulled' [facing political accusation]; and the third fear was of being unfair to [Xiao Hong's] children, friends and family."[55] Suddenly, their agenda of making their hometown more famous and visible became a political liability. Accordingly, the researchers recall that their first way of coping with this was to "study documents and leaders' speeches about *wenshi ziliao* work. This gave us further understanding of the significance of *wenshi ziliao* work, and we were determined to continue collecting materials about Xiao Hong."[56]

Having established a legitimate political framework in which to justify their research, the author of the report reverts to local identity as the primary basis for their endeavor, and rationalizes this commitment in terms of "seeking truth from facts." "Xiao Hong was a native of Hulan, and the people of Hulan know her best. It's our responsibility to clarify materials on her and write them into history. So long as we investigate carefully and deeply and seek truth from facts in writing, only then are we fulfilling our role." Accordingly, the researcher notes that after three months of persistent interviews of Xiao Hong's other relatives and

---

[53] Zhengxie hulan xian weiyuanhui, "women shi zenyang kaizhan wenshi ziliao de gongzuo" ("How Should We Carry Out *Wenshi Ziliao* Work?"), *Haerbin zhengxie* (*Harbin PPCC*), no. 3 (no. 13 overall) (1984) (Special Issue of the First [Harbin City] *Wenshi Ziliao* Work Conference) (Heilongjiang Provincial Archive): 81–84.
[54] Ibid.   [55] Ibid.   [56] Ibid.

neighbors, they were able to "resolve this issue"[57] and publish their account in a volume of Heilongjiang *wenshi ziliao*.[58] In this instance, local editors adapted the "seeking truth from facts" discourse to confer legitimacy to their local identity projects. By arguing that real truth seeking could only take place in the context of local relationships and knowledge, they privileged local cultural pride as the centerpiece of *wenshi ziliao* knowledge production.

Regional Interpretations of "Liberation" and Heroism

Armed with these reinterpretations and adaptations of "seeking truth from facts," local *wenshi ziliao* committees reevaluated historical events and people to construct a more inclusive version of history. In so doing, they subtly redefined "liberation" and heroism to suit and prioritize regional particularities over national Party orthodoxy. In their collection of materials about people and organizations who had competed for power at the local level with the Communist Party during the period between 1945 and 1949, editors adopted a nonjudgmental stance that avoided divisive "counterrevolutionary" rhetoric. This is evident in the open-ended questions that interviewers in Fujin asked elderly informants regarding some of the competing stakeholders jockeying for power during this transitional period:

4) When was the Preservation Society established? How was it established? Who presided over it, how many people joined, what were their names, and what role did it play?
5) When was the Grand Alliance established? How was it established? Who held the main responsibility? What was its main goal? What kind of influence did it have on society at the time?
6) When were the GMD and Three People's Principles Youth League organized in Fujin? Who was responsible? Where did they hold meetings? How many joined each?
7) How many major bandit bands were there in [the] area? What were the main leaders' names, and when, where and to whom did they surrender or meet their destruction?[59]

While the questions that the Fujin *wenshi ziliao* committee formulated in regard to Russian and Japanese imperialism (described later in the document) clearly direct the informants to provide evidence of foreign aggression, the foregoing questions simply prompt the interlocutor in a neutral

---

[57] Precisely what the problematic disparity was between the aunt's account and the official version of events in Xiao Hong's life is never disclosed in the report.
[58] Ibid.
[59] Fujin xian zhengxie, "Reference Outline for Asking Old Comrades to Write Memoirs," 1.

tone to provide information about the organizations' development. Item number two even includes a question about the group's influence on society, leaving the options for response relatively open and free of underlying assumptions.

To lend a redemptive perspective on this messy history of competing military and political organizations, and to incorporate multiple local identities more positively into the historical narrative, editors revised their definition of "liberation." Consider one of the questions on the Fujin committee's prescribed list: "what other major events and cases that stood out occurred between liberation in 1945 and the founding of the PRC in 1949?"[60] Deviating from the official Communist designation of 1949 as the moment of liberation, *wenshi ziliao* cadres in the northeast moved the date back to 1945 in order to give priority and recognition to their region's diversity and particularity above and beyond the Party itself. Indeed, editors took advantage of the atmosphere of political reconciliation and rehabilitation to glorify individuals who wielded military power and social influence outside the parameters of Party control in the aftermath of Japanese defeat, employing their life histories as a lens for celebrating local identity.

Stories of wild frontier migration played into this regional redefinition of "liberation." During the early twentieth century, the "bursting through the pass" discourse on migration reflected more than just popular perceptions of the dangers of venturing northeast. It also articulated modernizing elites' civilizing mission for the ethnic frontiers as well as their ambivalence about migrants' role in consolidating the border against Russian expansion. The concept of northern Manchuria as a desolate wilderness awaiting development fit into the civilizing mission that regarded migrants as agents of cultural and economic integration. At the same time, Qing officials were wary of migrants' unregulated movements in pursuit of economic opportunities across the borderland. Officials traveling through the region viewed the migrants as manifestations of a wild and dangerous frontier that defied the state's control. The mostly young men circulating among gold mines and lumber enterprises struck officials as a wild, unruly group whose energies shifted seasonally between productive labor and predatory violence.

The "wild frontier" reemerged in the *wenshi ziliao* with new political implications. In the context of a crisis of socialist ideology and devolving economic responsibility to the local and private realms, local identities and individual desires exploded onto the cultural scene. *Wenshi ziliao* reflected tension between this trend toward localization and the national

---

[60] Ibid., 2.

project of political consolidation. From initial planning to final publication, committees at the city and county levels took increasing initiative in producing memories. Interviewers and editors approached their work as an extension of other local culture revival projects. These included the preservation of ancient artifacts, the designation of historical sites for tourist consumption, the production of television series that popularized local cultural achievements, and the revival of local gazetteer writing. The *wenshi ziliao* became absorbed into this system of cultural projects promoting local interests. As local interests infused the *wenshi ziliao* planning and editing process, narrators and editors reimagined the migrant hero as wild outlaw and rootless wanderer whose exploits did not fit neatly into national ideology, resonating with desires unleashed by post-Mao reforms.

Fan Dechang's work as editor of the Yichun County *wenshi ziliao* in northeast Heilongjiang Province exemplified the local agendas that informed the content and structure of memory production. Prior to joining the *wenshi ziliao* committee, he had been an editor for the local gazetteer. A prominent expression of local identity that came under attack after 1949, the "new gazetteers" emerged in the early 1980s as part of the reorientation of historical inquiry toward the local level.[61] Adapting his role in gazetteer production to the *wenshi ziliao* editing process, Fan Dechang employed the migrant narrative as a means for incorporating local particularity within the project of national historical production. At the same time, his valorization of local exploits as a prominent feature of the migrant memoir stretched the boundaries of the Party's national discourse.

One of the informants from whom Fan Dechang solicited interviews for the *wenshi ziliao* in the early 1980s was Wang Ruiyi, a former gold miner, womanizing opium addict, and leader of a nomadic band of Oroqen hunters. Wang had been among the migrants drawn to state-sponsored mining initiatives along the Amur River. Following the collapse of the Qing in 1911, regional warlord governments assumed control over the mines on the Chinese side of the river before their transfer to Japanese management in 1933. The migrants fueling the mines' development also came into contact with Oroqens in the surrounding wilderness. Incorporated within the multiethnic Manchu banner system, the Oroqens had continued to pursue their nomadic livelihoods. With the

---

[61] For a discussion of the reemergence of gazetteer writing in the 1980s, see Stig Thøgersen and Søren Clausen, "New Reflections in the Mirror: Local Chinese Gazetteers (Difangzhi) in the 1980s," *Australian Journal of Chinese Affairs*, no. 27 (Jan. 1992): 161–184; Clausen, "Autobiography of a Chinese City: The History of Harbin in the Mirror of the Official City Gazetteer," *Historiography East & West* 2.1: 144–172.

intensification of Han Chinese migration, encounters with Chinese speculators, traders, and settlers became increasingly frequent. Arseniev and
Lattimore, in the course of their travels through the Ussuri and Amur
borderlands, observed Oroqens' growing dependence on opium, alcohol,
and other commodities that indebted them to the Chinese newcomers.[62]
At the same time, owing to their hunting skills and familiarity with the
rugged terrain, traders and mining speculators relied on them as guides,
while Japanese officers attempted to harness them as military assets in the
suppression of Chinese resistance. It was in this context that Wang had
left his home near the bustling port of Yantai in the 1920s as a young man,
alternating between mining for gold along the Amur River and wandering
through the wilderness with a group of Oroqens.

The production of his life story is a colorful example of the strategies
that local editors used to redirect the resources of the national *wenshi
ziliao* campaign toward the promotion of local agendas. Fan Dechang's
wenshi ziliao work overlapped with and became incorporated within other
local cultural programs with which he was concurrently engaged. He
recalls that "while editing *Jiayin County Gazetteer* I interviewed him
[Wang] many times. In July of this year, the County Government, the
United Front Committee, and the County Gazetteer office cooperated in
coordinating a two-day series of interviews."[63] Following the interviews,
Fan transcribed and edited Wang's recollections into a single written
narrative. In his introduction to the narrative, entitled "Gold-Mining
and 'Fuma' Life,"[64] the editor summarizes the highlights of Wang's life
story in a way that subtly displaces the CCP's nationalist narrative:

Early in the Republic he burst east of the pass. From 1923 he wandered from one
gold mine to another along the Jiayin River digging for gold. In 1934 an Oroqen
tribesman, Du Mude, adopted him as son-in-law. In 1945 he became head of the
Qilin[65] [Oroqen] force, and in late fall of 1946 he assumed the title of auxiliary
commander. People called him the Oroqen "fuma," and in his hands was
a military force of great bravery and fighting prowess.

In 1945 after the "August 15th" glorious restoration,[66] in Foshan County Ji
Hongfu and Wang Mingxuan led the Peace Preservation Army; the Niaoyun and
Xunke area was occupied by the Sixth Combined Division of the GMD's

---

[62] Lattimore, *Manchuria*; V. K. Arseniev, *Dersu the Trapper*. Translated by Malcolm Burr
(New York, NY: Dutton, 1941).
[63] Wang Ruiyi, "My Life as Gold Digger and 'Emperor's Son-in-Law,'" 146–147.
[64] *Fuma* is a combination of the characters meaning "horse" and "the extra horse straddled
up alongside the carriage," and is a term referring to the emperor's son-in-law. Amidst
ethnic intermingling in the northeast during the early twentieth century, migrants used
the term to refer to young Chinese men adopted into Oroqen families.
[65] *Qilin* means literally "forest dweller," and refers to the Oroqens.
[66] Referring to Japanese surrender at the end of the Second World War.

Expeditionary Army led by Liu Guangcai. Our People's Liberation Army's Hejiang Army carried out anti-banditry and political construction operations centered on the Jiamusi–Hegang areas. The Qilin Army that Wang Ruilin commanded maneuvered between these three military forces for as long as two years. It was not until winter 1947 that he joined our army.[67]

Later in his introduction Fan acknowledges Wang's eventual incorporation within the CCP's military structure, praising his role "in the People's Liberation Army's occupation of Foshan to rid the area of banditry and establish order, in the implementation of land reform, and in the struggle to harness the fighting capacity of the Oroqen people."[68]

Fan chooses to highlight Wang's independent exploits as the culmination of a wild and defiant migrant spirit and local identity unvanquished by larger national forces, GMD and CCP alike. He uses verbs such as "burst," "wandered," and "maneuvered between" to lend an aura of uncontrollable energy to Wang's movements. "Bursting through the pass," wandering among gold mines, and taking charge of Oroqen "tribesmen" work together to form the profile of a migrant hero unfettered by social or political control. Extending this narrative into the civil war period of the 1940s, the editor constructs an account of nationalist liberation centered on the nonconformist local hero that marginalizes the CCP's role.

While creating a lens for competing local and national definitions of heroism, the *chuang guandong* narrative of the wild frontier migrant also injected into historical discourse a raw and unfiltered assessment of the human condition that rejected political categories as irrelevant to the individual's struggle for survival. At a time when cynicism and disillusionment with politics had set in after a decade of unpredictable swings between ideological campaigns, memories of wilderness frontier migration offered a cultural space for celebrating the individual's survival as the sole remaining source of meaning, irrespective of political loyalties and ideological claims. Wang Ruiyi's reflections on his involvement in the Oroqens' politically ambiguous role in relation to the Chinese nation and the Communist Party create an alternative historical narrative privileging human survival over nationalist self-sacrifice and ideological partisanship.

Wang characterized his induction into a band of Oroqen hunters in the early 1930s as an initiation into a life of freedom and spontaneity in harmony with eternal rhythms of nature and uninhibited by societal attachments.

After I was taken in as son-in-law [of an Oroqen hunter], I spent a year living a nomadic life. Oroqen people generally went out on hunting expeditions four

---

[67] Wang Ruiyi, "My Life as Gold Digger and 'Emperor's Son-in-Law,'" 146–147.
[68] Ibid.

times each year: In February–March when the deep snow was starting to thaw and the deer fetus had just been formed, the hunters went deep into the mountains in small groups to catch the doe – this was called the "deer fetus hunt." In May–June when the green grass sprouted and the deer antlers grew out, they caught the stag in order to get the antlers – this was known as the "red hunt." In September–October, as the autumn wind picked up and the grasses and trees became dried up and yellow, this was the deer mating season. The sound of the does calling out for their mates went on without pause, and the stags would hastily come over when they heard the sound – because of this it was called the "calling deer hunt." In November–December, they would track the hoof prints in the snow and attack when they saw something – this was called "attacking the skin." In the course of a year they would move about through the wilderness for about seven to eight months, and the rest of the time they would go back to their huts.[69]

Wang's reveries about wandering through this virgin setting celebrate personal freedom, describing Wang himself playfully wandering through the mountains and rivers released from any responsibilities. "Now reflecting back, that kind of nomadic hunting life really was pretty exciting. All four seasons of the year wandering through the mountains and playing in the streams, with nothing to reap and nothing to manage, drinking from the mountain streams whenever I was thirsty and eating the wild animals whenever I was hungry, you could say I was pretty carefree."[70] Roaming freely through the landscape constitutes a complete removal of the self from the constraining framework of social demands and obligations.

Yet the political context for this return of the individual to a natural state of human freedom, the Oroqens' collaboration with the Japanese, was problematic from the perspective of the Chinese nationalist narrative. Since the late nineteenth century, intensifying waves of Chinese settlers hungry for land, market opportunities, and natural resources pressed against and sparked conflicts with Oroqen communities. Just as the British had used opium to open up the Chinese market, the Chinese settlers in the northeast used the drug to capture the market of wilderness goods in which the indigenous hunters specialized. The Oroqen word for "Han Chinese" was in fact the same as their word for "opium."[71] Through drawing the Oroqens into an addictive dependence on the commodity, Chinese traders were able to bind them into a pattern of economic indebtedness that could be exploited to demand favorable terms for acquiring goods with high market value like sable. Beginning at the turn of the century, contemporary travelers like Arseniev and Lattimore observed the rapid decline of the Oroqens into this state of drug addiction and perpetual indebtedness that put them at the mercy of a tightening Chinese commercial network. Chinese historians after 1949

[69] Ibid.   [70] Ibid.   [71] Duara, *Sovereignty and Authenticity*.

blamed this vicious cycle of indebtedness and drug addiction on a few "evil merchants" (*jianshang*), thereby deflecting any blame away from Chinese settlement and commercial expansion in the region as a whole.[72]

The systemic exploitation that ensued resulted in escalating resentment and hostility toward Chinese settlers. Arseniev encountered numerous cases of violence that erupted between the two groups, as commercial exploitation was exacerbated by the expansion of Chinese settlement into Oroqen hunting grounds.[73] After the Japanese occupation of Manchuria in 1931, Chinese who organized themselves into guerrilla resistance units, increasingly mobilized under Communist leadership, found themselves the targets of these long-standing grievances.

The Manchukuo government mobilized native ethnic groups' resentments and demands for the recovery of lost land and livelihoods in order to consolidate an autonomous Manchurian "nation" removed from Chinese influence. In accordance with their Concordia of Nationalities policy for Manchuria, the Japanese attempted to secure Oroqen loyalty by separating and isolating them from the surrounding Chinese population. The objective was to "de-Sinicize" them by returning them to their "primeval" way of life in the wilderness. Japanese ethnographers, anxious to preserve traces of a primordial past that they viewed as the primal roots of Japanese civilization, saw their role of protecting the Oroqens from Chinese corrupting influences as a justification for Japanese occupation of the region.[74]

Oroqen historical encounters with Chinese settlement in the frontier, combined with the ethnic mobilization policies of the new Manchukuo government, made them natural allies of the Japanese.[75] Oroqen "mountain forest units" (*shanlin dui*), each under the command of a Japanese "instructor," engaged in military exercises during peak hunting season in the spring and summer. Trained as sharpshooters targeting anti-Japanese and Communist forces, the Oroqen teams developed a fearful reputation. Communist fighters frequently "found it expeditious to eliminate Oroqen

---

[72] Ibid.

[73] Arseniev, *Dersu the Trapper*, 100–102, 105, 105–106, 107; Lattimore, *Manchuria*, 122–123.

[74] Nakao, "Japanese Colonial Policy."

[75] This is not to diminish the resentment that Oroqens felt against the Japanese for imposing severe restrictions on their livelihood and enforcing strict military discipline that frequently interfered with their own hunting rhythms and economic pursuits. Over the course of Japanese occupation, it certainly became clear that Japanese occupation had simply imposed tighter limitations on them, and the Manchukuo government adapted the *jianshang* opium addiction strategy for ensuring their compliance with Japanese military prerogatives. Katsumi Nakao states that Oroqen team members took advantage of the Soviet invasion in 1945 to have Japanese personnel killed. Nakao, "Japanese Colonial Policy."

hunters regardless of their political sensibilities." Lingering resentment at this indiscriminate killing found expression in sporadic Oroqen attacks on surrounding Chinese settlements at the end of the civil war.[76]

After 1949, the PRC government attempted to incorporate the Oroqens seamlessly into the Party-sanctioned history by emptying them of any historical agency and recasting their actions during the occupation in terms of passive subjection to Japanese exploitation. Wang draws on this discourse to empty out the political implications of his own involvement in these Oroqen military campaigns. He portrays the Oroqen lifestyle in terms of unchanging natural cycles, in opposition to which the Japanese enter the scene as intruders who trapped the native tribes with their nefarious schemes.

In the years of the Republic there were quite a few "forest-dwelling people" along the Jiayin River. Most of them set up huts in the vicinity of the gold valleys. When they went hunting they went off with their wives and children. When heavy snow made the mountains inaccessible, they spent the winter in their huts. During the time of Manchukuo, the dwarf devils used poisonous schemes to entice the "forest-dwelling people." They were well aware that the Oroqen people were skilled at shooting, knew the mountain trails well, and also smoked a lot of opium and drank a lot of alcohol. So they used opium and alcohol to buy the Oroqens off in order to deal with the Anti-Japanese United Army.[77]

Wang openly admits that the Oroqens actively collaborated with the Japanese military occupation, yet, according to his account, this did not stop him from playing off competing groups against each other when there was profit to be made. He secretly sold supplies to the leader of the early Communist resistance force in the area, Zhao Shangzhi, until the Russian wife of his Oroqen coconspirator allegedly exposed their dealings to Japanese authorities. He gives little account of his actions during the ensuing decade of Japanese occupation, only briefly mentioning his return to the gold mines as a successful labor boss under Japanese management. Skipping over the period of Japanese occupation, Wang devotes minutely detailed attention to the political transition period between Japanese surrender and Communist control. Minimizing his achievements prior to 1945, he claims that it was during this brief interlude that he made an important mark on the canvas of history.

Yet that mark as he describes it bears little resemblance to the mark of defiant heroism that the editor portrayed in the opening lines of the

[76] Lenore A. Grenoble and Lindsay J. Whaley, "Language Policy and the Loss of Tungusic Languages," *Language and Communication* 19.4 (Oct. 1999): 373–386; "Elunchun zu jianshi" bianxie zu, *Elunchun zu jianshi* (Huhehaote: Nei Menggu renmin chubanshe; Nei Menggu xinhua shudian faxing, 1983): 124–126.
[77] Wang Ruiyi, "My Life as Gold Digger and 'Emperor's Son-in-Law,'" 153.

account. Instead, Wang recounts in plain terms a series of pragmatic and often indecisive actions whose sole objective appears to be survival rather than heroic feats in a chaotic military environment. Caught between the then-dominant military force of the Peace Preservation Army and the expanding division of the Eighth Route Army, Wang recalls his vacillation as he weighed the relative costs and benefits of allying with one or the other. In the end, seeing no substantive evidence of a reliable Communist military strength in the region, Wang opted to "secretly join with the Communist Party while openly courting both. In the future I'd go along with whoever is strongest."[78] He shuttled back and forth between the two camps, attending the Peace Preservation Army's strategic meeting only to turn around and discuss military strategy with the Eighth Route Army, all the while remaining detached from both. When informed that the Eighth Route Army had dispatched a spy to convince the Peace Preservation Army to surrender, Wang recalls that he rushed off to disclose the truth about the spy to the Peace Preservation Army's commander, who forthwith had the spy executed. Meanwhile, when the Eighth Route Army passed through his area, Wang agreed to be their guide and warned the enemy camp to avoid confrontation with the superior Communist force. This double-agent identity nearly cost him his life when he was captured by a GMD-affiliated army division under the command of a former mining labor boss from Shandong. Relying on his connections with Oroqen fighters attached to the unit, he joined the division as an independent battalion commander and mining boss. When news of GMD military defeats reached his ears, he once again made overtures to the Eighth Route Army, yet he continued to hold back his Oroqen band of fighters until the tide of the civil war swung decisively in favor of Communist forces in 1948.

Wang closes his account with his eventual allegiance to the Communist army, yet the overall narrative that he presents privileges the period during which he operates in a continual state of shifting loyalties, fluid identities, and stealthy adaptations to an unpredictable political landscape. Instead of loyalty to the Party, communist ideology, or nationalist valor, Wang celebrates the triumph of the individual's chameleon-like cunning and survival instinct that overrides ideological concerns. The editor's introductory framing of the narrative in terms of bold local heroism differs from yet complements this emphasis on individual survival, both finding in post-Mao reforms a space for articulating a new vision of the relationship between individual agency, local and national identities, and the Communist Party-state.

---

[78] Ibid., 158.

Alongside this colorful, localized description of heroism that eschewed dominant nationalist and socialist interpretations, editors also resurrected and celebrated local customs, legends, songs, and religious practices that had been submerged beneath revolutionary discourse. This was again emphasized in the standard questionnaires assigned to interviewers in Fujin, which included the prompts "Collect and compile representative folk legends, stories, and songs" and "Describe every kind of seasonal custom and their concrete practices."[79] Many of the folktales that they collected employed images of the supernatural to highlight themes of economic opportunity. One story circulating in the area around Donggou in former southeast Manchuria describes an old migrant couple from Shandong who sets sail from Shandong across the Bohai Sea to a valley on the north side of a mountain that is uninhabited. They hire a male youth to help them work the land, and the high-quality grass that he feeds their donkey each day catches the old man's attention.

One day the old man asked the young helper, "Son, how is it that you find such excellent grass every day?" The youth replied, "I don't really know myself. There is a patch of grass in the valley, not very large. On the first day I cut some grass, then when I went back the next day to have a look, the exact same kind of grass had grown back. Over and over again and there is always more grass." When the old man heard this he exploded with laughter and said, "How could there be anything like that in this world?"[80]

Unbelievingly the old man follows the youth to this piece of land and, to his amazement, the following day all the grass they had cut the previous day had grown back in full. Determined to discover the secret to this mystery, he digs up a stone trough from underneath the grass and takes it back home with him. Seeing no use for it, he lays it down as a feeding trough for the pigs, which within a few days fatten up enormously despite being fed little.

Then one day, without thinking, the old man left the hoe inside the trough and told his young helper, "Today I want you to go and loosen up the soil." The young helper nodded in agreement. Before they knew it was afternoon, and the old man happened to notice that the hoe was still sitting in the trough. So he asked his wife, "The lad didn't go out to work the soil?" His wife answered, "What a memory you have! You were the one who sent him off early this morning, weren't you? He left early." The old man was really puzzled: "That can't be right, if he went out to work the land how come the hoe is still sitting there in the trough?" His wife stood

---

[79] Fujin xian zhengxie, "Reference Outline for Asking Old Comrades to Write Memoirs," 3.
[80] Qiu Yupeng and Gao Changyuan, "Jubao pen" ("The Treasure-Generating Trough"), Dongou xian minjian wenxue santao jicheng bianwei hui, *Dongou ziliao ben (Folk Literature Materials from Dongou County)* (Dongou, 1986): 272–274.

confounded when she saw it as well, and both felt that there was something very fantastical about this trough . . .

The old couple's lives grew more prosperous with each passing day.[81]

This example of the folktales collected during this time conveys a story of limitless possibilities for becoming rich that fed into the post-Mao narrative of economic development in a way that celebrated the historical glories of the northeast region as the leading frontier of agricultural and commercial expansion.

Historical accounts in the *wenshi ziliao*, while less fantastical, nevertheless drew on the same themes to describe migration to the northeast as a release from the shackles of previous economic despair and a space where one could fulfill ambitions and desires unconstrainedly. "There was no need to register one's household," as one article about eastern Manchuria put it, "nor any obligation to pay respects to the local village head . . . Possibly after the passing of a year or two the owner of the land might seek one out. Then he would be perfectly happy to let the tenant cultivate the land and work out an agreement whereby one is rent-free for the first three years" and "can pass the days focusing on one's own affairs."[82] According to a migrant recollection about Guandongshan Mountain in Jilin Province,

One can choose a nice sunlit spot protected from the wind, dig poles into the ground for a cabin and lay on straw tightly for the roof, put together a *keng* that heats easily, and it's enough to get by. The valley streams have water and the hills are covered with dry wood. In winter one can get a fire roaring and kids stay warm wearing a single layer of clothing. In spring the flowers blossom and one can cultivate the earth using primitive tools, sharpen a few oak branches.

Poke some holes with the sticks and insert corn seeds. Since the soil had over a hundred years' worth of decayed vegetation, loose and fertile, one can plant as much as one wants. As long as one can obtain seeds, there's no need to shovel the soil in summer, and come fall one would have a good harvest![83]

The celebration of the northeast as a magical, limitless, and wild frontier in these folktales and personal reminiscences brought to the fore a colorful and variegated assortment of characters and images that prioritized local diversity and particularity over national Party ideology.

Conclusion

The *wenshi ziliao* inherited earlier Chinese modernizing and revolutionary projects of (attempting to) align "objective" scientific research methodology with the "subjective" work of building national and revolutionary

---

[81] Ibid.   [82] *Tonghua wenshi ziliao*, 1: 41–42.   [83] Ibid.

consciousness. Neither cynically propagandist nor naïve about the trans-parency of historical truth, officials, editors, and writers creatively inter-vened in and reinterpreted Maoist concepts to add complexity and nuance to the historical record. Driven by their different agendas, parti-cipants at the national, provincial, and county levels adopted a wide range of abstract meanings and concrete applications of "seeking truth from facts" to recalibrate the relationship between complex historical realities and Party-centered national discourse. Disagreeing over the political implications of certain historical accounts and sparring over control of how the project was to be implemented, writers and editors selectively reappropriated ideas about locally based testimonial authenticity and systematic ordering of knowledge to assert their prerogatives and stake their claims. This spectrum of interpretations of "seeking truth from facts" informed the varied dimensions of *wenshi ziliao* content and accom-modated individualized and localized understandings of liberation and heroism that stretched the limits of the national Party-centered discourse.

   In the next chapter we move from scientific to affective discourses and strategies that *wenshi ziliao* organizers used to bring about healing and reconciliation.

5 Affective Community and Historical Rehabilitation
"Widely Making Friends" to Resecure Political Loyalty

Introduction

Along with "seeking truth from facts," post-trauma healing and reconciliation were core concerns of the *wenshi ziliao*. Capitalizing on the PPCC's lack of formal political power and its historical role as a United Front organization mediating between the Party and other organizations, officials presiding over the *wenshi ziliao* used the rhetoric of informal affective community to win the trust and compliance of individuals inducted into the PPCC. Masking the Party's close supervision over PPCC activities and downplaying their concurrent position as Party Committee officials, PPCC leaders attempted to create a sentimental, home-like atmosphere. At the same time, the acts of conducting interviews, collecting testimonies, and editing historical materials contributed to a broader itinerary of investigation and consultation that conferred on PPCC members a sense of privileged access and authority in the Party's decision-making process, implementation of reforms, and evaluation of local conditions. Through performing these acts along with writing their own personal narratives, PPCC members used the stages of *wenshi ziliao* memory work to re-suture the bond between the Party and members of their social class. This healing process was always a tenuous one that was predicated on these alienated individuals' constant suspense about their acceptance by the Party. Certain particularities in the history of the northeast borderland, such as its incorporation into the Japanese empire earlier than other parts of China, intensified debates and uncertainties about how to define the restored United Front and who belonged in it. As with shifting definitions of "seeking truth from facts," local cadres appropriated the healing dimension of *wenshi ziliao* to validate local identities that did not fit neatly into the Party-centered narrative and to reassert traditional native place values as an affective framework for attracting overseas investments in local development.

The *wenshi ziliao* mobilized historical testimonies to bring about healing and reconciliation in the aftermath of collective trauma, provide evidence supporting rehabilitation of and compensation to victims of state-orchestrated abuse, and pave the way for reintegrating society and rebuilding a unified nation. These characteristics situate *wenshi ziliao* within the international movement of truth and reconciliation that emerged in the 1980s, beginning in Latin America and then spreading to postcommunist Eastern Europe and postapartheid South Africa. Facing the challenge of securing the support of constituents who had suffered abuses under the former regime without alienating supporters of the previous government, a range of governmental and nongovernmental actors turned to truth and reconciliation commissions as a restorative justice approach to democratic transition and national reintegration.

In China, the *wenshi ziliao* version of restorative justice took place in a somewhat different context in which the regime sponsoring the project was overseeing its own transition, reinvention, and restoration. For this reason, there were several distinctive features of *wenshi ziliao* truth and reconciliation. First, *wenshi ziliao* participants did not directly address the traumatic events (i.e., the Cultural Revolution) that had transpired, given their dangerous implications for the Party's reputation. Instead, they reverted to a pre–Cultural Revolution and even pre-Communist past, indirectly acknowledging historical wrongdoings committed by the Party and compensating victims without undermining the overall historical legitimacy of the Party.

Second, unlike the clear delineation of victim and perpetrator that was central to other truth and reconciliation commissions, *wenshi ziliao* theorists emphasized complexity and multiple-sidedness in their evaluation of Chinese historical actors. This was in large part due to the Party's own multiple dimensions of victimhood and perpetration during the Cultural Revolution, which made the clear ideological designation of historical events and people as either right or wrong particularly difficult and politically unsound for the Party. The *wenshi ziliao*'s resulting emphasis on complexity and multiple dimensions was part of a larger cultural movement that some critical observers in China at the time referred to as "complexity fever." A proponent of this in the literary world explained that "there can be no 'black and white' judgments. Some readers are against complexity in characterization, but in fact complexity is richer than simplicity in literary creation, so long as the complexity is both artistic and realistic, and instructs as well as pleases the reader.'"[1] In the case of the *wenshi ziliao*, "complexity fever" translated into the absence of victim and perpetrator as categories. This not only contributed to a more

---

[1] Xiaoye You, "Ideology, Textbooks, and the Rhetoric of Production in China," *College Composition and Communication* 56.4 (June 2005): 640–641.

expansive and inclusive united front discourse but also implicitly protected the Party from historical liability for the recent political disasters.

Third, whereas especially in the case of South Africa the truth and
reconciliation commissions affirmed the authenticity and truthfulness of
victim testimonies, as Gillian Whitlock and others have shown, *wenshi
ziliao* editors had an ambivalent attitude toward their informants.[2] While
privileging the "three first-hands" (seeing, hearing, and experiencing) as
critical to *wenshi ziliao*, editors (as seen in the previous chapter) viewed
their informants as raw materials that needed to be "refined" and as
ideologically suspect. As a result, they used specific strategies in their
interviewing sessions to coax open-ended truth confessions from their
subjects while carefully containing their narratives within Party-approved
parameters.

These distinguishing features point to broader themes in the *wenshi
ziliao* approach to truth and reconciliation. Gil Eyal, in his comparative
study of postcommunist transitions in Slovakia and the Czech
Republic, identifies "individuation" and "embeddedness" as two
kinds of "wills to memory": "In one version [embeddedness], memory
is the guarantor of *identity* and maintains it through time – it is the
mechanism of *retention* responsible for the experience of being
a selfsame individual moving through time; in the other version [indi-
viduation], however, memory plays a role in overcoming psychic
trauma and the processes of dissociation it sets in motion. Individuals
are healed by remembering that which was repressed."[3] In the context
of Eastern Europe, he notes that the release of repressed memories
about abuses and suffering under the communist regime, or individuation, was the dominant mode of remembrance among dissident historians in the Czech Republic, whereas in Slovakia, where historians
employed under the previous government maintained their status
across the transition, the tendency was to forge a continuous historical
narrative emphasizing the preservation and continuity of national
identity.[4]

In China, the *wenshi ziliao*'s dual purposes of preserving and consolidating the Communist Party's monopoly on national authority while
opening a space for healing, reconciliation, and liberalizing reform
informed an approach to regime transition that integrated embeddedness
with individuation, or, to adapt Bakhtin's concept of intersecting

---

[2] Gillian Whitlock, "Review Essay: The Power of Testimony," *Law and Literature* 19.1
(Spring 2007): 139–152.
[3] Eyal, "Identity and Trauma," 7.   [4] Ibid.

tendencies of order and disruption in the cultural world, "centripetal" unifying and "centrifugal" decentralizing forces.[5]

This post-Mao model of memory work drew on Chinese Communist traditions of United Front, democratic centralism, mass line, and investigative research that built local flexibility and diversity into the equation of central Party control. At the same time, it was quite different from other modes of transitional justice and remembrance that characterized the early post-Mao period. On one extreme was the Gang of Four trial that prioritized retribution over reconciliation and intensively condensed all responsibility for the Cultural Revolution on four individuals. On the other extreme was the outpouring of "wounded literature," "towering wall literature," and other memoirs and fictional stories that filled in the gaps of widespread personal suffering left out of the official trial narrative. As Ban Wang writes, these literary expressions of traumatic suffering were, in contrast with the carefully framed trial verdict, incoherent, fragmented, and disjointed. "The traumatic memory is memory in wreckage. It is, as Shoshana Felman puts it, 'composed of bits and pieces of a memory that has been overwhelmed by occurrences that have not settled into understanding or remembrance, acts that cannot be construed as knowledge nor assimilated into full cognition, events in excess of our frames of reference.'"[6] These responses to the post–Cultural Revolution crisis dealt in a direct, detailed, and incisive way with the collective trauma, but between them they left open a gaping chasm between official and unofficial versions of history that could not be bridged without threatening the integrity of Party authority.

The *wenshi ziliao* of course did not deal directly with this traumatic historical experience, but it did provide a resolution to the dilemma of how to close the gap between state-sponsored and personal historical memories. Rather than the contrast between carefully orchestrated official spectacle and fragmented individualized recollections, the *wenshi ziliao* brought the state into the intimate domain of memory and healing and attempted to enfold the personal and incoherent into the "grand narrative" of Party and nation.

Given the state's sponsorship of the project, it can be easy to dismiss the *wenshi ziliao* as merely state propaganda with little or no real search for truth and justice. However, in its essence, even those truth and reconciliation commissions that have been generally recognized as successful in achieving these ends – most notably the one in South Africa – have been

---

[5] Gary Saul Morson and Caryl Emerson, *Mikhail Bakhtin: Creation of a Prosaics* (Stanford, CA: Stanford University Press, 1990), 30, cited and discussed in Michael Berry, *A History of Pain: Trauma in Modern Chinese Literature and Film* (New York, NY: Columbia University Press, 2008), 7.

[6] Wang, *Illuminations from the Past*, 114–115.

criticized for compromising truth in the pursuit of political reconciliation and national unity. Indeed, scholars such as Onur Bakiner have been troubled by the nation-centered and nation-building dimension of these institutions, and have noted the continual tension between the transformational aspect of truth telling and the conciliatory tendency to re-embed truth and reconciliation narratives within a stable political framework.[7] Theorizing more generally about the relationship between memory and reconciliation, Torsten Weber, drawing on the ideas of Aleida and Jan Assmann, notes that political reconciliation may only be possible through a conscious effort at "selective forgetting."[8]

These tensions were at the heart of the *wenshi ziliao*. At the same time, the *wenshi ziliao* project incorporated all three core elements of "mutual respect," including critical reflection on the past ("seeking truth from facts"), symbolic and material recognition (toward PPCC members and other alienated local elites), and political participation (through PPCC consultation processes), that Ernesto Verdeja identifies as defining characteristics of truth and reconciliation.[9] These criteria of critical truth seeking, symbolic and material recognition, and political participation were of course limited and enclosed significantly, and in respect to the first and second criteria, the concrete "legal-forensic" aspects of accountability, justice, and compensation for past abuses was much less evident that the more symbolic "narrative-historical" dimension of rewriting history.[10] Nevertheless, they were integral features of *wenshi ziliao* that were taken seriously by participants at all levels, and therefore deserve our serious consideration.

Another important issue with respect to the implementation of truth and reconciliation pertains to relations between different levels of society and the accommodation of multiple contesting voices. In their recommendations for effective practices of restorative justice, Erin Daly and Jeremy Sarkin-Hughes present a model of layered reconciliation that is centralized and nationally unified yet flexibly adapted and implemented locally.[11] Onur Bakiner points to the messiness of contesting voices and

---

[7] Onur Bakiner, "One Truth among Others? Truth Commissions' Struggle for Truth and Memory," *Memory Studies* 8.3 (July 2015): 346–350.
[8] Torsten Weber, "Forgetting and Forgiving: the Relation between Memory and Historical Reconciliation in Post–World War Two Japanese–Chinese Relations." Paper presented for panel "The Operations of Forgetting: Wars and the Making of the Asia-Pacific Region from the 17th Century to the Present" at AAS Conference, Toronto, March 18, 2017.
[9] Ernesto Verdeja, "Political Reconciliation in Postcolonial Settler Societies," *International Political Science Review* 38.2 (March 2017): 231–237.
[10] "Legal-forensic" and "narrative-historical" are terms that I borrow here from Bakiner, "One Truth among Others?" 346.
[11] Erin Daly and Jeremy Sarkin-Hughes, *Reconciliation in Divided Societies: Finding Common Ground* (Philadelphia, PA: University of Pennsylvania Press, 2007), 17.

perspectives that comprise these practices at the ground level.[12] Again, the structure and proliferation of *wenshi ziliao* committees at the county, city, provincial, and national levels, a dynamic discussed in more detail in Chapter 7, engendered a layered process of interpretations and narrative making. Political consolidation did not shut down contesting voices. Instead, the project of healing from the Cultural Revolution and producing a more inclusive united front with local elites required accommodating different perspectives and agendas of informants and editors at different levels whose liminal status in relation to the Party made them a constant source of transformation and reintegration.

"No Wearing Caps, No Beatings, No Pulling on Queues"

The Party reevaluated its relationship to society in terms of a more inclusive "revolutionary patriotic united front," and the United Front Office regarded the PPCC as a critical instrument for extending the Party's reach beyond narrow social class lines. In Fuyuan, the chair of the PPCC's work team committee, Wen Zhongkui, asserted in a speech at a local work conference on the United Front that the working class cannot stand alone and needs support from a broad social coalition. The PPCC, he argued, is the agent for building this coalition.[13]

In other reports, PPCC cadres justified the more inclusive approach by arguing that the socialist revolution had already succeeded in eradicating the capitalist class. As Dai Zhenhuan writes in his draft of the annual Fujin PPCC work report in 1980, "Socialist workers, farmers, intellectuals and other patriots who uphold socialism are [now] the mainstay of our country's society. Building and developing socialist enterprise and realizing the four modernizations is the shared interest and basic desire of all these people. So, the political foundation of united front in the new period [since 1978] is more developed and stronger than in any other period [and] is more expansive than in any other period. It is a revolutionary patriotic united front, a very expansive coalition."[14]

This redefinition of what constituted the revolutionary class was at the core of the PPCC's historical identity as an institution. Functioning as

---

[12] Bakiner, "One Truth among Others?"

[13] Wen Zhongkui, "Zai quanxian tongzhan gongzuo huiyi shang de jianghua" ("Speech at the United Front Work Conference for the Entire County") (April 28, 1987) (Fuyuan City Archives): 2.

[14] Dai Zhenhuan, "Zhongguo renmin zhengzhi xieshang huiyi fujin xian diwu jie weiyuanhui changwu weiyuanhui gongzuo baogao (caoan)" ("Draft of Work Report of [the] Fifth Session of [the] Standing Committee of Fujin County PPCC") (Delivered on Sept. 17, 1980, at the Fifth Session of the Fujin County PPCC) (Fujin City Archives): 4–5.

a mediator between Party and non-Party-affiliated organizations and selecting people largely on the basis of their training and expertise in various areas rather than on their Party credentials, the PPCC came under attack during the Cultural Revolution for harboring "counterrevolutionaries." Of the fifty-five people who were members of the Fujin PPCC at the start of the Cultural Revolution, according to Dai Zhenhuan, the "vast majority were wrongly attacked and vilified. Some were seized as capitalist roaders, some had to don hats as special suspects, some were framed as reactionary academics. Regardless, they all went through an excruciating ordeal," and he lauds them for never giving up on the Party's leadership or socialist vision.[15]

When the *wenshi ziliao* project was partially revived in the mid-1970s (full recovery did not take place until the early 1980s), it became an instrument by which a faction of central Party officials led by Zhou Enlai attempted to discredit the leftist "Gang of Four" as the Cultural Revolution began to wind down. To this end, Zhou helped orchestrate the release from prison and rehabilitation of political prisoners and their reassignment as PPCC members as early as 1972 when Nixon's visit inaugurated a somewhat more open atmosphere. While PPCC activities during these years were limited, confined to "arranging flowers, cleaning, and reading newspapers and central government directives," after 1975, former *wenshi ziliao* committee members reapplied the work of salvaging history to undermining the political credentials of the leftist faction. Shen Meijuan later recalled that her father, after spending five years in prison, returned to the desolate *wenshi ziliao* office of the PPCC in Beijing to write historical essays exposing the Gang of Four leaders' complicity with military authorities prior to 1949. Reemerging as discursive artillery against political rivals, *wenshi ziliao* was dangerous work in which political threats in the present and the reconstruction of pre-1949 events collided. According to Shen, so dire were the threats to her father's life during this period of *wenshi ziliao* production that he resided night and day within the PPCC headquarters.[16]

As Deng Xiaoping's reform leadership assumed a dominant foothold on power in 1978, the immediate political purposes of salvaging history changed from waging factional warfare to mobilizing broad-based support for the new regime. Referring back in the early 1980s to this violent period as a temporary aberration and setback, in line with the Party leadership's view on the Cultural Revolution as a whole, Fujin PPCC cadre Dai Zhenhuan redefined socialist revolution in terms of continuity

---

[15] Ibid., 3–4.
[16] Shen Meijuan, "National PPCC and Shen Zui Father and Daughter," 75.

and peaceful cooperation rather than class struggle and division. Essentially equating revolution with economic development, he argued that broad-based inclusivity in the form of a united front was critical to the success of both.[17]

Establishing connections beyond narrow Party circles to garner broader-based support for the Party constituted a primary purpose of the PPCCs at every level. To achieve this, PPCC leaders invoked a discourse of affective community that was tied to the institution's distinctive political function and organizational features. Unlike political organizations like the People's Congress and Party committees that vested in their members' policy-making responsibilities, the PPCC's role lacked concrete legal status and was limited to "political consultation, democratic supervision, and policy recommendation."

Yet it was precisely this informal, marginal role of the PPCC that created a flexible, politically safe space in which to simultaneously tolerate and contain grievances against and deviation from the Party line. It provided a semi-formal institutional channel, under Party supervision yet somewhat removed from the formal Party structure, through which alienated members of society could vent their anxieties about and criticisms of state policies in a relatively unfettered manner without spilling outside the Party's control. The casual and informal nature of many PPCC activities is reflected in common sayings that circulated among PPCC members, such as "if you think of it then consult, if you don't think of it then don't bother," and "whatever you say makes no difference." A common saying that expanded on the latter phrase indicates the combination of political pressure and powerlessness that PPCC members frequently felt: "if you don't say it then you simply don't say it, yet it's pointless when you do say it, and furthermore even though it's pointless to say it you still have to say it."[18] Moreover, People's Congresses and Party committees regularly made policy decisions before receiving recommendations from the PPCC. One schoolteacher recalled his school's recommendation that he join an education small group within the newly formed Harbin PPCC committee. In accordance with the PPCC principle of "no wearing caps, no beatings, no pulling on queues," in discussions on faculty housing and salaries he freely vented about teachers' low compensation. Aware that his words would have no concrete impact on policy

[17] Dai Zhenhuan, "Draft of Work Report of [the] Fifth Session of [the] Standing Committee of Fujin County PPCC," 5–6.
[18] Huang Feng, "Zai renmin zhengxie gongzuo de rizi li – huigu, ganshou yu sikao" ("The Days of Working at the PPCC – Reminiscences, Sentiments, and Reflections"), in *Wo yu zhengxie*, 56–65.

change, he nevertheless commented that "after all the infringements on democracy, this free space for expression already made us satisfied."[19]

The PPCC leaders reformulated the institution's lack of formal power in terms of a less tangible power of family-like harmony and unity. Intended to reforge a united front between the party-state and intellectuals, the PPCC disguised hierarchy and refashioned it as family paternalism. Even as they were closely monitored by the Party and frequently held concurrent posts in Party committees, PPCC leaders defined their role as embodying the true democratic spirit of the Party in contrast with the hierarchical constraints and political calculations that embroiled the formal party-state apparatus. A discourse of democratic unity and authentic expression naturalized ideological indoctrination and masked political coercion. From the outset, Zhou Enlai developed personal relationships with PPCC members as a way to reinscribe them within the political structure. He showed an interest in their everyday concerns like housing and medical issues while coaxing out of them political confessions and revealing memoirs.[20] As manager of the national PPCC reception room between 1959 and 1961, Geng Wenru recalled her role in creating a relaxing refuge from the political campaigns and attending to the members' everyday comforts, diversions, and amenities, including food and recreation.[21] Shen Meijuan reflected on her childhood days spent in the *wenshi ziliao* office in the early 1960s while her father, an amnestied former GMD officer, wrote articles commissioned by Zhou Enlai. She described the PPCC less as a political institution than as an affective familial community. In addition to having her meals in the PPCC cafeteria and studying and resting in the *wenshi ziliao* office, she recalls with nostalgia the festivities they celebrated with Zhou and other high-ranking Party officials as well as the affectionate attention she received from Deng Yingchao in spite of her youthful "shyness and barely muttered Hunan accent."[22]

Cultivating affective community was an important strategy by which Party leaders sought to bring about political healing and to reincorporate alienated scientists, intellectuals, and entrepreneurs. One of the initial goals of the restored PPCC committees was to coax people to tell their

[19] Zhu Xiufang, "Zhengxie wei wo dakai le canzheng yizheng de damen" ("My Introduction by the PPCC to Political Consultation"), in ibid., 178–180.

[20] Ma Yongshun, "Zhou Enlai xinian zhengxie dangwai weiyuan he gaoji minzhu renshi" ("Zhou Enlai's Concern for Non-Party PPCC Members and Prominent Democratic Leaders"), *Wenshi ziliao xuanji* 154: 50–64.

[21] Geng Wenru, "Sannian kunnan shiqi wo zai quanguo zhengxie litang de jingli" ("My Experiences in the Reception Hall of the National PPCC during Three Years of Hardship"), *Wenshi ziliao xuanji* 155: 92–100.

[22] Shen Meijuan, "National PPCC and Shen Zui Father and Daughter."

stories of hardship and persecution as a preliminary step toward rebuilding a broad-based Party-led coalition. However, given these individuals' recent experience with the dire consequences of telling the "wrong" story, conventional political study sessions were ineffective in breaking the wall of silence. Instead, the PPCC leadership used the discourse of "family" and "home" to depoliticize PPCC activities. In 1974, the Harbin PPCC assembled people from various economic, scientific, and intellectual sectors of society. As concurrent director of the United Front Bureau and the city PPCC, Ma Kaiyin led in the initiative to draw out people's Cultural Revolution stories and release pent-up grievances. In order to penetrate the veil of polite discourse, he invited them into an intimate emotional space by sharing with them his own experiences of psychological terror and confusion. Placing himself in this vulnerable and empathetic position temporarily suspended the political authority vested in his Party rank and elicited a more open discussion.[23] People who may have been reticent about opening themselves up to the PPCC often described their induction into the PPCC as a kind of conversion experience triggered by a PPCC leader's personal charisma. Asked to resume his collection of *wenshi ziliao* materials in 1981, Liu Feilin recalled the benevolent features of the PPCC vice-director's face.[24]

The PPCC leaders invoked this rhetoric of affective community to distinguish their role from that of formal Party committee officials even as they mediated between, if not concurrently serving, both roles. In memoirs published later by the Heilongjiang PPCC, former members of the organization wrote down recollections that were clearly idealized, yet reflect the strategic discourse of affective community that PPCC leaders employed to resecure and naturalize political loyalties. Recalling his induction into the Heilongjiang PPCC after the Cultural Revolution, a professor commented that the "upper and lower ranks were united in harmony" and "entering the room was like breathing in fresh spring air," contrasting it against the "yamen style" atmosphere of the government. Intellectuals who joined the PPCC articulated their indoctrination and reincorporation into the Party as a process of voluntary surrender that naturalized coercive mechanisms. The professor quoted earlier described himself as an "intellectual from the old society with many faults who did not give in easily when confronted. But in the big family setting of the PPCC he surrendered. If the PPCC could get someone like him to surrender, then it could win over anyone and draw them into united front."[25] Reconstructing a recent

[23] Ma Kaiyin, "Half of My Life with the Harbin City PPCC," 311–313.

[24] Liu Feilin, "Thirty Years' Reflections on Literary and Historical Work," 359.

[25] Chen Di, "Tuanjie xiyin zhishifenzi de hao defang" ("A Good Place for Uniting and Appealing to Intellectuals"), in *Wo yu zhengxie*, 136–139.

conversation among his peers at a gathering of Heilongjiang PPCC members, Zhang Wenda characterized the PPCC as a democratic space where communist egalitarianism finds its most authentic expression. In the conversation, a Heilongjiang University professor allegedly asked, "Why is it that the PPCC, which has no real power, has such great unifying and influential power?" In response, another professor pointed out its democratic nature: "From the chairman to the average member, there is no division between people and officials, no hierarchy. People can say what they want openly and whoever gives a good proposal will be taken seriously."[26]

In order to resecure the loyalties of alienated groups and individuals, therefore, PPCC organizations adopted strategies of "widely making friends," extending economic assistance, and tapping into non-Party members' social networks and organizational affiliations to expand the Party's influence. A work report of the PPCC in Fujin, drafted by Guan Chengzheng, describes efforts to make non-Party participants feel at home and develop a sense of communal solidarity and familiarity within the organization. "Last year we visited thirty-nine members' homes, visited their work units twenty-two times, and participated in member-organized activities thirty-one times. We organized members to participate in activities like a ping pong competition sponsored by the sports committee, qigong, elderly disco dancing, etc. in order to increase their connection and familiarity with each other and enrich their lives."[27]

Committee leaders at all levels had to strike a delicate balance between identifying with rank-and-file members and securing their conformity to Party dictates. Among the strategies employed to accomplish this was the coleadership of vice-directors with complementary political and economic credentials. Ma Kaiyin, who served as vice-chair of the Harbin PPCC from its founding in 1955, recalled the challenges of setting non-Party members to work on committee tasks. Concurrently director of the United Front Department of the city's Party Committee, Ma offset his close connection with the Party leadership by appearing alongside codirectors with non-Party backgrounds, including prominent entrepreneur and industrialist Wu Baixiang. Ma described this coleadership dynamic as a harmonious blending of Party and business interests.[28]

---

[26] Zhang Wenda, "Fenwei" ("Work Atmosphere"), ibid., 350–352.
[27] Guan Chengzheng, "Work Report of the First Session of the Fujin City PPCC's Standing Committee," 3–4.
[28] Ma Kaiyin, "Half of My Life with the Harbin City PPCC."

"Democratic Political Consultation and Supervision"

Alongside making them feel at home in spite of their marginality from the Party, local PPCCs conferred on these individuals a renewed sense of relevance and significance that recent political campaigns had stripped from them. Co-opting them through a process called "democratic political consultation and supervision," the Party designated PPCC members as at once beneficiaries of and participants in the formulation and implementation of policies. Recruiting them into the organization based on their expertise and access to social networks, Party officials incorporated them into the political process in a consultative capacity in order to reintegrate various social groups, demonstrate the Party's accommodating flexibility without risking redistribution of power, and lend persuasive legitimacy to Party directives. This consultative role provided a mechanism for linking non-Party members of the PPCC more closely to the Party apparatus. In a work report of the Fujin PPCC's standing committee in 1987, Xu Zhanhai framed the policy consultation process as a means of demonstrating the Party's concern and respect for accomplished people outside the Party. In particular, he writes that over the previous three years the standing committee had conducted 275 interviews with regular PPCC members to "understand their thoughts and needs," which they then communicated to relevant bureaus of the local Party and government. As an example of this concern and respect, Xu notes the county Party Committee's serious consideration of a proposal by Zhang Minghe, PPCC vice-chair and manager of a water heating fittings factory, that "the people's town should be managed by the people." The local government allegedly planned to implement this recommendation and even forwarded it to the "provincial city civilization inspection team as an experience in building civilization." In addition to this individual case, Xu also mentions that PPCC members attended two "political consultation meetings" held by the county Party to discuss more than thirty recommendations regarding issues such as "policies toward intellectuals, developing the Chinese medicine industry, and securing residential electricity usage." This, according to the report, "not only gave play to members' consultative role, but also tightened their ties to the county Party and government."[29]

The PPCC members performed a watchdog role, pointing out issues both in society at large and endemic to the Party organization itself that

[29] Xu Zhanhai, "Zhongguo renmin zhengzhi xieshang huiyi fujin xian diqi jie weiyuanhui changwu weiyuanhui gongzuo baogao" ("Work Report of the Seventh Session of the Fujin County PPCC's Standing Committee") (Delivered on Oct. 13, 1987, at the First Meeting of the Eighth Session of the Fujin County PPCC) (Fujin City Archives): 4–5.

needed to be addressed. The use of *wenshi ziliao* as historical evidence to justify the reversal of past policies against various groups was in fact part of an array of PPCC activities geared toward identifying and resolving festering social, economic, and political problems that posed a threat to the Party's standing in local society. These activities included, in 1988, recommendations by PPCC members in Fujin to "avoid hastily razing old bathhouses; organize old retired [PPCC] members [with experience] in politics and law to form a legal consultation office; repair the contagious disease clinic and the peace clinic in the center of the city; create a unified system of city construction; and quickly put an end to the gambling trend."[30] In the same year, PPCC members also produced thirty reports exposing corruption within the Party, with the result that "[s]ome problems were investigated and dealt with right away, and some cadres who did illegal things received their just punishment."[31]

The PPCC used a number of interconnected channels, therefore, from conducting on-site investigations and interviews to writing letters and reports, to keep tabs on social conditions while monitoring the Party organization to ensure its ability to secure people's loyalty and govern effectively. Nevertheless, the Party leadership within the PPCC routinely expressed worry that these consultative meetings and discussions held little substance and failed to give full play to the concerns and expertise of these non-Party members. Their reports indicate a lack of consensus within the Party about how accommodating and flexible the political process should be and, by extension, to what degree PPCC members' voices should be heard in that process. This is reflected in concerns expressed in an internal Fujin PPCC memo that "some people mistakenly believe that [the PPCC] is 'superfluous,' that it is a 'resting place,' an 'old people's home,' etc." The author goes on to argue against this perception, asserting the organization's importance as a "united front organization" critical to formulating policies and achieving national consolidation.[32] In a report several years later to the county Party, the Party Committee within the Fujin PPCC complained that there was an "excess of discussion and not enough supervision and oversight," noting in particular the scant "criticism of the overlapping functions of the Party and administration." The committee also noted that "little significant work or progress has been made in regard to how to maximize PPCC talent to serve the city's four modernizations development," PPCC work "lacks planning,"

---

[30] Guan Chengzheng, "Work Report of the First Session of the Fujin City PPCC's Standing Committee," 1–3.

[31] Ibid.

[32] "Zhengxie fujin xian weiyuanhui gongzuo zongjie" ("Wrap-Up Summary of Fujin County PPCC's Work") (Dec. 31, 1981) (Fujin City Archives): 9–10.

and regular members have little to do.[33] The Party leadership within the PPCC, therefore, envisioned a powerful role for the PPCC as a vehicle for mobilizing talent and expertise from outside the Party to serve the Party's economic, political, and cultural agendas. From their perspective, the residual marginalization of these groups as politically unreliable amounted to a waste of human resources and a detriment to the reformist goals of development and reconsolidation.

To utilize these human resources more fully, PPCC leaders assigned experts in various fields to fan out into local villages and towns to conduct inspections while gathering and disseminating information, with the purpose of regenerating and reconstructing the local culture and economy. According to later recollections, the vice-chair of the Heilongjiang provincial PPCC, Zhang Ruilin, led his crew of investigators to localities like Yichun, Jixi, and Mudanjiang to inspect developments in areas such as medicine, reforestation, and mining work conditions. The Harbin PPCC, meanwhile, was involved in the establishment of a "model civilized village" in 1984. After entering the village of Kangjiacun, medical and agriculture experts integrated their collection of data on local conditions with an intensive program designed to educate and mobilize the residents for the "civilizing" and modernization of their village. A participant recalled that the secretary of the Party Committee within the PPCC mingled with the villagers and sat on a *kang* while lecturing them about the use of scientific methods to enrich them. Agriculture and medical experts then went out to the fields to treat diseases and give advice to farmers on issues like raising livestock, while PPCC cadres, in a move that he likened to the old Eighth Route Army spirit, joined villagers in repairing roads, digging wells, planting trees, and improving sewage and trashcans.[34]

These inspections were critical to cementing the state's control over the allocation and distribution of resources and reconsolidating Party authority. During one inspection trip in the 1980s, Zhang Ruilin recalls having led a work team down to local villages at the end of the harvest season to oversee implementation of the grain procurement policy. In one case, when he arrived at the granary of a production team to inspect the grain set aside for state procurement, the production team leader and the local Party secretary had disappeared to avoid dealing with resistance to the policy from farmers. The report that he sent back to the provincial Party committee elicited a firm response from the government that strictly

[33] Zhonggong zhengxie fujin xian dangzu, "Shi zhengxie gongzuo zongjie" ("Wrap-Up Summary of the City PPCC's Work") (Jan. 5, 1989) (Documents of the Fujin County PPCC's Party Subcommittee) (Fujin City Archives): 4–5.
[34] Ma Kaiyin, "Half of My Life with the Harbin City PPCC," 319–320.

enforced the policy. Yet he recalls that this case of local resistance and evasion led him to reflect on the possible reasons for local discontent and ways to revise the government's approach to grain procurement in a way that would be more amenable to rural conditions and would lighten the burden on farmers.[35]

Undertaking such ventures comprised a strategy of revitalizing the Party's broad-based mass appeal by integrating scientific expertise and detached analysis with compassionate sensibility and affective bonds. Women who participated in these campaigns could be particularly effective in presenting the goal of reasserting central control in the more appealing light of empathetic concern for residents. Members of the provincial PPCC's women's group, for instance, cooperated with the Women's Federation to evaluate medical conditions in various villages. In her narrative of what took place, one of the inspection team members recalls their determination to experience firsthand the primitive rural conditions of the local village rather than follow the local leader's recommendation to return to the comfortable accommodations in the county seat. This, she claims, enabled them to appreciate the villagers' lack of medicine and medical facilities, with the result that they subsequently organized medical teams to do charitable visits several times a year. She touts the success of these visits in terms of the PPCC's cultivation of a relationship grounded in empathy and gratitude between the Party and the local population. Residents, she recalls, were now able to see firsthand the concrete contributions of the PPCC to the local community and its display of the Party's warm embrace of the people, while she followed up on these visits with reports that conveyed local residents' real needs to the government.[36] The perceived vulnerability of the female cadres heightened the local perception of disarming sacrifice and self-abnegation associated with this PPCC mission. Whereas Zhang Ruilin's strict enforcement of the grain procurement policy elicited fear and evasion, the women's medical tours reconsolidated Party control through affective community.

Local Party leaders regarded *wenshi ziliao* as a bridge linking the consultation/supervision and on-the-ground inspection/implementation aspects of the PPCC. This is evident in the way in which the Fujin Party vice-secretary, Luo Wenxiao, structured his speech to the PPCC in 1985, situating the *wenshi ziliao* in the middle as the link between policy consultation and inspection visits:

[35] Wang Jinling, "Mianhuai Zhang Ruilin tongzhi" ("Remembering Comrade Zhang Ruilin"), in *Wo yu zhengxie*, 32–36.

[36] Zhang Yu, "Zhengxie weiyuan shi rongyu, geng shi zeren" ("The Honor and Responsibility of Being a PPCC Member"), in *Wo yu zhengxie*, 347–349.

According to statistics, in the past year PPCC members proposed twenty-three recommendations and opinions regarding important aspects of the county's political life, including Party style, social order, economic development, etc.; twenty-one regarding assisting the county Party and government in implementing united front policy; organized other members and people in society to edit and publish Fujin *wenshi ziliao*, volume two; mobilized members to go deeply into eighteen townships and thirty-six villages to carry out forty-three consultation services, amounting to 344 "people-times" . . .

He goes on to mention the role of these inspection and consultation visits in assisting in the development of township and village enterprises, providing medical treatment and supplies, establishing cooking study sessions in the countryside, and contributing in other ways to promoting social and economic modernization in remote areas.[37]

As these details suggest, the work of historical reconstruction was an integral part of a comprehensive PPCC initiative to mobilize non-Party expertise for reconstructing the economic, social, and cultural fabric of society at the local and regional levels. It was critical to closing the loop from inspection and mobilization to policy formulation and implementation and back again, through a continual process of interviewing, writing, editing, publishing, and circulating.

Local PPCC leaders positioned *wenshi ziliao* at the center of comprehensive efforts in the economic, social, and cultural domains to implement and assess campaigns of modernization and reconsolidation. This is evident in how the authors of work reports situated *wenshi ziliao* production in relation to other PPCC activities. In his draft of the Fujin PPCC standing committee work report in 1985, for instance, Wang Xingkun seamlessly inserts his update on *wenshi ziliao* collection and publication between a description of progress on local economic and technical assistance and a summary of advances on the educational and religious fronts. These are all contained within a section of the report addressing how PPCC members' inspection visits to remote areas contributed to the implementation of Party policies. He begins the section by acknowledging the important role of PPCC members with business experience in facilitating the development of new enterprises, training personnel, and finding markets for products. He then demonstrates how individuals with expertise in various areas contributed to advances in local medicine, agriculture, forestry, and commerce through collecting technical information, attending conferences, and writing articles and books on topics

---

[37] Luo Wenxiao, "Zai zhengxie fujin xian weiyuanhui 1985 niandu xianjin gongzuo zu xianjin weiyuan biaozhang dahui shang de jianghua" ("Speech at the Fujin County PPCC's Gathering to Praise the Model Personnel and Model Work Teams for the Year 1985") (Dec. 20, 1985) (Fujin City Archives): 1–2.

ranging from agricultural mechanization and forest development to pricing information in relation to border trade.[38]

In this context, Wang makes reference to the *wenshi ziliao*, writing that "some old members devoted to doing *wenshi ziliao* work ... widely collected and enthusiastically 'rescued' materials," leading to the publication of Fujin's first issue.[39] Immediately following this, in the same section of the report, he shifts attention to the cultural sphere, education and religion in particular. In regard to education, he describes PPCC education committee members' devotion to raising teaching standards in the classroom and advancing the "three roads" (teaching, learning, and thinking) of education reform, while also mentioning how one member, a retired Russian language teacher, contributed his expertise to the promotion of border trade by training border trade service personnel. As for the subject of religion, Wang comments on efforts to mend relations with religious minority groups while incorporating them within a Party-controlled framework. He notes, for instance, that one standing committee member reached out to the Hui community by overseeing the repair of a mosque, while another PPCC member "enthusiastically publicized the 'Three Self-Patriotic Movement' to local Protestants, advised them not to join underground churches, and organized the collective body of believers in one village into an officially approved congregation.[40] Through structuring the report in this way, Wang envisioned *wenshi ziliao* as connecting projects of economic and cultural reconsolidation, united by the shared process of inspection, collection, and dissemination of specialized information.

Restorative Rites of Confession and Redemption

The invitation to participate in these consultative and inspection activities served as a restorative rite of confession and redemption for those who had suffered alienation. In the border town of Fuyuan, a former manager in the local construction industry, Zhang Jitai, gave expression to this sentiment in a speech that he gave at the county's first PPCC meeting in 1980:

I was born and raised in Fuyuan, and now I'm old. In the first half of my life I did some things that were not beneficial to the people; today, being specially invited

---

[38] Wang Xingkun, "Zhongguo renmin zhengzhi xieshang huiyi fujin xian diqi jie weiyuan-hui changwu weiyuanhui gongzuo baogao" ("Work Report of the Seventh Session of the Fujin County PPCC's Standing Committee") (Delivered on March 15, 1985, at the Second Meeting of the Seventh Session of the Fujin County PPCC) (Fujin City Archives): 5–8.
[39] Ibid.   [40] Ibid., 5–8.

by the county party to join the PPCC, my heart palpitates with excitement! I am even more honored and feel great responsibility about being able to consult with fellow [PPCC] members about major policy issues. I want to use all my remaining energy to give full play to my strengths.[41]

Formulaic-sounding and undoubtedly intended to ingratiate himself with the Party, Zhang's speech nevertheless follows a structure of confession and redemption that provided an important mechanism for recalibrating the relationship between local elites and the Party.

Policy consultation directly impacted PPCC members and their families, serving to co-opt them into the political process by engaging them simultaneously as participants in and beneficiaries of policy formulation. According to one report, "as soon as problems were discovered, [PPCC members] would investigate, analyze, raise suggestions, and send [their recommendations] to the appropriate bureaus." Their recommendations had concrete results, such as arranging for a work transfer that allowed a retired Chinese medicine doctor to be close to his son, supplementing life support expenses for a former PPCC vice-chair, and supplying housing for several PPCC members including a retired teacher and an engineer. The PPCC's involvement in the policy-making process, therefore, involved highly specific and personalized actions. Through facilitating the communication of its members' issues and grievances to other government agencies, in this case the county's economic commission and hygiene and education departments, the PPCC presented to its members an image of the party-state apparatus as both effective and attuned to individual concerns.[42]

Local PPCC leaders sought to win over these individuals by granting them special favors and privileges. According to Guan's work report:

Whatever personnel ask for, [the PPCC] does its best to carry out. For example, a member's friend, Liu Changji, who was a graduate of Tianjin medical school and a doctor of the Daqing urology department, wanted to return to Fujin to set up a private hospital. We made connections for him and helped create favorable conditions; when member Li Lianhai ran into building and financial problems with his dental hospital, we helped him with making connections above and below; when top chef Xu Zhaomao couldn't find an ideal location for expanding his craft, we made contacts all over and found a suitable place and also helped him set up over ten sessions for teaching families how to elevate their cooking style; etc.[43]

---

[41] "Wei jianzhu gongye shixian sige xiandaihua gongxian liliang – zhang jitai tongzhi zai xian shoujie zhengxie huiyi shang de fayan" ("Contributing Forcefully to the Realization of the Four Modernizations in the Construction Industry – Comrade Zhang Jitai's Speech at the First Session of the Fuyuan County PPCC") (Sept. 28, 1980) (Fuyuan City Archive): 2.

[42] "Wrap-Up Summary of Fujin County PPCC's Work," 9–10.

[43] Guan Chengzheng, "Work Report of the First Session of the Fujin City PPCC's Standing Committee," 3–4.

These forms of economic assistance went hand in hand with a more fundamental political rehabilitation and economic restitution for those who had lost both status and property during the Cultural Revolution. The PPCC acted as the mediator and reconciler between the Party and this aggrieved group, implementing restorative policies at the concrete, individual level. This involved systematic efforts to resolve individual cases of "grievous mistakes" during the Cultural Revolution such as "mistaken designation as rightists" and the confiscation of private property.[44] In this process, the PPCC functioned simultaneously as the agent and the object of political healing and rehabilitation, since the majority of its members were selected from outside the Party. While housed within the Party apparatus, the organization served as a selective microcosm of non-Party social elements and as a laboratory for experimenting with new social policies.

Members of the PPCC, therefore, had the ambiguous status of being at once consultants in policy formulation, targets of political reeducation, recipients of rehabilitative measures, and investigators carrying out state-sponsored campaigns like the *wenshi ziliao*. As the first line of people to benefit from restorative policies, they were utilized as a catalyst for expanding political allegiance to the Party. In Fujin, a "PPCC member policy investigation small committee" was formed to investigate and resolve non-Party members' economic and political grievances. This committee "convened meetings of [members'] work units to implement tasks," "meetings of people filing lawsuits," "discussion forums," "interview visits," and spot-checking inspections." The results of these meetings, interviews, and inspections included "over twenty instances of implementing and resolving the return of private residences and property, the repair of mosques, the enrollment of children in school, and other remaining problems." Those who had specialized skills that could be useful for the "four modernizations" were of particular interest to this committee, as reflected in its assistance in housing and income to twenty-five technicians.[45] According to his annual report on behalf of the Fujin PPCC's standing committee in 1987, Xu Zhanhai noted that he and his colleagues cooperated with the Party's United Front office and other departments to attend to eighty cases addressing past grievances, including "two policy documents regarding politics and history, seven on remaining problems with rectifying incorrectly labeled rightists, seven on residual problems regarding former businesspeople, three on the

---

[44] Wang Xingkun, "Work Report of the Seventh Session of the Fujin County PPCC's Standing Committee," 1–3.
[45] Ibid.

issue of returning private residences, three on the problem of material compensation, and one on the issue of old red army participants ... Among six [PPCC] personnel who were restored to their ranks, their children were given employment."[46]

These restorative measures drove the PPCC's expansion as an organization, which officials in the PPCC were quick to note as a measure of institutional vitality and influence. Itemizing the Fujin PPCC's main accomplishments in a work report in 1984, Xu Zhanhai noted that:

[T]he PPCC organization is gradually developing, and the scope of its networks and consolidation is broadening. At the first meeting of its sixth session [in 1980], the number of personnel, including chairs and vice-chairs, was triple what it had been at the first meeting of the fifth session prior to the "Cultural Revolution." The number of members more than doubled. Besides members, we have also invited people from various fields to attend activities. The PPCC has been directly and indirectly connecting with more and more people, and the number of people applying to become members and attending events is increasing each year. It is becoming a representative, fairly expansive patriotic united front organization.[47]

The "united front" policy of expanded political inclusion that infused *wenshi ziliao* revisionary history was the bloodline for the PPCC's survival and growth as an institution. Beyond other considerations of the Party leadership at various levels, therefore, the process of political reconciliation and reinterpretation became a self-sustaining vested interest for PPCC cadres who were continually seeking justification for additional resources and staff hires.

Vaunting the organization's contributions to the Party's influence and prestige, PPCC work reports proclaimed that "implementation of the Party's united front policy has incited people from all sectors to support and trust in the Party."[48] In Fujin, according to such reports, thirteen PPCC members had gloriously joined the party by 1985, increasing two years later to twenty, which "did away with the confused view that PPCC members 'cannot' join the Party."[49] In addition to entry into the Party, the report from 1985 notes that "some [of these individuals] are willing to devote their lives to serving the Party in the area of education ... some are

---

[46] Xu Zhanhai, "Work Report of the Seventh Session of the Fujin County PPCC's Standing Committee," 8–9.

[47] Xu Zhanhai, "Zhongguo renmin zhengzhi xieshang huiyi fujin xian diliu jie weiyuanhui changwu weiyuanhui gongzuo baogao" ("Work Report of the Sixth Session of the Fujin County PPCC's Standing Committee") (Delivered on Apr. 6, 1984, at the First Meeting of the Seventh Session of the Fujin County PPCC") (Fujin City Archive): 2.

[48] Wang Xingkun, "Work Report of the Seventh Session of the Fujin County PPCC's Standing Committee," 1–3.

[49] Ibid.; Xu Zhanhai, "Work Report of the Seventh Session of the Fujin County PPCC's Standing Committee," 8–9.

willing to devote themselves to 'opening up the 3 rivers and enriching the people with enterprise' to enliven Fuji's economy," and, referring to the *wenshi ziliao*, "some transmit their writings abroad to spread the Party's influence."[50]

Resecuring these individuals' political loyalties was the first step, therefore, toward utilizing their social connections to create, co-opt, and mobilize networks and organizations in the service of political consolidation. Guan Chengzheng reported that "many PPCC members have special talents and are core members of social mass organizations." To illustrate how these talents were put to use, he notes that two members who belonged to the provincial calligraphy association helped the city Party committee hold exhibits, one looking forward to the handover of Hong Kong and the other displaying information on "reproduction planning." Other PPCC members with overseas connections, meanwhile, assisted the local Party United Front office in organizing an association and stores dedicated to fostering ties with overseas Chinese.

Recruitment of individuals for the *wenshi ziliao* project was part of this effort to enlist support for the Party through the conferral of special attention and privileges. Reaching out to former educators and enterprise managers who had been sidelined from their positions first for political reasons and then on account of their age, PPCC committees offered them both material incentives and the psychological opportunity to feel relevant and significant in society again. Working closely with the local Party and the institution in which the individual had previously worked, the Party branch within the PPCC created contracts that provided detailed clarification of the economic benefits of doing *wenshi ziliao* work. A typical example is the following contract that the Party branch of the Raohe PPCC, with approval from the county Party committee and in consultation with the county's supply and marketing cooperatives, drew up for a former manager named An Linhai. It provides that:

1) After coming to the PPCC to work, An Linhai retains his status as the cooperatives' retired cadre. His retirement benefits, such as retirement money, local supplementary income and food provisions, as well as money for laundry, heating, medicine, etc., do not change and continue to be the responsibility of the original work unit. Major things concerning his life, such as housing, firewood, autumn harvest food, etc., continue to be the responsibility of the cooperatives.

2) As for An Linhai's income, before handling the retirement procedure, the PPCC office starting in October will send monthly the income difference of 23.32 yuan, filling in the gap with the original salary.

---

[50] Wang Xingkun, "Work Report of the Seventh Session of the Fujin County PPCC's Standing Committee," 1–3.

3) The PPCC office will assess and provide expenses for his official work travels.
4) To avoid affecting his health, his work and rest hours can be appropriately flexible and relaxed. According to health-related issues and other conditions, he can propose to end his work with the PPCC at any time without any conditions or constraints.
5) There are five copies of this agreement. The county cooperatives, PPCC office, Personnel Affairs Department, Finance Administration Department, and An Linhai each get a copy.
   "Signed by the PPCC office and the County Cooperatives Federation, May 14, 1983."[51]

This *wenshi ziliao* work contract, while not greatly enriching the prospective editor, did represent in concrete terms the individual's rehabilitation and reintegration into society and into the embrace of the Party. Along with modest material compensation, the document provides an expression of the Party's affective concern for the individual's well-being. Careful to avoid any perception of compulsion or exploitation on the PPCC's part, the drafters of the contract present *wenshi ziliao* work as a relaxing and carefree way to serve the nation under the Party's benevolent gaze.

Breaking Down the Barriers of Silence: Historical Production, Affective Community, and the Forging of Sentimental Bonds between Interviewer and Interviewed

The imperative of resecuring political loyalty also informed the *wenshi ziliao* interviewing process. The strategies that interviewers use to collect material from informants are a critical part of any officially sponsored oral history project, as demonstrated by scholars who have examined state-orchestrated oral history. In Singapore's Oral History Unit established in 1978, for instance, the state imposed carefully prescribed restrictions on the interactions between interviewer and interviewee and the kinds of information that could be presented in the interviews. As Kevin Blackburn describes, these interactions involved "highly structured questionnaires to pose a series of predetermined questions" that conformed to the state's nationalist narrative.[52] Lysa Hong characterizes these interviews as more like "debriefing sessions" that "relegate the interviewees as

<hr/>

[51] Zhonggong raohe xian zhengxie dangzu, "Guanyu qingqiu zengpei zhuanzhi wenshi ziliao renyuan de zengbian baogao" ("Organization Expansion Report Regarding the Request to Add Full-Time *Wenshi Ziliao* Personnel") (Aug. 19, 1983) (Raohe County Archive).
[52] Kevin Blackburn, "History from Above: The Use of Oral History in Shaping Collective Memory in Singapore," in Paula Hamilton and Linda Shopes, eds., *Oral History and Public Memory* (Philadelphia, PA: Temple University Press, 2008), 36.

individuals to the background; their role is largely to provide the anecdote, the local color that would give the 'objective picture' flesh and detail
and the trappings of the 'voice of the ordinary person.'"[53] Looking back to
the 1950s, the CCP adopted a more subtle and flexible approach to
conducting interviews. Thomas Mullaney describes a set of strategies in
the 1954 Ethnic Classification Project in Yunnan that he calls "participant transformation," and that interviewers called "persuasion work," in
which "scholars carefully orchestrated the interview process, gathering
together representatives of those [ethnic] candidate groups that it
intended to merge and then ... setting the conditions under which these
candidates came to 'realize' (seemingly on their own) the bonds they
shared with one another." Mullaney adds that in cases where there was
"entrenched opposition," interviewers would "draw upon an even more
complex, covert, and epistemically violent repertoire."[54]

Like the field workers of the 1954 project in their pursuit of ethnic
categorization, *wenshi ziliao* interviewers adopted a complex, flexibly
designed repertoire of interviewing strategies to obtain the information
that they needed for reclassifying people and events historically. But unlike
the earlier project, the individuals conducting the interviews were not sent
down from Beijing to carry out central Party directives in a hasty, forced
manner. *Wenshi ziliao* investigators were local elites interviewing other local
elites in their social circles. In this localized context, a complex dynamic
ensued between interviewer and interviewee that was more individualized,
more varied, and more ambivalently situated between shared local complicity and subjection to and imposition of national Party guidelines. Rather
than focusing on group classification or relegating the individual to the status
of anecdote, detail, or background color, *wenshi ziliao* cadres were interested
in highlighting the individuality of the informant as a way to recalibrate in
more localized terms the relationship between state and society.

The *wenshi ziliao* also grew out of a Chinese Communist tradition of
transforming the individual's thought processes and consciousness.
As Uradyn Bulag points out, Mao used a method of intense study sessions,
deep inner thought exposure, and a continual process of telling and retelling (in oral and written form) life histories, for the ultimate purpose of
"destroying vestiges of individualism" and making sure everyone conformed tightly to the militant Party organization.[55] Fangchun Li describes

---

[53] Lysa Hong, "Ideology and Oral History Institutions in Southeast Asia," in Patricia Pui
Huen Lim and Chong Guan, eds., *Oral History in Southeast Asia: Theory and Method*
(Singapore: Institute of Southeast Asian Studies, 1998), 33–46, cited in Blackburn,
"History from Above," 38.
[54] Mullaney, *Coming to Terms with the Nation*, 11.
[55] Bulag, "Can the Subalterns Not Speak?" 98–99.

the individualized process of literally "turning the mind" (*fanxin*) that accompanied mass "speaking bitterness" (*suku*) struggle sessions during land reforms in northern China in the 1940s. In regard to the encounter between Party visitor and poor peasant, Li writes about "the power of education-and-transformation (*jiaohua*)" in bridging the "huge gap between the peasants' individual experiences (*ku*) and the revolutionary Party's transcendent 'knowledge' (of, for example, class exploitation)" and "infus[ing] particularized 'experience' with universal 'knowledge.'"[56] This educating and transforming process, as Yu Liu notes, included "three techniques of discourse propagation – personalization, magnification, and moralization – that induced the individual to 'translate the national discourse into personal stories'; 'politicize all aspects of life, including petty thoughts or behaviors, with a grand political discourse'; and 'moralize revolutionary discourse.'" Liu writes that "in Mao's China, every person was supposed, through small-group meetings, confession-writing, and so on, to internalize the collective discourse by reproducing it in individual stories. Instead of simply being 'indoctrinated' in the official discourse, the masses were also urged to join in the authorship of it by adding their own 'raw materials.'"[57]

The *wenshi ziliao* was in certain respects a continuation of these individualized strategies for "turning the mind" and bridging the gap between personal thoughts and official discourse. The tactics used to induce local elites' cooperation in producing individualized accounts that would reflect and illustrate national ideology on a micro level echoed Mao's efforts to foster the internalization and joint authorship of official discourse. As with Mao's demand that Investigative Research investigators reduce the psychological distance between themselves and their subjects by immersing themselves in the local community, *wenshi ziliao* interviewers similarly made great efforts to win over the hearts and minds of their informants. The resulting tension between listening to and faithfully recording individual perspectives and fitting these voices into an acceptable discursive framework was a continuing concern, as outlined in the following discussion.

Collectors and interviewers adopted specific strategies to connect with informants on an individual level and persuade them to divulge information that was often personal and at times politically sensitive. Their efforts in securing informants' trust and extracting from their mouths the

---

[56] Fangchun Li, "Making Revolution on the Mind: Fanxin and the Exercise of Thought-Power in the Land Reform Movement of Northern China (1946–48)," *Frontiers of Literary Studies in China* 6.4 (2012): 598–620, at 617–618.

[57] Yu Liu, "Maoist Discourse and the Mobilization of Emotions in Revolutionary China," *Modern China* 36.3 (2010): 334–335.

historical evidence they desired demonstrates on the micro level the Party's approach to healing political wounds and reconsolidating control. Those who had experience conducting interviews described the challenges in dealing with interviewees who feared political reprisal and refused to open up about their past. Writing on behalf of the national PPCC in 1983, a modern history researcher named Rong Mengyuan recalled such difficulties he had encountered as an interviewer in the early 1960s prior to the Cultural Revolution. Entrusted with the task of collecting information about the Beiyang warlord government, he found the elderly survivors he interviewed extremely reticent and unwilling to disclose sensitive details. For instance, Rong recounts with chagrin, beyond talking about "playing chess, playing cards, and how his mistresses quarreled," the interviewee was silent when asked about warlord Duan Qirui's political life. "They [the informants] had hesitation in their thinking, and we didn't know how to remove their hesitation. So, we couldn't retrieve valuable materials." Rong expresses the hope that interviewers will share their experiences and lessons in regard to this challenge and move forward.[58]

Participants in local *wenshi ziliao* work conferences did share their experiences and views on how to break down these barriers of silence that confronted investigators. In one case in Harbin, an interviewer named Tong Zhenyu recalls multiple attempts to convince a former prostitute to disclose "painful areas" of her past.

I visited 13 times. [Twelve] times I was cursed away. The final time I visited she along with her adopted daughter and son-in-law were all at home, and I made dumplings with them. When she saw me enter the room, she was very anxious. After eating the dumplings, her daughter and son-in-law left the room, and only then did she say: "You are quite a friend. You scared me 'til I was sweating." At this point I patiently explained to her the significance of *wenshi ziliao* and said to her, "if it's not so good to talk at home, we can find another place. When talking about past things, I definitely won't use your name."[59]

Collecting materials, therefore, was frequently an arduous process of relationship building, in which the Party's determination to break down the barriers of popular distrust was embodied in the interviewer's patient and methodical approach to overcoming the informant's hesitation. Just as the PPCC leadership attempted to gain the support of non-Party inductees by creating a home-like atmosphere for them, interviewers took great lengths to represent the Party machinery in an intimate, personalized light.

[58] Rong Mengyuan, "Commentary on Working with Historical Materials," 6.
[59] Tong Zhenyu, "How I Collected *Wenshi Ziliao*," 75–77.

The process of conducting personal interviews and eliciting testimonies could forge sentimental bonds between interviewer and interviewed that fused historical production with affective community. While collecting information in 1984 about the history of one of the women's academies in Heilongjiang, a Qiqihar *wenshi ziliao* team member developed close relationships to twenty former students who sang old academic songs for him to record and shared with him photos preserved over the years. He recalls being particularly moved during the lantern festival that year when one of the women gave him a handmade paper gourd for good luck and health.[60]

In their visits to informants' homes, interviewers cultivated an attitude of relaxed friendship and sincere affection that masked their role in conducting Party-orchestrated inspections. Behind this casual demeanor lay carefully devised methods for incrementally acquiring the targeted materials. Tong Zhenyu describes a six-part methodology for conducting interviews, as follows:

1) During the first meeting explain the reason for coming. You don't need to talk for a long time, and when it's over set a time for the next meeting. This way you avoid the problem of not being able to find the old person in the next interview, and he can be prepared with what to say.

2) During the second visit, first let him talk about his experiences, then converse with the interviewee about the main aspects of his experience without constraints on the scope of content. In the course of conversing, listen patiently and sincerely, and make the atmosphere lively and relaxed.

3) After conversing in this way three to five times, becoming mutually familiar and intimate, set a topic framework and converse in a questionnaire format, talking and taking notes. After talking, I organize materials that the interviewee himself is not able to organize by arranging in an orderly way the materials I wrote down. I then immediately submit these to him to examine and revise. This way after repeating this several times, I can gradually make the materials complete.

4) Make the most of your time to work with a sense of urgency. In order to quickly grasp into one's hands the materials, conduct dialogue and complete a draft step by step in a planned fashion.

5) After completing the draft, first hand it to the interviewee to check wording, make revisions to notes, and corroborate the truthfulness of the materials.

6) It's not possible to include all materials that are collected in the article [publication]. What should be done? My method is to divide according to categories and record them on notecards, keeping them for later use.[61]

This methodology for conducting interviews involved a gradual progression from open-ended conversation to a more focused questionnaire-style dialogue that homed in on the specific aspects of history that *wenshi ziliao*

---

[60] Liu Feilin, "Thirty Years' Reflections on Literary and Historical Work," 361–362.
[61] Tong Zhenyu, "How I Collected *Wenshi Ziliao*," 75–77.

committees were targeting. This approach allowed the interviewer to create an inclusive, inviting atmosphere in which to ease the interviewee's fears while at the same time prompting the informant to highlight issues and events that fit into the broader historical narrative that cadres were attempting to construct. The combination of free-style and question-naire-format interaction also balanced the priorities of inclusive accommodation of multiple perspectives on one hand and exclusionary political control on the other.

This strategy had some success, judging from anecdotal accounts. After the thirteenth "dumpling-making" visit, Tong Zhenyu finally softened the resistance of the interviewee who allegedly helped track down and arrange for meetings with eight other former prostitutes. "Later," Tong adds, "they voluntarily told me their occupational names at that time. So you see, the process of collecting *wenshi ziliao* is a process of publiciz-ing and educating people about Party policy. In collecting materials, one should not only respect them [the informants], but also differentiate between different circumstances and utilize different approaches in doing interviews."[62] Tong conceives of *wenshi ziliao* as a bilateral exchange between Party and subject, in which the Party educates and enlightens its subjects in exchange for obtaining resources and loyalty from them. In this exchange, *wenshi ziliao* workers saw themselves partly as mediators and partly as proselytizing agents on behalf of the party-state.

Ambivalent Mediators: Mobilizing Agents, Mobilized Subjects

While functioning as agents of the state, interviewers were themselves targets of local Party efforts to cultivate support from influential indivi-duals outside the Party. At the heart of the Party's united front agenda lay a tension between mobilizing people's active participation as both inter-viewers and interviewees within a unified ideological framework, and the injection of diverse and ambivalent voices onto the interviewing, writing, and editing process which risked spilling over the boundaries of that framework. Their involvement in inspections of local conditions and interviews with local residents placed PPCC members in an ambivalent position as simultaneously mobilized subjects and mobilizing agents, mediating between the state that they were officially representing and the individuals they were sent to investigate.

Unlike the presumption in truth commissions like the one in South Africa that the victims of the former regime deserved full acceptance and

[62] Ibid.

that the authenticity of their testimonies should not be questioned, the recently traumatized local elites who participated in the *wenshi ziliao* did not receive this unreserved embrace by the Party.[63] While implicitly repudiating the Maoist political campaigns that had ostracized them, the pre–Cultural Revolution ambivalence of the Party toward intellectuals and other elites as unreliable risks that needed to be closely supervised and always proving their political loyalty did not fundamentally change in the 1980s. Treated as an asset to the Party through their incorporation into the *wenshi ziliao* project, these individuals were at the same time continually subjected to political study sessions, were constantly in suspense about their Party status, and were pressured to reaffirm how good the Party had been to them while maintaining silence about the specific abuses they had experienced under its leadership. This continued political vulnerability and uncertainty made the *wenshi ziliao* experience an act of negotiating between the Party's united front agenda and local elites' mixed fear and determination to demonstrate their loyalty.

Like the people they interviewed, newly inducted PPCC members were initially hesitant to write articles about the past. Having recently endured political vilification and in many cases still barred from Party membership, they were understandably anxious about divulging sensitive historical details about themselves. Even as interviewers collecting, writing down, and editing other people's testimonies, uncertainty about the new regime's expectations and policies drove lingering fear and unwillingness to participate wholeheartedly in the project. This prompted PPCC leaders to ramp up political study sessions to ensure that the ideological framework for writing and conducting interviews was clearly ingrained in all PPCC members.

These study sessions integrated political philosophy with practical issues that addressed intellectuals' everyday material concerns, and reports sent back to the Party Committee at the end of each session put intellectuals' "progress" under indirect Party supervision. One of the first initiatives of PPCC committees around the country after 1978 was to invite ex-GMD officials and others previously labeled as counterrevolutionary. Many people viewed PPCC membership in rather unfavorable terms as signifying one's politically marginal status. Rather than embracing the invitation to join the PPCC as an affirmation of accomplishments and expertise in certain areas, intellectuals and others faced their recruitment with a sense of foreboding about their tenuous relationship to the Party and the political reeducation to which they would likely be subjected during meetings. In idealized recollections published later by the Heilongjiang

---

[63] Whitlock, "Review Essay," 145.

PPCC, a former professor professed his initial reservations about joining the PPCC after becoming a Party member in 1983. He recalled his resentment toward being pressured by his academic work unit in 1981 to attend meetings regularly at the Heilongjiang provincial PPCC. Viewing the meetings as a distraction from his academic research and dismissing as "deviant" other members of the PPCC, he found excuses to avoid the meetings during the first few years. He goes on in his account, however, to describe the transformative effect of participating in study sessions and inspection tours as "cleansing his political mindset."[64] During its fifth session from March 1983 to May 1985, Heilongjiang PPCC chair Li Jianbo transmitted orders to the city and county levels to establish specific study sessions, schedule reports and lectures, and print out reference readings to go along with the original writings. Li's training at Yanan Marxist Academy informed this top-down ideological command structure, and he invited classmates from the academy like Yang Chao, head of the Sichuan PPCC, to give guest lectures reconciling Maoist and Dengist philosophies.[65] Besides promoting ideological clarity, meetings held by the provincial PPCC and attended by more than 200 intellectuals in the early 1980s addressed practical issues such as work assignment and compensation, housing, married couples living apart, education and employment for children, and access to Party membership.[66]

Those who did the mobilizing through interviewing, writing, and editing, therefore, were also the targets of a continual process of political study, clarification, and indoctrination carried out by Party leaders within the PPCC. Lü Mingyi, vice-chair of the Raohe PPCC, advised other leading Party cadres within the organization to "thoroughly do the thought work of *wenshi ziliao* article writers, help them raise their level of understanding, liberate their thoughts, and give them the courage to write straightforwardly."[67] Lü's suggestion is that political study under Party guidance would "liberate" non-Party participants from their muddled uncertainties or inaccurate notions about what the new standards of political correctness were. The "courage to write straightforwardly" would result not from indiscriminate freedom to address

---

[64] Wang Zhilu, "Wo dang zhengxie weiyuan de huigu" ("My Recollections of Becoming a PPCC Member"), in *Wo yu zhengxie*, 174–177.

[65] Li Jianbo, "*Wo yu zhengxie* de jidian huiyi" ("Some Reminiscences on My Experiences with the PPCC"), in *Wo yu zhengxie*, 1–10.

[66] Lin Shangli, *The Chinese Communist Party and the People's Political Consultative Conference*, 74–76.

[67] Lü Mingyi, "Zhongguo renmin zhengzhi xieshang huiyi diyi jie weiyuanhui changwu weiyuanhui gongzuo baogao" ("Work Report of the Standing Committee of the First Session of the [Raohe County] PPCC") (Mar. 20, 1983) (Raohe County Archive): 13.

whatever comes to mind, but rather from firmly drawn boundaries that clarify for the individual what is acceptable to include.

Unlike many of the interviewees, interviewers regarded their participation in the *wenshi ziliao* process as an opportunity to prove their political loyalty to the Party. The act of mobilizing others to tell their stories, therefore, was in part a demonstration and measure of their capacity to serve the Party. The PPCCs' recruitment of these individuals to serve on *wenshi ziliao* work teams reflected a dual strategy of reaching out with open arms to people outside the Party while capitalizing on their political vulnerabilities to exact demands on them. This approach left these individuals feeling grateful and beholden to the Party yet in a constant state of suspense about their status. One such individual was An Linhai, a retired division head of Raohe's supply and marketing cooperatives, who joined the local *wenshi ziliao* committee in 1983. Two years later, having been honored with the title of "PPCC exemplary worker," he gave a speech summarizing his experience with *wenshi ziliao* at the county's second *wenshi ziliao* work conference. "After arriving in the PPCC," he recalls, "everyone from the chair to office comrades treated me with familiarity and took care of me in all respects. They were caring toward me and made me feel that the PPCC is a very warm place. I won't go into detailed discussion about how I was taken care of and cared for in my living situation. Most moving to me is the political caring and concern [they showed me]."[68]

His expression of gratitude is laden with a continuous need to prove his Party credentials in the absence of a definitive status as Party member. He reflects on how "the interference of the 'leftist' line" regarding "my so-called historical problem" had prevented him from joining the CCP despite his multiple attempts since the early 1950s. By the early 1980s, "I had lost heart. I thought, it was not resolved before retirement and now I don't even have a work position, so who will care about me?" When the PPCC recruited him in 1983, the Party subcommittee within the PPCC was aware of this history and approached him with encouragement but no clear resolution, telling him, according to An's recollection, "'the Party has never abandoned any comrades who desire to enter this organization. As long as one has this desire one should work hard to pursue it and not be frustrated and lose heart,'" and "encouraged me to struggle to become a true CCP member. This concern and encouragement from the PPCC Party organization stirred up my courage and I once more submitted an application to the Party."[69] In spite of these exchanges, at the time that

---

[68] Raohe zhengxie bangongshi, "An Linhai's Speech to the Second Session of the Raohe PPCC," 1–2.
[69] Ibid.

An delivered this speech the issue of his Party membership had yet to be resolved, though he insists that "it's been encouraging to me and my mood is very relaxed, feeling deeply the Party's warmth."[70]

In recruiting people like An Linhai to participate in the *wenshi ziliao* process, therefore, local PPCCs used their tenuous political status as leverage over them to ensure their conformity to the dictates of the project. Their dual position both as agents of the Party and as politically suspect aliens outside the Party also made them uniquely qualified to act as mediators between the formal party-state and the informants they interviewed. While collecting information from them, these interviewers could simultaneously communicate their own experiences of political redemption as personal testament to the Party's enlightening policies and concern for people's well-being.

Rendering the Editor Visible and Invisible

As important as the interviewer was in accessing sources and shaping the way informants reflected on their past, *wenshi ziliao* committees were careful to minimize, if not leave out altogether, acknowledgment of their role in the published version. While the interviewing and editing process was critical to ensuring that informants' recollections fit into the prescribed narrative, PPCCs presented the published accounts as authentic, unaltered historical truth by putting the informants' names front and center as the sole authors. The majority of the recollections that were included in the 1984 published account of the Blagoveshchensk Massacre, for instance, were the narratives of three individuals, Yin Xingwen, Jin Baichuan, and Liu Qingqi. While intervening significantly in the organization and writing of the overall text, the editor, Liu Banghou, made himself invisible from the text's production. Only the names of the three main informants interviewed in 1965 (who, as the editor notes in the introduction, were no longer alive during the editing process) appeared under the title of the published article to indicate the authorship of the text. The name of the editor, however, is absent from the article's authorship on the title page. On one hand, this can be understood as due to the temporal gap between the moments of narration and editing, as Liu Banghou had no part in conducting the interviews or in shaping and transcribing the content of their narratives. At the same time, however, the absence of any reference to the editor's role downplayed his intervention in shaping the perceived historical significance of the text in order to

[70] Ibid.

lend it an authenticity derived from the firsthand experience conveyed through the voices of the original eyewitnesses, while concealing the role of the editor in retrospectively superimposing onto the narratives the state-sponsored nationalist ideology. The title of the article, "What was seen and heard of the great Hailanpao [Blagoveshchensk] massacre," reinforces this aura of authenticity, referring to the firsthand experience of "what was seen and heard."

This pursuit of authenticity through the production of firsthand accounts has a long tradition in Chinese literary and historical writings. The most conspicuous examples of this in imperial China were the *biji* (miscellaneous journal records). In addition to extemporizing on contemporary political and cultural developments, the authors would describe unusual encounters or strange phenomena that they had seen or heard. These spontaneous and miscellaneous accounts constituted a personal, authentic alternative to the carefully crafted and politically censored official dynastic histories. In the early twentieth century, this tradition of firsthand experiential writings converged with new ideas relating to social scientific research imported from the West. These Western ideas stressed the need for objective survey data and field research interviews that would enable the state to obtain more accurate and systematic knowledge of conditions at the local level. Liang Qichao once theorized the importance of collecting firsthand experiential accounts of watershed moments in modern China such as the Boxer Uprising and the Hundred Days Reform. A systematic investigation along these lines, Liang suggested, would mobilize a living history in the service of national consciousness.[71]

Chinese socialists adapted this *diaocha* (investigation) or *kaocha* (inspection) method of social scientific research for their political agendas. They employed the oral history methodology as a way to simultaneously mobilize the past and those retelling it for the project of socialist transformation. During the 1950s and 1960s, teams of investigators, ranging from professional researchers to students engaged in school projects, fanned out into villages where key events such as the Taiping and Boxer Uprisings had taken place. The objective of these "campaigns" was to "rectify" history based in the authentic firsthand testimonies of the masses, while simultaneously serving as an exercise for educated elite in "learning from the masses" and acting out new socialist class relations through the interview process.[72]

Wenshi ziliao adapted these politically inspired pursuits of authenticity to the context of post-Mao historical production. The standard *wenshi*

---

[71] Kwong, "Oral History in China," 29–30.   [72] Ibid., 31–33.

ziliao practice of rendering the editor invisible from the text was apparently not always easy to swallow for the interviewers who invested so much of their time in writing down and organizing into a coherent narrative the often-fragmented information they gleaned during the interviews. While informants viewed the interviewers, at least initially, as threatening agents of state extractive power, the interviewers regarded their own role as a commitment to self-sacrifice and renouncement of personal gain for the collective good. Referring to the "special requirement regarding spoken materials" that privileges the informant as sole author, Tong Zhenyu commiserates with fellow interviewers that "[w]e all want to have our names appear in the articles we write. How can we resolve this problem? I feel we need to look at it from the perspective of the enterprise and raise our understanding of the long-term significance of *wenshi ziliao*. And each of us needs to be willing to be the nameless *wenshi ziliao* collector."[73]

In order to create an aura of authentic immediacy of firsthand historical perspective, PPCCs concealed the extensive and deliberate processes entailed in the production of *wenshi ziliao*. The project's goals of social mobilization thus involved contradictory impulses: at the collection and writing stage, the interviewers' visible and highly personal interactions with informants were critical both to securing the materials themselves and remodeling the relationship between Party and subject. On the other hand, the use of *wenshi ziliao* for the purpose of social mobilization at the publication and circulation stage, particularly in the areas of education and propaganda, required the erasure of that process and the presentation of the materials as an unmediated expression of historical experience.

Borderland History and the Pursuit of Overseas Chinese Loyalties

Editors mobilized historical evidence from firsthand testimonies to rehabilitate and restore privilege and dignity to non-Party PPCC members and other individuals whose political support and expertise the Party sought. The selection process was by no means a predetermined given and at times sparked impassioned debate. Deciding what life stories to include in the final publications brought to the fore debates about the substantive meaning of post-Mao reforms and their ramifications for who and what aspects of history belonged within the nation. It involved a relatively open-ended process shaped by differing opinions among local actors on how to interpret national directives. Interviewers, writers, and editors had to circumscribe and tailor central government guidelines

---

[73] Tong Zhenyu, "How I Collected *Wenshi Ziliao*," 75–77.

regarding what defined nationalism, what constituted the United Front, and who belonged in the nation to the historical particularities of the region in which they conducted their work. One controversial case pertained to the historical memory of seven men executed by GMD authorities as underground agents of the CCP. After 1949, the Party recriminalized them as spies for the authorities. According to Shen Meijuan, her father participated in this initiative following his own reinstatement in the PPCC in 1977. In the absence of archival evidence, Shen Zui's compilation of firsthand testimonies, including that of the vice-premier, put forward evidence that posthumously exonerated them.[74]

The earlier impact of Japanese occupation in the northeast compared to other parts of China in the 1930s provoked struggles in the 1980s within the Heilongjiang PPCC over the question of which "resistance patriots" qualified for inclusion in the nationalist narrative, bringing to the surface disagreements over the relative importance of socialist revolutionary and nationalist elements in the Party's historical identity. A former *wenshi ziliao* team member in Qiqihar recalled some examples of these ideological battles over content selection. He explains that, after the author's "objective evaluation" of a "patriotic figure," a certain person protested and demanded that this individual not be memorialized. This incited an argument over what constituted being patriotic, and the author proudly concludes that his side eventually won out and furthered the cause of expanding the United Front and national consolidation. In other cases, the cross-purposes of *wenshi ziliao* as historical materials and political propaganda caused rifts among editors over what content was salutary and acceptable for release. One site of substantial disagreement was the issue of whether to acknowledge and commemorate the "Tianbai Incident" in which the Manchukuo government exposed and arrested 110 underground CCP activists in 1941. A debate ensued among Qiqihar *wenshi ziliao* members concerning what kind of impact retelling this story might have on the political consciousness of prospective readers. Did the Tianbai activists deserve historical acknowledgment as patriots on the front lines of resistance, as one group argued, or would reference to this incident have a negative, demoralizing effect? In the end those in favor of including an account of this event won the debate.[75]

By utilizing materials and testimonies to confer special honors on former anti-imperialist activists, editors highlighted their region's nationalist significance. In so doing, they integrated the borderland region's historical reconstruction with the project of resecuring political loyalties to the Party at

---

[74] Shen Meijuan, "National PPCC and Shen Zui Father and Daughter," 75–76.
[75] Liu Feilin, "Thirty Years' Reflections on Literary and Historical Work," 364–365.

the local level. Information about a man named Ni Yuande that the Raohe *wenshi ziliao* committee located while collecting materials on the Seventh Division of the Allied Anti-Japanese Army provides a case in point. Ni, a member of the Chaoyang production brigade of Xilinzi commune at the time of the investigations, had been a former head of the Raohe County branch of the Anti-Japanese Salvation Association, was imprisoned, and allegedly remained resolute and refused to expose any of the association's members. With this evidence in hand, the *wenshi ziliao* committee submitted a proposal to the county's Civil Administration Department, which was promptly approved and implemented, to formally recognize him for his contributions to the anti-Japanese resistance.[76] Similarly, the Qiqihar's *wenshi ziliao* committee's published account of a general's role in the Jiangqiao campaign against the Japanese led to government recognition of him as a revolutionary martyr along with economic assistance to his descendants. Another published narrative about the life of Li Yinghuan, organizer of a local anti-Japanese force in Lindian County at the start of the Japanese occupation who came under attack during the Cultural Revolution, had a similar impact. City and county courts, in cooperation with the Lindian PPCC and Qiqihar *wenshi ziliao* committee, used evidence from the *wenshi ziliao* account to "rectify" earlier verdicts on him.

Participants used the collection, writing, and editing of historical materials as a vehicle for rectifying "politics and history," and thereby "rectifying incorrectly labeled rightists." As mentioned earlier, the legal-forensic aspect of this rectification, while significant in its own right, was less central to the project than the symbolic dimension of revising the historical narrative and by extension redefining who and what was worthy of historical inclusion and commemoration. Through the act of historical rehabilitation, *wenshi ziliao* editors celebrated the local particularity of national political and cultural figures. In some cases, they deviated from the official name that the Party's history ascribed to a given individual, assigning instead a name that tied that person's identity exclusively to the editors' county or city. In Fujin County, situated along the northeast reaches of the Songhua River, local PPCC reports in the early 1980s repeatedly refer to a man named Zhang Jinsi as the most important "revolutionary hero" subject of historical research and commemoration.[77] A short biographical summary is revealing of the kinds

[76] Raohe zhengxie bangongshi, "Raise High the Banner of Patriotism," 2–3.
[77] Zhengxie fujin xian changwu weiyuanhui, "Yong duozhong fangshi fadong weiyuan yu gejie renshi jiji 'qiangjiu' woxian 'wenshi ziliao'" ("Use All Kinds of Methods to Mobilize Personnel and People from All Spheres to Enthusiastically 'Rescue' Our County's '*Wenshi Ziliao*'"), *Zhengxie gongzuo* (*PPCC Work*), no. 10 (Aug. 20, 1982) (Fujin City Archives): 2; Cao Mingren, "Work Report of the Sixth Session of the Fujin County PPCC's Standing Committee," 5–6.

of characteristics that local cadres were now defining as "revolutionary." According to one biographer's description of his life, Zhang's original given name was Jiazhou, and he was born into a landlord family in Bayan County near Harbin. Involved in anti-Japanese student demonstrations during his youth in the 1920s, he joined the Communist Party after being admitted to Beijing University and returned to the northeast after the Japanese occupation in 1931 to engage in underground resistance. However, in 1933, his anti-Japanese guerrilla unit suffered losses and the Party leadership criticized his "rightist" mistakes. In consequence, he appears to have been removed from a formal position in the Party organization and relocated on his own to Fujin. In an attempt to start a new life as a schoolteacher and principal, he adopted an alias, Jinsi, met the woman he married, and settled down as a family man. At the same time, he maintained connections with the Party and resumed underground activities, leading eventually to his death from a gunshot wound in 1937.

Immediately after the founding of the PRC, memorial exhibits and monuments at Beijing University and in his native county of Bayan honored Zhang as a martyr.[78] Zhang's period of residence in Fujin, on the other hand, bore ambiguous political associations. It was during this period of his life that he was cut off from the Party organization, labeled as a "rightist." His alias of "Jinsi" symbolically marked this formal rupture from the Party, though he allegedly continued to harbor informal Party connections. By redeeming him posthumously as the centerpiece of their commemorations of revolutionary heroes, local PPCC and *wenshi ziliao* cadres were making an explicitly political manifesto about the need for political redemption and rehabilitation of those who had been persecuted during the Maoist years.

At the same time, by celebrating his identity as Zhang Jinsi rather than his birth name of Zhang Jiazhou (by which the other exhibits and monuments had referred to him), they were making a statement affirming the distinctness of Fujin both from its neighbors in the northeast and from the rest of China. This distinctness had a subtle tone of subversiveness toward the central Party leadership, implying that what was being celebrated was an identity that was separate from the Party's and defiant of the Party's ideological doctrine.

These local agendas driving historical reevaluation were also important in shaping PPCC and *wenshi ziliao* activities overseas. The international context shifted dramatically between the two phases of PPCC and *wenshi ziliao*

---

[78] Yu Shaoxiong, "The Northeast Anti-Japanese United Army Generals." Heilongjiang People's Publishing House, 2009. Retrieved online at www.biographypdf.cc/military-fig ures/86579633145039193276.html.

production in the 1960s and 1980s. In the early 1960s, at the height of military tensions with both the Soviet Union and the Nationalist government in Taiwan, Party committees and the political arm of the PLA directed PPCC committees to mobilize historical and cultural resources for the war effort. Activities associated with this task included monitoring, reeducating, and utilizing individuals whose ties to overseas defectors made them politically suspect. By 1980, in the context of market liberalization and thawed relations with the Soviet Union and Taiwan, PPCC committees adapted their investigative methods and united front discourse toward the economic and diplomatic pursuits of seeking out overseas sources of foreign investment and publicizing Party reforms abroad. *Wenshi ziliao* committees employed historical commemoration as an affective instrument for tying local economic interests to an expanded international project of political integration.

In 1962, the PPCC national committee contributed to cultural mobilization for the impending war effort by commemorating the 300th anniversary of Zheng Chenggong's conquest of Taiwan. At the same time, the PLA's northeast political section sent members from the three provincial PPCC committees in northeast China who specialized in Taiwan-related issues on a fifteen-day visit to the front lines in Fujian Province. There military officers put them through a boot camp experience of educational propaganda and hands-on field action that included visiting Zheng Chenggong's monument, inspecting enemy lines through binoculars, and firing cannons (some with real gunpowder and others with propaganda materials).[79] This experience formed part of a close relationship between the PPCC and the military during the early 1960s. As a 1963 report by the standing committee of the Jilin City PPCC indicates, a significant portion of *wenshi ziliao* work was devoted to collecting historical materials useful for military propaganda, a priority reflected in the "Sixty-Four Villages" project conducted along the Sino–Russian border.[80]

The PPCC's work in mobilizing cultural resources against the foreign enemy was closely tied to its project of neutralizing perceived political threats domestically. Local and provincial committees used the threat of foreign invasion as an impetus for tracking down and investigating individuals whose connections abroad made their loyalties to the Party suspect. Inspections, reeducation study sessions, and *wenshi ziliao* production went hand in hand as tools for identifying potential threats

---

[79] Guo Chunhua, "Indelible Memories," 294–295.
[80] Ma Yilin, "Zhongguo renmin zhengzhi xieshanghuiyi jilin sheng jilin shi dierjie weiyuan-hui changwu weiyuanhui gongzuo baogao" ("Work Report of the Standing Committee of the Second Jilin City PPCC Committee") (Presented at the First Full Meeting of the Third Jilin City PPCC Committee, Nov. 28, 1963), "Appendix Documents" Section, *Jilin shizhi*, 314–321.

to the Party, subjecting these threats to intense ideological pressure, and then mobilizing them as cultural resources for crafting stories that supported the official narrative of Communist success. The Jilin City branch of the PPCC demonstrated this during the period from 1963 to 1965 when it rounded up relatives of defectors to Taiwan and subjected them to a series of "panel discussions" and speeches. During these events, officials from the Propaganda Department of the city's Party Committee and the Jilin military's political division "educated" them regarding policies toward Taiwan and Taiwan's present conditions. These reeducation sessions included visits to agricultural production brigades, factories, schools, and historical sites such as monuments to officially recognized Communist heroes in the region like Yang Jingyu. Following this indoctrination, the targeted individuals were expected to make the transition from being passive recipients of Party education to taking an active role in disseminating propaganda abroad via "any channels available," such as sending letters to relative and friends in Taiwan.[81] By 1965, in the final stage of their political reintegration, some of them joined *wenshi ziliao* teams in writing and compiling manuscripts that tailored their personal and family experiences to official Communist history.[82]

Following the Cultural Revolution, China's diplomatic and economic opening to the outside world relied in part on the continuation and adaptation of pre–Cultural Revolution approaches to social and cultural mobilization. The PPCC applied its roles in political mediation and integration to facilitating the internationalization of regional and national economic policies. "National unification" work groups within PPCC committees at the city, county, and provincial levels tied together native place sentiment, local economic interests, national integration, and overseas connections. In the northeast, these work groups recruited individuals with overseas connections, arranged family reunions, and appealed to the nostalgia of natives of the region living abroad to attract their investment in local enterprise.[83]

The reappointment of pre–Cultural Revolution personnel to these new committees reflected the combination of continuity and change in the PPCC's political role. Having participated in the inspection/

---

[81] *Jilin shizhi*, 32–33.

[82] Ma Yilin, "Zhongguo renmin zhengzhi xieshanghuiyi jilin sheng jilin shi disanjie weiyuanhui changwu weiyuanhui gongzuo baogao" ("Work Report of the Standing Committee of the Third Jilin City PPCC Committee") (Presented at the First Full Meeting of the Fourth Jilin City PPCC Committee, Dec. 24, 1965), "Appendix Documents" Section, *Jilin shizhi*, 327–331.

[83] Xu Huiqing, "Jiji zuo hao haiwai tongzhan gongzuo" ("Enthusiastic Implementation of United Front Work Overseas"), in *Wo yu zhengxie*, 392–401.

propaganda trip to the front lines of the cross-straits conflict in the 1960s, in 1980, Guo Chunhua resumed his activities as a member of the "National Reunification" subcommittee of the Heilongjiang PPCC. Instead of aiming cannons across the straits and acknowledging heroic Chinese conquests of the island, he hosted former "enemies" like a Mr. Yang who had worked in the Nationalist government's Defense Department in Taiwan during the 1960s. Guo and the provincial PPCC capitalized on Yang's visit as an opportunity to publicize abroad the Party's reform policies. One of the anticipated outcomes was Yang's "surprise" to find that a former GMD general was now in the office of the vice-chair of the provincial PPCC. According to Guo's account, "intimate meetings with friendly PPCC officials felt like coming home to family."[84]

Relatives of defectors to Taiwan were once again targets of PPCC reeducation campaigns intended to bring about political reintegration and to mobilize dissemination of Party propaganda abroad via various personal channels. "National Unification" subcommittees within regional branches of the PPCC tied the political goals of reeducating and reintegrating this recently ostracized group to the economic agenda of stimulating local development via new sources of overseas investment. In Jiamusi, a city along the Sino–Soviet border, relatives of overseas Chinese attended meetings organized by the local PPCC national unification work committee in 1981. Starting as reeducation sessions disseminating information about new state policies, these meetings expanded into reunions with relatives and friends abroad that were intended to generate local access to overseas capital.[85]

As part of Party leaders' attempt to improve ties with Taiwan and to resecure the loyalty of those living on the mainland who had overseas family connections, *wenshi ziliao* teams recruited former GMD officials or their surviving relatives and colleagues to tell their stories and prioritized their inclusion in publications. *Wenshi ziliao* reports generally included anecdotes describing the profuse gratitude toward the Communist Party that friends and relatives living overseas felt upon seeing these redemptive historical accounts of individuals formerly labeled as counterrevolutionary. As Dai Zhenhuan, in his work report on behalf of the standing committee of the Fujin PPCC, notes in 1980, "the united front in the new period also includes the great span of fellow Chinese in Taiwan, Hong Kong, Macao, and abroad, and includes all patriotic people.

[84] Guo Chunhua, "Indelible Memories."
[85] Jiamusi difangzhi bianzuan weiyuanhui, "Zhengxie zuzhi" ("PPCC Structure"), Jiamusi shizhi (Zhonghua shuju, 1996): 1332–1333.

Supporting national unification is all that is required for us to come together."[86]

Appropriating for local economic gain the national post-Mao policy of gradually opening China up to overseas investment and thawing ties with Taiwan, local PPCC cadres directed their efforts of reconciliation with particular energy toward those who had overseas connections in Taiwan, Hong Kong, and elsewhere. Reversing the counterrevolutionary labels that affiliation with Taiwan had earned them in the past, local PPCCs now regarded them as key channels for attracting human talent and economic resources from successful overseas Chinese. Co-opting them with the economic and political privileges described earlier, PPCC leaders used members of the organization with overseas ties as instruments of extending Party propaganda abroad and as conduits facilitating "three connections" to "compatriots" in Taiwan, Hong Kong, and other locations overseas.[87] In Fujin, in addition to encouraging members to send letters to their overseas friends and relatives, PPCC leaders held "three overseas compatriots" meetings and talks every holiday.[88] Combining their overseas pursuits with an effort to mobilize people from around the country with ties to Fujin, they also created a "friendship list" of seventy-one people scattered in different parts of the country who, according to the Party subcommittee of the PPCC, "devote themselves to important positions and some have lots of energy and capacity to do things. In the past half year, they provided over a hundred documents of information to promote their hometown's development. Some cooperated to attract funds, technology, and talent for the city's economic development."[89]

In his work report for the Fujin PPCC in 1987, Xu Zhanhai described the potential for rehabilitative acts to generate new loyalties and commitments of resources from abroad. He illustrates this with an example in which the PPCC restored a private residence to a man named Yuan Fulin, whose family was in Taiwan. Yuan allegedly

wrote a letter to tell his relatives living in the U.S. and Taiwan. After reading the letter, his uncle, aunt, and relatives wrote a letter to the county government saying ... "Our five residence buildings in Fujin city have been returned to our

---

[86] Dai Zhenhuan, "Draft of Work Report of [the] Fifth Session of [the] Standing Committee of Fujin County PPCC," 4–5.

[87] Zhou Zuojun, "Zhongguo renmin zhengzhi xieshang huiyi fujin xian diliu jie weiyuanhui changwu weiyuanhui gongzuo baogao" ("Work Report of the Eighth Session of the Fujin County PPCC's Standing Committee") (Delivered on Mar. 21, 1988, at the Second Meeting of the Eighth Session of the Fujin County PPCC) (Fujin City Archives): 4.

[88] Zhonggong zhengxie fujin shi dangzu, "Wrap-Up Summary of the City PPCC's Work," 3–4.

[89] Ibid.

family, converted to renminbi. Thank you for your help, and for your upright policies toward the people ... after recovering from illness we plan to visit our hometown of Fujin to pay respects to the graves [of our ancestors] and see relatives and friends after being away for forty years away. At that time we will again thank the government!" This letter expresses the feelings of overseas Chinese toward their hometown in China.[90]

Here Xu Zhanhai draws on pre-Communist ideals of native place loyalty and attachment to conceive of the PPCC's role in generating economic and political loyalties from overseas. In this way, he re-grounded the post-Mao modernization project in traditional local-centered networks and sentiments. At the same time, he articulated the effort to resecure political loyalties and economic resources in terms of familial devotion and reunion.

The PPCC committees also used the discourse of healing to reincorporate these individuals into society. The PPCC-arranged reunions of ex-GMD officials with overseas relatives provided forums for incorporating Chinese abroad into an extended conception of Chinese nation. This rearticulation of political goals was evident in the role that Li Yongning played as a relative of defectors to Taiwan. Relegated to forest and farm labor on account of his family background in the late 1950s, after 1980, the Heilongjiang provincial PPCC dispatched him to towns and villages where he met with other groups of people with overseas connections. As in the past, these meetings involved a combination of reeducation/indoctrination and mobilization. But now PPCC cadres represented the Party in affective familial terms intended to generate overseas investment. Li Yongning made clear this connection between political reintegration and economic investment. Recalling his efforts to resolve the difficulties that relatives of overseas "defectors" faced in reentering the workforce, educating their children, reuniting with relatives abroad, and even dealing with disputes over claims to property overseas, he claimed that "the people would thank the government heartily and put their hearts in investing in China's reforms ... and attracting funds from abroad."[91] Whether or not he personally believed in this claim, the rhetoric of healing and compassion was an important discourse used to mobilize new international networks in the service of economic modernization.

The reunited family embodied metaphorically the reconstitution of the Chinese polity. Along with sending New Year's greetings to former GMD officials in Taiwan, starting in 1980, the national PPCC began organizing

---

[90] Xu Zhanhai, "Work Report of the Seventh Session of the Fujin County PPCC's Standing Committee," 8–9.

[91] Li Yongning, "Wo zai zhengxie de gangwei shang" ("My Role in the PPCC"), in *Wo yu zhengxie*, 181–183.

family reunion visits in Hong Kong between defectors to Taiwan and relatives who had remained in China. The personal sentiment exchanged between long-separated family and friends symbolized the healing process of re-suturing the fractured political base of the Party. Shen Meijuan, the editorial secretary for the national *wenshi ziliao* office, recalled her father Shen Zui's reunion with relatives and friends from Taiwan, Canada, and the United States beginning in 1980. She described the initial apprehension of a former GMD officer and his wife during their visit from New York City to see him. Intimidated by soldiers guarding the PPCC building, they allegedly paced around outside for a long time in the cold before a neighbor of Shen Zui's led them to the residence attached to the PPCC in which he lived. She describes her father's reassuring words to them that official attitudes toward Taiwanese defectors had changed and "gradually their fears were washed away and they visited again in 1984 to take part in cultural activities like Beijing opera, which they had feared were not permissible."[92] The mixing of politics and personal sentiment was evident in the Jilin provincial PPCC vice Party chair's orchestration of a reunion between two former GMD generals, one of whom was his father-in-law. When the meeting took place in Hong Kong in 1988, organized by another former GMD officer-turned-businessman and partially funded by the Xinhua news organization, he recalls his wife tearfully kneeling at her father's feet.[93]

The content, distribution, and circulation of *wenshi ziliao* materials facilitated and in some cases drove these overseas connections. *Wenshi ziliao* articles were distributed in partially or fully reprinted form to a variety of organizations ranging from schools and theater production companies to factories, banks, and commercial enterprises. During the early 1980s, the widening circulation of *wenshi ziliao* extended abroad, with articles reprinted in overseas Chinese newspapers and transmitted through informal personal channels. Viewing the historical documents both as material objects with a certain commodity value and as affective vehicles of social and political bonds, PPCC cadres devised multiple forms of compensation, including "storing funds domestically, transferring funds to domestic relatives or friends, donating to relevant departments, substituting books [for money], and purchasing valuable gifts with commemorative value."[94]

---

[92] Shen Meijuan, "National PPCC and Shen Zui Father and Daughter," 77–80.

[93] Xiao Shanyin, "Sishi nian hou chongfeng zai xianggang" ("Reunion in Hong Kong after Forty Years"), *Wenshi ziliao xuanji* 154: 65–69.

[94] "Zhengxie diwuci quanguo wenshi ziliao gongzuo huiyi jingyan xuanbian" ("Selected Experiences from the Fifth National *Wenshi Ziliao* Work Conference), Summary Report, 1986 (Heilongjiang Provincial Archive).

Reprinted articles disseminated in overseas Chinese newspapers could trigger long-lost connections between former GMD officials who saw in the revisionist history an opportunity for personal reunion and political healing. The reprinting of a former GMD military officer's memoir in a Chinese newspaper in New York City, for instance, prompted a fellow GMD officer to visit the mainland and reunite with his former comrade in the national PPCC office.[95] The selective commemoration of individuals whose lives spanned geographic and political boundaries facilitated this internationalization of regional memories. *Wenshi ziliao* articles highlighted, for instance, the accomplishments of former Heilongjiang governor-general Zhu Qinglan. Zhu's migration from southeast China along with his wide-ranging military activities and political relationships made his story a site of shared celebration regionally, nationally, and overseas. In 1986, Qiqihar *wenshi ziliao* commemorating Zhu's life appeared not only in museum exhibits and book publications in other regions of China, including Shanxi, Zhejiang, and Shanghai, but also became publicized in Taiwan through the promotional activities of a Taiwanese film celebrity.[96]

The *wenshi ziliao* role in building an expanded united front overseas involved reinvoking native place discourse. In 1987, the Heilongjiang *wenshi ziliao* research committee formed an eleven-member subcommittee devoted to the task of collecting materials from overseas, particularly Taiwan. According to the resolutions of the first meeting held in May of that year, the subcommittee's task was to "mobilize overseas relatives and old friends to write *wenshi ziliao*, and through them expand contacts overseas and open up collection avenues; at the same time, broadly contact PPCC and democratic party members and utilize their overseas connections to open up channels for collecting materials from overseas; we also need to examine and validate these overseas materials."[97] Extending the methods and goals of *wenshi ziliao* social mobilization overseas, the report articulated the purpose of this project as "advancing cross-straits 'connections,' inspiring overseas Chinese native-place sentiment, increasing their affections for the ancestral country, and thereby advancing implementation of 'one country, two systems.'" These words echoed the resolution, drawn up a year earlier in Beijing at the fifth national *wenshi ziliao* conference, to "call forth the nationalist homeland sentiment of overseas Chinese."[98] The act of collecting historical

---

[95] Shen Meijuan, "National PPCC and Shen Zui Father and Daughter," 78–81.

[96] Liu Feilin, "Thirty Years' Reflections on Literary and Historical Work," 363–364.

[97] Heilongjiang sheng zhengxie weiyuanhui, "Haiwai zhengji zu diyici huiyi jiyao" ("Main Contents of [the] First Conference of [the] Overseas Collection Group") (1987) (Heilongjiang Provincial Archive).

[98] "Selected Experiences from the Fifth National *Wenshi Ziliao* Work Conference."

materials was seen, therefore, as an important vehicle for cultivating overseas Chinese loyalties to the Party, using the traditional cultural trope of native place rather than communist ideals to articulate these goals.

The provincial and national PPCC leaders present at the conference envisioned their organizations as go-betweens facilitating deepening relationships across the straits. To this end, they encouraged the exchange of letters and sponsored personal as well as business, academic, and tourist-related visits in both directions.[99] The project of collecting historical materials was, therefore, equally concerned with mobilizing participants' social and political affections as it was about the sources themselves.

Wenshi ziliao committees used historical accounts and memoirs to reawaken native place attachments, catalyze return visits and reunions, and propel foreign investment. The reevaluation of local historical figures within the context of economic liberalization expanded into an international project that was then tied back to local economic interests. *Wenshi ziliao* cadres noted the impact of historical revisions on individuals overseas as a way to illustrate just how powerful and effective the project was as a mobilization tool. The Heilongjiang *wenshi ziliao* office demonstrated this in a report entitled "*Wenshi ziliao* is spiritual food that inspires people to struggle for shared ideals." The authors assert that by "releasing materials that no one would have dared to release before" and "including the accomplishments of anyone who historically benefited the nation," *wenshi ziliao* "exhibit how incomparably accommodating the party is, moving people powerfully in China and abroad."[100] To illustrate this, they point to the far-reaching impact of a *wenshi ziliao* account produced in Qiqihar. Historically rehabilitating a former GMD-affiliated educator named Wang Binzhang who was honored as a patriot in Taiwan, the article allegedly moved his niece, a professor in Hong Kong, to "express the intention to work to help China."[101] Similarly, a descendant of Zhang Tingge, after visiting Harbin several times, allegedly decided to invest in the Shuanghesheng wine factory and revive the flour mill that Zhang had founded.[102]

While *wenshi ziliao* organizers at the national level regarded this effort as an integrative project to construct a united greater China, they were wary about the potential political dangers that materials collected overseas

[99] Ibid.
[100] Heilongjiang sheng zhengxie wenshi ban, "*Wenshi Ziliao* Is Spiritual Food That Inspires People to Struggle for Shared Ideals," 6–7.
[101] Ibid.
[102] *Haerbin shizhi* (*Harbin City Gazetteer*) (Haerbin shi difangzhi bianzuan weiyuanhui, 1993): 204–205.

might pose. Urging researchers to collect materials from overseas, particularly Taiwan, they envisioned a joint venture of mainland–Taiwan historical production that would lead to integration of the two countries on the Communist Party's terms. In this vein, participants at the fifth national work conference on *wenshi ziliao* held in Beijing in 1986 concluded that:

We should welcome Taiwan's recent re-printing and publication of a lot of mainland *wenshi ziliao*. We should also enthusiastically collect historical materials published in Taiwan, from among those with more objective and accurate content, and selectively reprint or publish as separate volumes. [This is] in order to mutually supplement missing materials, advance mutual understanding among historical materials workers on both sides of the straits, and work together to compile historical artifacts of the ancestral country. We should do the same toward Hong Kong, Macao, and overseas.[103]

The national policy of liberalizing China's ties with Taiwan and other countries created a problem that was familiar to PPCC and *wenshi ziliao* cadres: how to balance inclusivity and accommodation with Party control. In the case of expanding *wenshi ziliao* overseas, PPCC cadres viewed with particular sensitivity the connection between historical writing and political reconsolidation. Their attention to the potential volatility of this work is evident in the resolution of the fifth national *wenshi ziliao* conference. Encouraging the acquisition and publication of materials produced in Taiwan, it urges researchers and editors to "approach materials collected from overseas with tolerance, upholding the principle of seeking common ground and preserving what is different."[104] At the same time, it calls for "selective reprinting and publication" of materials "with more objective and accurate content" that are "useful for advancing a united China."[105] Applying the *wenshi ziliao* editing principle of "refining" materials, leaders at the national level sought to incorporate Taiwan into the project in a way that would inscribe diversity within a cohesive Party-approved narrative.

Conclusion

The Party exhibited a continued ambivalence toward local elites in the process of healing and reconciliation. This was manifested in the rhetoric of affective community combined with the continual tensions and

---

[103] "Outline of Report Regarding [the] Situation and Spirit of [the] PPCC's Fifth National *Wenshi Ziliao* Work Conference," 8–9.
[104] "Selected Experiences from the Fifth National *Wenshi Ziliao* Work Conference."
[105] Ibid.; "Outline of Report Regarding [the] Situation and Spirit of [the] PPCC's Fifth National *Wenshi Ziliao* Work Conference," 8–9.

apprehension created by political study sessions and uncertainty about Party status. This ambivalence shaped the *wenshi ziliao*'s controlled, selective approach to social mobilization and the hybrid strategies of interviewing that combined open-ended, unreserved expression of views with carefully circumscribed questionnaire-like sessions.

As with truth commissions in other countries, the *wenshi ziliao* accounts had a legal as well as historical significance and function. In numerous cases, detailed research into the lives of individuals formerly labeled as counterrevolutionaries served as legal evidence used by friends and relatives to obtain material compensation as well as symbolic historical rehabilitation. As a result, participants in the project carried out healing and reconciliation in multiple stages that included the social mobilization of writers and informants, the legal rehabilitation of commemorated individuals, and, as described more in the next chapter, the distribution of *wenshi ziliao* for propaganda and educational purposes.

In the specific context of the northeast borderland, the early influence of Russian and Japanese colonialism sparked sensitive questions about who belonged within an acceptable national narrative and brought to the fore local identities that deviated from the Party-centered version of history.

We now turn our attention in more depth to the role and impact that *wenshi ziliao* had in social and political mobilization.

6   Mobilizing a "Patriotic United Front"

Introduction

The mixture of lingering suspicion and mutual interests in the Party's attitude toward local elites informed *wenshi ziliao* organizers' ambivalence about the project's role as an instrument of social and political mobilization. Differentiating the project from other more "passive" historical endeavors such as gazetteers and Party histories, PPCC leaders attributed the special importance of *wenshi ziliao* to its "active" characteristic of mobilizing United Front social forces through collecting and writing historical materials. *Wenshi ziliao* organizers measured the success, accuracy, and comprehensiveness of their mission of "salvaging the past" in terms of *wenshi ziliao* committees' capacity to link up with other social organizations and penetrate into every sector of society. At the same time, the Party exhibited concern about the political "safeness" of the materials collected and the range of perspectives expressed in them. Pursuing a delicate balancing act of containing the Pandora's box of meanings and interpretations within the Party's control, organizers sought new channels for expanding the reach and impact of *wenshi ziliao* while experimenting with hybrid *neibu/gongkai* (internal/open) approaches to publishing and circulating the materials.

This profound ambivalence about local elites and the role of *wenshi ziliao* in social mobilization marked both continuity with and departure from earlier attempts by the Party to mobilize and secure the support, loyalty, and expertise of economic, social, and cultural elites for its program of socialist transformation and development. As had been the case in United Front ventures during the 1950s, PPCC and *wenshi ziliao* organizers in the 1980s continued to hold mixed views of this social class as on one hand a valuable asset for the Party deserving privileged treatment and on the other hand a potentially dangerous source of ideological confusion and an object of criticism and reeducation.

At the same time, the context had changed dramatically between the two periods of United Front work. During the first decade of PRC rule, as Eddy U describes in detail, the Party sought the assistance of individuals who possessed expertise in administrative management and cultural and economic production, occasionally lavishing on them privileged position and access in order to co-opt and incorporate them into the new national polity.[1] In doing so, however, the Party's authority, control, and confidence in its vision for socialist reconstruction was rarely in question, and as Gerry Groot's research shows, its use of a more expansive national framework to incorporate this group of elites served as an instrumental means of achieving a more comprehensive and less politically costly hegemonic control over society.[2] In the aftermath of the profound trauma, confusion, and intra-Party disarray of the Cultural Revolution, the Party used the revived *wenshi ziliao* to experiment with a much more loosely organized, ideologically varied approach to political mobilization that gave participants in the project wider room to articulate diverse social and regional identities that did not always match up with or conform to Party-centered nationalism. These dynamics of producing *wenshi ziliao* in the 1980s reveal a moment of profound ambivalence about historical and ideological truth that made the mobilization of local elites a more ambiguous and delicate venture, with the "objects" of mobilization (the local elites) having a greater say in dictating the terms of producing historical memory and discourse.

Along with this United Front dimension, the *wenshi ziliao*'s integration of historical research with social mobilization was in many respects not a new phenomenon in modern China. In the early twentieth century, activist intellectuals regarded the collection and analysis of social facts as integral to the transformation and production of new social group identities that could collectively constitute and consolidate the Chinese nation.[3] As Leigh Jenco observes, Yan Fu's concept of *qunxue* "reflected a broader attempt by elites to identify the Chinese nation as grounded in a multiplicity of interests." According to Liang Qichao's interpretation of *qunxue*, "although in a nation there may be 10,000 differences of status, purpose, and ability, the knowledge and will that governs these 10,000 differences is one – resulting in the mutual communication, intersecting strengths, and infinite points of contact that unite 10,000 paths in one shared direction."[4] The nationalist united front concept that was at the

---

[1] Eddy U, "Dangerous Privilege," 32–57.   [2] Groot, *Managing Transitions*.
[3] See Tong Lam, *A Passion for Facts*.
[4] Leigh Jenco, "New Communities for New Knowledge: Theorizing the Movement of Ideas across Space," in Jenco, ed., *Chinese Thought as Global Theory: Diversifying Knowledge Production in the Social Sciences and Humanities* (Albany, NY: State University of New York Press, 2016), 140–142.

core of the *wenshi ziliao* initiative drew on a Chinese communist tradition that went back to the 1940s. Its roots, however, go back further to this earlier intellectual movement that sought to replace the Confucian family and clan-centered paradigm with a new vision of society as a composite of diverse social groups and interests that together constituted the nation.

While that movement had been driven by and centered on local elites, Mao's communist movement directed its attention to peasants as the core target of political transformation and mobilization through its version of social fact collecting, the mass line and "investigative research." As described in Chapter 4, the mass line was a mechanism by which the Party used the collection and ideological "processing" of raw human experiences to access and mobilize the peasant masses through cultivating and unleashing class struggle. The Party cadres who implemented the mass line were simultaneously agents and objects of social transformation. As Aminda Smith notes in her discussion of the mass line as applied to "vagrants," "the self-critical cadre whose own 'incorrect mind-set' was transformed through reeducation was a narrative trope ... The official rhetoric insisted that the CCP's own agents were as prone to 'mistaken worldviews' as anyone else, and this claim evidenced the pervasiveness of Old Society ideological damage while cadres' renunciation of 'wrong thoughts' testified to the transformative power of reeducation." Smith describes an idealized triangular relationship between people with incorrect views or vagrants, ordinary people with correct views, and Party cadres in need of correction themselves, with "each person's ideological transformation" depicted "as the result of the mutually beneficial encounter between the Party and the People."[5]

Intellectuals had an ambiguous role in relation to the state in the empirical research and social mobilization processes of investigative research. The Party relied on them for their scientific expertise, yet at the same time used the investigations to reeducate and discipline them through making them "learn from the peasants" and endure physical hardship. As Ping-Chun Hsiung has pointed out, the purpose of these investigations was to closely connect the central Party organization to the grassroots population and thereby facilitate political mobilization of the masses, to demonstrate the Party's genuine concern about local conditions, and to collect social facts that could inform policy formulation and provide empirical evidence supporting the Party's decisions and actions. In practice, as Hsiung points out, swings in Party politics and the caprices of Mao's leadership made investigative research a perilous venture for the investigators, whose research findings came to light only after consensus

---

[5] Smith, *Thought Reform and China's Dangerous Classes*, 91–92.

among the research team members and approval by Party and state agencies at multiple levels.[6]

Like these earlier methods, the *wenshi ziliao* combined the objectives of social fact collecting, empirical research, and social mobilization. Deng Yingchao's formulation of *wenshi ziliao* as having mutually reinforcing "passive" and "active" characteristics of "passive" research and "active" United Front work hearkened back to mass line attempts to integrate fact finding and mass mobilization. Like the Party cadres implementing the mass line in the 1950s, *wenshi ziliao* organizers were simultaneously agents and objects of social transformation. As with investigative research, *wenshi ziliao* utilized local elites with research expertise to conduct the investigations, which similarly had the purpose of reinvigorating ties between the Party and grassroots organizations and thereby facilitating the Party's mobilization of certain social groups, demonstrating to local society that the Party cared earnestly about improving their situation, and providing a mechanism for evaluating and collecting social facts about local conditions that could inform policy formulation and revision while providing hard evidence to justify the Party line.

There were also differences from past practices. An obvious distinction was between the groups being mobilized, with peasants and vagrants in the 1950s and local elites in the 1980s being the objects of mobilization. In both cases, particularly with regard to vagrants and local elites, the Party viewed those at the front line of social mobilization and transformation with a degree of ambivalence and suspicion. In the case of the vagrants, the Party resorted, at least initially, to reeducation internment camps as one way to carry out thought reform in an intensive, focused, and contained way.[7] In the context of the *wenshi ziliao*, the Party's interaction with and attitude toward local economic and cultural elites was more complicated, viewing them as objects of reeducation, victims of mass line mobilization excesses who deserved conciliatory redress, and valuable sources of economic and cultural capital for post-Mao market reform development. Given these sensitivities and complexities, *wenshi ziliao* organizers in the 1980s were much more ambivalent about the social mobilization aspect of the project. This ambivalence was manifested in several ways. First, rather than the principle of full immersion in local society, investigators were instructed to interact selectively with particular individuals whose historical experience fit specific criteria that would be useful for market reform and the nationalist United Front agenda. Second, their half-open, half-closed approach to publishing and circulating the materials placed stringent

[6] Ping-Chun Hsiung, "Pursuing Qualitative Research from the Global South," 10–18.
[7] See Smith, *Thought Reform and China's Dangerous Classes*, 12.

limitations and controls on the parameters of social mobilization. This ambivalence is not surprising given that Deng himself had been a victim of social mobilization gone wild in the Cultural Revolution. But it is important to note that, at least in the case of the *wenshi ziliao*, the Deng regime did not abandon the fundamental principles of research and mobilization that Mao had innovated, but introduced hybrid features that placed limits and constraints on the mobilization aspect.

Second, while *wenshi ziliao* practices reveal the Party's continued ambivalence toward local elites, as discussed in detail in the previous chapter, compared to the Maoist period these elites, rather than the peasants, were now the privileged focus of mobilization efforts. Even as PPCC members conducting investigations were in continued suspense about their Party status, the entire program of *wenshi ziliao* work was centered on regaining local elites' trust and loyalty, listening to their trials and tribulations, and, in mostly symbolic but occasionally material ways, redistributing resources to them. As Alexander Day notes, the Maoist portrayal of peasants as a socially radical population that could be mobilized for revolution was transformed after 1978, when the new post-Mao discourses generally depoliticized the social category of the peasantry, portraying peasants in conservative terms that would conform to market rationale.[8] In contrast, the *wenshi ziliao* re-politicized the local elites as the leading force in the Party's modernization project.

As part of the effort to remobilize this group, the *wenshi ziliao* drew on and reformulated the "speaking bitterness" (*suku*) and "recalling bitterness and reflecting on sweetness" (*yiku sitian*) historical memory campaigns of the past. Instead of peasants' bitter memories of past exploitation, the *wenshi ziliao* invoked local elites' memories of bitter past experiences (generally pre-Communist, so as to remove the Party from any historical responsibility for wrongdoing). But while the narrative of bitterness followed by Party-induced salvation was still present in these accounts, a more prevalent theme in *wenshi ziliao* was how these individuals had overcome hardships through their own enterprising efforts. This illumination of self-agency was a new phenomenon in *wenshi ziliao* that tied into post-Mao market reforms emphasizing local initiative and private enterprise.

"Accurately Recording History Expands the United Front"

In their effort to resecure political loyalties at home and abroad, PPCC leaders at all levels regarded the *wenshi ziliao* as a process not simply of

---

[8] Day, *The Peasant in Postsocialist China*.

recovering historical artifacts, but of mobilizing all elements of society into a patriotic united front under the Party's leadership. In her speech to the national *wenshi ziliao* work conference in 1983, Deng Yingchao referred to this as the "active" side of *wenshi ziliao* work. "It appears to be just literary work, but in fact it is not since after being released the materials will have an instant active impact. This literary work is the same as other kinds of united front work and is an indispensable kind of work."[9] Emphasizing the connection between reconstruction of the past and political reconsolidation in the present, a summary report from the fifth national *wenshi ziliao* work conference held two years later made the observations that "describing an individual serves as integrative education for the masses," "justly evaluating history serves to stimulate patriotic sentiment," and "accurately recording history expands the united front."[10] Former national *wenshi ziliao* committee vice-chair Du Jianshi, quoted in an interview with another committee member, expressed the urgency of salvaging pre-1949 historical experiences before the last of these individuals died. In order to do so, he suggested that the PPCC mobilize all sectors of society in conducting surveys, drawing up lists of names, and immediately sending committee personnel to their residences to interview and collect personal memories.[11]

In a 1983 report, the Heilongjiang provincial *wenshi ziliao* office characterized the entire process of collecting and writing materials as active mobilization of a united front.

In practice we discovered that *wenshi ziliao* work is not only about collecting, researching, editing, and publishing materials, but more importantly it forms part of the Party's united front work. Compared to other departments' work on historical and literary materials, the PPCC's *wenshi ziliao* contains a more all-encompassing people's characteristic. Its content covers almost all phenomena, its sources include old comrades within the Party as well as people from all areas outside the Party, and the process of *wenshi ziliao* work involves ... bringing together people from all areas of society to undertake this venture with united spirit and ethic. This is a unique characteristic of *wenshi ziliao* work.[12]

To illustrate this united front work, the report goes on to give examples of the wide spectrum of characters who participated in the project, including leading members of the provincial People's Industrial and Commercial

---

[9] Haerbin shi zhengxie weiyuanhui mishuchu, "Comrade Deng Yingchao's Speech at the National PPCC's Fourth National *Wenshi Ziliao* Work Conference," 4–5.

[10] "Selected Experiences from the Fifth National *Wenshi Ziliao* Work Conference."

[11] Chen Min, "My Part in the Work on *Wenshi* Materials."

[12] Heilongjiang sheng zhengxie wenshi bangongshi, "Yikao shehui liliang kaizhan wenshi gongzuo" ("Rely on Social Forces to Carry Out *Wenshi Ziliao* Work") (July 1983) (Heilongjiang Provincial Archives 56:1:298):18–19.

Federation, former industrialists, famous actors, and former GMD generals.[13] By soliciting these individuals' involvement and "bringing out their enthusiasm" as informants and writers, *wenshi ziliao* committees signaled the Party's inclusive policy and attempted to utilize them as agents for constructing a new post-Mao economic, cultural, and political identity.

The PPCC cadres who oversaw this work distinguished *wenshi ziliao* from other kinds of history production such as gazetteers and Party histories. What made *wenshi ziliao* uniquely significant, in their view, was its comprehensive integration of the writing and editing process with social mobilization. Indeed, they viewed the two processes as inseparable: the establishment of extensive social networks outside the Party was vital to the collection of large amounts of historical material, while the interactions involved in collecting these materials in turn garnered new social connections for the Party.

In the case of *wenshi ziliao*, the goal of maximizing access to historical sources with only a small team of researchers went hand in hand with the question of how to maximize the Party's reach across different sectors of society with limited human and material resources. "As the saying goes," the Heilongjiang report continues,

"a diligent wife has difficulty making a meal without rice." In *wenshi ziliao* work, collecting is the first priority. Without collecting materials, there's no way to edit or publish. *Wenshi ziliao* are hidden among old Party comrades and people outside the Party. If we rely solely on *wenshi ziliao* office comrades, we will have no capacity to dig up large amounts of material. In this regard, the mass line is very important. To mobilize *wenshi ziliao* collection work ... we need to place lots of it in the hands of mass organizations.[14]

Judging from this report, the provincial *wenshi ziliao* committee regarded the act of collecting historical materials as a measure of its ability to extend its influence and mobilizing force into every sector of society, Party and non-Party alike. Its organizational gaze dissolves the boundary between person and object, between historical artifact and the person conveying that artifact, and melds the two together as social resources to be harnessed for the party-state's reconsolidation. Echoing this sentiment, a Fujin PPCC report asserted that "we need to maximize forces for collecting *wenshi ziliao*. With the support of relevant work units, we need to recruit people with a certain amount of cultural and historical knowledge, writing ability, and enthusiasm

---

[13] Ibid., 19–20.
[14] Heilongjiang sheng zhengxie wenshi bangongshi, "Rely on Social Forces to Carry Out *Wenshi Ziliao* Work," 18–19.

from the Party, government administration, mass organizations, and enterprises to do extra service outside their jobs as *wenshi ziliao* collection personnel."[15] *Wenshi ziliao* organizers viewed the Party as just one among a wide spectrum of organizations and agencies that needed to be mobilized for the collection and writing process. The Party, therefore, was at once the mobilizing and mobilized organization, providing guidance and resources to the PPCC while at the same time serving as one among many sources of historical materials and expertise.

Local PPCC leaders reported mixed results in this broad mobilization effort. Zhang Zhenbang, PPCC chair in Raohe, while noting progress, was critical of the insufficient efforts made thus far to extend the mobilizing capacity of *wenshi ziliao*.

First, there has not been enough propaganda about the importance of *wenshi ziliao* work, for which reason many in society don't know what it is, why the PPCC does it, and so some leaders and people don't pay much attention to it.

Second, there has not been enough going deep into mobilizing the masses. Collection work stops at the general call level, *wenshi ziliao* work relies on a small number of people, and many people have not been activated (6–7). Even if all ninety county PPCC members were to take out a pen and write or submit materials, they are still a tiny number. As for other draft writers, they are utilized even less. As a result of this, there are many mistakes and gaps in Volume One of Raohe *wenshi ziliao*.[16]

As seen from this passage, local PPCC cadres drew equivalence between the accuracy and comprehensiveness of the historical materials they produced and their organization's ability to mobilize all sectors of society in a concerted effort. In their view, there was no distinction between claims to historical veracity and political unifying will.

The Urgency of "Salvaging the Past"

The *wenshi ziliao* project represented the constant danger of the nation's extinction as embodied by the impending death of those who had lived through key historical events. Leaders of the PPCC at the national level frequently invoked a sense of urgency about tracking down survivors of major historical events and collecting their memories before it was too late. In a national PPCC-sponsored article about *wenshi ziliao* written by Rong Mengyuan, the editor of *Modern Historical Materials*, Rong laments the time

---

[15] Zhengxie fujin xian changwu weiyuanhui, "Use All Kinds of Methods to Mobilize Personnel and People from All Spheres to Enthusiastically 'Rescue' Our County's '*Wenshi Ziliao*,'" 2.

[16] Zhang Zhenbang, "Struggle to Pioneer *Wenshi Ziliao* Work," 6–7.

lost since the previous stage of production in the early 1960s when survivors of events like the Revolution of 1911 had still been alive. He expresses concern that at this point it may be difficult to find written materials on these topics, let alone living witnesses. He gives examples of two former secretaries, one in Shanxi who had worked under warlord Yan Xishan, and another in Sichuan who had been involved in the North–South political negotiations in 1919, who, in their fear of persecution during the Cultural Revolution, burnt all the official documents in their possession. Fortunately, in the latter case, the Sichuan provincial PPCC had made copies of the original papers, but Rong concludes that similar cases of loss or near loss are likely prevalent in places all over the country.[17]

One lesson in this regard from the perspective of the Raohe *wenshi ziliao* committee took place in early 1984 when several committee members traveled to a nearby county to interview a man who was in the know about the activities of the Allied Anti-Japanese Army's Seventh Division, only to find when they got there that he had lost his memory and ability to talk due to a brain hemorrhage.[18] In his later reminiscences, Liu Feilin recalled the Qiqihar *wenshi ziliao* committee's repeated frustrations when their efforts to secure testimonies came too late. One instance of this was when they identified a man who had been intimately familiar with the workings of the Manchukuo secret police in the 1930s, only to find from his family registry that he had died ten days earlier. In another case that he recalls, the *wenshi ziliao* committee collaborated with the city culture bureau and art institute to interview a former director and acting star in films shot in Harbin during the 1930s. He died before they were able to obtain any written testimony from him.[19]

Seeking to construct a compellingly authentic narrative to verify the Party's nationalist credentials, local teams of collectors viewed the premature death of informants as the irretrievable loss of vital building blocks in the Party's historical identity. Zhang Zhenbang expressed his regret in a speech in 1985 about one such missed opportunity to verify the patriotic activities of Party cadres on the eve of Japanese occupation. He recalled, "Cui Yongjian, prior to the Japanese devils' occupation of Raohe, under the disguise of setting up a school, set up a Party cadre training class in Sanyicun village, training a core force for fighting the Japanese and for revolution. Apparently only Li Chengxia in Yongfengcun village knew much about this. But since we were not proactive, by the time we went to find out about this he had passed away."[20] The passing of this local

---

[17] Rong Mengyuan, "Commentary on Working with Historical Materials," 5.
[18] Zhang Zhenbang, "Struggle to Pioneer *Wenshi Ziliao* Work," 11–12.   [19] Ibid.
[20] Ibid., 12–13.

villager before the interviewers could reach him marked a failure in the Party's attempt to access and mobilize local society in the service of salvaging political legitimacy.

While these unforeseen deaths posed a problem for *wenshi ziliao* implementation, the urgency of salvaging a soon-to-be-lost past also served a discursive function. During the Cultural Revolution, frenzied political campaigns destroyed thousands of lives, particularly those of elderly survivors of important historical events in the prerevolutionary period. The attack on the "four olds" included a mass persecution of those whose lives harbored too much history. The idea of salvaging the past before it went extinct, therefore, obliquely referenced this massive loss of lives without directly bringing up the events of the previous decade, much less the Party's complicity in them. The "salvaging the past" discourse thus recast the Party's role as one of rescuer and healer, while circumventing and eliding an all-too recent history of Party-approved persecution by reframing that loss and the need to heal from it in terms of salvaging the pre-1949 past.

Social Mobilization as a Measure of Historical Productivity

The team structures that the provincial PPCC put in place to carry out this work reflected an attempt to harness diverse social forces in an efficient and integrative way. These consisted of three teams: one was composed of "PPCC personnel, democratic parties, people's organizations, people from every sector of society outside the Party, and old Party comrades who were in contact with mass organizations." This team, according to the *wenshi ziliao* office's report, "not only is the main source of *wenshi ziliao*, but also guarantees its special character and is the most basic force that *wenshi ziliao* work relies on." The second component of this structure is made up of "experts from history research and academic departments and other relevant departments" who "not only expand the source of drafts for us, but also more importantly serve as consultants guaranteeing the continual rise in quality of *wenshi ziliao* work." The final layer in this structure consists of the *wenshi ziliao* committees at the local level who "guarantee that provincial *wenshi ziliao* work can, in a relatively short period, develop more deeply and widely."[21]

Local PPCCs adopted parallel structures linking core *wenshi ziliao* work teams with intellectuals and potential non-Party informants.[22]

[21] Heilongjiang sheng zhengxie wenshi bangongshi, "Rely on Social Forces to Carry Out *Wenshi Ziliao* Work," 22–23.
[22] Raohe zhengxie bangongshi, "Raise High the Banner of Patriotism," 13.

This way of structuring *wenshi ziliao* work approached the compilation of large amounts of materials as a process of integrating Party committees, academic institutions, and non-Party organizations into a single all-encompassing framework. Zhang Zhenbang, chair of the Raohe PPCC, extended his vision beyond these three teams to include a comprehensive mobilization campaign in the service of producing historical accounts. He writes that: "Besides assigning a group of full and part-time *wenshi ziliao* personnel, we also need to recruit comrades from Party and administrative departments, people's organizations, factories and enterprises, cultural and educational institutions, and medical units to collect and write *wenshi ziliao*. Their task is to approach Party comrades and people from outside the Party who have first-hand experiences and conduct interviews with them on specialized historical events and people."[23] At the county's first *wenshi ziliao* work conference in 1984, a work team leader named Li Rongchun gave a speech reinforcing this mobilization scheme. "We must mobilize the masses, getting those who can write to write and those who can talk to talk. Everyone should contribute to the *wenshi ziliao*." To this end, he stressed the need for a systematic campaign organized by Party branches in all work units to assign people to produce historical materials, subsidize and provide any equipment necessary for this work, and submit to the *wenshi ziliao* committee an updated list of names of those assigned to participate.[24]

The process of accessing historical sources, therefore, involved and justified the extension of the Party's apparatus into every corner of society and provided a channel for intellectuals to participate in the project of producing history within carefully prescribed limits. Provincial-level staff gave this system credit for enabling a small *wenshi ziliao* staff of only two or three people "who were all strangers to *wenshi ziliao* work" to progress "from having nothing to substantial achievement ... This achievement, though in its initial stage, has made us realize that supporting the Party's united front direction and relying on social forces from every sector of society is the spirit of *wenshi ziliao* work."[25] *Wenshi ziliao* cadres regarded the number of materials collected, characters written, and volumes published and circulated as an indicator not simply of historical productivity but, more important, also of the Party's capacity to intervene in and mobilize society to carry out its policies and projects.

[23] Ibid.
[24] Raohe zhengxie bangongshi, "Comrade Li Rongchun's Speech at Raohe County's First *Wenshi Ziliao* Work Conference," 3–4.
[25] Heilongjiang sheng zhengxie wenshi bangongshi, "Rely on Social Forces to Carry Out *Wenshi Ziliao* Work," 22–23.

Diversity and Unity: The Debate on Internal versus Open Circulation of *Wenshi Ziliao*

The use of *wenshi ziliao* as an instrument in social and political mobilization also informed debates among organizers about the relative merits of open and restricted circulation of the materials. The *neibu* (internal) circulation of *wenshi ziliao* created a zone of cultural creativity in which Party authorities could celebrate inclusivity and plurality of expression while containing that heterogeneity within a tightly bounded framework of controlled distribution. The tension between promoting and containing diversity speaks to Alexander Cook's observation about the contradiction between Deng's instruction to "emancipate the mind" and the Party's Four Cardinal Principles of "following the socialist path, supporting the dictatorship of the proletariat, following the leadership of the CCP, and upholding the CCP's official ideology."[26] In the early 1980s, PPCC committees generally designated *wenshi ziliao* within the category of "internal circulation" (*neibu faxing*), as opposed to open circulation (*gongkai faxing*). This meant that the PPCC restricted distribution of *wenshi ziliao* to a select group of government, Party, and academic institutions along with work units in targeted industries. In addition to controlling the channels of circulation within the ranks of a specific core audience, *neibu* classification made the materials off-limits to foreigners. In the early to mid-1980s, more than 300 Chinese journals along with various books in the humanities and social sciences carried this designation. The content of these *neibu* publications was far-reaching, but particularly prone to fall under this category were materials dealing with sensitive topics in the domestic realm, such as Party history, and in the international arena, such as relations with the Soviet Union and the Sino–Soviet border.[27]

The limited distribution of *neibu* materials, besides being restrictive, was ironically appealing in some ways to writers and editors. It provided a "safe space" in which to develop fields of study, address certain issues, or give voice to views at an early, premature stage when it was not clear how they would fare in the broader political environment or in front of an international audience. In regard to writing "between the lines" of acceptable official discourse, Geremie Barmé quotes Hungarian writer Miklós Haraszti: "'Debates between the lines are an acceptable launching ground for trial balloons, a laboratory of consensus, a chamber for the expression of manageable new interests, an archive of weather reports. The opinions expressed there are not alien to the state but perhaps simply premature.'"[28]

---

[26] Alexander Cook, *The Cultural Revolution on Trial*, 29–30.
[27] Rozman, "China's Soviet Watchers in the 1980s," 436–437.
[28] Geremie Barmé, *In the Red: On Contemporary Chinese Culture* (New York, NY: Columbia University Press, 1999), 5–6, cited in Cook, *The Cultural Revolution on Trial*, 29–30.

While Haraszti describes the imperative for writers to formulate a "between the lines" discourse, *neibu faxing* provided *wenshi ziliao* writers with a "between the lines" structural framework within which they could experiment more freely with historical discourses. It provided a degree of protection for authors and publishers from personal responsibility for the content of their publications, and in some cases it gave writers the freedom to publish without having to face the tight scrutiny of the local Party secretary. Counterbalancing the constraints on range of circulation was a relaxation in control of unofficial, divergent points of view that might otherwise have been construed as representative of the official government stance.

This was particularly relevant for historical writing, accommodating a sliding of multiple layers of history in dynamic tension with each other as the Party delicately negotiated the legacy of its recent political mistakes. Observing how *wenshi ziliao* negotiated the tumultuous history of ethnic conflict and rebellion in the culturally Tibetan Qinghai (Amdo) region, Benno Weiner describes "glimpses," "buried notes," and references to histories of Party oppression and violence that are "just off the page."[29] As discussed earlier, the northeast borderland did not pose the same kind of ethnic danger that the northwestern and southwestern regions posed for the Party. Instead, the "glimpses" of different histories that the *neibu* framework allowed, whether colonialist or nationalist, Party-centered or borderland-centered, occupied a "safe space" in which to experiment with and develop a new post-Mao narrative.

There were also practical economic and bureaucratic considerations. *Neibu* designation provided attractive cost-cutting benefits in cases where the publication appealed mainly to a specialized readership, or when the sponsors of a serial publication were not willing to make a long-term commitment of resources required for public status. *Neibu* status also allowed for speedier process of publication release.[30]

These issues surrounding *neibu* classification are revealing of the political conditions and calculations that drove *wenshi ziliao* production during this period. The framework of limited circulation allowed for a period of experimentation while lingering ideological debates shaped and reshaped the terrain of historical production. It enabled PPCC authorities to carefully channel and direct these materials to a select audience, retaining some control over how they were used and who used them while averting the risk of their appropriation by other groups for alternative proposes.

There was general agreement about the merits of using *wenshi ziliao* as reference materials for other offices and organizations involved in various

[29] Weiner, "State Commemoration of Tibetan Anti-State Resistance."
[30] Rozman, "China's Soviet Watchers in the 1980s," 438.

kinds of cultural production. The idea was that *wenshi ziliao* would serve
as raw materials that experts in various fields could selectively utilize and
reshape into processed cultural works. Speaking at the provincial work
conference in 1983, Li Jianbai asserted that:

historical research is inseparable from historical materials, artistic creation
requires raw materials, and other social science research [in areas like] politics,
economics, law, ethnic nationalities, religion, etc. all must draw materials from
wenshi ziliao. Historical research in particular, without a sufficient amount of
accurate, lively, and objective materials, becomes water without a source, tree
without root. In the past three years many divisions have used *wenshi ziliao*
released by the provincial PPCC. Editors of Party history, military history, economic history, and local history have all used related materials.[31]

The Harbin PPCC's release of its first volume of *wenshi ziliao* in 1982
reflected these goals. Securing approval for publication from the provincial publishing bureau, the city PPCC was left with the task of printing
and circulating the materials internally. The primary readership in the
first couple of years consisted of provincial and city-level Party committees, people's congresses, governors and vice-governors, and PPCC
members, who received the *wenshi ziliao* as "gifts." The PPCC also sent
book order notifications to libraries, universities, and specialized educational and historical research institutes in major cities around the country,
as well as to major work units in Harbin and various political and economic organizations comprising the CCP's "united front."

At the same time, provincial and national PPCC leaders envisioned
a wider and more direct role for *wenshi ziliao* in mass education and
propaganda efforts. One strategy was to tie the release of *wenshi ziliao*
publications to major regional and national commemorative events. This
practice had precedent in the early 1960s. In September 1961, for
instance, *wenshi ziliao* committees at the central, provincial, and local
levels used the PPCC's official commemoration of the 1911 Revolution
as a unifying theme for mobilizing the collection of life history accounts.
The reminiscences that emerged out of this commemorative project
appeared on the pages of *People's Daily* and *Guangming Daily*, and the
PPCC sent copies to news organs in Hong Kong, Macao, and overseas
Chinese communities to create a United Front community across
national borders.[32] In the early 1980s, *wenshi ziliao* organizers revisited
this approach, calling for the release of "relevant books at the right time"
to accompany major commemorative events. They also advocated for

[31] Haerbin shi zhengxie weiyuanhui mishuchu, "Comrade Li Jianbai's Speech at
the Second Provincial *Wenshi Ziliao* Work Conference," 38–39.
[32] Zhang Tong, "Zhou Enlai and the PPCC's *Wenshi Ziliao* Work."

publishing "a large number of socially beneficial volumes rich in content" for use as "historical, patriotic, and revolutionary tradition education for the people."[33]

Even within the *neibu* classification, efforts to extend the public visibility and influence of the materials steadily increased during the early to mid-1980s. As a case in point, while constrained to a limited printing and circulation capacity, maintained at an average of 5,000 copies per volume between 1982 and 1986, the Harbin City PPCC used alternative avenues for extending the project's reach to a wider readership beyond immediate government and Party circles. One strategy was the use of newspapers and journals like *Harbin Daily News* to publicize the contents of upcoming publications. The tailoring and release of special commemorative volumes to coincide with the celebration of national anniversary events also gave the *wenshi ziliao* more relevance and wider appeal. The fortieth anniversary of Japanese defeat and Harbin's liberation in the mid-1980s provided this opportunity, as commemorative volumes became incorporated into special media events designed to mobilize patriotic fervor and loyalty to the Party. Newspapers and journals reprinted *wenshi ziliao* articles for their special propaganda segments, and various work units from Communist Youth League academies and children's TV programming to industry bureaus purchased *wenshi ziliao* as educational texts for employees and youth.

While remaining officially *neibu*, local *wenshi ziliao* committees found alternate channels for enhancing and broadening the reach and influence of their historical projects. As the *wenshi ziliao* became better known, their use as specialized historical reference materials by disparate organizations from military bureaus to theater and film companies became increasingly common. The Changchun Film Company, for instance, while filming a movie about a military insurrection, bought twenty copies of *wenshi ziliao* and drew upon the materials to render certain details such as clothing style more authentic.[34] Other writers sought out *wenshi ziliao* as new raw materials for their creative works.

As production and "internal" circulation expanded and diversified, organizers pushed for a transition to "open" circulation to maximize the project's social and political impact. In 1983, national PPCC vice-chair Yang Chengwu noted an important change that was taking place in the social application of *wenshi ziliao*. Whereas in the past the materials had "primarily been given to history research units and leadership cadres for

---

[33] "Outline of Report Regarding [the] Situation and Spirit of [the] PPCC's Fifth National *Wenshi Ziliao* Work Conference," 4.

[34] *Haerbin shizhi* (1993), 205–207; Liu Feilin, "Thirty Years' Reflections on Literary and Historical Work."

reference, [they are now] gradually expanding to ordinary readers. Some provinces and cities have already begun circulating openly domestically and abroad." He emphasizes the importance of widening public access to and consumption of *wenshi ziliao*, noting that "there needs to be a shift from internal to open circulation to facilitate educating young cadres and the masses while building bridges overseas." He thus perceives the opening of public circulation channels as part of the effort to build a broad united front as the basis for national consolidation, including unification with Taiwan. At the provincial work conference in 1983, Wang Mingkui gave a speech entitled "Raising high the banner of patriotism in opening up the new stage of *wenshi ziliao* work." He argued that the current scale of distribution of the historical materials was insufficient for this patriotic purpose. "In the past three years," he said, "*wenshi ziliao* have been circulated internally, or the amount printed and circulated has been small and the scope of circulation has been narrow. This is far from satisfying requirements in various areas. We need to advance in the work of publicizing and expand circulation." To this end, he directs local committees to take the initiative in "building a circulation network" while remaining subject to provincial supervision in the recommendation and selection of "circulation personnel."

Local and provincial leaders of the project nevertheless highlighted progress in extending production and circulation levels. A provincial report in 1983, entitled "Rely on social forces to expand *wenshi ziliao* work," used statistics to illustrate these gains: "Up to the present [the provincial PPCC] has collected 542 historical materials, about 5,150,000 characters; edited and published nine volumes of Heilongjiang *wenshi ziliao*, about 1,390,000 characters; and circulated 47,500 books."[35] Within a year the Harbin City PPCC made a similar claim on a smaller local scale, reporting that in the previous two years it had edited and published two volumes of "Harbin *wenshi ziliao*, altogether twenty-four articles, about 200,000 characters, and circulated 8,000 copies."[36]

Aside from spouting numbers, organizers also used anecdotes to illustrate the widening educational impact of *wenshi ziliao*. Another speaker at the provincial conference, Li Jianbai, described "a lecturer in the Provincial Chinese Medicine Institute who bought every issue of Heilongjiang *wenshi ziliao* because her son, who studies in middle school, loves reading 'Heilongjiang *wenshi ziliao*.' She says after reading it, her understanding of history increases and her thought is opened up." He

---

[35] Heilongjiang sheng zhengxie wenshi bangongshi, "Rely on Social Forces to Carry Out *Wenshi Ziliao* Work," 23.

[36] Niu Naiwen, "Raise High the Banner of Patriotism," 56.

follows this with another anecdote about a young participant in the *wenshi ziliao* project in Mudanjiang whose mother had fought in the Long March. He allegedly told his *wenshi ziliao* office colleagues that "whenever I lift the pen to write these materials, the events of the former generation's heroic struggle to make the revolution successful move my heart. When I think about what they endured, I love our socialist country and want to contribute my all to building socialism. Otherwise, I will let down the former martyrs long asleep in their graves."[37] By juxtaposing these two anecdotes, Li attempted to demonstrate that the entire process of production, from the initial stages of collecting and writing to the final circulation of published materials, was geared toward educating, mobilizing, and transforming people through historical writing.

From this standpoint, adopting the "insiders only" policy of "internal circulation" as reference materials for Party cadres failed to address a fundamental political and educational objective of the project. *Wenshi ziliao* accounts were infused into local and provincial news, entertainment, and education. Radio, TV, and newspaper stations used them as raw materials for programs, particularly during major moments of national commemoration such as the fortieth anniversary of Japanese surrender.

Highlighting local uniqueness and promoting nationalist unity were simultaneous educational goals that were intended to, and frequently did, reinforce each other. The infusion of local flavor into stories of anti-Japanese nationalist heroes made them more real and compelling to their readers, lending to the party-state a concrete localized character to which residents of villages and small towns could relate. From this perspective, the *wenshi ziliao* were a powerful state propaganda tool that transmuted statist political goals into locally authentic historical narratives. This combination of historical authenticity, literary flavor, and political philosophy reflects the modern Chinese definition of the humanities as *"wenshizhe"* (literature, history, philosophy). More broadly, it situates the *wenshi ziliao* within a longer Chinese syncretic tradition that fused history, literature, and philosophy into what Ji Xianlin has described as "a mode of inquiry in pursuit of the 'union of heaven and humanity'" that regarded "the very coherence of the universe as a whole and all things within it," to use Peter Bol's words. This epistemological tradition going back to the Song, as Gloria Davies notes, "gave special importance to exemplars of self- and social improvement, perceived as acting in accord with 'natural laws' to benefit others." The *wenshi ziliao*

---

[37] Haerbin shi zhengxie weiyuanhui mishuchu, "Comrade Li Jianbai's Speech at the Second Provincial *Wenshi Ziliao* Work Conference," 35–36.

carried on these tendencies toward syncretic writing, infusing literature and philosophy into history and encoding the individual life story with a broader coherency of national political meaning and truth. Instilling in youth, in particular, a sense of regional patriotism tied to broader nationalist concerns was a major objective of *wenshi ziliao* circulation. The Tangyuan Communist Youth League's newsletter, *Tangyuan tongxun*, for instance, created a special section where selected *wenshi ziliao* were displayed. Local children's theaters incorporated them into educational performances.[38] Schools were a major target of *wenshi ziliao* distribution, indicating that a systematic effort to integrate a new nationalist historiography in the classroom was well under way throughout the 1980s. In Raohe, *wenshi ziliao* cadres were reportedly invited numerous times to middle schools, electricity factories, technical schools, and agriculture schools to speak about anti-Japanese heroes. Reading *wenshi ziliao* accounts inspired teachers and students at one elementary school to build a monument to a local anti-Japanese martyr.[39] At Longjiang County's Number One Middle School, teachers assigned the "History that cannot be forgotten" special volume on oppressive Japanese rule as class material. After reading a survivor's account of a massacre that had taken place in Longjiang, students allegedly responded by saying that "slaves in a destroyed country are worse off than dogs and pigs. This history can't be forgotten and Chinese people can't allow themselves to be mutilated. We will always hold onto our life destiny into the future."[40]

At the same time, *wenshi ziliao* cadres sought to instill in youth a sense of distinctive local identity in a way that only these materials could effect. According to Raohe's PPCC chair, Zhang Zhenbang, these historical accounts "do not have any words that would amaze anyone, but they are filled with local atmosphere ... middle school teachers invited *wenshi ziliao* comrades to go to their schools to report on [the latest issue]."[41] Organizers regarded the "local atmosphere" in the historical writings as important both for instilling local pride in youth and for rekindling native place loyalties in those who had left the region to work in other parts of China and beyond. In 1987, Xu Zhanhai, standing committee member of the Fujin PPCC, reported the city's progress in publishing three *wenshi*

---

[38] Heilongjiang sheng zhengxie wenshi ban, "*Wenshi Ziliao* Is Spiritual Food That Inspires People to Struggle for Shared Ideals."

[39] Yang Lixin, "Zhongguo renmin zhengzhi xieshang huiyi dierjie weiyuanhui changwu weiyuanhui gongzuo baogao" ("Work Report of the Second Session of the [Raohe] PPCC's Standing Committee"). Delivered on Mar. 26, 1987, at the Fourth Meeting of the Second Session of the Raohe PPCC. Raohe County Archive

[40] Heilongjiang sheng zhengxie wenshi ban, "*Wenshi Ziliao* Is Spiritual Food That Inspires People to Struggle for Shared Ideals," 3.

[41] Zhang Zhenbang, "Struggle to Pioneer *Wenshi Ziliao* Work," 4.

ziliao collections and distributing 5,000 copies. In assessing the significance of this achievement, he writes that these books "not only enriched
the contents of our county's local elementary and middle school teaching
materials, but also stirred up the love of hometown felt by all people in the
county. For Fujin natives who work elsewhere, they are even more
strongly affected than those living at home by these materials."[42]
Though the funds available for printing copies were limited, organizers
of the project had an ambitious vision to promote local pride in and
devotion to the city's past heritage and future development.

Meeting the political demands of widening mobilization efforts
required not only political will but also economic resources. *Wenshi ziliao*
offices increasingly thrust themselves into a more market-oriented role as
"product" distributors. By the mid-1980s, the Harbin City PPCC began
to expand its circulation and marketing operations. In December 1984, it
took part in the creation of a city-level *wenshi ziliao* circulation network
and an extension of a similar network at the national level, and in the
following year, a specialized bookstore went into business selling Harbin
wenshi ziliao while also brokering the sale of *wenshi ziliao* from other major
cities like Wuhan and Chongqing. Reflecting this expansion of distribution operations, the Harbin *wenshi ziliao* committee assigned two additional personnel to oversee circulation by 1986. That same year, the
provincial *wenshi ziliao* office announced that it would "clear accounts"
with a "service provider company" and assume the responsibility of
circulating the Heilongjiang *wenshi ziliao*.[43] By the end of the year, the
wenshi ziliao research committee claimed that in spite of "conditions
being somewhat lacking," they had "overcome all kinds of difficulties"
and had "basically taken care of debts to the service company, established
five hundred basic subscribers, and distributed 12,000 copies of provincial *wenshi ziliao* volumes."[44]

Expanding circulation stemmed from both a top-down integrative
agenda and a bottom-up desire to promote regional identity on the
national stage. Organizers saw a direct link between marketization of
the state apparatus and political and administrative cohesion across
local, provincial, and national lines. They envisioned a national system
of local and regional circulation networks that would unify distribution

---

[42] Xu Zhanhai, "Work Report of the Seventh Session of the Fujin County PPCC's Standing
Committee," 10.

[43] Heilongjiang sheng zhengxie wenshi bangongshi, "Heilongjiang Provincial PPCC's
Plans for *Wenshi Ziliao* Work in 1986."

[44] Heilongjiang sheng zhengxie wenshi ziliao yanjiu weiyuanhui, "1986 nian wenshi gongzuo zongjie, 1987 nian wenshi gongzuo jihua" ("Heilongjiang Provincial *Wenshi Ziliao*
Research Committee's Summary of *Wenshi Ziliao* Work in 1986 and Plans for Work in
1987") (Heilongjiang Provincial Archive 56:2:332) (1986): 3–4.

vertically across political levels and horizontally across regions. To this end, in 1986, the provincial office assigned several retired personnel to "set up a service office for circulating Heilongjiang *wenshi ziliao* and brokering the circulation of the national PPCC's *wenshi ziliao* publications." In addition, it directed cadres to "strongly establish circulation personnel in each city and county, building a network across the whole province to open up avenues and enlarge the volume of circulation."[45] Heilongjiang may have been lagging behind some other provinces in this effort, since a report from the national PPCC's conference on *wenshi ziliao* that same year notes that "to deliver these books into the hands of readers and expand their social influence, in recent years quite a few local PPCCs, in situations where releasing, selling, and buying books was difficult, have set up circulation service departments. Some have even established *wenshi ziliao* bookstores."

Organizers of the Heilongjiang *wenshi ziliao* expressed pride in what they saw as the prominence of their province's publications in the national circulation network, announcing that the national PPCC had ordered 1,000 sets of selected Heilongjiang *wenshi ziliao*, "which is among the largest number of volumes ordered from any province by the national PPCC."[46] The result of this drive to expand distribution, according to the national PPCC report in 1986, was that "in the past three years national and local PPCCs have published over 530 kinds of *wenshi ziliao* reading materials, [amounting to] 72,080,000 characters."[47] Nevertheless, the authors urge PPCCs at every level to find economically efficient ways to accelerate the publication and release of materials, instructing them to "proactively contact publishing offices" to publish the books at a "reasonable cost" and "shorten the timetable of publication."[48]

In practice, local PPCCs pursued a hybrid approach to distributing materials that combined features of internal and open circulation. Constrained by funding from the local Party committee, *wenshi ziliao* offices were limited in the number of copies they could produce, designating a portion of them for market distribution and a portion for internal circulation among political and administrative units. In Fujin, for instance, the Party branch within the PPCC issued a letter in 1986 to the local Party committee asking for its approval of a plan to print 2,500

---

[45] Heilongjiang sheng zhengxie wenshi bangongshi, "Heilongjiang Provincial PPCC's Plans for *Wenshi Ziliao* Work in 1986."

[46] Heilongjiang sheng zhengxie wenshi ziliao yanjiu weiyuanhui, "Heilongjiang Provincial *Wenshi Ziliao* Research Committee's Summary of *Wenshi Ziliao* Work in 1986 and Plans for Work in 1987," 3–4.

[47] "Outline of Report Regarding [the] Situation and Spirit of [the] PPCC's Fifth National *Wenshi Ziliao* Work Conference," 4–5.

[48] Ibid., 10.

copies of the third volume of Fujin *wenshi ziliao*. "Besides a portion being given free by the publisher [Heilongjiang Provincial Publishing House] and sold by bookstores," the authors propose to distribute the books to "all committees and branches of the Party in the city; in the countryside send them to village and town Party committees, town and village enterprises (TVEs), village Party branches, and village culture and reading rooms."[49]

The use of *wenshi ziliao* internally within the Party as reference and educational materials for local cadres remained a top priority throughout the 1980s. This indicates that, while United Front mobilization was a key concern, equally important in the application of *wenshi ziliao* was the objective of bringing all levels and local branches of the Party into ideological conformity with post-Mao policy. Whether the readers were Party cadres or town and village enterprise managers, the narratives presented, through the retelling of the past, a set of discourses on economic and political reform, instructive lessons for implementing these reforms, and models of appropriate behavior and attitudes. In addition, the distribution of *wenshi ziliao* served both internal and external purposes for the PPCC, promoting outreach to a broad United Front while facilitating the political transformation and indoctrination of members within the organization. Reflecting these dual agendas, Xu Zhanhai, in his work report on behalf of the PPCC standing committee in Fujin, listed progress in *wenshi ziliao* work as the fifth and final category of the organization's achievements for the year 1987. Here he describes the circulation of 5,000 copies of *wenshi ziliao* as an "important piece of the patriotic united front [that] stimulates people to come together, unify, and build a socialist spiritual civilization." He includes within this category the "study work" assigned to PPCC members to make sure they "keep up with the times and adapt to social developments in the new period." This study, according to Xu,

ties together the present situation with the key characteristics of each time period; pushes members to study Marxist, Leninist, and Maoist thought; clarifies the Party's direction and policies at particular periods of time; and [instructs members to] listen to county Party and government reports and inspection studies on industrial and agricultural production development, etc. [This is intended] to make members aware of the upper-level situation so that they are better able to contribute to building socialist civilization and carry out political consultation.[50]

---

[49] Zhonggong zhengxie fujin xian dangzu, "Report on the Publication of the Third Volume of 'Fujin *Wenshi Ziliao.*'"

[50] Xu Zhanhai, "Work Report of the Seventh Session of the Fujin County PPCC's Standing Committee," 9–11.

While attempting to expand circulation as widely as possible, PPCC leaders regarded these historical accounts as part of a political study repertoire that constituted an ongoing and internal political consolidation drive within the PPCC. The wide array of contents that *wenshi ziliao* encompassed, from stories of nationalist and revolutionary self-sacrifice to accounts celebrating entrepreneurial success, was conducive to the range of purposes that study sessions fulfilled, from indoctrinating members politically to updating them on economic conditions.

This vision of a broad educative and propaganda role for the historical materials, however, was tempered by concern about the issue of political sensitivity. *Wenshi ziliao* occupied an ambiguous position at the interstices of public and private, official and personal, that made these materials both powerful and dangerous to the state politically. Yang Chengwu, vice-chair of the national PPCC, followed his words of encouragement about broadening circulation with a warning about the limits on how far this should go:

Open circulation will also bring some problems, such as bringing up historical problems of authorities and well-known people in Taiwan, historical issues that are controversial and debated within the Party, etc. These problems, while to some extent unavoidable, do need to be considered in regard to their potential political impact. In regard to this, we need to take the approach of being faithful to facts and strictly assessing and clearly differentiating between opposing perspectives. Absolutely no condemnation and vilification, no hiding things secretively, and don't pursue low-class tastes. As for high-quality materials that are politically sensitive, you can make copies and strictly restrict the scope of circulation.[51]

The inclusiveness and diversity of contents, while essential to the tasks of building a united front and bringing about political healing and reconciliation, also made it difficult for the Party to control the political message that they conveyed. Were the individuals commemorated in these historical accounts, such as former GMD officials, nationalist heroes or counterrevolutionaries? As teams of interviewers, writers, and editors lent their local agendas and interpretations to their accounts of various historical events and people, how could the central Party leadership ensure that there was absolute consistency to the political views expressed? This was of particular concern when the Party leadership itself was in a transitional state of disagreement over how inclusive and accommodating the United Front should be. Yang's approach to resolving this issue was laden with contradictions between an inclusive attitude of "being faithful to facts" and "absolutely no condemnation and vilification" on one hand, and

---

[51] Yang Chengwu, "Speech at the Closing Ceremony of the Fourth National *Wenshi Ziliao* Work Conference," 30–31.

a politically restrictive view of "strictly assessing and clearly differentiating between opposing perspectives" and "don't pursue low-class tastes" on the other. He added, as well, the necessity of "strictly restricting the scope of circulation" in the case of politically sensitive topics.

A similar ambivalence characterized provincial cadres' attitude toward opening up circulation. In Heilongjiang Province, in particular, the proximity to the Russian border and the pre-1949 history of Sino–Russian interactions made the *wenshi ziliao* a particularly charged site of discourse in relation to recently reopened economic relations between the two countries. Like Yang Chengwu, Wang Mingkui conditioned his enthusiasm about expansion with instructions to "carefully select the best of the materials, raise quality, and create conditions" for this transition from internal to open circulation.[52] Precisely what factors determined the designation of an article as "best" and "quality" is left open to interpretation. The complex discourse on and application of "seeking truth from facts," discussed elsewhere, are an indicator of how up for grabs these labels were in different contexts. As in other areas of *wenshi ziliao* production, therefore, competing agendas and latent anxieties about the project's political sensitivity and mobilizing capacity shaped the ambiguity in policies on circulation.

Conclusion

Wenshi ziliao organizers introduced an innovative approach to social and political mobilization that integrated the Maoist methods of mass line and investigative research with a more controlled, selective mobilization process. The *neibu/gongkai* hybrid framework for *wenshi ziliao* publishing and circulation provided a politically safe space for Party officials, informants, writers, and editors to experiment locally with different variations of reform discourse in the realm of history. This hybrid structure also allowed Party cadres to get their feet wet in the market through brokering the limited sale of *wenshi ziliao* and building regional circulation networks. More broadly, the *wenshi ziliao* reveals a Party anxious to reanimate socialist discourse with a new grassroots historical-literary movement yet equally anxious to contain this animus within a tightly controlled editing and circulation process.

In the next chapter, we look at how these tensions informed participants' interactions at different levels of the PPCC's local-regional-national structure.

---

[52] Wang Mingkui, "Raise High the Banner of Patriotism," 52.

7 Local, Regional, and National Dynamics of *Wenshi Ziliao* Production

Introduction

Along with mobilizing local elites, *wenshi ziliao* organizers used the collection of historical materials as a means for reconsolidating the party-state bureaucratic apparatus. *Wenshi ziliao* committees' solicitation of materials from a wide range of official organizations demanded cooperation across departments and agencies. The coordinated act of submitting accounts on particular topics and the comprehensiveness of the materials thus collected operated as a test and measure of the post-Mao state's capacity to behave in a rational, systematic, and specialized fashion. This integrative project played out in complex ways through the interactions between county, city, provincial, and national levels of the PPCC. Provincial organizers' efforts to consolidate county-level work into a unified and coherent process was met with mixed responses from participants at the city and county levels who at times resisted but more often appropriated interventions from above to resituate themselves and their localities in the wider regional and national cultural arena. These interactions and integrative pressures ironically provided a new framework for rationalizing and rearticulating pre-national concepts of northeast regionality.

The effort to infuse a higher level of efficiency, cooperation, and integration into the bureaucracy was part of a broader post-Mao project of replacing highly emotional political campaigns and personal charisma with rational expertise and impersonal standardization. As Alexander Cook observes, this strategy for obtaining "stability, continuity, and great authority," as a 1978 Party communiqué put it, follows Max Weber's reasoning that bureaucratic rationalization is the most effective means of modernization and industrialization, and involved "the institution of a well-ordered hierarchy of offices, staffed by skilled technocrats capable of efficiently and impersonally executing tasks according to clear rules and procedures."[1] *Wenshi ziliao* organizers expressed concern about

[1] Cook, *The Cultural Revolution on Trial*, 26–27.

what they perceived as scattered and disorganized activities emanating out of different offices. Using the terms "systematization" and "specialization," they tied bureaucratic rationalization to the comprehensive and accurate collecting, organization, editing, and publication of historical materials. This agenda was consistent with the communiqué's stated goals of "stability, continuity, and great authority," in this case to be achieved by constructing a more robust historical narrative of the Party and the nation.

At the same time, the integrative localization or localized integration of the *wenshi ziliao* process speaks to the flexibility and resilience that scholars have attributed to post-Mao governance strategies, as referenced earlier. The combination of broad conceptual guidelines proposed by the national PPCC, publishing and circulation prerogatives devolved to the county and city levels, and provincial and interprovincial efforts to develop coherent northeast regional narratives contributed to and allowed room for an interlayered process of initiative and reappropriation. As with the hybrid *neibu/gongkai* approach to circulating *wenshi ziliao*, the embeddedness of flexible design into the vertical structure of PPCC committees balanced grassroots-based practice with top-down hierarchical control.

This raises more fundamental questions about the relationship between the party-state and local practices of knowledge production. Here it may be useful to consider Henri Lefebvre's decentering perspective on modern industrial capitalism through the lens of space produced by lived everyday practices and contingencies. In the post-Mao Chinese context, the party-state was attempting to recenter political authority and discourse through producing a new national Party-centered history. The "lived practices" of memory production exposed the limits of this homogenizing "monologue of the state."[2] But these contradictions and contingencies of *wenshi ziliao* practice were a built-in feature of the Party's design of the project. Deng's innovative spin on Chinese communist approaches to social mobilization, investigative research, and democratic centralism purposefully created the conditions for contingency and contradiction to emerge and proliferate within layers of organizational and discursive structuring and control.

The relationship between state power and political identity formation has been a fraught issue in twentieth-century Chinese history. In his analysis of student movements, Fabio Lanza has argued that in both 1919 (the May Fourth period) and the early stage of the Cultural

---

[2] Kristin Ross, "Streetwise: The French Invention of Everyday Life," *Parallax* 2 (1996): 73, cited in Lanza, *Behind the Gate*, 6–7.

Revolution (1966), the production of student identities grew out of the tensions that resulted from students' continual but always incomplete distancing from the disciplinary and hierarchical authority of the state, which in turn "continuously attempted to reabsorb the challenge of 'students.'"[3] On the other end of the spectrum were the participants in investigative research during the Great Leap Forward who, as Ping-Chun Hsiung has shown, operated squarely within the confines of the party-state apparatus and were subject to multiple levels of Party supervision.[4]

The *wenshi ziliao* constitute a mode of memory politics and identity formation that falls between these two ends of the spectrum in regard to distancing from or proximity to the state. Organizers at each level used their proximity to and position within the party-state structure to revise and produce local and regional historical identities. Politicization, in this case, was the result of state mobilization and local participants' reappropriation of the Party's mobilizing agenda and resources. Rather than either distance from or total immersion within the party-state, *wenshi ziliao* writers and editors negotiated a multilayered space within the state, maneuvering the tension between hierarchical structure and decentralized localization that was itself the product of a post-Mao state strategy to balance the needs of healing, reconciliation, and Party control.

Mending Fractures within the Party-State

The mobilization of people and resources for the production of *wenshi ziliao* materials was as much about integrating different sectors of the state under tight Party control as it was about linking the party-state to society at large. Local PPCC leaders perceived fractures within the party-state that were just as problematic from the standpoint of producing history as were the divisions between Party and non-Party elements of society. In Raohe, Zhang Zhenbang noted positive trends toward greater cooperation among different agencies and work units in the collection of *wenshi ziliao*. Particularly noteworthy for their "selfless and sincere help" were the "County Gazetteer Office, the Party History Office, the Public Security Bureau, the court system, the Bureau of Water Resources, Yongle Village, and Xiaojiahe Township."[5] He argued that interagency cooperation was essential for the successful completion of special-topic *wenshi ziliao* issues. Writing on the histories of transferred soldiers' development of the "Great Northern Wilderness" and the battle

[3] Lanza, *Behind the Gate*, 6–7.
[4] Ping-Chun Hsiung, "Pursuing Qualitative Research from the Global South," 10–15.
[5] Zhang Zhenbang, "Struggle to Pioneer *Wenshi Ziliao* Work," 6.

with the Soviet Union over Zhenbao Island, for instance, would demand the *wenshi ziliao* office's collaboration with state-run farms and the "81679 Army Unit," respectively. Similarly, collecting materials on Li Baoman, the founder of Raohe's anti-Japanese guerrilla unit, "must be done in cooperation with the Party History Office, the Gazetteer Office, and each township."

The range of Party- and state-run organizations that influenced and participated in the project is evident from the identities of those to whom the PPCC submitted its *wenshi ziliao* work conference reports. Besides the district, provincial, and national PPCC offices, recipients of the third Harbin work conference report at the city level included the following extensive list: every department office of the Party, the People's Congress, the court, the government office, the Historical Gazetteer Office, the Overseas Chinese Affairs Office, the Discipline and Inspection Office, the All-Workers' Union, the Women's Federation, each democratic party, the Industry and Commerce Federation, the Taiwan Federation, the Overseas Chinese Federation, the Harbin Daily Newspaper, and radio and TV stations.[6] The order of contents in this official "mailing list" reflects a political vision of the *wenshi ziliao* as centered on the party-state, fanning out to various United Front social and economic organizations, and finally extending to the general mass audience.

Local PPCC cadres expressed their concern about the standing and reputation of the PPCC, bemoaning the perception of some that the organization was "superfluous" and "dead waters." To combat this, they advocated not only "raising the self-consciousness" of members and mobilizing them to engage more actively in various projects such as the *wenshi ziliao*, but also tightening the relationship between the PPCC and the Party. The authors of a work report in Fujin describe a three-step plan for accomplishing this: the first is to "proactively report on work" to the county Party office. "If problems are encountered, immediately indicate this to the county Party." The second step is to "put into full play the role of the Party Committee" by "educating the collective membership on Party directives and policies," organizing discussions of policy issues, and ensuring that each work committee within the PPCC carries out appropriate tasks. The third part to this plan emphasizes the PPCC's role as bridge between the Party and local society, citing as examples the conversations and "plenum meetings" that the Fujin PPCC convened on issues such as education and national unification. These activities, according to the

---

[6] Zhengxie haerbin shi weiyuanhui bangongting, "Shi zhengxie zhaokai disanci wenshi ziliao gongzuo huiyi" ("The City PPCC Convenes Its Third *Wenshi Ziliao* Work Conference"), *Zhengxie qingkuang* (*Developments with the PPCC*), no. 23 (Nov. 9, 1987). Harbin City Archive.

report, "were all appreciated and supported by branches of the central Party."[7] Conscious of their potentially politically suspect and marginal position as a "united front" organization outside the Party, PPCC leaders were anxious to provide evidence of their loyalty and usefulness to the Party as agents of mobilizing wider social support for its policies.

At the same time, they criticized Party and government leaders for not paying them enough attention and respect, and demanded that these officials work harder to incorporate the PPCC more substantively into decision-making processes. The metaphor that Guan Chengzheng, a Fujin PPCC standing committee member, used to describe the ideal relationship between the PPCC and the Party was "both ends warm" – "the warmth of the city Party Committee and government on one end stimulates the PPCC's warmth on the other." Developing the metaphor, he writes: "Judging from our city's experience, in order for the Party and government to be truly 'warm,' it is not enough for just one or two leaders to be warm; the whole collective organization needs to be warm. It doesn't mean being warm momentarily as a passing thought, but being continually warm." He praises the city Party leadership for visiting the PPCC "over forty times, on average three times per month," and for inviting PPCC leaders to six on-site office meetings, a science and technology conference, work report meetings, and spring festival celebrations. However, he contends that the Party neither offers sufficient concrete guidance and support nor allows the PPCC to play an important political role, with the result that "work has lacked planning, moving in sporadic pushes." In particular, he notes that "there is not enough time given to consultation, and decisions are made hastily without proper examination," and consequently "there has been fairly little criticism and recommendations" on issues like overlapping Party and government responsibilities.[8] In spite of the official discourse and apparent Party objectives of broad-based political consolidation, the actual interactions between the PPCC and the Party indicate that United Front workers often found themselves short of resources, ignored by Party officials, and demoralized with the sense that their efforts in projects like the *wenshi ziliao* were without substantial purpose and recognition.

That said, *wenshi ziliao* collection involved a mobilization of state agencies, demonstrating their compliance with and implementation of Party policy through their active submission of historical materials to the *wenshi ziliao* office. To this end, local committees drafted outlines that listed

---

[7] "Wrap-Up Summary of Fujin County PPCC's Work," 9–10.
[8] Guan Chengzheng, "Work Report of the First Session of the Fujin City PPCC's Standing Committee," 5–6.

historical topics according to the agencies involved. The following is an example of one such outline drafted in Raohe, showing the name of the agency on the left side of the colon and the description of the historical topics for which that agency was responsible on the right side. For the sake of brevity, the topic descriptions have in most cases been paraphrased:

> **Public Security Bureau:** Public security conditions in old China and Manchukuo periods; Manchukuo police brutality; and the anti-opium drive after 1949.
>
> **Hygiene:** Historical developments in medicine/hygiene and model cases of hard work to develop the medical enterprise.
>
> **Education:** Historical developments in education.
>
> **Civil Administration:** Accounts of those who fought on or provided assistance to the front line in the war after land reform; mobilization for the Korean war; cases of social relief like taking care of soldiers and their families, fighting fire, and supporting the poor.
>
> **Women's Federation:** Women's involvement in the revolutionary struggle and cases of model revolutionary women in history.
>
> **Culture:** Cultural activities in old Raohe and the activities of the culture workers' team on the #859 Farm.
>
> **Electric:** Development of the electric industry.
>
> **Industry:** History of industrial development and model cases of hard work opening factories.
>
> **Agriculture:** History of agricultural development and production in old Raohe.
>
> **Water Production:** Historical development of the fishing industry.
>
> **Postal/Telegraph:** Historical development of the postal/telegraph industry.
>
> **Business:** Historical development of business.
>
> **Supply and Distribution:** Historical development of agricultural commerce and establishment of the supply and distribution cooperative.
>
> **Banks:** Historical development of finance.[9]

In addition to these items, the outline also organizes general historical themes, including "anti-Japanese activities and organizations; Manchukuo

---

[9] "Raohe wenshi ziliao zhuanxie xieshang tigang" ("Consultation Outline for Drafting Raohe *Wenshi Ziliao*") (Materials of Raohe County's Second *Wenshi Ziliao* Work Conference) (1985) (Raohe County Archive).

period organizations, exploitation, and suffering; land reforms; and post-land reform development of mutual aid," according to particular villages that were selected as key points for collecting materials on each of those themes. Dajiahe, Datonghe, Yongle, Xiaojiahe, and Xilinzi villages, for instance, were the "writing work units" assigned to write on the local history of the Anti-Japanese Allied Guerrilla Army Unit and the Anti-Japanese National Salvation Association, while two villages, Datonghe and Xilinzi, were given the task of producing materials on the "conditions of refugees crossing the [Ussuri] [R]iver during the false Manchukuo period."[10]

The process of reconstructing the past, therefore, went hand in hand with the reintegration of the local political, social, and economic structures, demanding that they both cooperate efficiently and specialize in certain areas that together would constitute a unified system. This administrative cooperation was seen as essential to the effective application and circulation as well as production of *wenshi ziliao*. In addition to "summoning cadres and employees, especially young cadres and employees, to read and study them," Raohe's Party vice-secretary, He Baojun, instructed the Education Bureau to work with the PPCC to make sure that every student from the fifth year of elementary school on up had a *wenshi ziliao* book to read.[11] Administrative cooperation between different agencies was viewed by Party officials like He as critical for maximizing the impact of the Party's new nationalist education campaign through efficiently enabling the dissemination of *wenshi ziliao* to various groups, including schoolchildren, employees, and Party cadres themselves.

Yet PPCC leaders expressed concern about the reluctance of different state agencies to act in a collaborative manner, hoarding materials for themselves, regarding other agencies as competitors and potential threats, and thus inhibiting administrative integration and systematic work efficiency. In Raohe, Zhang Zhenbang wrote that: "If people shut their doors and do their own thing, each holding onto their materials and not sharing them, there is no way to attain substantive specialization or to be systematic." To offset this problem, he gives the following instructions to cadres: "first, you cannot be afraid that you will lose out in cooperation; second, you cannot 'put yourself at the center' and put materials you have collected behind locked doors." He was not alone in his concern. The central Party

---

[10] Ibid.
[11] "Xianwei fushuji he baojun zai raohe xian dierci wenshi ziliao gongzuo huiyi de jianghua" (County Party Vice-Secretary He Baojun's Speech at Raohe County's Second *Wenshi Ziliao* Work Conference) (Aug. 6, 1985) (Raohe County Archive): 5.

organization formulated a "sixteen-character" slogan to address this issue: "Look at the big picture, voluntarily share mutual benefit, democratically discuss, and make agreements."[12] The *wenshi ziliao* collection process was an attempt to bring about administrative consolidation of the party-state both vertically (across local, regional, and central lines) and horizontally (across different agencies at the same level). Ironically, the emphasis on "firsthand" individual histories went hand in hand with the drive for collective unity, systematic productivity, and bureaucratic efficiency.

While reintegration was a key objective, different history-producing agencies divided up their work in a way that reinforced differentiation between Party and non-Party actors in history. This was particularly evident in the division of labor between the PPCCs and Party history research institutes. Wang Jing, the director of the Provincial Party History Research Institute, was quoted as saying, "doing *wenshi ziliao* work is significant. Using history to educate youth to love the party, love the ancestral country, and love socialism is a most persuasive way." Yet as part of a drive to specialize and be more systematic, the two organizations in Heilongjiang decided to split responsibilities, with the PPCC "getting social materials from old people who had been in political positions in Manchukuo, while the Party History Research Institute should focus on getting Party history materials from old comrades who had joined the revolution fairly early." "Allocating work in this way," wrote the PPCC secretary's office, "each with its own focus, mutually complementing one another, will benefit provincial *wenshi ziliao* work."[13] This "mutual complementarity" also sharpened the boundary in historical projects between revolutionary Party insiders and "united front" outsiders who had problematic if not outright hostile relationships historically to the Party.

While the *wenshi ziliao* served the purpose of accommodating a variety of different groups under a unified political umbrella, the structure of historical production continued to set apart, if not marginalize, individuals who lacked the revolutionary Party credentials. PPCC leaders, however, did not regard this approach as marginalizing in any way to non-Party elements of society. On the contrary, they celebrated the unique character of *wenshi ziliao* and the PPCC's role and purpose in creating them. In Harbin, an editor named Niu Naiwen reflected on the special

[12] Zhang Zhenbang, "Struggle to Pioneer *Wenshi Ziliao* Work," 16–17.
[13] Zhongguo renmin zhengzhi xieshang huiyi Heilongjiang sheng diwujie weiyuanhui dierci huiyi mishu chu, "Gezu weiyuan taolun hui dui gongzuo qingkuang baogao" ("Report from Discussion Meetings of Each Small Group of Heilongjiang PPCC Members Regarding *Wenshi Ziliao* Work Conditions"), *Jianbao* (*Brief Report*), no. 4 (Mar. 21, 1984) (Heilongjiang Provincial Archive 56:1:315).

characteristics of *wenshi ziliao* at a work conference held in the city. He begins with a detailed discussion of the contributions that entrepreneurs and industrialists had made to the city's economic development in the pre-1949 period. He even casts the city's Russian colonial legacy in positive terms as a special feature of the city's unique cultural flavor.[14]

He then goes on to clarify what qualities distinguish this *wenshi ziliao* work from historical work conducted by other organizations such as "social science research departments, teaching work units, news and publication departments; there are also Party history materials collection offices and local gazetteer offices." All these work units, he writes, "collect, research, or release historical materials on all aspects of Harbin, including military, politics, economy, industry/commerce, culture, education, nationalities, religion, society, etc. In this respect we are alike and have close ties to these work units." "But the PPCC," he continues, "has its unique character, which needs to be paid attention to during the collection process." He describes five main points of difference that set *wenshi ziliao* apart from these other projects: first, collecting materials involves mainly "inviting people outside the Party to write about aspects other than Party history. As for Party history-related materials, it is better for the Party history collection office to collect these, but we can continue to collect materials related to Party-led united front and mass movements." Second, *wenshi ziliao* must be firsthand eyewitness materials. Third, due to the requirement of firsthand experience, the time frame for these materials was set between 1898 (the Hundred Days Reforms) and the Cultural Revolution. Fourth, since *wenshi ziliao* serve in part as reference materials for other historical texts like the local gazetteers, "there are no demands that the materials be systematic or comprehensive, and there are no restrictions on length, structure, or perspective." Last, *wenshi ziliao* are uniquely accommodating to those who submit historical materials. "As long as they are first-hand, not copied or fabricated, not submitted twice or multiple times, not scholarly essays or fictional literature, and regardless of their historical value and whether they will be included in a publication, [the authors] will all be given compensation according to regulations and the situation."[15]

While acknowledging the interconnectedness of the party-state's overall project of historical reconstruction, Niu highlights the unique character of the PPCC's *wenshi ziliao* as an inclusive project unfettered by politics and ideology, an "invitation" to people outside the Party to lend their voices to the historical narrative. These "special characteristics" gave local editors like Niu the freedom to explore and celebrate different

---

[14] Niu Naiwen, "Raise High the Banner of Patriotism," 56–62.   [15] Ibid., 63.

aspects of the city's economic history and cultural heritage that deviated from the Party-centered revolutionary narrative. The locally distinctive accounts of commercial vitality and colonial flavor that Niu celebrates were at once in tension with the standard revolutionary Party history and necessary for the multifaceted nationalist and market reform agendas of post-Mao historical identity. The balance between cross-departmental integration and differentiation in the administrative organization of *wenshi ziliao* production played an important role in shaping these competing tendencies in historical writing.

"Two Legs Facing Outside and Two Eyes Directed Down": Relationships across Local, Provincial, and National Lines

The challenge of balancing integration and differentiation also informed the vertical relationships between *wenshi ziliao* offices at the county, city, provincial, and national levels. Leaders at the national level encouraged local and regional initiative and reported exuberantly on county, city, and provincial achievements in collecting and publishing *wenshi ziliao*. In his speech at the fourth national *wenshi ziliao* work conference in 1983, Yang Chengwu congratulated PPCCs at these levels for cooperating with each other to hold regional conferences and forming a "national *wenshi ziliao* work network" for collecting materials and producing publications.[16] He emphasizes the need for collaboration among PPCCs and other offices across different localities and regions to ensure higher quality, reduce "wasteful redundancy," and effectively tackle historical issues and events that extended beyond local boundaries. At the same time, in cases where a city or county lacks the resources or manpower, he advises the provincial office to intervene and publish *wenshi ziliao* on their behalf. This, he says, "will avoid getting in the way of localities' enthusiasm and will raise the quality of publications."[17]

These statements indicate that the national PPCC leadership was eager to devolve responsibility to the local level, consistent with a trend that was evident in other areas of post-Mao governance in the 1980s. Yang Chengwu envisioned a constellation of local initiatives that would drive national political reintegration from the bottom up. But this vision also promoted the strengthening of local and regional identities, whereby the goals of national reconsolidation became remobilized for the regional project of revitalizing a distinctive northeast historical consciousness.

[16] Yang Chengwu, "Speech at the Closing Ceremony of the Fourth National *Wenshi Ziliao* Work Conference," 20–21.
[17] Ibid., 31–32.

Wenshi ziliao cadres at the provincial level regarded the reintegration of localities under centralized provincial leadership as a key requirement for implementation of the project. In assessing its achievements over the previous year, the author of a Heilongjiang *wenshi ziliao* committee report in 1986 boasted that the committee had sent personnel down to the local level fifteen times, spending a total of seventy-seven days carrying out inspections and meetings to ensure conformity with provincial guidelines.[18] The process of determining what materials to collect in each county was, from the provincial party's standpoint, an opportunity to demonstrate upper levels' attention to local concerns and needs while enforcing local implementation of central Party directives.

These inspection team trips alternated with periodic work conferences at each level that "invited" PPCC leaders from the level below to study and discuss policy documents, listen to speeches, and compare their work performance with upper-level expectations. The fourth and fifth national *wenshi ziliao* work conferences held in 1983 and 1986, for instance, brought together provincial PPCC chairs and vice-chairs with their coun-terparts at the national level to align the "spirit" of central policies with provincial cadres' approach to implementation. At the fifth meeting in 1986, the vice-chair of the central PPCC, Yang Jingren, opened with an explanation of the central Party's decision regarding the role of *wenshi ziliao* in building "socialist spiritual civilization," following which provin-cial leaders gave their own speeches explaining how their approaches conformed to national guidelines. In the case of Heilongjiang, the title of the speech was "*Wenshi ziliao* is spiritual food nourishing people's struggle for a shared ideal."[19] These meetings were replicated structurally at the provincial and local levels. A year after the fifth national work conference held in Beijing, the Heilongjiang PPCC convened its fourth provincial *wenshi ziliao* work conference in Harbin. Over a period of three and a half days, PPCC vice-chairs who oversaw *wenshi ziliao* work at the county and city levels assembled to hear about and discuss the results of the national meeting, exchange experiences, and put together a provincial work report.[20]

Provincial PPCC cadres regarded their counterparts at the local county and city levels as generally ignorant, backward, and in need of concrete guidance from above. From their perspective, *wenshi ziliao* was a top-

---

[18] Heilongjiang sheng zhengxie wenshi ziliao yanjiu weiyuanhui, "Heilongjiang Provincial *Wenshi Ziliao* Research Committee's Summary of *Wenshi Ziliao* Work in 1986 and Plans for Work in 1987," 3–4.

[19] "Outline of Report Regarding [the] Situation and Spirit of [the] PPCC's Fifth National *Wenshi Ziliao* Work Conference," 3–4.

[20] Ibid., 9–10.

down initiative that could only be properly implemented if the provincial and national leadership intervened forcefully at the local level to enlighten, reeducate, and activate *wenshi ziliao* teams. They referred to this approach of "deeply penetrating the base level and providing concrete guidance" as having "two legs facing outside and two eyes directed down."[21]

One aspect of the "backwardness" and "confusion" that frustrated reform-minded cadres at both the provincial and county levels was the refusal of "leftist"-leaning Party members to accept reconciliation with those outside the Party who had only recently been condemned as counterrevolutionary. Facing this residual resistance at the local level to the new post-Mao reform policies, central and provincial United Front leaders used top-down measures to incorporate these outsiders into the political process by enforcing their exposure to upper-level Party documents. Between 1977 and 1985, national and provincial leaders of the PPCC carried out frequent inspection campaigns directed at lower echelons to assess and enforce political conformity at all levels of the PPCC.

The frequency of these inspections is indicative of the intensity of disagreement and resistance that upper-level committees of the PPCC faced from local branches. The head of the Heilongjiang provincial PPCC committee during its fifth session from 1983 to 1985 oversaw 1,820 investigations into conflicts within PPCC local units. According to his recollections, a major source of grievances was discrepancies at the local level in PPCC units' handling of the new "united front" policy regarding treatment of intellectuals, former GMD officials, and former businessmen, as well as in the areas of religion, ethnic minorities, and overseas relations. Blaming the "leftist" tendencies of local unit cadres for inhibiting top-down Party reform, he used temperature gradients as a metaphor for characterizing the relationship between different levels of the PPCC. While the upper-level leadership was "hot" in its embrace of the new policy toward intellectuals, middle echelons were "cool" and lower-level cadres were downright cold in their unabated hostility toward intellectuals.[22] In 1982, the Heilongjiang *wenshi ziliao* office organized meetings in six different regions within the province, claiming to have mobilized seventy cities and counties to collect almost 100 source materials and produce articles on 500 topics.[23]

---

[21] Heilongjiang sheng zhengxie wenshi bangongshi, "Rely on Social Forces to Carry Out *Wenshi Ziliao* Work," 22–23.

[22] Li Jianbo, "Some Reminiscences on My Experiences with the PPCC," 3–5.

[23] Heilongjiang sheng zhengxie wenshi bangongshi, "Rely on Social Forces to Carry Out *Wenshi Ziliao* Work," 19–20.

Observing in a work report that "comrades doing *wenshi ziliao* work at the base levels are very ignorant about the task and really need concrete help and guidance," provincial cadres analyzed the strategies they used at these meetings to educate and instruct their lower-level "comrades." In order to explain to them the policy of "preserving accuracy and seeking truth from facts," help them "grasp the correct direction for *wenshi ziliao* work," and "enthusiastically proclaim the need to 'rescue' materials about to be lost," provincial leaders adopted the procedure of "one person giving a speech and then everyone else filling in to examine and clarify ideas, identify special characteristics, and decide on the main points." They also brought in provincial leaders from other departments, such as the Party History Research Institute, the Local History Research Office of the Social Science Academy, and the Provincial Publishing Bureau's Academic Editing Office, to provide instruction in topics of regional history and the Party's role in it, as well as guidance in the methodological issues of how to compile, write, and edit materials. The meetings also brought cadres from different counties together to exchange experiences and learn from each other. At one of these events in Jiamusi, attended by forty people from twenty cities and counties, ten *wenshi ziliao* collection personnel shared their experiences with their peers. According to the organizers of the meeting, participants came away from these discussions with a new awareness that they needed to "diligently study modern and contemporary history, elevating their level of specialized knowledge; establish a style of work based in modesty and carefulness; uphold the 'three first-hands' and the policy of 'preserving truth and seeking truth from facts'; and gain a full grasp of the materials, get rid of the vulgar and keep the refined, get rid of the fake and preserve the authentic, and raise the quality of materials."

Congratulating themselves on the success of these endeavors, provincial *wenshi ziliao* leaders claimed that local cadres "hoped that provincial *wenshi ziliao* office comrades would often come down and convene this kind of meeting to give face to face guidance." In addition, they claimed that these regional meetings had a transformative and inspiring impact on local *wenshi ziliao* work, writing that:

[C]omrades who used to feel that *wenshi ziliao* work "had no connection to the four modernizations and really had no significance" changed their minds; those who in the past had no understanding about doing extra work in the evenings[24] gradually gained knowledge and grew into a core force; cities and counties that had not yet started *wenshi ziliao* work enthusiastically pursued it; work units which

---

[24] The author is referring to those who were asked to take on *wenshi ziliao* work as an extra task beyond their normal daily workload.

in the past had achieved a certain amount of work raised it to a higher level, and *wenshi ziliao* work in the entire province became lively.[25]

To further mobilize broad-based participation at the county level, provincial- and national-level leaders made the determination that not only Party cadres but also non-Party PPCC members should have access to upper-level Party documents. In a report sent down "regarding the scope of central Party documents to be distributed to non-Party members," the central Party United Front office instructed that any materials read by county-level Party cadres should also be disseminated to PPCC members outside the Party. In accordance with this new rule, the standing committee of the Fujin PPCC received relevant documents from upper-level agencies five times per year and distributed them to all the other PPCC members two times per year. This practice, according to Fujin standing committee member Wang Xingkun, would "resolve the issue of members' '*zhiqing*' (awareness of the situation) and create favorable conditions for their '*chuli*' (expenditure of effort)."[26]

Projects of Integration and Particularism

These positive views of upper-level initiative were not always shared at the local level. Perhaps not too thrilled about the condescending, arrogant attitude of their provincial superiors, and frustrated with a constant barrage of disruptive intervention, local PPCC leaders made formal complaints to the provincial level. In Fujin, the PPCC's vice-chair, Huang Yunmu, was also concurrently a representative on the Provincial People's Congress. Applying the PPCC's consultative and supervisory function of "organizing and mobilizing members to draft proposals and recommendations," Huang sent a letter to the Standing Committee of the Provincial People's Congress about "the problem of all kinds of upper-level agency inspection teams creating havoc." Provincial Party Secretary Sun Weiben allegedly "read it himself and responded with affirmation."[27] In contrast with the "ignorance, backwardness, and confusion" that provincial cadres observed, county and city-level PPCC officials had, in some cases at least, an equally diminutive regard for their provincial comrades. They attempted to use whatever influence they had at higher levels to assert

---

[25] Heilongjiang sheng zhengxie wenshi bangongshi, "Rely on Social Forces to Carry Out *Wenshi Ziliao* Work," 22–23.

[26] Wang Xingkun, "Work Report of the Seventh Session of the Fujin County PPCC's Standing Committee," 2–4.

[27] Guan Chengzheng, "Work Report of the First Session of the Fujin City PPCC's Standing Committee," 1–2.

autonomy in how they ran local affairs and to keep at bay the inspection teams coming from above.

Provincial-level cadres, therefore, had a different perspective on the dynamics of *wenshi ziliao* work from their local counterparts. While county-level PPCC leaders viewed the collection and writing of *wenshi ziliao* as an opportunity to project the historical and cultural significance of their local identities on center stage and as a justification for the reallocation of resources to the local level, their provincial superiors regarded historical writing as a project of bringing remote areas of the province into alignment with national and provincial objectives through reeducative campaigns. In this way, provincial and central leaders of the Party and PPCC attempted to enforce vertical consolidation through a combination of sending down work teams and sending up local PPCC leaders. The project of historically reintegrating border regions into the nation involved a concomitant project of administrative reintegration of the political structure across local, provincial, and national lines.

The conjoining of historical reintegration with administrative consolidation was evident in the meetings to determine how to incorporate the contents of local *wenshi ziliao* into provincial and national-level publications. Upper-level work conferences functioned not only as reeducation training seminars for lower cadres but also as planning sessions for designing special topic volumes at the local level that would be suitable, in excerpted form, for republication at the national level. At the 1983 national work conference held in Shanxi, for instance, the PPCC delegates from Heilongjiang reached an oral agreement with the national PPCC to produce a special publication on the life of anti-Japanese general Ma Zhanshan.[28]

National-level meetings also became a space for provincial leaders from the northeast to forge and reassert older regional identities. Provincial PPCC leaders from Heilongjiang, Jilin, and Liaoning took advantage of the national conference held in Shanxi, for instance, to revive and reaffirm a distinctive conceptualization of northeast regional history. They expressed this through another special volume dedicated to the "history that cannot be forgotten" of Japanese occupation and anti-Japanese resistance in former Manchuria.[29] The Heilongjiang PPCC leadership used this meeting as an opportunity to celebrate the regional history on the national stage and to resituate the northeast region at the front and center of the nationalist narrative. In his speech to the fifth national work

[28] Heilongjiang sheng zhengxie wenshi ban, Cooperate Greatly and Thoroughly Specialize, 1–2.
[29] Ibid.

conference, "*Wenshi ziliao* is spiritual food nourishing people's struggle for a shared ideal," the vice-chair defined this "spiritual food" as historical materials that would remind people of the borderland's tragic and heroic experience of imperialism and anti-imperialist struggle. He notes that the Heilongjiang PPCC led the three northeast provinces in producing the "History that cannot be forgotten" special volume, released as Volume Nineteen in the Heilongjiang *wenshi ziliao*, which, he claims, was useful for patriotic education and earned positive reviews in China and overseas.

While appropriating national forums to reconstruct regional historical identities, provincial leaders expressed anxiety about their new responsibilities. Though the Heilongjiang PPCC had established a *wenshi ziliao* committee in 1962, prior to the Cultural Revolution its tasks were limited to collecting, writing, and editing materials. The national office had assumed the responsibility and financial burden of publication and circulation. After creating a research team in 1963, the Heilongjiang committee guided the Harbin PPCC in recruiting twenty-one people, including former industrialist and entrepreneur Wu Baixiang, to start collecting and writing accounts. Among the forty-three articles on issues ranging from politics and education to commerce and industry that were completed by 1965, the provincial committee recommended seven to the national level.[30]

That changed after 1978, when new national PPCC regulations called for local and provincial offices to produce their own materials and cover the costs of every stage of production from collecting sources to circulating books. The Heilongjiang *wenshi ziliao* office made its concerns about these new expectations clear in a 1980 letter to the national PPCC. To begin with, the authors indicate that they are overwhelmed by the enormity of the task and feel that they have no firm foundation on which to build. They complain that, of the 170 article drafts the provincial office collected before the Cultural Revolution, the vast majority were lost in the chaos. Aside from a small number that had been sent on to the national office, only about ten materials, which were sorely incomplete, remained.[31]

Adding to their own lack of preparation, the provincial staff point to the structural deficiencies below them at the county and city levels. By the time of this letter fifty-five counties and cities had already restored PPCC apparatuses. However, only those in major cities like Harbin, Qiqihar, Jiamusi, Mudanjiang, and Daqing had set up *wenshi ziliao* committees, and even these did not have their own formal office structures and instead

---

[30] *Haerbin shizhi*, 199.
[31] Untitled report on *wenshi ziliao* by Heilongjiang provincial wenshi ziliao office (Oct. 10, 1980).

fell under the dual management of the study committee office or the PPCC secretary's office. Furthermore, the work of collecting materials had only just begun.[32] In spite of these deficits, the provincial office leadership expressed its determination to publish and circulate 5,000 copies of the first volume of Heilongjiang *wenshi ziliao* by late December of that year (the letter was written in mid-October), and from then on planned to publish two issues per year. The leadership calculated that the expenses for the entire year, including an estimated 2,000 yuan for each issue's publication, would be approximately 10,000 yuan, all covered at the provincial level. The method of compensating authors for their work would be in accordance with the national *wenshi ziliao* office's "provisional regulation regarding compensation for collecting *wenshi ziliao* drafts," and would also refer to the "No. 14 document" (1980) of the CCP's Central Propaganda Department.[33]

Given these organizational and financial challenges, the authors conclude their letter with a request for more guidance and support from the national *wenshi ziliao* office in establishing offices at the local level; clarifying financial costs; understanding better how to collect, edit, and publish materials; and determining methods for mobilizing people to participate.[34] Judging from these sources, the initial impetus for *wenshi ziliao* appears to have come from above, with the central *wenshi ziliao* office demanding that lower levels pull themselves together and move forward with producing local history.

As time went on, however, local and provincial *wenshi ziliao* cadres made the project their own, appropriating national guidelines in subtle ways to advance their local and regional agendas. Local *wenshi ziliao* committees envisioned the provincial level as a space for exhibiting the highlights of their locally produced history and as a resource for supplementing materials they lacked. Whereas before the Cultural Revolution, provincial PPCCs dictated the editing and publication of *wenshi ziliao* materials, by the 1980s, a shift toward increased local autonomy had taken place whereby county- and city-level committees were encouraged to take initiative in and responsibility for all stages of the process from planning and collection to editing and publication. Notwithstanding these changes, an obligation persisted on the part of local committees to send up to the provincial level for republication certain articles that were deemed to have wider regional value. In 1988, in preparation for the commemoration of the fortieth anniversary of the PRC's founding, the Harbin *wenshi ziliao* committee collected and published materials pertaining to the United Front. At the same time, in accordance with

---

[32] Ibid.   [33] Ibid.   [34] Ibid.

national PPCC directives, it selected twenty articles previously published in Harbin that were considered of particularly "high value." After making "further improvements," the Harbin committees submitted these articles to the national level, where they were incorporated into the "Chinese *wenshi ziliao* archives."[35] In addition, the provincial office generally stored copies of all issues published at the county and city levels.[36] In this way, provincial cadres continued to view historical production at the "base levels" as subordinate and instrumental to provincial-level concerns.

Editors at the county level reinterpreted this requirement as an opportunity to show off the "best hits" from their collection of local histories. One account in Raohe, for instance, describes two such articles compiled by the *wenshi ziliao* research committee's vice-chair and submitted to the provincial office as the "first fresh flowers in the *wenshi ziliao* garden."[37] In addition, local investigators utilized upper-level supervision as an avenue for obtaining additional source materials. Raohe's team of researchers, while working on the commemoration of anti-Japanese battles, "realized that the Provincial Party History Institute had more materials and knew more about the situation." For this reason they visited the institute to "ask for their suggestions. They made many valuable suggestions, some of which we have already taken up."[38] A negotiation took place, therefore, between local and provincial agencies involved in historical production, with local participants balancing the search for a distinctive identity with reliance on provincial resources.

The upper-level leadership took steps to ensure that local production fit into overall provincial priorities. One way to accomplish this was to establish a broad framework of historical questions and topics to circumscribe the parameters of county-level work. It was then the responsibility of local editors to tie the specific characteristics of their local history to these provincial goals. In 1983, the Heilongjiang *wenshi ziliao* committee drew up a "discussion draft" of its "Heilongjiang *wenshi ziliao* collection outline" and sent out directives to all the city and county PPCCs in the province to study local conditions, tie them to this provincial outline, and

---

[35] *Haerbin shizhi*, 201–202.
[36] Zhengxie raohe xian weiyuanhui, "Zhengxie di baci changweihui (kuoda)" ("The Eighth (Expanded) Meeting of the Standing Committee of the PPCC") (Aug. 24, 1982) (Raohe County Archive).
[37] Zhengxie raohe xian weiyuanhui bangongshi, "Chen lei shengzhang dui kanglian diqijun junzhang chen rongjiu lieshi mudi de pishi" ("Governor Chen Lei's Instructions Regarding the Gravesite of the Martyr Chen Rongjiu, Commander of the Seventh Division of the Anti-Japanese Allied Army"), *Raohe zhengxie (Raohe PPCC)*, no. 26 (Nov. 13, 1982) (Raohe County Archive).
[38] Zhang Zhenbang, "Struggle to Pioneer *Wenshi Ziliao* Work," 3.

then submit detailed versions of their outlines to the provincial office by May of the following year.[39]

The upper-level initiative intended for the national and provincial agendas of political integration prompted and emboldened local cadres to assert the political and cultural significance of their border towns on a larger regional and national stage. Statements made by the Raohe PPCC's vice-chair, Lü Mingyi, illustrate this. In regard to "united front" work, he complained that in spite of the national PPCC work conference's resolutions to the contrary, "some people think 'central, provincial, and city [levels] are important, while county seats are dispensable,' or 'a small county on the border has nothing to consolidate with.'"[40] Dispelling this assumption was one of the implicit agendas at Raohe's first *wenshi ziliao* work conference in 1984, where PPCC chair Zhang Zhenbang reported that he had combined the items on the "Heilongjiang *wenshi ziliao* collection reference outline" with the county's actual historical conditions to create the "Raohe *wenshi ziliao* collection reference outline." In his report, he begins with reference to the broad national PPCC guidelines for collecting materials across a wide range of spheres from the period between 1898 and the Cultural Revolution. He then describes how the county's materials "are not only rich but also have a special character," particularly in regard to its history of imperialism and resistance, and indicates that this realization resulted from comparing local conditions to the key points of the provincial outline.[41]

Local cadres like Lü appropriated the policies sent down by central and provincial PPCCs to demarginalize and demand more attention and resources for their counties. These local, provincial, and national agendas reinforced each other. *Wenshi ziliao* provided a mechanism for fusing local particularism and regional identity with central Party objectives of political consolidation. At the same time, Zhang and Lü's assertion of Raohe's historical significance aligned quite neatly with the provincial office's agenda. After all, the provincial report giving instructions about these topic outlines provided the following justification for *wenshi ziliao* work: "Through careful analysis of our province's situation, we have come to the realization that the belief that our province lies on the border, developed late, and doesn't have any significant events or people and nothing to write about doesn't conform to reality. Our province not only has a copious amount of rich materials, but also has its special character."[42] Both the county and provincial levels, therefore, shared

---

[39] Wang Mingkui, "Raise High the Banner of Patriotism," 51–52.
[40] Lü Mingyi, "Work Report of the Standing Committee of the First Session of the [Raohe County] PPCC," 13.
[41] Raohe zhengxie bangongshi, "Raise High the Banner of Patriotism," 9–10.
[42] Wang Mingkui, "Raise High the Banner of Patriotism," 51–52.

the objective of using *wenshi ziliao* to promote their significance on the national stage by simultaneously integrating their histories into the national narrative and highlighting regional distinctiveness. County-level participants' efforts to promote their local heritage constituted building blocks in a broader provincial campaign to construct a new image of Heilongjiang's nationalist and revolutionary credentials.

This provincial agenda, in turn, provided local PPCCs with persuasive rationale for demanding more resources from the Party and expanding their organizations. Specifically, county-level PPCC cadres, in their reports to the relevant Party bureaus, emphasized the key position that their county's *wenshi ziliao* materials occupied in the province-wide scheme of things. This was apparent in the rhetorical strategy that the Party subcommittee within the Raohe PPCC used in a letter to the county Party asking for its approval of increasing the number of full-time personnel assigned to *wenshi ziliao* work. The authors begin with a reference to the general importance that recent national and provincial work conferences had ascribed to *wenshi ziliao*, calling it "a glorious enterprise for building socialist spiritual culture and benefiting the next generation." Following this statement, they go on to identify the specific importance of their county to this endeavor, writing that the "provincial PPCC has affirmed that our county's materials on the anti-Japanese resistance and the opening of the Great Northern Wilderness are two focus points of the provincial *wenshi ziliao*." For this reason, they conclude, "we urgently need to be allocated a full-time *wenshi ziliao* personnel, so please promptly approve this expansion."[43] County PPCC leaders, therefore, were quick to reappropriate provincial-level objectives as leverage for pressuring reluctant and bare-boned local Party committees to hand over scarce resources and underwrite the PPCC's modest organizational expansion.

Local cadres' promotion of their counties' distinctive contributions to the national narrative frequently arose in response to provincial initiative, especially in cases where human and financial resources at the county level were inadequate and writing on certain topics carried large and potentially risky political implications. In Hulan, for instance, PPCC cadres dutifully read the guidelines for *wenshi ziliao* work that had been drafted at national- and provincial-level conferences, but the county PPCC had a total of only two personnel and lacked any independent funds. As the author of one report wrote, "What could be done without people or funds?"[44] In Harbin, the city office faced a similar reaction from cadres at the district level. A *wenshi ziliao*

[43] Zhonggong raohe xian zhengxie dangzu, "Organization Expansion Report Regarding the Request to Add Full-Time *Wenshi Ziliao* Personnel."
[44] Zhengxie hulan xian weiyuanhui, "How Should We Carry Out *Wenshi Ziliao* Work?"

small group was created in the Daoli district PPCC at the request of the city leadership, but according to a district report, those who were assigned to the group were skeptical about the process. Among their "problematic ways of thinking" were the perceptions that retrieving materials from the pre-1945 period would be "exceedingly difficult" and that "even if there were materials to write, it would be hard to find people to take it up." For these reasons, "since we felt there were many difficulties, work was put on hold." The city office pushed harder, however, and in 1983 mandated that the district formally establish and regularly convene a *wenshi ziliao* committee. By August of that year, the committee had studied the speeches delivered at city and national work conferences for advancing *wenshi ziliao*, and drafted an outline of topics to guide the collection process.[45]

Local PPCC officials, while demanding more attention and resources from the Party, also faced pressure to implement *wenshi ziliao* in accordance with upper-level directives. In Suiling, PPCC cadres credited local cooperation between the PPCC and other Party organizations for enabling their completion of the first volume of *wenshi ziliao*. However, given that the provincial office "demanded" that they hold another editorial meeting to evaluate their progress and make plans for the second volume, the momentum appeared to come from above.[46] In Raohe, the *wenshi ziliao* committee appeared to be more active, sending people on study tours to other counties and producing twelve articles by 1984. Nevertheless, the local PPCC office acknowledged that "*wenshi ziliao* work is still far behind the Party's expectations and requirements, and far behind other counties and cities." As a result, the county branch of the Party organized a work conference to "transmit the spirit of the national and provincial *wenshi ziliao* work conferences."[47]

When historical controversies emerged in the process of collecting testimonies, local *wenshi ziliao* cadres turned to upper-level directives for guidance and authorization before proceeding further on the project. In Hulan, in spite of their complaints about scarce resources, researchers did manage to begin work on evaluating the early life of novelist Xiao Hong. Like their Suiling counterparts, they expressed gratitude for assistance from other local government and Party institutions, including the county gazetteer, Party Academy, and Party propaganda offices. However,

[45] "Gongzuo xin jumian jiji kaichuang woqu wenshi ziliao" ("Enthusiastically Move Forward with *Wenshi Ziliao* in the New Phase of Work"), in Haerbin shi zhengxie weiyuanhui mishuchu, *Haerbin zhengxie* (*Harbin PPCC*), no. 3 (no. 13 overall) (1984) (Special Issue of the First [Harbin City] *Wenshi Ziliao* Work Conference): 85–87.
[46] Zhengxie heilongjiang sheng weiyuanhui bangongting, Suiling xian zhengxie bangongshi, "Wenshi ziliao diyiji chukan" ("Release of the First Volume of [Suiling] *Wenshi Ziliao*") (1983) (Heilongjiang Provincial Archive 56:1:298).
[47] Raohe zhengxie bangongshi, "Comrade Li Rongchun's Speech at Raohe County's First *Wenshi Ziliao* Work Conference," 1–2.

controversial testimonies about the writer's life elicited fears about the political repercussions of the project and prompted them to reexamine national and provincial PPCC instructions on *wenshi ziliao* methodology and significance. Moreover, the article that resulted from this endeavor appeared not at the county level but in the provincial series.[48]

A combination of lack of resources, fear of entanglement in wider controversies, and interest in publicizing the life histories of regionally and nationally prominent individuals informed this local deference to and dependence on upper-level instructions and initiative. In cases where the historical event or person had wider national prominence, county and city committees occasionally performed localized pieces of a larger project directed from above that involved the participation of various regions in the northeast and other parts of the country. In 1982, the PPCC in Wangkui County was instructed by the provincial office to conduct interviews and write up a piece on "the early youth years of Lin Feng."[49] Lin Feng, whose birthplace was in Wangkui, traveled widely in northern China and became a nationally and regionally prominent Party official, including a stint as second in command of the Northeast Bureau of the CCP in the early 1950s. Cadres in the Wangkui PPCC promptly formed an "Early Youth Years of Lin Feng" writing and editing committee and made trips "inside the pass" as far away as Beijing and Tianjin to track down sources.[50]

The upper-level push to mobilize *wenshi ziliao* activities, as described earlier, involved a process of integrating local participants into a broader regional and national framework through inspection and research visits. In still other cases, *wenshi ziliao* were a part of a broader repertoire of commemorative activities that fanned out across various counties from the provincial PPCC and government. In January 1985, the Heilongjiang PPCC attempted to highlight its importance as a leader in China's national development by announcing that it would hold an exhibition displaying its contributions to the Four Modernizations later that year in Harbin. The timing of the exhibition coincided with the release of a special volume of *wenshi ziliao* to commemorate the fortieth anniversary of Japan's defeat. As part of the overall exhibition, the provincial committee required that city, district, and county offices raise funds and recruit personnel to create designs and set up booths for their own exhibits.[51]

---

[48] Zhengxie hulan xian weiyuanhui, "How Should We Carry Out *Wenshi Ziliao* Work?"

[49] Zhengxie heilongjiang sheng weiyuanhui bangongting, Wangkui xian zhengxie bangongshi, "Zhengxie gongzuo" ("PPCC Work"), no. 2 (no. 6 overall) (June 4, 1983) (Heilongjiang Provincial Archive 56:1:298).

[50] Ibid.

[51] Wang Yesheng, "Zai zhengxie hegang shi diwujie weiyuanhui gongzuo shi de huiyi" ("Recollections during the Work of the Fifth Session of the Hegang City PPCC"), *Hegang wenshi ziliao* 8 (1995): 13–33, at 28–29.

Attempts by county-level committees along the northeast borderland to promote their region's national significance became co-opted by and incorporated into the provincial government's project of producing a unified, undifferentiated narrative of Heilongjiang's leading role in the nationalist struggle against imperialism. Illustrating this tendency was the Heilongjiang governor's call for local PPCCs across the province to locate, restore, and formally recognize the burial sites of the Allied Anti-Japanese Army's commanders. In 1982, the Raohe PPCC office reported that Tangyuan County was the first to respond to Governor Chen Lei's initiative, but that Raohe was quick to follow. Leading this effort in Raohe were Zhang Zhenbang, the county's PPCC chair and concurrent Vice Party Secretary; the chair of the local United Front office; and Yao Zhongyin, a member of the PPCC's standing committee and head of the Gazetteer Office. According to the report, Yao led a team of investigators to dig up historical materials and interview surviving army officers and their relatives until finally, after two months of determined search, they found the exact location of the burial site and the complete skeletal remains of Chen Rongjiu, former commander of the Allied Anti-Japanese Army's Seventh Division. With this task accomplished, after their allegedly energetic efforts in spite of old age and physical frailty to forge across mountains and forests, the members of this investigation team reported their findings to the Provincial Party History Research Institute and "other relevant offices."[52]

Wenshi ziliao production was closely integrated with other nationalist commemorative projects sponsored by the PPCC and was carefully coordinated across Party and government bureaus both at the local level and between the local and provincial levels. The local Party and government leadership worked closely with the PPCC on these projects. Zhang Zhenbang, in his capacity as concurrent county PPCC chair and Vice Party Secretary, formed a small leadership group to supervise the search for Chen Rongjiu's burial site. This group consisted of leading cadres from a number of different sections of the Party and government at the county level, including the county gazetteer, archive, Party propaganda, culture, civil affairs, grain provisions, and finance administration. Those who joined the "Commander Chen grave inspection team" included cadres from the PPCC, gazetteer, library, civil affairs, United Front offices, the crematory, and the local branch of the Association of Science and Technology. Following the discovery of the burial site, the county Party leadership

---

[52] Zhengxie raohe xian weiyuanhui bangongshi, "Zongli canguan dongbei lieshi jinianguan shi de zhishi" ("Observations during the Premier's Visit to the Northeast Martyrs Memorial"), *Raohe zhengxie* (*Raohe PPCC*), no. 23 (Sept. 22, 1982) (Raohe County Archive): 1–2.

246 Dynamics of *Wenshi Ziliao* Production

"highly evaluated and praised the PPCC's investigation" and instructed the civil administration department of the county government to manage the relocation of the burial site to an expanded martyrs' gravesite, the establishment of a monument, and various commemorative activities. As these tasks were completed, the head of the civil administration department promptly reported its progress to the provincial level. At the same time, as mentioned earlier, the vice-chair of the Raohe's *wenshi ziliao* research committee completed two articles on the topic of anti-Japanese resistance to coincide with these other projects and sent them to higher levels, where one of the articles was featured in a special volume published by the provincial PPCC.[53]

County PPCCs imaginatively appropriated regulations and campaign initiatives from the central and provincial levels to fit into their local identity-building projects. National regulations intended to address environmental degradation resulting from decades of deforestation, for instance, were reinterpreted by local and provincial PPCC leaders as an opportunity to further embellish their assertions of regional distinction in the anti-imperialist historical narrative. In 1982, in response to the National People's Congress decision to "initiate a nation-wide obligatory tree planting movement," the Raohe PPCC chair and vice-chair, Zhang Zhenbang and Lü Mingyi respectively, led a group of twenty-two PPCC members to establish a "PPCC patriotic woods" next to the martyrs' gravesite. The expressed purpose of this "patriotic woods" was to "express appreciation for past martyrs and create prosperity for future generations," and "old retired cadres, old workers, teachers, doctors, science and technology experts, notable people from every sector, and representatives of minorities and women were all united in the effort of planting the four hundred trees."[54] It is worth noting that this description is taken from a speech given by the vice-chair of the Heilongjiang PPCC, Zhang Ruilin, during a conference for exchanging experiences of PPCC work across the province. The tree-planting project, therefore, grew out of interactions between the national, provincial, and local levels of the

---

[53] Zhengxie raohe xian weiyuanhui bangongshi, "Xian zhengxie lingdao he liangming changwei canjia chen rongjiu junzhang xishengdi shubei he lieshi zhonggu qianyi huo-dong" ("Participation by the County PPCC Leadership and Two Standing Committee Members in the Engraving of Army Commander Chen Rongjiu's Martyrdom Site Monument and the Relocation of His Remains"), *Raohe zhengxie* (*Raohe PPCC*), no. 25 (Oct. 25, 1982): 1–2; Lü Mingyi, "Work Report of the Standing Committee of the First Session of the [Raohe County] PPCC," 6–7.

[54] Zhengxie raohe xian changwu weiyuanhui, "Zhishu zaolin, mianhui xianlie, yinji zisun – xian zhengxie weiyuan yingzao 'aiguo lin'" ("Plant Trees and Create a Forest, Commemorate Past Martyrs, and Protect the Next Generations – County PPCC Members' Establishment of the 'Patriotic Forest'") (May 10, 1982) (Raohe County Archive).

state. They did this by tying in tree planting to their ongoing projects of commemorating local martyrs.

A similar pattern of tailoring national and provincial directives to local needs characterized the implementation of campaigns to promote national and Party loyalty through the "study" and emulation of model individuals. Adapting the selfless motif of the Lei Feng-style hero to the post-Mao context, the national PPCC and United Front office made an "announcement regarding learning from and publicizing advanced models."[55] Implicitly addressing concern about liberalization policies that were making it easier for people to leave the country in search of better opportunities, the resulting campaign's list of models to emulate included individuals who had overseas connections yet remained committed to serving China. In the northeast, one of these models was a physician born in Hong Kong who, after graduating from medical school in Dalian in 1958, served at the Taian County hospital in Liaoning Province until his death in 1984. The following year, the national PPCC, in coordination with the national hygiene bureau, set off the "study Pan" campaign with an article in its newspaper, "The warm blood of a Hong Kong person spilt in Taian county, Liaohe peninsula." The PPCC's commemoration of Pan Enliang's life highlighted the Party's restorative actions toward him to make amends for unjust treatment during the Cultural Revolution, extending to him the opportunity to visit and reunite with his family in Hong Kong. According to this narrative, his unswerving loyalty to Party and nation inspired him to turn down alluring offers in Hong Kong and devote the rest of his life to improving medical conditions in Taian.[56]

Local cadres in the northeast reappropriated the national Party's concern with the implications of mending ties with Hong Kong and Taiwan toward their goal of resituating the borderland at the center of China's modernization efforts. Responding to the initiative from above, by 1986, the Heilongjiang PPCC joined Liaoning in implementing the "decision to study Comrade Pan Enliang" by sending down directives to the county and city levels. Unlike the provincial governor's initiative described earlier to promote counties' commemoration of their own local heroes, in this case the national and provincial offices were imposing outsiders on their

[55] "Fujin xian zhengxie qijie sanci huiyi guanyu jinyibu kaizhan xiang pan enliang tongzhi xuexi de jueding" ("Decision by the Third Meeting of the Seventh Session of the Fujin County PPCC Regarding Advancing Further with the Study of Pan Enliang") (Mar. 28, 1986) (Fujin City Archives).
[56] Zhengxie raohe erjie xian weiyuanhui, "Guanyu shenru yibu xiang pan enliang tongzhi xuexi de jueding" ("Decision Regarding Deepening Study of Comrade Pan Enliang) (Mar. 16, 1986) (Raohe County Archive): 1–2.

local counterparts. Yet county PPCCs along the northeast borderland adapted these campaigns to reaffirm regional identities. In its own interpretation, the Raohe PPCC concluded that "we should learn from comrade Pan Enliang, rooting ourselves in the borderland, giving our lives to Raohe, and devoting all our strength to revitalizing Raohe."[57]

While county PPCC committees adapted Lei Feng-style national and provincial campaigns to promote local economic development and political loyalty, *wenshi ziliao* writers and informants drew on the political tradition of model emulation to justify and imbue with significance their own life histories. In comparison with PPCC officials' focus on features of the individual that fit into the narrative of self-sacrifice for the nation, memoirists appropriated the model emulation formula to magnify the importance of their personal achievements. In his self-written preface, former industrialist Xing Jinghuan reflects this in his explanation of what motivated him to record his past experiences:

I thought, I am a seventy-eight-year old man of experience who had ventured through the business world ... While my head is still clear, writing about my experiences in the old and new kinds of society is not just a tribute for myself and my close friends. It should also be beneficial for people in the business community and for many more people living after [the recounted time period] to understand the historical situation, to gain an appreciation of present-day life, and to pursue future enterprise. Having thought through these things, I set my mind to writing down truthfully what I consider to be an autobiography.[58]

In presenting his life story as model businessman and as a lesson for the younger generation on how to manage a business successfully, Xing Jinghuan was at once drawing upon and inverting the well-established didactic model, originating in Confucian historical writing and actively employed by the CCP to mobilize political loyalty. The Party leadership had circulated stories about heroic individuals, such as the (forged) diary of Lei Feng, that encapsulated the Communist virtues of self-sacrifice and duty to the collective, while drawing on the Confucian didactic tradition of enshrining virtuous individuals as paragons of moral virtue for the rectification of society. In spite of, or perhaps because of, market reforms that shifted emphasis away from collective duty toward individual interest, the invocation of "model workers" to be emulated persisted as a device employed by the state to encourage collective conformity in the implementation of official campaigns. In the project of compiling the *New City Gazetteer* for Harbin, for instance, Lei Feng-style slogans urged

---

[57] Ibid.
[58] Xing Jinghuan, "My Over Sixty Years' Experience with Commercial Enterprises," 80.

gazetteer writing and editorial committee members "on the national level, to learn from Yan Juqian; at the local level, learn from Zhao Tian."[59]

The *wenshi ziliao* project aimed to highlight local achievements and distinctiveness as a way to demonstrate the Party's inclusive tolerance of diversity while at the same time enclosing that diversity and particularity within an overall path of national progress overseen by the CCP. According to this framework, local and individual particularity was expected to illustrate on a microcosmic level the Party's national ideological principles. Xing Jinghuan adapted and redeployed official didactic representations of the model worker to valorize his own life as a testament to enterprising spirit, individual achievement, and economic self-gain. *Wenshi ziliao* contributors thus rescued their individuality from the local, regional, and national politics of these campaigns.

"Learn from Our Brother Counties": Conflating Local, Regional, and National Interests

While informants and writers made these efforts to expand the historical and geographical importance of their life events, *wenshi ziliao* cadres sought institutional means of capturing historical events that extended beyond the administrative limits of their jurisdiction. To this end, they voiced the need for greater horizontal cooperation and integration among PPCC organizations in different localities. Given that the geographical scope of certain historical events and people extended beyond any one locality, beginning in 1983, national and provincial organizers instructed local PPCCs to reach out to each other and collaborate in collecting and writing materials. This geographically integrative dimension of *wenshi ziliao* production was tied to a broader PPCC push to enhance its consolidative impact through cross-local cooperative initiatives. Networks connecting PPCC committees from different areas of the country emphasized cross-regional interdependence in economic, cultural, and technological development. One of the advocates for this trend, a leading member of the Qiqihar PPCC committee, recalled using a meeting convened by the national PPCC in 1986 to gain support for building a network of city-level committees. Later that year, he hosted a conference in Qiqihar that brought together PPCC leaders from ten cities, preparing the groundwork for an annual conference on economic and technological cooperation that included officials from various government bureaus.[60]

---

[59] Clausen, "Autobiography of a Chinese City."
[60] Huang Demin, "Yici nanwang de huiyi" ("An Unforgettable Meeting") in *Wo yu zhengxie*, 309–313.

At the same time, organizers of *wenshi ziliao* viewed this collaborative push as a measure for increasing bureaucratic productivity and efficiency while minimizing waste and redundancy. This was a challenging proposition and reflected the simultaneous organizing principles of political consolidation and localized devolution that informed *wenshi ziliao* work. Speaking to his colleagues at a Heilongjiang work conference in 1983, Wang Mingkui announced that a prerequisite for making *wenshi ziliao* more specialized and systematic was "to strengthen cooperation in areas of collecting, organizing, researching, editing, publishing, etc. work within the PPCC system." As illustrations of this, he refers to several historical events and individual lives that spanned multiple counties. "Regarding materials on the big exposure of illegal activity in Bayan, Mulan, and Tonghe counties during the Manchukuo period, these three counties must cooperate; as for materials on [Heilongjiang governor] Shou Shan, Heihe and Nenjiang districts need to cooperate, etc." To achieve this collaboration, he declares that "from now on the provincial PPCC should, in planned fashion, convene cooperation and specialization conferences and organize the exchange and discussion of collection outlines. [The purpose of this is] to facilitate communication about conditions, mutually advance, and at the same time avoid redundant collecting, releasing the same article many times, scattering materials, and wasting labor and money."[61] Perhaps influenced by this provincial vision, county teams of investigators set off on "study tours" to other counties where they met and exchanged experiences with their counterparts. In early July 1983, for instance, four *wenshi ziliao* participants from Raohe, including a PPCC vice-chair, made trips to Tangyuan, Yilan, and Baoqing Counties "to learn from our brother counties' experiences in initiating *wenshi ziliao* work and to synthesize the experiences of other places."[62]

Provincial organizers saw their role in terms of bringing about a wider political and administrative consolidation across the region, using the lens of history as a vehicle for breaking down localized, bureaucratic silos. This integrative drive extended across provincial lines as well, reflecting that a significant part of the initiative originated from the national level, specifically a national *wenshi ziliao* work conference held in Beijing in 1983. The Heilongjiang PPCC responded by receiving study tours from

[61] Wang Mingkui, "Raise High the Banner of Patriotism," 53.
[62] Zhengxie heilongjiang sheng raohe xian weiyuanhui, "Yijiubasan nian zhengxie gongzuo zongjie he basi nian zhengxie gongzuo anpai yijian de baogao" ("Report Giving Summary of PPCC Work for the Year 1983 and Recommendations for Arranging PPCC Work for the Year 1984"), *Rao zhengxie fa* (*Raohe PPCC*), no. 2 (1983) (Raohe County Archive): 7.

PPCCs in Bayan, Fangzheng, and Tangyuan Counties within the province as well as the cities of Changchun, Qingdao, and Hangzhou "to exchange experiences and tighten relations between brother PPCCs."[63]

The "wasted labor" and "redundant collecting" that national and provincial organizers sought to avoid was a by-product of the search for and affirmation of local identity that partly drove the collection of *wenshi ziliao*. Upper-level leaders faced the quandary of how to incentivize local participants to enthusiastically produce materials while ensuring that their efforts conformed to national and provincial guidelines. Shared local and national memories could, in certain cases, open up collaborative avenues of cultural production to alleviate, at least temporarily, this tension between centralized administrative control and local initiative. The commemoration of certain incidents conflated local, regional, and national interests by allowing localities to lay privileged historical claims to events that had a broader national significance, facilitating cooperation between levels of the PPCC. The commemoration of the fortieth anniversary of Harbin's "liberation" was one such incidence of collaborative memory that privileged Harbin local identity by tying its history to a wider nationalist storyline. As part of the preparations for this event, members of the Harbin *wenshi ziliao* committee extended their commemorative narrative to the founding of the national PPCC in Harbin in 1948. One of the members of this committee recalled the assistance that the national committee gave him in tracking down and interviewing the sole surviving signer of the PPCC's founding charter. Commemorating this milestone also expanded the Harbin *wenshi ziliao* committee's scope of operations to other parts of China, including the native places of the nine remaining founders of the national PPCC.[64] Similarly, the Qiqihar *wenshi ziliao* committee's decision in 1986 to compile a special biographical volume on the life and career accomplishments of Zhu Qinglan, former Heilongjiang governor-general, expanded into a nationwide project on account of Zhu's multiple associations with various regions in China, including his birthplace of Shaoxing in Zhejiang Province. As mentioned earlier, a complete reprint of the Qiqihar publication appeared in a book released by the Shaoxing PPCC, while a museum in Shanxi Province in north China displayed photos from the publication in

[63] Haerbin shi bianzhi weiyuanhui, "Guanyu shi zhengxie zengshe wenshi ziliao bangongshi de tongzhi" ("Notice Concerning the City PPCC's Establishment of a *Wenshi Ziliao* Office"), *Ha bianzi* (Harbin numbering), no. 134 (Dec. 22, 1981) (Harbin City Archive): 8.
[64] Zhang Tong, "Dacheng 'guanyu zhaokai xin de zhengzhi xieshang huiyi zhu wenti de xieyi' de qianqian houhou" ("The Process of Completing 'Agreement Regarding Some Questions on Establishing the New PPCC'"), *Heilongjiang wenshi ziliao* 41: 330–342.

a special exhibit on Zhu's life. The project even extended across the Taiwan straits, popularized in Taiwan by a Taiwanese pop star who had hosted the spring festival television production in China the previous year.[65]

Nationalist Reintegration and Pre-National Concepts of the Northeast Borderland

Ironically, however, the integrative initiative from the national level also fostered the reemergence of a northeast regional identity. The conception of the northeast as a separate political and cultural space permeated administrative approaches to implementing the project. During August 20–26 in 1985, national PPCC leaders, in coordination with provincial leaders from all three provinces in the northeast, convened the "Three Northeast Provinces PPCC and *Wenshi Ziliao* Work Cooperation Conference" in Jilin City. Thirty-four leaders from the city and provincial levels attended the meeting, guided by national PPCC leaders.[66] While subsuming regional divisions under national directives, the conference reaffirmed the designation of the "Northeast" as an entity distinctive from the rest of China. Reinforcing this, Heilongjiang *wenshi ziliao* committee members resurrected in their reports the pre-1949 concepts and terminologies of the "Three Northeast Provinces" (Liaoning, Jilin, and Heilongjiang) and "east of the pass" that had delineated the northeast region as its own separate entity distinct from "China proper." In early 1986, the Heilongjiang *wenshi ziliao* office staff laid out their plan to organize a series of work conferences in the upcoming year. Beginning with internal meetings of the provincial *wenshi ziliao* research committee, the plan called for a step-by-step progression from local to regional in the scale of the conferences. During the "second season," they would "convene small *wenshi ziliao* work symposia" to foster cooperation between localities in the collection of materials to "push forward *wenshi ziliao* work across the province." Following this stage, in the third season, they envisioned a "Northeast Three Provinces *wenshi ziliao* cooperation meeting."[67] This regionwide conference appears to have been an annual event and to have played a central role in overall *wenshi ziliao* planning, as attested by references to it in other annual reports. One provincial-level report produced a year earlier indicates that this

---

[65] Liu Feilin, "Thirty Years' Reflections on Literary and Historical Work," 363–364.

[66] *Jilin shizhi*, 69–70.

[67] Heilongjiang sheng zhengxie wenshi bangongshi, "Heilongjiang Provincial PPCC's Plans for *Wenshi Ziliao* Work in 1986."

conference determined the overarching topics that *wenshi ziliao* committees in all three provinces would pursue. In 1984, according to this report, the participants in the conference reached a consensus on choosing the CER, which Russia had constructed for its expansion into Manchuria, as the special topic for that year (later revised on account of insufficient availability of materials).

Local *wenshi ziliao* committees paradoxically utilized pre-national concepts of inside and outside China to characterize and even emphasize their diligent attention to carrying out a nationalist project. Organizers at the county and city levels, through framing *wenshi ziliao* work in collaborative planning events along the lines of a shared historical context and colonial past, reinforced a concept of cohesive regional identity. Alongside the "Northeast Three Provinces," terms such as "inside the pass" and "outside the pass" that had been used to describe the northeast as a strange, remote, and wild frontier beyond the pales of Chinese civilization reemerged in local *wenshi ziliao* reports, testifying to the editors' strong lingering sense of separate northeast identity. In the fourth issue of its special publication, *Harbin PPCC*, published in 1982, a short article summarizing a study tour organized by the city's PPCC refers to the departing team's destination as "inside the pass."[68] The language the author uses here to bring attention to Harbin PPCC cadres' effort to extend themselves beyond their locality to other parts of the nation ironically resonates with associations of otherness and difference. In the county of Wangkui, meanwhile, the PPCC's summary of local *wenshi ziliao* work describes the lengths taken to collect materials and conduct interviews concerning the life of an anti-Japanese revolutionary martyr named Lin Feng. A special amount of effort was required because Lin had spent his youth in a variety of places, including Tianjin and Beijing, for which reason the research team had to travel "inside the pass" to conduct further research and interviews.[69] In this instance, the county PPCC's report reappropriates this historical terminology to highlight the great distances and difficulties researchers had to overcome in order to complete their tasks. In so doing, local PPCC cadres inverted the original meanings associated with inside and outside the pass, implying that the area "inside the pass" was the strange and foreign land they must encounter in the fulfillment of their duty.

[68] Xueweihui bangongshi, "Shi zhengxie zuzhi bufen weiyuan fu guannei xuexi canguan xiaojie" ("Short Report on Study Tour Inside the Pass That the Harbin City PPCC Organized for a Group of Its Personnel"), in Haerbin shi zhengxie weiyuanhui bangongshi, *Haerbin zhengxie* (*Harbin PPCC*), no. 4 (no. 4 overall) (1982): 31–41.

[69] Zhengxie heilongjiang sheng weiyuanhui bangongting Wangkui xian zhengxie bangongshi, "Zhengxie gongzuo."

Conclusion

This chapter suggests that the *wenshi ziliao* slogans of "systematization" and "specialization" were integral to a larger post-Mao project of bureaucratic rationalization and modernization. Organizers reframed this modernization project as a measure of the comprehensiveness, accuracy, and coherence of the historical materials they collected. They also reappropriated this terminology as a discursive tool with which to demand more resources, attention, and respect from the Party. Frustrated at times with what they perceived as a lack of sufficient support and acknowledgment from the Party leadership, participants capitalized on the Party's efforts toward political and administrative consolidation to rationalize bureaucratic compliance with their own demands for a steady supply of historical materials to add to their collections and publications.

These efforts involved an interlayered process of interactions across county, city, provincial, and national levels. The entangled tendencies of localized devolution of responsibilities to the county and city levels alongside top-down integrative actions, imposed especially by provincial cadres, created a complex dynamic. Local editors sought more direction and support from their superiors while attempting to shield themselves from the periodic instructional and inspection tours sent down by the provincial office. Initiative shifted between these different levels at different times and in different contexts, depending on the political implications of specific projects, the geographical expanse and significance of the subjects being commemorated, and the resources that *wenshi ziliao* offices had at their disposal. This shifting terrain of interdependence and negotiation between different administrative levels of the project gave rise to local projects that, to varying degrees, overlapped with, diverged from, and reappropriated the national Party-centered narrative. In this complex web of maneuverings, the integrative drive of provincial *wenshi ziliao* editors did not necessarily conform to the national Party-centered vision. Their efforts to bring county-level activities into orderly conformity with a single coherent framework resulted in a reaffirmation of pre-national northeast regional identities that perpetuated an idea about northern Manchuria, and the northeast more broadly, as a place lying outside or beyond the nation's borders.

Conclusion

During my research for this book, a librarian commented on the continuing production of *wenshi ziliao* in China today. His evaluation was that the new crop of *wenshi ziliao* is not as high in quality or as valuable as the materials produced in the earlier phase. He reasoned that most of the people who had experienced important historical events had passed away, and that the historical writing is not as rich. Was there an implicit suggestion that *wenshi ziliao* "truths" about the post-1949 period are less authentic and more contrived than memories of the pre-Communist period that could be articulated more flexibly and with less stringent political constraints? In the post-transition period of a rising neoliberal authoritarianism, have *wenshi ziliao* lost their capacity to accommodate, mobilize, and reconcile multiple "truths" about the past? Benno Weiner has suggested that this is the case, observing a shift in the latest iteration of *wenshi ziliao* away from United Front reconciliation toward a more uncompromising Party-centered authoritarianism.[1]

Looking back at my conversation with the librarian, I am struck by how his words echoed *wenshi ziliao* cadres' urgent call to "salvage the past" before it is lost forever. In the 1980s, the urgency of this call was based in the transitional post-Mao Party's crisis of political and historical legitimacy. This sense of imminent danger for the Party opened up a momentary space where a wider spectrum of representation was possible and indeed required for resecuring the political loyalties of alienated elites and for working out contradictions between Maoism and the post-Mao reform agenda.

One area in which the Maoist legacy continues to creep up from time to time is in the realm of social science research and "seeking truth from facts." Reflecting and reappropriating the political tensions that have always ridden Mao's approach to seeking truth, the investigative research discourse has been variously mobilized by the Party leadership to demand

---

[1] Weiner, "State Commemoration of Tibetan Anti-State Resistance."

fact-based rigor and efficiency from bureaucrats, by dissident intellectuals to investigate and draw attention to social conditions, and by the Chinese Academy of Social Sciences to celebrate and reaffirm its importance as a state-sponsored research institution.[2] This flexibility of interpretation and diversity of reappropriation was also a defining characteristic of the *wenshi ziliao*, with its accommodation of local, regional, and national agendas. This is what made the *wenshi ziliao* a flexible resource for the state, creating an enclosed space for airing different voices and agendas at different levels. Its principles of "seeking truth from facts," locally and regionally based initiative, and United Front reconciliation opened it up to tensions and negotiations that were at once integral to and risky for Party consolidation.

This brings me back to my earlier question about whether this flexible, adaptive nature of *wenshi ziliao* can be sustained, or if authoritarianism is undermining this dimension and fundamentally changing its character into a more rigid form of Party propaganda. Answering this question will require more research. But for now it is worth considering what is really at stake here. In his discussion of the Ethnic Classification Project, Thomas Mullaney observes that the ethnic categories put in place needed to be continually reinforced and sustained in various ways by the state.[3] In the case of the *wenshi ziliao*, what needed to be sustained was the delicate balance between central Party control and localized diversity and initiative through enclosing diverse voices and meanings within a unified framework. The principles of the "three first-hands," "seeking truth from facts," United Front reconciliation, and localized memory production were integral to maintaining this balance and set the *wenshi ziliao* apart from other Party-orchestrated historical writing. If the Party's direction is toward increasing authoritarianism and suspicion of alternative histories and narratives, then this powerful feature of the *wenshi ziliao* may be weakened.

Since the 1980s in China there has been a revival and intensification, in new forms, of 1930s and Maoist-era obsessions with collecting social facts. During the 1980s, this was reflected in Deng's slogan "emancipating the mind and seeking truth from facts" and in the reemergence of Li Jinghan's comprehensive Republican-period survey of Ding County as obligatory reading for a new generation of social scientists.[4] Since then, the collection of social facts in the form of social and opinion surveys has become a pervasive feature of contemporary Chinese society. As Tong

[2] Ping-Chun Hsiung, "Pursuing Qualitative Research from the Global South," 7–8.
[3] Mullaney, *Coming to Terms with the Nation*, 146.
[4] Tong Lam, *A Passion for Facts*, 144–146.

Lam argues, this new social survey movement is revolutionary in the sense that the state is now directing social facts for public consumption to support Party legitimacy, to promote a discourse of *suzhi* (human quality), and to penetrate to the "soul" of the people even as it is retreating from society in other (mostly economic) areas.[5]

Compared to this partly state-managed and partly consumer market-oriented mobilization of social facts in contemporary China, the *wenshi ziliao* marked a moment of profound ambivalence situated between Maoist mobilization and market liberalization. Like the social surveys conducted today, *wenshi ziliao* writing was prescriptive of social values and not just descriptive of historical events and people, and it was designed to reevaluate the "human quality" needed for modernization and to penetrate to and transform the soul of the people, at least local elites. But unlike the consumptive social surveys pervading society today, *wenshi ziliao* was a hybrid internal/open process that was more selectively directed and contained and was always hinged between popular mobilization and Party secrecy.

The post-Mao transition also marked a crossroads in historical thought and discourse. As Gloria Davies argues, the Chinese approach to writing about the past has historically been more concrete, human-centered, and referential to positive examples than the more abstract Hegelian history-as-philosophy. Even with the embrace of social scientific method in the 1980s and the popular idea that Maoist thought was an aberration in its exploitation of theory to prescribe social behavior and ideals, Davies observes that intellectuals continued to "express a yearning for an ideal 'pattern of conduct.'"[6] The *wenshi ziliao* embodies this tension in post-Mao thought between demonstrating objective scientific methodology and prescribing social and political ideals. As China asserts itself as a global power, the direction and outcome of this tendency will be increasingly critical. In the midst of international criticism of the Chinese government for propaganda and distortion of truth, it should be kept in mind that "truth" has always been in part about prescribing social ideals and "life-strategies."[7] From this perspective, the *wenshi ziliao* might just be a compelling model for a Chinese approach to and conceptualization of truth seeking.

In regard to historical discourse, the twentieth century saw a swing back and forth between modernization and revolutionary narratives. As Huaiyin Li observes, since the late 1980s and 1990s, Chinese historians have jettisoned the revolutionary narrative in favor of the modernization narrative. In the context of China's rapid economic

---

[5] Ibid.   [6] Davies, "Knowing How to Be," 34–37.   [7] Ibid.

development and international integration, the new historiography has optimistically reassessed not only modernizing efforts in the past, but also Chinese tradition as favorable for rather than a hindrance to modernization.[8] As Ban Wang and Davies suggest, this revisionist lens involved a positive reinterpretation of *chuantong* (tradition) as referring to "China's premodern cultural legacy as a whole" and informed a shift away from critical inquiry into the past toward a new uncritical nostalgia for an idealized past.[9]

This shift had not yet fully taken place during the 1980s, during which time the *wenshi ziliao* provided space for reconciliation and accommodation. Participants in the project were intent on finding ways to integrate revolutionary and modernization narratives, navigating between positive and negative reevaluations of the pre-1949 past. The more recent removal of the revolutionary narrative from historical discourse could be a dangerous proposition for the Party. If the *wenshi ziliao* in the 1980s demonstrated a recognition of the contradictions that needed to be reconciled, it appears that recent successes in economic development and international status have placed the Party in a more confident position where it is no longer willing to recognize this need for reconciliation and accommodation. Whatever the reasons may be, it might be prudent for the Party to look back to this earlier transitional phase of historical production.

In the northeast borderland, this shift in historical discourse has informed a reevaluation of Russian colonialism, ethnic minority traditions, and regional historical concepts of northern Manchuria and "inside" and "outside" the pass. As in other aspects of historiography, the positive revisionism and even exoticization of Russian colonialism has become especially prevalent since the 1990s, as Yukiko Koga demonstrates.[10] But it had already become an important feature of *wenshi ziliao* writing, which juxtaposed nationalist narratives of anti-Russian resistance and victimization with accounts that celebrated Russian cultural influences to stake out distinctive local and regional identities. This, combined with the celebration of ethnic minority cultures and the revival of a "northern Manchuria" discourse, provided representational avenues for negotiating between county, city, provincial, and national agendas in the debate on tradition and modernization. It documents how, in this transitional moment, shifts in historiography took specific shape in the interstices between local, regional, and national contexts of historical production.

[8] Huaiyin Li, *Reinventing Modern China*, 24–26.
[9] Ban Wang, *Illuminations from the Past*, 119–123; Davies, "Knowing How to Be," 39.
[10] Koga, "The Atmosphere of a Foreign Country."

It also speaks to a comparative perspective on China's borderlands. As Benno Weiner, Dasa Mortimer, Sandrine Catris, and others have shown, the volatility of ethnic issues in the northwest and southwest borderlands precluded certain avenues of historical memory.[11] In Xinjiang, as Catris notes, inclusion of pre-1949 Uighur rebellions required labeling the GMD specifically, and not Chinese state control generally, as the enemy.[12] Uradyn Bulag similarly discusses how, in the case of Inner Mongolia, recent reconciliation with the GMD as a "benign force working for the interest of the Mongols" has narrowed the possibilities for how to represent Mongol uprisings.[13]

In the northeast borderland, the absence of an imminent threat to Chinese state control from the indigenous population opened up a broader and more flexible portfolio of memory strategies for *wenshi ziliao* writers and editors. Reconciliation with the GMD, for instance, has simply meant a broader united front and has opened up rather than closed off integrative narratives. The more looming issue has been relations with Russia and how to remember the region's complicated position in respect to Russian colonial schemes. In certain contexts and sites of memory production the Chinese state has taken a one-sided and uncompromising stance. The Aihun Historical Relics Museum, designated as a patriotic education site, uses life-size dioramas to depict the 1900 Blagoveshchensk massacre in stark terms of Chinese victimization and Russian brutality, which contrasts with the absence of any reference to the massacre in its counterpart on the Russian side (in Blagoveshchensk).[14] Juxtaposed with this anti-Russian nationalism are local exoticized celebrations of Russian cultural influence as an integral part of the commercial history of border towns and the distinctive character of cities like Harbin.[15] The *wenshi ziliao* managed to integrate and reconcile these tendencies, turning this problematic history into an opportunity to construct a narrative accommodating local and regional identity-forming projects alongside nationalist historiography.

This brings us finally to the question of how the *wenshi ziliao* relate to the broader trend of rising nationalism and nationalist historiography in

[11] Weiner, "State Commemoration of Tibetan Anti-State Resistance"; Mortimer, "Wenshi Ziliao Narratives of Anti-Communist Resistance"; Catris, "Searching for the Elusive Past."
[12] Catris, "Searching for the Elusive Past."
[13] Bulag, "Can the Subalterns Not Speak?" 107–108.
[14] Victor Zatsepine, "The Blagoveshchensk Massacre of 1900: The Sino–Russian War and Global Imperialism," Norman Smith and James Flath, eds., *Beyond Suffering: Recounting War in Modern China* (Vancouver, BC: University of British Columbia Press, 2011): 107–129.
[15] See Koga, "The Atmosphere of a Foreign Country."

East Asia since the 1980s and especially the 1990s.[16] While anti-imperialist nationalism was a significant theme in *wenshi ziliao* history production, it is important to clarify this theme's implications for the broader goals and character of the project. The nationalist strain in *wenshi ziliao* was entangled with and sewn onto a discourse of international integration, manifested partly in the interfusion of narratives of anti-imperialism and colonial nostalgia. Nationalism by itself certainly does not suffice as a framework for characterizing the project. *Wenshi ziliao* accommodated an interlayered and nuanced process, a centrally orchestrated yet localized network and mosaic of strategies of historical production and representation.

---

[16] For a number of case studies documenting this trend, see Edward Vickers and Alisa Jones, eds., *History Education and National Identity in East Asia* (New York, NY: Routledge, 2005).

References

Archives

Fujin City Archive (Fujin shi danganguan), Fujin, Heilongjiang.
Fuyuan City Archive (Fuyuan shi danganguan), Fuyuan, Heilongjiang.
Harbin City Archive (Haerbin shi danganguan), Harbin.
Heilongjiang Provincial Archive (Heilongjiang sheng Danganguan), Harbin.
Raohe County Archive (Raohe xian danganguan), Raohe, Heilongjiang.
Tongjiang City Archive (Tongjiang shi danganguan), Tongjiang, Heilongjiang.

Primary Sources

Arseniev, V. K. 1923. Transl. Malcolm Burr. *Dersu the Trapper*. New York, NY: Dutton, 1941.
Bian Ji. "Bi Fengzhi de gongxian" ("Bi Fengzhi's Contributions"). Heihe wenshi ziliao – Lü e huaqiao shiliao xuan, vol. 8, *Zhengxie heilongjiang sheng heihe shi weiyuan hui wenshi ziliao yanjiu gongzuo weiyuan hui* (1991): 89–90.
Cao Mingren. "Zhongguo renmin zhengzhi xieshang huiyi fujin xian diliu jie weiyuanhui changwu weiyuanhui gongzuo baogao" ("Work Report of the Sixth Session of the Fujin County PPCC's Standing Committee"). Delivered on March 21, 1983, at the third meeting of the sixth session of the Fujin County PPCC. Fujin City Archives. (Note: The numbers [*juanzong hao* or *dangan hao*] were not listed on some of the archival files and documents cited in this study. The numbers may have appeared in other locations that were not observed and recorded at the time of archival research. The author takes full responsibility for any unintentional omissions.)
Cao Tingjie. 1885. *Eguo xiboli dongpian jiyao (Account of Russian Eastern Siberia)*. Reprinted in Shen Yunlong, comp. *Jindai zhongguo shiliao congkan xubian (Collection of Modern Chinese Historical Materials)*, vol. 52. Taibei xian, Yonghe zhen: Wenhai chubanshe, 1978.
Chen Di. "Tuanjie xiyin zhishifenzi de hao defang" ("A Good Place for Uniting and Appealing to Intellectuals"). Heilongjiang sheng zhengxie lianyihui. *Wo yu zhengxie (The PPCC and I)*. Internal circulation, 2002: 136–139.

Chen Kezheng and Pang Guowen. "Xiang you shengming de wangmazi gaoyao" ("The Celebrated Pockmarked Wang's Medical Ointment"). *Harbin wenshiziliao* 10. Harbin shi weiyuan hui wenshi ziliao yanjiu weiyuan hui, 1986.

Chen Min. "Wo yu wenshi gongzuo – fang du jianshi" ("My Part in the Work on *Wenshi* Materials – My interview with Du Jianshi"). *Liaowang*, no. 13 (1986).

Chen Zhankui and Chen Zhanyuan. "Chenshi zhenggu yuan de chuangjian he fazhan" ("The Founding and Development of Chen's Osteopathic Clinic"). *Harbin wenshiziliao* 5. Harbin shi weiyuan hui wenshi ziliao yanjiu weiyuan hui, 1984.

Dai Zhenhuan. "Zhongguo renmin zhengzhi xieshang huiyi fujin xian diwu jie weiyuanhui changwu weiyuanhui gongzuo baogao (caoan)" ("Draft of Work Report of the fifth Session of the Standing Committee of the Fujin County PPCC"). Delivered on September 17, 1980, at the fifth session of the Fujin County PPCC. Fujin City Archive.

"Elunchun zu jianshi" bianxie zu. *Elunchun zu jianshi*. Huhehaote: Nei Menggu renmin chubanshe; Nei Menggu xinhua shudian faxing, 1983.

Feng Hefa. *Zhongguo nongcun jingji lun: nongcun jingji lunwen xuanji* (*Selected Articles on the Chinese Rural Economy*). Shanghai: Liming shudian, 1934.

Fujin xian zhengxie. "Guanyu dui yuan gongshangyezhe anpai shiyong qingkuang de diaocha" ("Investigation Regarding the Assignment and Use of Former Participants in the Business and Industry Sectors"). April 1, 1981. Fujin City Archives.

Fujin xian zhengxie. "Qing lao tongzhi xie huiyilu cankao tigang" ("Reference Outline for Asking Old Comrades to Write Memoirs"). August 8, 1981. Fujin City Archives.

"Fujin xian zhengxie qijie sanci huiyi guanyu jinyibu kaizhan xiang pan enliang tongzhi xuexi de jueding" ("Decision by the Third Meeting of the Seventh Session of the Fujin County PPCC Regarding Advancing Further with the Study of Pan Enliang"). March 28, 1986. Fujin City Archives.

Gao Ruzhang. "Mingpai chu zi zhen gongfu – 'sanshenglu' caidao de youlai yu fachan" ("A Famous Brand Arises from True Diligence – The Origins and Development of the 'Sanshenglu' Kitchen Knife"). *Harbin wenshiziliao* 12. Harbin shi weiyuan hui wenshi ziliao yanjiu weiyuan hui, 1987.

Geng Wenru. "Sannian kunnan shiqi wo zai quanguo zhengxie litang de jingli" ("My Experiences in the Reception Hall of the National PPCC during Three Years of Hardship"). *Wenshi ziliao xuanji*, vol. 155. Beijing: Zhongguo wenshi chubanshe, 2009, 92–100.

"Gongzuo xin jumian jiji kaichuang woqu wenshi ziliao" ("Enthusiastically Move Forward with *Wenshi Ziliao* in the New Phase of Work"). Haerbin shi zhengxie weiyuanhui mishuchu. *Haerbin zhengxie* (*Harbin PPCC*), no. 3 (no. 13 overall). Special issue of the First [Harbin City] *Wenshi Ziliao* Work Conference (1984): 85–87.

Guan Chengzheng. "Zhongguo renmin zhengzhi xieshang huiyi fujin shi diyi jie weiyuanhui changwu weiyuanhui gongzuo baogao" ("Work Report of the First Session of the Fujin City PPCC's Standing Committee). Delivered on March 14, 1989, at the second meeting of the first session of the Fujin City PPCC. Fujin City Archive.

"Guanyu zhengxie diwuci quanguo wenshi ziliao gongzuo huiyi de qingkuang he jingshen de huibao tigang" ("Outline of a Report Regarding the Situation and Spirit of the PPCC's Fifth National *Wenshi Ziliao* Work Conference"). Heilongjiang Provincial Archive 56:2:263 (1987).

Guo Chunhua. "Nanwang de huiyi" ("Indelible Memories"). In *Wo yu zhengxie*, 292–299.

Guo Zhaoyan and Zhang Xiaoyun. "Tieling deshenghao xingshuai shimo" ("The History of the Flourishing and Decline of the Deshenghao Enterprise in Tieling"). *Liaoning wenshi ziliao* 26. Liaoning renmin chubanshe, 1989.

Haerbin shi bianzhi weiyuanhui. "Guanyu shi zhengxie zengshe wenshi ziliao ban-gongshi de tongzhi" ("Notice Concerning the City PPCC's Establishment of a *Wenshi Ziliao* Office"). *Ha bianzi* (Harbin numbering), no. 134 (December 22, 1981). Harbin City Archive.

"Haerbin shi minjian gongshang lian shiliao xiaozu" ("Harbin City Democratic Construction and Industrial and Commercial Federation's Historical Materials Small Group"). Haerbin shi zhengxie weiyuanhui mishuchu. *Haerbin zhengxie (Harbin PPCC)*, no. 3 (no. 13 overall). Special issue of the First [Harbin City] *Wenshi Ziliao* Work Conference) (1984): 71–74.

Haerbin shi zhengxie weiyuanhui mishuchu. "Deng yingchao tongzhi zai quan-guo zhengxie disici quanguo wenshi ziliao gongzuo huiyi shang de jianghua" ("Comrade Deng Yingchao's Speech at the National PPCC's Fourth National *Wenshi Ziliao* Work Conference"). September 24, 1983. (Recorded and orga-nized without the speaker's inspection.) Special issue of the First [Harbin City] *Wenshi Ziliao* Work Conference. *Haerbin shi zhengxie (Harbin City PPCC)*, no. 3 (no. 13 overall). (January 8, 1984).

Haerbin shi zhengxie weiyuanhui mishuchu. "Li jianbai tongzhi zai dierci quan-sheng wenshi ziliao gongzuo huiyi shang de jianghua" ("Comrade Li Jianbai's Speech at the Second Provincial *Wenshi Ziliao* Work Conference"). Special issue of the First [Harbin City] *Wenshi Ziliao* Work Conference. *Haerbin shi zhengxie (Harbin City PPCC)*, no. 3 (no. 13 overall). (January 8, 1984).

Haerbin shizhi (Harbin City Gazetteer). Haerbin shi difangzhi bianzuan weiyuan-hui, 1993.

Heilongjiang sheng zhengxie weiyuanhui. "Haiwai zhengji zu diyici huiyi jiyao" ("Main Contents of the First Conference of the Overseas Collection Group"). 1987. Heilongjiang Provincial Archive.

Heilongjiang sheng zhengxie wenshi ban. "Kaizhan da xiezuo, gaohao zhuanti-hua" ("Cooperate Greatly and Thoroughly Specialize"). August 19, 1985. Heilongjiang Provincial Archives 56:1:290.

Heilongjiang sheng zhengxie wenshi ban. Untitled report on *wenshi ziliao* by Heilongjiang provincial wenshi ziliao office. Harbin: Heilongjiang sheng danganguan, October 10, 1980. Heilongjiang Provincial Archive 56:1:195.

Heilongjiang sheng zhengxie wenshi ban. "Wenshi ziliao shi huanqi renmen wei gongtong lixiang er fendou de jingshen shiliang" ("*Wenshi Ziliao* Is Spiritual Food That Inspires People to Struggle for Shared Ideals"). November 1986. Heilongjiang Provincial Archives 56:2:263.

Heilongjiang sheng zhengxie wenshi bangongshi. "1986 nian sheng zhengxie wenshi gongzuo jihua" ("Heilongjiang Provincial PPCC's Plans for *Wenshi Ziliao* Work in 1986"). March 26, 1986. Heilongjiang Provincial Archive.

Heilongjiang sheng zhengxie wenshi bangongshi. "Yikao shehui liliang kaizhan wenshi gongzuo" ("Rely on Social Forces to Carry Out *Wenshi Ziliao* Work"). July 1983. Heilongjiang Provincial Archives 56:1:298.

Heilongjiang sheng wenshi ziliao yanjiu weiyuanhui. "1986 nian wenshi gongzuo zongjie, 1987 nian wenshi gongzuo jihua" ("Heilongjiang Provincial *Wenshi Ziliao* Research Committee's Summary of *Wenshi Ziliao* Work in 1986 and Plans for Work in 1987"). 1986. Heilongjiang Provincial Archive 56:2:332.

Heilongjiang sheng zhengxie wenshi ziliao yanjiu gongzuo weiyuanhui. "Heilongjiang sheng shaoshu minzu wenshi ziliao zhengji tigang" ("Outline for Collection of Heilongjiang Provincial *Wenshi Ziliao* Materials about Ethnic Minorities"). 1987. Heilongjiang Provincial Archive.

Huadian wenshi ziliao 6. Huadian shi weiyuan hui wenshi ziliao yanjiu weiyuan hui, 1992.

Huang Demin. "Yici nanwang de huiyi" ("An Unforgettable Meeting"). *Wo yu zhengxie*, 309–313.

Huang Feng. "Zai renmin zhengxie gongzuo de rizi li – huigu, ganshou yu sikao" ("The Days of Working at the PPCC – Reminiscences, Sentiments, and Reflections"). *Wo yu zhengxie*, 56–65.

Jiamusi difangzhi bianzuan weiyuanhui. *Jiamusi shizhi* (*Jiamusi City Gazetteer*) 2. Zhonghua shuju, 1996.

Jiaohe wenshi ziliao 1. Zhongguo renmin zhengzhi xieshang huiyi jilin sheng jiaohe xian weiyuanhui wenshi ziliao yanjiu weiyuanhui, 1985.

"Jilin shi zhengxie zuzhi jigou" ("Organizational Structure of the Jilin City PPCC"). *Jilin shizhi* (*Jilin City Gazetteer*). Jilin shi zhengxie weiyuanhui, 1997: 78–92.

Jin Zonglin. "Zhang tinge qiren qishi" ("Zhang Tingge, Who He Was and What He Did"). *Harbin wenshi ziliao*. Harbin shi weiyuan hui wenshi ziliao yanjiu weiyuan hui 2 (1983).

Lattimore, Owen. *Manchuria: Cradle of Conflict*. New York, NY: Macmillan Company, 1932; republished, New York, NY: AMS Press, ca. 1975.

Li Shutang. *Dongjiao jixing* (*Records of Travels along the Eastern Borderland*). s.l.: s.n., 1899.

Li Xingchang. "Huiji houshi de guangrong shiye – mantan wenshi ziliao gongzuo" ("A Glorious Enterprise Benefiting Later Generations – Some Comments about *Wenshi Ziliao* Work"). Haerbin shi zhengxie weiyuanhui mishuchu. *Haerbin zhengxie* (*Harbin PPCC*), no. 2 (no. 6 overall). 1983.

Liu Feilin. "Wenshi gongzuo de sanshinian jiyi" ("Thirty Years' Reflections on Literary and Historical Work"), in *Heilongjiang wenshi ziliao*, vol. 41. Heilongjiang renmin chubanshe, 2010: 359–66.

Liu Wenfeng. *Dongchui jixing* (*Travels to the Eastern Frontier*). China: s.n., 1901.

Liu Yiwang. "Jingdong liujia yu changchun yifahe" ("The Liu Clan of Jingdong and Yifahe of Changchun"). *Jilin wenshi ziliao*. Jilin sheng weiyuan hui wenshi ziliao yanjiu weiyuan hui 15 (1987).

Lü Lingui. "Zhongdong shijian fasheng qianhou de lishi qingkuang ji qi genyuan" ("On the Historical Circumstances and Causes of the CER Incident"). *Haerbin shizhi (Harbin History and Gazetteer)* 2 (1985): 44–53.

Lü Mingyi. "Zhongguo renmin zhengzhi xieshang huiyi dier jie weiyuanhui changwu weiyuanhui gongzuo baogao" ("Work Report of the Standing Committee of the Second Session of the [Raohe] PPCC"). March 17, 1985 at the second meeting of the Second Session of the Raohe PPCC. Raohe County Archive.

Lü Mingyi. "Zhongguo renmin zhengzhi xieshang huiyi diyi jie weiyuanhui changwu weiyuanhui gongzuo baogao" ("Work Report of the Standing Committee of the First Session of the [Raohe County] PPCC"). March 20, 1983. Raohe County Archive.

Luo Wenxiao. "Zai zhengxie fujin xian weiyuanhui 1985 niandu xianjin gongzuo zu xianjin weiyuan biaozhang dahui shang de jianghua" ("Speech at the Fujin County PPCC's Gathering to Praise the Model Personnel and Model Work Teams for the Year 1985"). December 20, 1985. Fujin City Archives.

Ma Kaiyin. "Wo yu Haerbin shi zhengxie bansheng yuan" ("Half of My Life with the Harbin City PPCC"). *Heilongjiang wenshi ziliao* 41: 304–321.

Ma Yilin. "Zhongguo renmin zhengzhi xieshanghuiyi jilin sheng jilin shi dierjie weiyuanhui changwu weiyuanhui gongzuo baogao" ("Work Report of the Standing Committee of the Second Jilin City PPCC Committee"). Presented at the first full meeting of the third Jilin City PPCC Committee, November 28, 1963. "Appendix documents" section. *Jilin shizhi*, 314–321.

Ma Yilin. "Zhongguo renmin zhengzhi xieshanghuiyi jilin sheng jilin shi disanjie weiyuanhui changwu weiyuanhui gongzuo baogao" ("Work Report of the Standing Committee of the Third Jilin City PPCC Committee"). Presented at the first full meeting of the Fourth Jilin City PPCC Committee, December 24, 1965. "Appendix documents" section. *Jilin shizhi*, 327–331.

Ma Yongshun. "Zhou Enlai xinian zhengxie dangwai weiyuan he gaoji minzhu renshi" ("Zhou Enlai's Concern for Non-Party PPCC Members and Prominent Democratic Leaders"). *Wenshi ziliao xuanji* 154. Zhongguo wenshi chubanshe, 2009: 50–64.

Niu Naiwen. "Gaoju aiguo zhuyi qizhi kaichuang woshi wenshi ziliao gongzuo xin jumian" ("Raise High the Banner of Patriotism to Pioneer the New Phase of Our City's *Wenshi Ziliao* Work"). Haerbin shi zhengxie weiyuanhui mishuchu. *Haerbin zhengxie (Harbin PPCC)*, no. 3 (no. 13 overall). Special issue of the First [Harbin City] *Wenshi Ziliao* Work Conference. (1984).

Qiqihaer shi zhengxie wenshiban. "'Qiqihaer wenshi tongxun' chuban" ("Publication of 'Qiqihar *Wenshi* Report'"). 1983. Heilongjiang Provincial Archive 56:1:298.

Qiu Yupeng and Gao Changyuan. "Jubao pen" ("The Treasure-Generating Trough"). Dongou xian minjian wenxue santao jicheng bianwei hui. *Donggou ziliao ben (Folk Literature Materials from Donggou County)*. Donggou, 1986: 272–274.

"Raohe wenshi ziliao zhengji cankao tigang" ("Reference Outline for Collecting Raohe *Wenshi Ziliao*"). Materials of Raohe County PPCC's Second *Wenshi Ziliao* Work Conference. 1985. Raohe County Archive.

"Raohe wenshi ziliao zhuanxie xieshang tigang" ("Consultation Outline for Drafting Raohe *Wenshi Ziliao*"). Materials of Raohe County's Second *Wenshi Ziliao* Work Conference. 1985. Raohe County Archive.

Raohe zhengxie bangongshi. "An linhai tongzhi zai zhengxie raohe dierjie xian weiyuanhui" ("An Linhai's Speech to the Second Session of the Raohe PPCC"). March 21, 1985. Materials of Raohe County PPCC's Second *Wenshi Ziliao* Work Conference. Raohe County Archive.

Raohe zhengxie bangongshi. "Gaoju aiguo zhuyi qizhi kaichuang woxian wenshi ziliao gongzuo de xin jumian – zhang zhenbang tongzhi zai raohe xian diyici wenshi ziliao gongzuo huiyi shang de jianghua" ("Raise High the Banner of Patriotism to Pioneer the New Phase of *Wenshi Ziliao* Work in Our County – Comrade Zhang Zhenbang's Speech at Raohe County's First *Wenshi Ziliao* Work Conference"). March 7, 1984. Raohe County Archive.

Raohe zhengxie bangongshi. "Li Rongchun tongzhi zai raohe xian diyici wenshi ziliao gongzuo huiyi shang de jianghua" ("Comrade Li Rongchun's Speech at Raohe County's First *Wenshi Ziliao* Work Conference"). March 6, 1984. Raohe County Archive.

Raohe zhengxie bangongshi. "Wenshi ziliao zhengji cankao tigang (taolungao)" ("Discussion Draft of Reference Outline for Collecting *Wenshi Ziliao*"). March 1984. Raohe County Archive.

Rong Mengyuan. "Mantan shiliao gongzuo" ("Commentary on Working with Historical Materials"). Qiqihaer shi zhengxie weiyuanhui wenshi ziliao yanjiu weiyuanhui. *Wenshi tongxun (Culture and History Newsletter)*, no. 3 (no. 7 overall). 1984. orig. from national PPCC's *Wenshi tongxun*, no. 4. 1983.

Shen Meijuan. "Shen Zui funü yu quanguo zhengxie" ("National PPCC and Shen Zui Father and Daughter"). *Wenshi ziliao xuanji*. 154. Zhongguo wenshi chubanshe, 2009: 70–86.

Smith, Arthur Henderson. *Village Life in China: A Study in Sociology*. New York, NY, and Chicago, IL: F. H. Revell Company, 1889.

Tonghua wenshi ziliao 1. Tonghua shi weiyuan hui wenshi ziliao yanjiu weiyuan hui, 1987.

Tong Zhenyu. "Wo shi zenyang zhengji wenshi ziliao de" ("How I Collected *Wenshi Ziliao*"). Haerbin shi zhengxie weiyuanhui mishuchu. *Haerbin zhengxie (Harbin PPCC)*, no. 3 (no. 13 overall). Special issue of the First [Harbin City] *Wenshi Ziliao* Work Conference (1984).

Wan Fulin, Zhang Boying, and Li Yushu. *Heilongjiang zhigao (Heilongjiang Gazetteer)*. "Kuangchan." Taibei xian, Yonghe zhen: Wenhai chubanshe, 1965, 1933.

Wang Chunsheng. "'Yuji huomo' de bianqian" ("Evolution of the 'Yuji Flour Mill"). *Jixi wenshi ziliao* 2. Jixi shi wenshi ziliao weiyuanhui, 1986.

Wang Hui, *Wang Hui zi xuan ji (Selected Writings of Wang Hui)* (Guilin: Guangxi shifan daxue chubanshe, 1997, translated in Viren Murthy, "Modernity against Modernity: Wang Hui's Critical History of Chinese Thought," *Modern Intellectual History* 3.1 (April 2006): 137–165.

Wang Jinling. "Mianhuai Zhang Ruilin tongzhi" ("Remembering Comrade Zhang Ruilin"). *Wo yu zhengxie*, 32–36.

Wang Mingkui. "Gaoju aiguo zhuyi qizhi kaichuang wosheng wenshi ziliao gong-zuo xin jumian" ("Raise High the Banner of Patriotism in Pioneering the New Stage of *Wenshi Ziliao* Work in Our Province"). Haerbin shi zhengxie weiyuan-hui mishuchu. *Haerbin zhengxie* (*Harbin PPCC*), no. 3 (no. 13 overall). Special issue of the First [Harbin City] *Wenshi Ziliao* Work Conference (January 8, 1984).

Wang Ruiyi. "Taojin yu 'fuma' shenghuo" ("My Life as Gold Digger and 'Emperor's Son-in-Law'"). *Yichun wenshi ziliao* 1. Yichun shi weiyuan hui wenshi ziliao yanjiu weiyuan hui, 1984.

Wang Xingkun. "Zhongguo renmin zhengzhi xieshang huiyi fujin xian diqi jie weiyuanhui changwu weiyuanhui gongzuo baogao" ("Work Report of the Seventh Session of the Fujin County PPCC's Standing Committee"). Delivered on March 15, 1985, at the second meeting of the Seventh Session of the Fujin County PPCC. Fujin City Archives.

Wang Yesheng. "Zai zhengxie hegang shi diwujie weiyuanhui gongzuo shi de huiyi" ("Recollections during the Work of the Fifth Session of the Hegang City PPCC"). *Hegang wenshi ziliao* 8 (1995): 13–33.

"Wei jianzhu gongye shixian sige xiandaihua gongxian liliang – zhang jitai tongzhi zai xian shoujie zhengxie huiyi shang de fayan" ("Contributing Forcefully to the Realization of the Four Modernizations in the Construction Industry – Comrade Zhang Jitai's Speech at the First Session of the Fuyuan County PPCC"). September 28, 1980. Fuyuan City Archive.

Wen Zhongkui. "Zai quanxian tongzhan gongzuo huiyi shang de jianghua" ("Speech at the United Front Work Conference for the Entire County"). April 28, 1987. Fuyuan City Archives.

Wu Baixiang. "Wushi nian zishu" ("Recalling Fifty Years"). *Harbin wenshi ziliao* 3. Harbin shi weiyuan hui wenshi ziliao yanjiu weiyuan hui, 1983.

"Xianwei fushuji he baojun zai raohe xian dierci wenshi ziliao gongzuo huiyi de jianghua" ("County Party Vice Secretary He Baojun's Speech at Raohe County's Second *Wenshi Ziliao* Work Conference"). August 6, 1985. Raohe County Archive.

Xiao Shanyin. "Sishi nian hou chongfeng zai xianggang" ("Reunion in Hong Kong after Forty Years"). *Wenshi ziliao xuanji* 154: 65–69.

Xing Jinghuan. "Wo congshi shangye liushi duo nian de jingli" ("My Over Sixty Years' Experience with Commercial Enterprises"). *Jiamusi wenshi ziliao*. Jiamusi shi weiyuan hui wenshi ziliao yanjiu weiyuan hui 8 (1989).

Xu Chengbei. "Wenshi san ti" ("Three Points Regarding *Wenshi Ziliao* Materials"). *Beijing guancha* (*Beijing Observation*), no. 8 (2000).

Xu Huiqing. "Jiji zuo hao haiwai tongzhan gongzuo" ("Enthusiastic Implementation of United Front Work Overseas"). *Wo yu zhengxie*, 392–401.

Xu Shuqiu. "'Kai jiaotong' shiqi de (bu) shi, huashang, lü e qiaomin ji qita" ("Blagoveshchensk during the Period of 'Open Transportation,' Chinese Merchants, Chinese Residing in Russia, and Other Matters"). *Heihe wenshi ziliao – Lü e huaqiao shiliao xuan* 8. Zhengxie heilongjiang sheng heihe shi weiyuan hui wenshi ziliao yanjiu gongzuo weiyuan hui, 1991.

Xu Zhanhai. "Zhongguo renmin zhengzhi xieshang huiyi fujin xian diliu jie weiyuanhui changwu weiyuanhui gongzuo baogao" ("Work Report of the

Sixth Session of the Fujin County PPCC's Standing Committee"). Delivered on April 6, 1984, at the first meeting of the Seventh Session of the Fujin County PPCC. Fujin City Archive.

Xu Zhanhai. "Zhongguo renmin zhengzhi xieshang huiyi fujin xian diqi jie weiyuanhui changwu weiyuanhui gongzuo baogao" ("Work Report of the Seventh Session of the Fujin County PPCC's Standing Committee"). Delivered on October 13, 1987, at the first meeting of the Eighth Session of the Fujin County PPCC. Fujin City Archives.

Yang Chengwu. "Zai di sici quanguo wenshi ziliao gongzuo huiyi shang bimuhui de jianghua" ("Speech at the Closing Ceremony of the Fourth National *Wenshi Ziliao* Work Conference"). Sept. 24, 1983. *Haerbin zhengxie (Harbin PPCC)*, no. 3 (no. 13 overall). Special Issue of the First [Harbin City] Wenshi Ziliao Work Conference (1984).

Yang Lixin, "Zhongguo renmin zhengzhi xieshang huiyi dierjie weiyuanhui changwu weiyuanhui gongzuo baogao" ("Work Report of the Second Session of the [Raohe] PPCC's Standing Committee"). Delivered on March 26, 1987 at the fourth meeting of the Second Session of the Raohe PPCC. Raohe County Archive.

Yang, Martin. *A Chinese Village: Taitou, Shantung Province.* New York, NY: Columbia University Press, 1945.

Ye Jinghuan. "Qu puchen yu fuzengqing shangchang" ("Qu Puchen and Fuzengqing Market"). *Jiamusi wenshi ziliao* 6. Jiamusi shi weiyuan hui wenshi ziliao yanjiu weiyuan hui, 1987.

Yin Xingwen, Jin Baichuan, and Liu Qingqi. "Hailanpao da tusha jianwen" ("Firsthand Accounts of the Blagoveshchensk Massacre"). *Heilongjiang wenshi ziliao* 12 (1984).

You Zhixian. "Zhongguo renmin zhengzhi xieshang huiyi tongjiang xian dier jie weiyuanhui changwu weiyuanhui gongzuo baogao" ("Work Report of the Standing Committee of the Second Session of the Tongjiang County PPCC"). From the speech at the first meeting of the First Session of the Tongjiang City PPCC. March 29, 1987. Tongjiang City Archive.

Youhao district government, Youhao lumber bureau. *Shizhi ziliao huibian (Historical Gazetteer Compilation).* Yichun: Youhao District Gazetteer Committee, 1986–1987, 182–185.

Young, Walter C. "Chinese Colonization in Manchuria." *Far Eastern Review* 24.6 (June 1928).

Zhang Fushan. "Tantan cunzhen qiushi" ("Some Observations about Preserving Authenticity and Seeking Truth"). Haerbin shi zhengxie weiyuanhui mishu-chu. *Haerbin zhengxie (Harbin PPCC)*, no. 3 (no. 13 overall). Special issue of the First [Harbin City] *Wenshi Ziliao* Work Conference (1984).

Zhang Jitai. "Biancheng maoyi de yanbian – fuyuan xian jiefang qian de shangye xiao shi" ("The Evolution of Border Town Trade – A Short History of Commerce in Fuyuan County Prior to 1949"). *Jiamusi wenshi ziliao.* Jiamusi shi weiyuan hui wenshi ziliao yanjiu weiyuan hui 6 (1986).

Zhang Pingfu, Zhang Weijiang, and Dong Yuanchao. *Renmin zhengxie gailun (General discussion of PPCC).* Beijing United Front Teaching Materials. Beijing: Zhongyang bianyi chubanshe, 2008.

Zhang Tong. "Dacheng 'guanyu zhaokai xin de zhengzhi xieshang huiyi zhu wenti de xieyi' de qianqian houhou" ("The Process of Completing 'Agreement Regarding Some Questions on Establishing the New PPCC'"), *Heilongjiang wenshi ziliao* 41: 330–342.

Zhang Tong. "Ershi niandai shouhui zhongdong tielu bufen liquan shi shulue" ("A Brief Historical Account of the Partial Recovery of Rights on the CER"). *Haerbin shizhi* (*Harbin History and Gazetteer*) 1 (1984): 23–32.

Zhang Tong. "Zhou enlai yu PPCC wenshi ziliao gongzuo" ("Zhou Enlai and the PPCC's *Wenshi Ziliao* Work"). *Shihai cunzhen* (*Gems of Culture and History*), no. 2 (2009).

Zhang Yu. "Zhengxie weiyuan shi rongyu, geng shi zeren" ("The Honor and Responsibility of being a PPCC Member"). *Wo yu zhengxie*, 347–349.

Zhang Zhenbang. "Zai aiguo zhuyu de qizhi xia, jiaqiang nuli xiezuo, wei kaichuang wenshi ziliao gongzuo er fendou" ("Struggle to Pioneer *Wenshi Ziliao* Work through Strengthening Diligent Cooperation under the Banner of Patriotism"). Office of the Raohe PPCC. Materials of the County PPCC's Second *Wenshi Ziliao* Work Conference. August 6, 1985. Raohe County Archive.

Zhang Ziyu. "Jingying shanhai zahuo de tianfengyong" ("Tianfengyong Specializing in Wild-Harvested Products"). *Harbin wenshi ziliao* 12 (1988).

"Zhengxie diwuci quanguo wenshi ziliao gongzuo huiyi jingyan xuanbian" ("Selected Experiences from the Fifth National *Wenshi Ziliao* Work Conference"). Summary Report, 1986. Heilongjiang Provincial Archive.

Zhengxie fujin xian changwu weiyuanhui. "Yong duozhong fangshi fadong weiyuan yu gejie renshi jiji 'qiangjiu' woxian wenshi ziliao" ("Use All Kinds of Methods to Mobilize Personnel and People from All Spheres to Enthusiastically 'Rescue' Our County's '*Wenshi Ziliao*'"). *Zhengxie gongzuo* (*PPCC Work*), no. 10 (August 20, 1982). Fujin City Archives.

"Zhengxie fujin xian weiyuanhui gongzuo zongjie" ("Wrap-Up Summary of Fujin County PPCC's Work"). December 31, 1981. Fujin City Archives.

Zhengxie fuyuan xian weiyuanhui. "Jiaqiang dui zhengxie gongzuo de lingdao, chongfen fahui zhengxie zhineng zuoyong" ("Strengthen Leadership of PPCC Work and Fully Realize the Functional Potential of the PPCC"). October 1988. Fuyuan City Archives.

Zhengxie fuyuan xian weiyuanhui bangongshi. "Guanyu erjie erci huiyi de cai-liao" ("Regarding the Materials of the Second Meeting of the Second Session of the Fuyuan County PPCC"). March 15, 1985. Fuyuan City Archives.

Zhengxie haerbin shi weiyuanhui bangongting. "Shi zhengxie zhaokai disanci wenshi ziliao gongzuo huiyi" ("The City PPCC Convenes Its Third *Wenshi Ziliao* Work Conference"). *Zhengxie qingkuang* (*Developments with the PPCC*), no. 23 (November 9, 1987). Harbin City Archive.

Zhengxie heilongjiang sheng raohe xian weiyuanhui. "Yijiubasan nian zhengxie gongzuo zongjie he basi nian zhengxie gongzuo anpai yijian de baogao" ("Report Giving Summary of PPCC Work for the Year 1983 and Recommendations for Arranging PPCC Work for the Year 1984"). *Rao zheng-xie fa* (*Raohe PPCC*), no. 2 (1983). Raohe County Archive.

Zhengxie heilongjiang sheng weiyuanhui bangongting. Suiling xian zhengxie bangongshi. "Wenshi ziliao diyiji chukan" ("Release of the First Volume of [Suiling] *Wenshi Ziliao*"). 1983. *Heilongjiang Provincial Archive* 56:1:298.

Zhengxie heilongjiang sheng weiyuanhui bangongting. Wangkui xian zhengxie bangongshi. "Zhengxie gongzuo" ("PPCC Work"), no. 2 (no. 6 overall). June 4, 1983. Heilongjiang Provincial Archive 56:1:298.

Zhengxie hulan xian weiyuanhui. "Women shi zenyang kaizhan wenshi ziliao de gongzuo" ("How Should We Carry Out *Wenshi Ziliao* Work?"). *Haerbin zhengxie* (*Harbin PPCC*), no. 3 (no. 13 overall). Special Issue of the First [Harbin City] *Wenshi Ziliao* Work Conference. Heilongjiang Provincial Archive (1984).

Zhengxie raohe erjie xian weiyuanhui. "Guanyu shenru yibu xiang pan enliang tongzhi xuexi de jueding" ("Decision Regarding Deepening Study of Comrade Pan Enliang"). March 16, 1986. Raohe County Archive.

Zhengxie raohe xian changwu weiyuanhui. "Zhishu zaolin, mianhui xianlie, yinji zisun – xian zhengxie weiyuan yingzao 'aiguo lin'" ("Plant Trees and Create a Forest, Commemorate Past Martyrs, and Protect the Next Generations – County PPCC Members' Establishment of the 'Patriotic Forest'"). May 10, 1982. Raohe County Archive.

Zhengxie raohe xian weiyuanhui. "Zhengxie di baci changweihui (kuoda)" ("The Eighth [Expanded] Meeting of the Standing Committee of the PPCC"). August 24, 1982. Raohe County Archive.

Zhengxie raohe xian weiyuanhui bangongshi. "Chen lei shengzhang dui kanglian diqijun junzhang chen rongjiu lieshi mudi de pishi" ("Governor Chen Lei's Instructions Regarding the Gravesite of the Martyr Chen Rongjiu, Commander of the Seventh Division of the Anti-Japanese Allied Army"). *Raohe zhengxie* (*Raohe PPCC*), no. 26 (November 13, 1982). Raohe County Archive.

Zhengxie raohe xian weiyuanhui bangongshi. "Xian zhengxie lingdao he liangming changwei canjia chen rongjiu junzhang xishengdi shubei he lieshi zhonggu qianyi huodong" ("Participation by the County PPCC Leadership and Two Standing Committee Members in the Engraving of Army Commander Chen Rongjiu's Martyrdom Site Monument and the Relocation of His Remains"). *Raohe zhengxie* (*Raohe PPCC*), no. 25 (October 25, 1982). Raohe County Archive.

Zhengxie raohe xian weiyuanhui bangongshi. "Zongli canguan dongbei lieshi jinianguan shi de zhishi" ("Observations during the Premier's Visit to the Northeast Martyrs Memorial"). *Raohe zhengxie* (*Raohe PPCC*), no. 23 (September 22, 1982). Raohe County Archive.

Zhengxie tongjiang xian weiyuanhui bangongshi. "Duanxun" ("Brief Report"). *Tongjiang zhengxie* (*Tongjiang PPCC*), no. 14 (no. 109 overall). December 10, 1985. Tongjiang City Archive.

Zhengxie tongjiang xian weiyuanhui bangongshi, wenshi xuexi shi. "Wenshi ziliao zhengji gongzuo jianxun" ("Brief Report on Work of Collecting *Wenshi Ziliao*"). *Tongjiang zhengxie* (*Tongjiang PPCC*), no. 2 (no. 96 overall). February 10, 1985. Tongjiang City Archive.

Zhengxie weiyuan shouce (Handbook for PPCC Personnel). Zhengxie heilongjiangsheng weiyuanhui bangongting, 2008: 163–167.

"Zhongdonglu zhuanti shiliao xiezuo hui huiyi jiyao" ("Main Points from Meeting of Committee on CER Special Topic Historical Materials"). 1986. Heilongjiang Provincial Archives 56:2:263.

Zhonggong raohe xian zhengxie dangzu. "Guanyu qingqiu zengpei zhuanzhi wenshi ziliao renyuan de zengbian baogao" ("Organization Expansion Report Regarding the Request to Add Full-Time *Wenshi Ziliao* Personnel"). August 19, 1983. Raohe County Archive.

Zhonggong zhengxie fujin xian dangzu. "Guanyu chuban 'fujin wenshi ziliao' di sanji de baogao" ("Report on the Publication of the Third Volume of 'Fujin *Wenshi Ziliao*'"). Documents of the Fujin County PPCC's Party subcommittee, no. 5. November 24, 1986. Fujin City Archives.

Zhonggong zhengxie fujin xian dangzu. "Shi zhengxie gongzuo zongjie" ("Wrap-Up Summary of the City PPCC's Work"). January 5, 1989. Documents of the Fujin County PPCC's Party Subcommittee. Fujin City Archive.

"Zhongguo renmin zhengzhi xieshang huiyi fujin xian zhengxie gongzuo de jiben huodong banfa (caoan)" ("Draft of Plan for Fujin County PPCC's Basic Work Activities"). October 10, 1980. Fujin City Archives.

Zhongguo renmin zhengzhi xieshang huiyi Heilongjiang sheng diwujie weiyuan-hui dierci huiyi mishu chu. "Gezu weiyuan taolun hui dui gongzuo qingkuang baogao" ("Report from Discussion Meetings of Each Small Group of Heilongjiang PPCC Members Regarding *Wenshi Ziliao* Work Conditions"). *Jianbao (Brief Report)*, no. 4 (March 21, 1984). Heilongjiang Provincial Archive 56:1:315.

Zhongyang yanjiuyuan jindaishi yanjiusuo. *Chi Yich'iao xiansheng fangwen jilu (Records of Interviews with Ji Yiqiao)*. Taipei, Taiwan: Academia Sinica, Institute of Modern History, 1964.

Zhou Zuojun. "Zhongguo renmin zhengzhi xieshang huiyi fujin xian diliu jie weiyuanhui changwu weiyuanhui gongzuo baogao" ("Work Report of the Eighth Session of the Fujin County PPCC's Standing Committee"). Delivered on March 21, 1988, at the second meeting of the Eighth Session of the Fujin County PPCC. Fujin City Archives.

Zhu Xiufang. "Zhengxie wei wo dakai le canzheng yizheng de damen" ("My Introduction by the PPCC to Political Consultation"). *Wo yu zhengxie*, 178–180.

Other References Cited

Anagnost, Ann. "A Surfeit of Bodies: Population and the Rationality of the State in Post-Mao China." In Faye D. Ginsburg and Rayna Rapp, eds., *Conceiving the New World Order: The Global Politics of Reproduction*. Berkeley, CA: University of California Press, 1995, 22–41.

Anzaldua, Gloria. *Borderlands/La Frontera: The New Mestiza*. 4th edition. San Francisco, CA: Aunt Lute Books, 2012.

Aron, Stephen and Jeremy Adelman. "From Borderlands to Borders: Empires, Nation-States, and the Peoples in Between in North American History." *American Historical Review* 104 (June 1999): 814–841.

Bakiner, Onur. "One Truth among Others? Truth Commissions' Struggle for Truth and Memory." *Memory Studies* 8.3 (July 2015).

Baranovitch, Nimrod. "Others No More: The Changing Representation of Non-Han Peoples in Chinese History Textbooks, 1951–2003." *Journal of Asian Studies* 69.1 (February 2010): 85–122.

Barmé, Geremie. "History for the Masses." In Jonathan Unger, ed., *Using the Past to Serve the Present: Historiography and Politics in Contemporary China*. New York, NY: Routledge, 1993: 260–286.

Barmé, Geremie. *In the Red: On Contemporary Chinese Culture*. New York, NY: Columbia University Press, 1999, 5–6.

Behar, Ruth. *Translated Woman: Crossing the Border with Esperanza's Story*. Boston, MA: Beacon Press, 2003.

Benjamin, Walter. "Theses on the Philosophy of History." In Hannah Arendt, ed. Harry Zohn, trans. *Illuminations*. New York, NY: Schocken, 1969.

Benton, Gregor. "Dissent and the Chinese Communists before and since the Post-Mao Reforms." *International Journal of China Studies* (Special Issue *Dissent before and since Post-Mao Reforms*) 1.2 (October 2010): 311–329.

Blackburn, Kevin. "History from Above: The Use of Oral History in Shaping Collective Memory in Singapore." In Paula Hamilton and Linda Shopes, eds., *Oral History and Public Memory*. Philadelphia, PA: Temple University Press, 2008: 31–46.

Blouin, Francis X. and William G. Rosenberg, eds., *Archives, Documentation, and Institutions of Social Memory*. Ann Arbor, MI: University of Michigan Press, 2007.

Bodnar, John. "Public Memory in an American City: Commemoration in Cleveland." In John R. Gillis, ed., *Commemorations: The Politics of National Identity*. Princeton, NJ: Princeton University Press, 1994.

Bodnar, John. *Remaking America: Public Memory, Commemoration, and Patriotism in the Twentieth Century*. Princeton, NJ: Princeton University Press, 1993.

Brown, Jeremy and Paul Pickowicz. "The Early Years of the People's Republic of China: An Introduction." In Jeremy Brown and Paul Pickowicz, eds., *Dilemmas of Victory: The Early Years of the People's Republic of China*. Cambridge, MA: Harvard University Press, 2007, 1–18.

Brown, Kate. *A Biography of No Place: From Ethnic Borderland to Soviet Heartland*. Cambridge, MA: Harvard University Press, 2003.

Bulag, Uradyn E. "Can the Subalterns Not Speak? On the Regime of Oral History in Socialist China." *Inner Asia* 12.1 (2010): 95–111.

Burns, John B. "Civil Service Reform in Contemporary China." *Australian Journal of Chinese Affairs*, no. 18 (July 1987): 47–83.

Catris, Sandrine. "Searching for the Elusive Past: The Production of Historical Narratives in Post-Mao Xinjiang." Paper presented at Association of Asian Studies Conference. Toronto, March 18, 2017.

Chen Yong. *Chinese San Francisco 1850–1943: A Trans-Pacific Community*. Stanford, CA: Stanford University Press, ca. 2000.

Clausen, Søren. "Autobiography of a Chinese City: The History of Harbin in the Mirror of the Official City Gazetteer." *Historiography East & West* 2.1 (2004): 144–172.

Clausen, Søren and Stig Thøgersen, eds., *The Making of a Chinese City: History and Historiography in Harbin*. Armonk, NY: M. E. Sharpe, 1995.

Cook, Alexander C. *The Cultural Revolution on Trial: Mao and the Gang of Four.* Studies of the Weatherhead East Asian Institute, Columbia University. Cambridge: Cambridge University Press, 2016.

Cook, Haruko and Theodore Cook. *Japan at War: An Oral History.* New York, NY: New Press; Distributed by W. W. Norton, 1992.

Croizier, Ralph. "Qu Yuan and the Artists: Ancient Symbols and Modern Politics in the Post-Mao Era." In Jonathan Unger, ed., *Using the Past to Serve the Present: Historiography and Politics in Contemporary China.* New York, NY: Routledge, 1993, 124–150.

Daly, Erin and Jeremy Sarkin-Hughes. *Reconciliation in Divided Societies: Finding Common Ground.* Philadelphia, PA: University of Pennsylvania Press, 2007.

Davies, Gloria. "Knowing How to Be: the Dangers of Putting (Chinese) Thought into Action." In Leigh Jenco, ed., *Chinese Thought as Global Theory: Diversifying Knowledge Production in the Social Sciences and Humanities.* Albany, NY: State University of New York Press, 2016, 29–54.

Davis, Natalie. *Fiction in the Archives: Pardon Tales and their Tellers in Sixteenth Century France.* Stanford, CA: Stanford University Press, 1987.

Day, Alexander F. *The Peasant in Postsocialist China: History, Politics, and Capitalism.* Cambridge: Cambridge University Press, 2013.

Denton, Kirk. *Exhibiting the Past: Historical Memory and the Politics of Museums in Postsocialist China.* Honolulu, HI: University of Hawaii Press, 2014.

Dickinson, Greg, Carole Blair, and Brian L. Ott, eds., *Places of Public Memory: The Rhetoric of Museums and Memorials.* Tuscaloosa, AL: University of Alabama Press, 2010.

Diemberger, Hildegard. "Life Histories of Forgotten Heroes? Transgression of Boundaries and the Reconstruction of Tibet in the Post-Mao Era." *Inner Asia* 12.1 (2010): 113–125.

Duara, Prasenjit. *Sovereignty and Authenticity: Manchukuo and the East Asian Modern.* Lanham, MD: Rowman and Littlefield, 2003.

Dynon, Nicholas. "'Four Civilizations' and the Evolution of Post-Mao Socialist Ideology." *China Journal*, no. 60 (July 2008): 83–109.

Eddy U. "Dangerous Privilege: The United Front and the Rectification Campaign of the Early Mao Years." *China Journal*, no. 68 (July 2012): 32–57.

Eyal, Gil. "Identity and Trauma: Two Forms of the Will to Memory." *History & Memory* 16.1 (2004): 5–36.

Flath, James. "Managing Historical Capital in Shandong: Museum, Monument, and Memory in Provincial China." *Public Historian* 24.2 (Spring 2002): 41–59.

Giersch, Charles Patterson. "Afterword: Why Kham? Why Borderlands? Coordinating New Research Programs for Asia." *Cross-Currents: East Asian History and Culture Review* (Honolulu, Hawaii), no. 19 (2016): 202–213.

Guyot-Réchard, Bérénice. "Reordering a Border Space: Relief, Rehabilitation, and Nation-Building in Northeastern India after the 1950 Assam Earthquake." *Modern Asian Studies* 49.4 (July 2015): 931–962.

Goldstone, Jack A. "Ideology, Cultural Frameworks, and the Process of Revolution." *Theory and Society* 20.4 (1991): 405–454.

Gottschang, Thomas R. and Diana Lary. *Swallows and Settlers: The Great Migration from North China to Manchuria*. Ann Arbor, MI: Ann Arbor Center for Chinese Studies, University of Michigan, ca. 2000.

Grenoble, Lenore A. and Lindsay J. Whaley. "Language Policy and the Loss of Tungusic Languages." *Language and Communication* 19.4 (October 1999): 373–386.

Groot, Gerry. *Managing Transitions: The Chinese Communist Party, United Front Work, Corporatism, and Hegemony*. New York, NY: Routledge, 2004.

Grundlingh, Albert. "Reframing Remembrance: The Politics of the Centenary Commemoration of the South African War of 1899–1902." In Hans Erik Stolten, ed., *History Making and Present Day Politics: The Meaning of Collective Memory in South Africa*. Uppsala: Nordiska Afrikainstitutet, 2007.

Hämäläinen, Pekka and Samuel Truett. "On Borderlands." *Journal of American History* 98.2 (September 2011): 338–361.

He, Baogang and Stig Thøgersen. "Giving the People a Voice? Experiments with Consultative Authoritarian Institutions in China." *Journal of Contemporary China* 19.66 (2010): 675–692.

Heilmann, Sebastian. "From Local Experiments to National Policy: The Origins of China's Distinctive Policy Process." *China Journal*, no. 59 (January 2008): 1–30.

Heilmann, Sebastian and Elizabeth J. Perry. "Embracing Uncertainty: Guerrilla Policy Style and Adaptive Governance in China." In Sebastian Heilmann and Elizabeth J. Perry, eds., *Mao's Invisible Hand: The Political Foundations of Adaptive Governance in China*. Cambridge, MA: Harvard University Press, 2011, 1–29.

Hershatter, Gail. *Dangerous Pleasures: Prostitution and Modernity in Twentieth Century Shanghai*. Berkeley, CA: University of California Press, 1997.

Hershatter, Gail. "Forget Remembering: Rural Women's Narratives." In Ching Kwan Lee and Yang Guobin, eds., *Re-envisioning the Chinese Revolution: The Politics and Poetics of Collective Memories in Reform China*. Washington, DC: Woodrow Wilson Center Press; Stanford, CA: Stanford University Press, ca. 2007, 69–92.

Hershatter, Gail. *Gender of Memory: Rural Women and China's Collective Past*. Berkeley and Los Angeles, CA: University of California Press, 2011.

Hong, Lysa. "Ideology and Oral History Institutions in Southeast Asia." In Patricia Pui Huen Lim and Chong Guan, eds., *Oral History in Southeast Asia: Theory and Method*. Singapore: Institute of Southeast Asian Studies, 1998, 33–46.

Jenco, Leigh. "New Communities for New Knowledge: Theorizing the Movement of Ideas across Space." In Leigh Jenco, ed., *Chinese Thought as Global Theory: Diversifying Knowledge Production in the Social Sciences and Humanities*. Albany, NY: State University of New York Press, 2016, 135–162.

Jones, Alisa. "Policy and History Curriculum Reform in Post-Mao China." *International Journal of Educational Research* 37 (2002): 545–566.

Koga, Yukiko. "'The Atmosphere of a Foreign Country': Harbin's Architectural Inheritance." In Anne Cronin and Kevin Hetherington, eds., *Consuming the*

Entrepreneurial City: Image, Memory, Spectacle. New York, NY: Routledge, 2008, 221–254.

Koga, Yukiko. *Inheritance of Loss: China, Japan, and the Political Economy of Redemption after Empire*. Chicago, IL: University of Chicago Press, 2016.

Kwong, Luke S. K. "Oral History in China: A Preliminary Review." *Oral History Review* 20.1/2 (April 1, 1992): 23–50.

Lanza, Fabio. *Behind the Gate: Inventing Students in Beijing*. New York, NY: Columbia University Press, 2010.

Lean, Eugenia. *Public Passions: The Trial of Shi Jianqiao and the Rise of Popular Sympathy in Republican China*. Berkeley and Los Angeles, CA: University of California Press, 2007.

Lee, Ching Kwan. "What Was Socialism to Chinese Workers? Collective Memories and Labor Politics in an Age of Reform." In Ching Kwan Lee and Yang Guobin, eds., *Re-envisioning the Chinese Revolution: The Politics and Poetics of Collective Memories in Reform China*. Washington, DC: Woodrow Wilson Center Press; Stanford, CA: Stanford University Press, ca. 2007, 141–165.

Lefebvre, Henri. *The Production of Space*. Transl. by Donald Nicholson-Smith. Blackwell, Oxford, 1991. Originally published in 1974.

Li Fangchun. "Making Revolution on the Mind: Fanxin and the Exercise of Thought-Power in the Land Reform Movement of Northern China (1946–48)." *Frontiers of Literary Studies in China* 6.4 (2012): 598–620.

Li Huaiyin. *Reinventing Modern China: Imagination and Authenticity in Chinese Historical Writing*. Honolulu, HI: University of Hawaii Press, 2012.

Lin Shangli. *Zhongguo gongchandang yu renmin zhengxie (The Chinese Communist Party and the People's Political Consultative Conference)*. Shanghai: Dongfang chuban zhongxin, 2011.

Liu, Lydia H. *Translingual Practice: Literature, National Culture, and Translated Modernity – China, 1900–1937*. Stanford, CA: Stanford University Press, 1995.

Lukin, Alexander. *The Bear Watches the Dragon: Russia's Perceptions of China and the Evolution of Russian–Chinese Relations since the Eighteenth Century*. Armonk, NY: M. E. Sharpe, 2003: 58–59.

Ma, Shu-Yun. "The Role of Power Struggle and Economic Changes in the 'Heshang Phenomenon' in China." *Modern Asian Studies* 30.1 (February 1996): 29–50.

Makley, Charlene. "'Speaking Bitterness': Autobiography, History, and Mnemonic Politics on the Sino–Tibetan Frontier." *Comparative Studies in Society and History* 47.1 (January 2005): 40–78.

Maynes, Mary Jo, Jennifer Pierce, and Barbara Laslett. *Telling Stories: The Use of Personal Narratives in the Social Sciences and History*. Ithaca, NY: Cornell University Press, 2008.

Min, Lin. "The Search for Modernity: Chinese Intellectual Discourse and Society, 1978–88 – The Case of Li Zehou." *China Quarterly*, no. 132 (December 1992): 969–998.

Mitter, Rana. "Behind the Scenes at the Museum: Nationalism, History and Memory in the Beijing War of Resistance Museum, 1987–1997." *China Quarterly* 161 (March 2000): 279–293.

Moore, Aaron William. "The Problem of Changing Language Communities: Veterans and Memory Writing in China, Taiwan, and Japan." *Modern Asian*

Studies. Suppl. China in World War II, 1937–1945: Experience, Memory, and Legacy. 45.2 (March 2011): 399–429.

Morson, Gary Saul and Caryl Emerson, *Mikhail Bakhtin: Creation of a Prosaics.* Stanford, CA: Stanford University Press, 1990, 30. Cited and discussed in Michael Berry, *A History of Pain: Trauma in Modern Chinese Literature and Film.* New York, NY: Columbia University Press, 2008, 7.

Mortimer, Dasa. "Wenshi Ziliao Narratives of Anti-Communist Resistance in Northwest Yunnan." Paper presented at Association of Asian Studies Conference, Toronto, March 18, 2017.

Mullaney, Thomas. *Coming to Terms with the Nation: Ethnic Classification in Modern China.* Berkeley and Los Angeles, CA: University of California Press, 2011.

Nakao, Katsumi. "Japanese Colonial Policy and Anthropology in Manchuria." In Jan van Bremen and Akitoshi Shimizu, eds., *Anthropology and Colonialism in Asia and Oceania.* Richmond, Surrey: Curzon, 1999, 245–256.

Naoki Sakai, "Introduction," in Naoki Sakai and Yukiko Hanawa, eds., *Traces I: Spectres of the West and Politics of Translation.* Hong Kong: Hong Kong University Press, 2002, v–xiii.

Nathan, Andrew J. *History of the China International Relief Commission.* Cambridge, MA: East Asian Research Center, Harvard University, 1965.

Perdue, Peter C., Helen F. Siu, and Eric Tagliacozzo, eds., *Asia Inside Out: Changing Times.* Cambridge, MA: Harvard University Press, 2015.

Perry, Elizabeth. "Studying Chinese Politics: Farewell to Revolution?" *China Journal,* no. 57 (January 2007): 1–22.

Pfoser, Alena. "Between Russia and Estonia: Narratives of Place in a New Borderland." Nationalities Papers. *Journal of Nationalism and Ethnicity* 42.2 (2014): 269–285.

Pickowicz, Paul G. "Memories of Revolution and Collectivization in China: The Unauthorized Reminiscences of a Rural Intellectual." In Rubie S. Watson, ed., *Memory, History, and Opposition under State Socialism.* Santa Fe, NM: School of American Research Press, 1994, 127–148.

Pieragastini, Steven. "Circular Lines: the History and Memory of Imperial Railways in Sino-Vietnamese Borderlands." Paper presented for panel "Memory-Making and the Construction of Collective Memory across East Asia's Twentieth Century." Association of Asian Studies Conference, Toronto, March 18, 2017.

Pincus, Leslie. "The Founding of the National Diet Library in Occupied Japan." In Francis Blouin and William G. Rosenberg, eds., *Archives, Documentation, and Institutions of Social Memory: Essays from the Sawyer Seminar.* Ann Arbor, MI: University of Michigan Press, 2007, 382–392.

Ping-Chun Hsiung. "Pursuing Qualitative Research from the Global South: 'Investigative Research' during China's 'Great Leap Forward' (1958–62)." *Forum: Qualitative Social Research* 16.3 (2015).

Prins, Gwyn. "Oral History." In Peter Burke, ed., *New Perspectives on Historical Writing.* University Park, PA: Pennsylvania State University Press, 2001, 120–155.

Reardon-Anderson, James. *Reluctant Pioneers: China's Expansion Northward, 1644–1937.* Stanford, CA: Stanford University Press, 2005.

Reilly, James. "Remember History, Not Hatred: Collective Remembrance of China's War of Resistance to Japan." *Modern Asian Studies* 45.2 (March 2011): 463–490.

Rozman, Gilbert. "China's Soviet Watchers in the 1980s: A New Era of Scholarship." *World Politics* 37.4 (July 1985): 435–474.

Schwarcz, Vera. "Strangers No More: Personal Memory in the Interstices of Public Commemoration." In Rubie S. Watson, ed., *Memory, History, and Opposition under State Socialism*. Santa Fe, NM: School of American Research Press, 1994, 45–64.

Selden, Mark. *China in Revolution: The Yenan Way Revisited*. Armonk, NY: M. E. Sharpe, 1995.

Shao Dan. *Remote Homeland, Recovered Borderland: Manchus, Manchoukuo, and Manchuria, 1907–1985*. Honolulu, HI: University of Hawaii Press, 2011.

Siegelbaum, Lewis H. "Another 'Yellow Peril': Chinese Migrants in the Russian Far East and the Russian Reaction before 1917." *Modern Asian Studies* 12.2 (1978): 307–330.

Silber, Irina. "Commemorating the Past in Postwar El Salvador." In Daniel J. Walkowitz and Lisa Knauer, eds., *Memory and the Impact of Political Transformation in Public Space*. Durham, NC: Duke University Press, 2004, 211–231.

Simon, Roger. *Gramsci's Political Thought: An Introduction*. London: Lawrence and Wishart, 1982.

Smith, Aminda M. *Thought Reform and China's Dangerous Classes: Reeducation, Resistance, and the People*. Lanham, MD: Rowman and Littlefield, 2012.

Spence, Donald P. *Narrative Truth and Historical Truth: Meaning and Interpretation in Psychoanalysis*. New York, NY: W. W. Norton, 1980.

Strauss, Julia. "Morality, Coercion and State Building by Campaign in the Early PRC: Regime Consolidation and after, 1949–1956." *China Quarterly*, no. 188 (December 2006). Special Issue: History of the PRC (1949–1976): 891–912.

Su Xinliu. "Lüping henan zhenzai hui huodong shimo" ("History of the Activities of the Henan-in-Beiping Disaster Relief Organization"). *Nandu xuetan* (February 2004).

Suleski, Ronald. "Regional Development in Manchuria: Immigrant Laborers and Provincial Officials in the 1920s." *Modern China* 4.4 (October 1978): 419–434.

Sullivan, Lawrence. "The Controversy over 'Feudal Despotism': Politics and Historiography in China, 1978–82." In Jonathan Unger, ed., *Using the Past to Serve the Present: Historiography and Politics in Contemporary China*. New York, NY: Routledge, 1993, 174–204.

Tagliacozzo, Eric. *Secret Trades, Porous Borders: Smuggling and States along a Southeast Asian Frontier, 1865–1915*. Reprint edn. New Haven, CT: Yale University Press, 2009.

Taylor, Charles. "Social Theory As Practice," *Philosophical Papers* 2 (1985): 98. Cited in Leigh Jenco, ed., *Chinese Thought as Global Theory: Diversifying Knowledge Production in the Social Sciences and Humanities*. Albany, NY: State University of New York Press, 2016, 4–5, 7–8.

Thøgersen, Stig and Søren Clausen. "New Reflections in the Mirror: Local Chinese Gazetteers (Difangzhi) in the 1980s." *Australian Journal of Chinese Affairs* 27 (January 1992): 161–184.

Tian Fang. *Zhongguo yimin shilue* (Brief History of Chinese Migration). Beijing: Zhi shi chubanshe: Xinhua shudian, Beijing faxing suo faxing, 1986.

Tong Lam. *A Passion for Facts: Social Surveys and the Construction of the Chinese Nation-State, 1900–1949*. Berkeley and Los Angeles, CA: University of California Press, 2011.

Townsend, James R. *Political Participation in Communist China*. Berkeley and Los Angeles, CA: University of California Press, 1969.

Tsai, Kellee. "Adaptive Informal Institutions and Endogenous Institutional Change in China." *World Politics* 59.1 (October 2006): 116–141.

Tucker, David. "City Planning without Cities: Order and Chaos in Utopian Manchukuo." In Mariko Tamanoi, ed., *Crossed Histories: Manchuria in the Age of Empire*. Honolulu, HI: Association for Asian Studies and University of Hawaii Press, 2005, 53–81.

Unger, Jonathan. "The Class System in Rural China: A Case Study." In James L. Watson, ed., *Class and Social Stratification in Post-Revolution China*. London: University of London and the Contemporary China Institute, Joint Committee on Contemporary China, 1984.

van Slyke, Lyman. *Enemies and Friends: The United Front in Chinese Communist History*. Stanford, CA: Stanford University Press, 1967.

Verdeja, Ernesto. "Political Reconciliation in Postcolonial Settler Societies." *International Political Science Review* 38.2 (March 2017): 227–241.

Vickers, Edward and Alisa Jones, eds., *History Education and National Identity in East Asia*. New York, NY: Routledge, 2005.

Waldron, Arthur. "China's New Remembering of World War II: The Case of Zhang Zizhong." Special Issue: War in Modern China. *Modern Asian Studies* 30.4 (October 1996): 945–978.

Wang Ban. *Illuminations from the Past: Trauma, Memory, and History in Modern Cinema*. Stanford, CA: Stanford University Press, 2004.

Wang Xiting. *Xiangma yingzhang zong siling: wang delin zhuan (Bandit, Regiment Head and Supreme Commander: A Biography of Wang Delin)*. Harbin: Heilongjiang renmin chubanshe, 1987.

Wang Zheng. *Never Forget National Humiliation: Historical Memory in Chinese Politics and Foreign Relations*. New York, NY: Columbia University Press, 2012.

Weber, Torsten. "Forgetting and Forgiving: The Relation between Memory and Historical Reconciliation in Post–World War Two Japanese–Chinese Relations." Paper presented for panel "The Operations of Forgetting: Wars and the Making of the Asia-Pacific Region from the 17th Century to the Present." Association of Asian Studies Conference, Toronto, March 18, 2017.

Wei, C. X. George. "Mao's Legacy Revisited: Its Lasting Impact on China and Post-Mao Era Reform." *Asian Politics & Policy* 3.1 (January 2011): 3–27.

Weigelin-Schwiedrzik, Susanne. "In Search of a Master Narrative for 20th-Century Chinese History." *China Quarterly*, no. 188. History of the PRC, 1949–1976 (December 2006): 1070–1091.

Weiner, Benno. "State Commemoration of Tibetan Anti-State Resistance in Qinghai's *Wenshi Ziliao*: Rebellion in Three Frames." Paper presented at Association of Asian Studies Conference. Toronto, March 18, 2017.

Wemheuer, Felix. "Dealing with Responsibility for the Great Leap Famine in the People's Republic of China." *China Quarterly* 201 (March 2010): 176–194.

Whitlock, Gillian. "Review Essay: The Power of Testimony." *Law and Literature* 19.1 (Spring 2007): 139–152.

Wolff, David. *To the Harbin Station: The Liberal Alternative in Russian Manchuria, 1898–1914*. Stanford, CA: Stanford University Press, 1999.

Womack, Brantly. "Modernization and Democratic Reform in China." *Journal of Asian Studies* 43.3 (May 1984): 417–439.

Wright, Tim. "'The Spiritual Heritage of Chinese Capitalism': Recent Trends in the Historiography of Chinese Enterprise Management." In Jonathan Unger, ed., *Using the Past to Serve the Present: Historiography and Politics in Contemporary China*. New York, NY: Routledge, 1993, 205–238.

Xu Chenggang. "The Fundamental Institutions of China's Reforms and Development." *Journal of Economic Literature* 49.4 (December 2011): 1076–1151.

Yan Xiaojun. "Regime Inclusion and the Resilience of Authoritarianism: The Local People's Political Consultative Conference in Post-Mao Chinese Politics." *China Journal*, no. 66 (July 2011): 53–75.

Yan Yunxiang. "The Impact of Rural Reform on Social and Economic Classification in a Chinese Village." *Australian Journal of Chinese Affairs* 27 (January 1992): 1–23.

Yang, Lijun and Lim, Chee Kia. "Three Waves of Nationalism in Contemporary China: Sources, Themes, Presentations and Consequences." *International Journal of China Studies*. Special Issue *Dissent before and since Post-Mao Reforms* 1.2 (October 2010): 461–485.

You, Xiaoye. "Ideology, Textbooks, and the Rhetoric of Production in China." *College Composition and Communication* 56.4 (June 2005): 632–653.

Yu Liu. "Maoist Discourse and the Mobilization of Emotions in Revolutionary China." *Modern China* 36.3 (2010): 329–362.

Yu Shaoxiong. "The Northeast Anti-Japanese United Army Generals." Heilongjiang People's Publishing House, 2009. Retrieved online at http://www.biographypdf.cc/military-figures/86579633145039193276.html.

Zatsepine, Victor. *Beyond the Amur: Frontier Encounters Between China and Russia, 1850–1930*. Vancouver: UBC Press, 2017.

Zatsepine, Victor. "The Blagoveshchensk Massacre of 1900: The Sino–Russian War and Global Imperialism." In Norman Smith and James Flath, ed., *Beyond Suffering: Recounting War in Modern China*. Vancouver, BC: University of British Columbia Press, 2011, 107–129.

Zhang, Xiaoling. *The Transformation of Political Communication in China: From Propaganda to Hegemony*. Series on Contemporary China, vol. 29. Singapore: World Scientific Publishing Company, 2011.

Index

agriculture, 27, 37, 49, 52, 53, 63, 76, 82, 83, 94, 105, 123, 152, 167, 169, 170, 191, 217, 220, 228
Aihun, 68, 259
All-Workers' Union, 226
Amur Province, 66
Amur River, 1, 54, 69, 101, 102, 144
An Linhai, 97, 98, 174, 175, 183, 184, 266
Anti-Japanese Salvation Association, 188
Anti-Rightist Campaign. *See* campaigns
Anti-Spiritual Pollution Campaign. *See* campaigns
Anzaldua, Gloria, 10, 46
apartheid, 13, 155
Arseniev, V.K., 145, 147
Assam, 95, 273
Assmann, Aleida, 158
Assmann, Jan, 158
Association of Science and Technology, 245
authoritarianism, 4, 19, 22, 255, 256

Bakhtin, Mikhail, 156, 157
Bakiner, Onur, 158
banditry, 49, 52, 56, 93, 104, 142, 146
Banner system, 11, 144
Baoqing, 97, 250
Barmé, Geremie, 211
Bayan, 189, 250, 251
Beijing, 12, 27, 32, 38, 40, 55, 68, 93, 120, 160, 162, 176, 189, 195, 196, 198, 233, 244, 250, 253, 262, 267, 268, 275, 278
Beiyang, 178
Benjamin, Walter, 15
big character poster (*dazibao*), 41
Blackburn, Kevin, 175

Blagoveshchensk, 1, 66, 67, 68, 69, 70, 71, 72, 73, 100, 102, 135, 184, 259, 267, 268, 279
Blagoveshchensk Massacre, 68
Bohai Sea, 70, 151
Bol, Peter, 216
bourgeoisie, 65, 79, 111, 130
Boxer Uprising, 68, 104, 117, 185
Buddhism. *See* religion
Bukui (Qiqihar), 87
Bulag, Uradyn, 9, 48, 78, 176, 259
Bureau of Water Resources, 225
bureaucracy
    "bureaucratic capitalism," 30
    "quality control," 116
    accountability, 21
    and migration, 58
    and political mobilization, 207, 210
    and United Front, 5, 21, 201
    influence on local identities, 252–253, 254
    overlap with Party, 166
    PPCC's place in and collaboration with, 32, 105, 175
    professionalization and rationalization, 20, 110, 223, 254, 256
    re-integration, 223, 225–232, 250
    role in publishing and circulation, 212, 218, 219
    top-down and bottom-up, 232–236
business. *See* commerce

campaigns
    "Great Northern Wilderness" (*Beidahuang*), 53
    "speaking bitterness" and "recalling bitterness and reflecting on sweetness," 123, 204
    and intellectuals, 181
    and United Front, 21, 37

Anti-Rightist Campaign, 3, 6
Anti-Spiritual Pollution Campaign, 22
Campaign to Wipe Out Hidden
  Counterrevolutionaries, 6
Hundred Flowers Campaign, 32
legacies and memories, 83
local appropriation of, 242, 246
Maoist campaigns, 15, 32, 116
mobilization for, 43
model emulation, 247, 248
nationalist education, 229
oral history, 185
Rectification Campaign, 14
re-education, 32, 192, 237
retreat from, 146, 162, 165, 223
Canada, 195
Canton (Guangzhou), 37
Cao Mingren, 120, 188, 261
capitalism
  "red capitalists," 22
  "bureaucratic capitalism," 30
  and Soviet Union, 130, 136
  post-Mao re-evaluation, 27, 54–56, 59,
    62–66, 79–85, 90, 121
  target of socialist campaigns, 30, 32, 37
  theories of, 224
Central Party Committee (Central
  Committee), 38, 47, 132
CER Incident (Chinese Eastern Railroad
  Incident), 131, 132, 265
Changchun, 62, 93, 214, 251, 264
Chaoyang, 188
Chen Rongjiu, 240, 245, 246, 270
Chen Yun ("Feeling the stone while
  crossing the river"), 21
Chengji Needle Factory, 65
China Democratic League, 35
Chinese Academy of Social Sciences
  (CASS), xi, xiii, 256
Chinese Communist Party
  and borderland identities, 60–66
  cultural production, 23–25, 28–29
  historical identity, 36–42, 46–53,
    130–140
  ideology, 22–23
  nationalist turn, 79–82, 85–87,
    95–104, 109
  overseas connections, 186–198, 200–204
  political mobilization, 4–9, 20–22
  post–Cultural Revolution
    reconsolidation, 1–3, 13–16
  professionalization, quality control, and
    education, 20, 110–113, 115–116
  re-education and rehabilitation, 82–84,
    180–184

Chinese Medicine Institute, 215
Chinese-American, 61
Chongqing, 218
chuang guandong ("bursting east of the
  pass"), 146
churches. See religion
citizenship, 86
Civil Administration Department, 105, 246
civil war
  GMD-CCP, 146, 149, 150
  Soviet Union, 130
clan, 66
class struggle, 8, 30, 41, 47, 60, 64, 85, 121,
  124, 161, 202
classification, 104, 122, 123, 176, 211,
  212, 214
collaborators, 27
colonialism. See also imperialism
  and ethnic minorities, 107, 109
  and regional identity, 46
  anti-colonial resistance, 18, 49
  borderland characteristics, 4, 10, 16, 45,
    73, 74, 75, 81, 253, 258
  Chinese colonialism, 77–78
  colonial modernity, 12, 113
  enclaves and concession areas, 37
  nationalist history of, 97, 101, 108
  nostalgia for, 87–90, 231, 232, 260
Comintern, 5, 36
commerce, 1, 16, 35, 42, 48, 60–74, 79–84,
  87–95, 105, 109, 128, 133–137, 169,
  228, 231, 238
communism
  historical conceptualizations, 37, 38,
    51–52
  Maoist practices, 202–204
  post-communist transitions, 156–157
  post-Mao re-evaluation, 7, 20, 22, 26,
    53–58, 100, 113, 118, 121, 124,
    131–138, 248
Communist Youth League, 214, 217
"complexity fever", 155
Concordia of Nationalities, 148
Confucius, 26, 52, 131
Constitution (People's Republic of
  China), 23
corruption, 49, 54, 166
cosmopolitanism, 104
Cossack, 66
County Cooperatives Federation, 175
Cui Yongjian, 208
cultural capital, 106, 203
Cultural Revolution, 1, 2, 3, 6, 7, 8, 13, 14,
  15, 20, 21, 22, 24, 26, 28, 33, 34, 35,
  41, 42, 43, 52, 82, 83, 85, 101, 106,

113, 115, 118, 122, 124, 140, 155, 157, 159, 160, 163, 172, 173, 178, 181, 188, 191, 201, 204, 208, 209, 225, 231, 238, 239, 241, 247, 273
currency, 58
Czech Republic, 156

Dagurs, 11
Dai Zhenhuan, 159, 160, 161, 192, 193, 262
Dalian, 247
Daoism. *See* religion
Daqing, 171, 238
Dayang. See currency
democracy. *See also* democratic centralism; People's Political Consultative Conference
  "democratic revolution," 48
  consultation and supervision, 165–170, 230
  Maoist interpretations, 8
  parties, 29, 31, 32, 35, 196, 209, 226
  political transition, 13, 155
Democracy Wall, 21
democratic centralism, 30, 119, 157, 224
Democratic National Construction Alliance, 79
Democratic National League, 29
Democratic People's Youth League. *See* youth leagues
Deng Jiemin, 61
Deng Xiaoping, 21, 111, 123, 160
Deng Yingchao, 42, 125, 126, 162, 203, 205, 263
Dengist, 7, 182
dialectical materialism, 26, 116, 119, 124, 125, 126, 138
diaocha (investigation), 5, 82, 83, 185, 262
Ding County, 256
Discipline and Inspection Office, 226
discourses. *See* ideology
Dongbei. See Harbin; Heilongjiang; Jilin; Liaoning; Manchuria; Three Northeast Provinces
dragon wings, 2, 101
Du Jianshi, 40, 205, 262
Duan Qirui, 178
Duluhe, 55

Eastern Europe, 13, 155
education, 2, 42, 48, 49, 61, 86, 97, 169, 170, 199, 226, 228, 231, 238
  "civilizing" and modernizing campaigns, 167
  agencies, 171, 210
  educators, 80, 161, 173, 174, 197

local identity, 217–218
party reform, 20, 115
Party, PPCC, and bureaucracy, 34–35, 220, 226
patriotic education, 119, 120, 205, 238, 259
re-education, 6, 14, 15, 29, 30, 31–33, 57, 111, 113, 172, 177, 181–184, 190, 192, 194, 200, 202–203, 234, 235, 237
rehabilitation and re-evaluation of past, 39, 41
schools and school curricula, 27
social mobilization, 180, 186, 217–218, 221
youth, 59, 62, 229, 230
education bureaus, 27
elites
  civilizing mission, 12, 111, 143
  identities, 28
  mobilization, 9, 43, 176–177, 255
  persecution and rehabilitation, 8, 13–15, 158, 171–175, 181–184
  relationship to party-state, 78, 112, 198, 200–204
  United Front, 5–8, 21, 86, 159
enterprise. *See* entrepreneurs
entrepreneurs
  historical representations, 46, 50, 51–74, 90–95, 103–104, 122–124, 231
  rehabilitation, 18, 22, 26, 79–84
  United Front, 5, 162
Ethnic Classification Project, 110, 176, 256
ethnicity
  classification, 176, 256
  discourses and representation, 27, 101, 104–109, 145–149
  issues in borderlands, 4, 10–11, 18, 24, 45, 46, 77–78, 212, 258, 259
  minorities, 75
  nationalism, 41
European, 87
evidential learning (*kaozheng*), 12, 111
Expeditionary Army, 146
expertise, 5, 20, 21, 34, 43, 81, 83, 87, 110, 112, 115, 116, 160, 165, 166, 168, 169, 170, 181, 186, 200, 201, 202, 203, 207, 223
exploitation, 26, 55, 57, 67, 68, 70, 86, 96, 108, 137, 148, 149, 175, 177, 204, 229, 257

factories, 28, 48, 72, 79, 88, 191, 195, 210, 217, 228
famines, 124
Fan Dechang, 144, 145

Fan Wenlan, 117
Fangzheng County, 251
fanxin (turning the mind), 177
Feng Yuxiang, 131
feudalism, 26, 30, 41, 48, 51, 52, 54, 91, 93, 95, 118
film, 102, 196, 214
Finance Administration Department, 175
foreigners, 54
forestry, 169
Foshan County, 145, 146
Four Cardinal Principles, 211
Four Modernizations, 35, 87, 171, 244, 267
Fujin, 16, 17, 48, 61, 62, 81, 82, 83, 84, 97, 98, 115, 120, 133, 134, 136, 142, 143, 151, 159, 160, 164, 165, 166, 167, 168, 169, 170, 171, 172, 173, 188, 189, 192, 193, 206, 217, 219, 220, 226, 227, 236, 247, 261, 262, 265, 267, 268, 269, 271
Fuma, 145
Fuyuan, 16, 17, 47, 106, 134, 159, 170, 171, 261, 267, 268, 269
Fuzengqing, 81, 268

gambling, 49, 56, 57, 166
Gang of Four, 15, 20, 157, 160, 273
gazetteers, 2, 27, 28, 35, 55, 99, 144, 231, 245, 249, 266, 268
German, 65, 71, 72
Guomindang (Nationalist Party), 2, 5, 26, 29, 37, 39, 40, 48, 52, 78, 112, 117, 131, 132, 138, 142, 145, 146, 150, 162, 181, 187, 192, 194, 195, 196, 197, 206, 221, 234, 259
gongkai (open), 9, 25, 200, 211, 222, 224
gongtong zhangling (Common Program), 30
governance. *See also* ethnicity; Truth and Reconciliation; People's Political Consultative Conference
    "feudal oppression," 54
    "handling contradictions," 37
    ethnic mobilization, 149
    famine relief, 58
    gender, 92
    local practices, 22, 101
    Manchukuo, 148
    multi-party, 29
    post-Mao, 22, 43, 77, 224, 232
    regime transition, 155, 156

rehabilitation, 81
scientific rationality as principle, 111
social classification, 123
social ills, 56
Soviet Union, 130
state building in borderlands, 53, 55, 75, 144
grain procurement, 167, 168
Gramsci, Antonio, 5, 6, 277
Grand Alliance, 142
Great Britain, 93, 147
Great Leap Forward, 3, 6, 13, 28, 33, 37, 38, 110, 225, 276
Great Northern Wilderness, 53, 225, 242
Guan Chengzheng, 115, 164, 166, 171, 174, 227, 236, 262
Guandi, 87
Guandongshan, 152
Guandu Mining Company, 54, 55
Guangdong, 72
Guangming Daily (*Guangming ribao*), 213
Guangxu, 54
Guanyinshan, 55
guerrilla (guerrilla-style politics), 4, 5, 21, 43, 148, 189, 226
Guo Chunhua, 39, 190, 192, 263

Han (Han Chinese), 11, 18, 108, 145, 147
Hangzhou, 251
Haraszti, Miklós, 211, 212
Harbin
    commemorative events, 214, 251
    commerce and industry, 61–66, 79–81, 238
    revisionist narratives, 75, 89–95, 230, 259
    Russian colonial identity and anti-Russian activities, 16, 75
    Sino–Russian CER conflict, 130–137
Harbin Daily News, 214
Harbin Daily Newspaper, 226
Harbin Progressive Women's League, 61
He Baojun, 229, 267
Hebei Province, 1, 70, 72, 80, 81, 90, 91, 93, 117, 122, 131, 134
Heihe, 1, 17, 66, 68, 69, 102, 103, 250, 261, 267

Heilong River, 55, 66, 67, 69
Heilongjiang
    and Chinese nation, 219, 244–247,
        249–252
    anti-colonial resistance, 88, 98–101
    commerce and industry, 55, 59, 64
    cross-border encounters, 101–104,
        222
    ethnic relations, 11, 104–109
    inter-regional cooperation, 247
    local-regional identities, 237–241,
        252
    multifaceted historical
        representations, 60
    northern Manchuria, 9, 17
    overseas connections, 189–197
    Russian presence, 45
Heilongjiang Provincial Publishing
    House, 220
Heilongjiang University, 164
Hejiang, 146
Heshang, 24, 275
Hezhe. *See* ethnicity
Hong Kong, xii, 114, 174, 192, 193, 195,
    197, 198, 213, 247, 267
Hong Xiuquan, 118
Hu Shi, 119
Huachangtai, 70, 71
Huaihai (Battle of), 117
Huang County, 81
Huang Yunmu, 236
huiyi lu (record of memories), 28
Hulan, 140, 141, 242, 243
Hulin, 97
Hunan, 162
Hundred Days Reform, 185
Hundred Flowers Movement, 14
Hungarian, 211
hygiene, 48, 171, 228, 247

ideology. *See* Chinese Communist Party;
    communism; dialectical materialism;
    imperialism
imperialism. *See also* Japan, Russia
    and borderland, 89–90, 96–101, 241,
        245–246
    and ethnic minorities,
        104–107
    and railroads, 93–94
    anti-imperialism, 11, 27, 28, 30, 61,
        84–87, 119, 187–189, 238, 260
    Chinese, 78
    economic, 63–65
in memoriam literature, 28
India, 95, 273

indoctrination. *See also* education; ideology;
    People's Political Consultative
    Conference
    "refinement," 121
    affective means, 161–164, 194
    model emulation, 247–248
    political study, 3, 31, 32, 116, 120, 177,
        181, 182, 191, 221
    within Party and PPCC organizations,
        220, 233, 235
industrialization, 48, 54–55, 63, 223,
        224, 228
    impact on ethnic minorities, 105
    in early PRC period, 30, 37
    industrialists, 61, 62, 63, 79–84, 101,
        128, 164, 165, 170, 206, 231, 238, 248
    nationalist discourses, 65, 69–73
    northern Manchuria, 89–95
industries. *See* commerce
Industry and Commerce Federation
    (Industrial and Commercial
    Federation), 79, 80, 206, 226, 263
intellectuals
    May Fourth Movement, 92
    mobilization, 209, 210
    political campaigns, 3, 32
    re-education, 31
    rehabilitation, 35
    relationship to party-state, 14, 18, 37–38,
        162–164, 165, 180–184, 234
    truth seeking movements, 12–13,
        111–112, 201–204, 256, 257
    United Front, 5, 29, 33, 159
internationalism, 31
Investigative Research (*diaocha yanjiu*), 5,
    8, 9, 12, 112, 113, 114, 157, 202, 203,
    222, 224, 255
Islam. *See* religion

Japan
    and ethnic minorities, 11, 104–108, 109,
        145, 147–149
    anti-Japanese struggle and narratives, 26,
        37, 47, 49, 52–53, 60–62, 64, 78, 79,
        85, 88–89, 93, 96–98, 100–101, 119,
        127, 131, 140, 187–189, 208, 214,
        217, 226, 229, 237, 240, 242,
        244–246, 253
    in Manchuria, 4, 17, 73, 75, 76, 154, 187
    oral history in, 28
    research ventures, 67
    trade with, 65, 103
Ji Hongfu, 145
Ji Wanshan, 64
Ji Xianlin, 216

Jiamusi, 51, 192, 235, 238
Jiang Jieshi (Chiang Kaishek), 118, 130, 131
Jiangqiao Campaign, 101, 188
jiangtie. *See* currency
Jiangxi Soviet, 37
Jianshang (evil merchant), 148
jiaohua (education-and-transformation), 177
Jiayin River (also, Jiayin County), 145, 149
Jilin, 17, 35, 62, 63, 93, 138, 152, 190, 191, 195, 237, 252, 264, 265
Jin Baichuan, 66, 184, 268
Jinchang Flourmill, 134, 135, 136
Jingqili River, 66
Jinman Valley, 58
Jixi, 63, 97, 167, 266
journals, 26, 28, 211, 214
Jurchen, 27

Kang Yefu, 80
kaocha (inspection), 185
Khabarovsk, 133
Kham, 10, 46, 77, 273
Korea, 78

labor
agriculture, 27
borderland development, 53, 96
discourse, 23
historical and literary representations, 28
migrant, 54–58, 67, 70–71, 75, 94, 143, 149–150
political classification, 82–83, 123
re-education and rehabilitation, 14, 112, 194
Lamaism. *See* religion
land development, 55, 56, 58
land reform, 48, 53, 60, 85, 123, 146, 228, 229
laobaixing, 92
Latin America, 13, 155
Lattimore, Owen, 56, 94, 145, 147, 148, 264
"learning from the masses", 185
Lefebvre, Henri, 11, 12, 76, 224, 275
Lei Feng, 23, 247, 248
Leting County, 62, 81
Li Baoman, 226
Li Chenglin, 84
Li Dazhao, 37
Li Hongzhang, 54
Li Jianbai (Li Jianbo), 64, 213, 215, 263
Li Jinghan, 256
Li Rongchun, 96, 210, 243, 266

Li Xingchang, 59, 60, 89, 128, 129, 264
Li Yichun, 138
Li Yongning, 194
Li Yunting, 81
Li Zehou, 23, 275
Liang Qichao, 111, 185, 201
Liaohe, 247
Liaoning Province, xi, 17, 62, 91, 93, 237, 247, 252, 263
liberalization
and local elites, 81–84
and party control, 257
and socialism, 63
bureaucracy, 20
cross-border interactions, 101–104
discourses, 10, 22
historical revisionism, 2, 45, 53–60, 79–81, 95
overseas connections, 189–198, 247
regime transition, 156
liberation. *See also* communism; imperialism; nationalism; revolution; socialism
Lin Feng, 244, 253
Lindian County, 188
Liu Banghou, 1, 2, 66, 68, 184
Liu Feilin, 34, 87, 101, 163, 179, 187, 196, 208, 214, 252, 264
Liu Guangcai, 146
Liu Qingqi, 66, 184, 268
Long March, 37, 216
Longjiang County, 217
Lü Lingui, 132, 265
Lü Mingyi, 105, 182, 241, 246, 265
Luan County, 122, 124
Luo Wenxiao, 168, 169, 265

Ma Kaiyin, 35, 163, 164, 167, 265
Ma Zhanshan, 101, 127, 237
Macao, 192, 198
Manchukuo, 47, 48, 49, 52, 53, 61, 73, 100, 105, 108, 147, 148, 149, 187, 208, 228, 228, 230, 250, 273, 278
Manchuria. *See also* Heilongjiang; Three Northeast Provinces; Three Eastern Provinces; *Dongbei*
border conflicts with Russia, 130–137
colonization and anti-colonial resistance, 73, 148, 237, 253
ethnic relations, 11, 18
migration and migrant enterprise, 54–55, 56, 70, 123, 124, 151–152
Northern Manchuria (*Bei Man*), 1, 5, 9, 11, 16, 17, 76–81, 87–104, 143, 254, 258

Manchus. *See also* ethnicity
Mao Zedong, 68
Maoism. *See also* Investigative Research;
    Mass Line; campaigns; United Front
market reform. *See* liberalization
Marriage Law, 92
martyr, 188, 189, 217, 240, 253,
    270
Marxism. *See* communism
Mass Line (*qunzhong luxian*), 4, 5, 7, 8, 9,
    112, 113, 157, 202, 203, 206, 222
masses, 8, 27, 58, 68, 92, 96, 112, 177, 185,
    202, 205, 207, 210, 215
May Fourth Movement, 92
mechanization, 170
medicine, 35, 48, 49, 65, 165, 167, 168,
    169, 171, 174, 228
Memorial Hall of the People's War of
    Resistance against Japan, 26
memorials, 87, 189
merchants. *See* entrepreneurs
migration
    border conflict, 2
    cross-border encounters, 101–104
    discourses, 143–145, 151–152
    enterprises and commerce, 16, 45–47,
        65, 79–81, 134
    ethnic encounters, 1, 66–74
    native place and clan, 123
    personal narratives, 50–52, 53–60,
        66–74, 90–95, 143–145, 196
    push factors, 124
    refugees, 58, 124, 229
    state-sponsored, 52, 53, 75
military, 4, 34, 40, 41, 42, 48, 66, 67, 68,
    69, 75, 76, 80, 86, 89, 91, 92, 101, 105,
    108, 124, 127, 130, 131, 134, 138,
    139, 143, 145, 146, 148, 149, 150,
    160, 189, 190, 191, 196, 213, 214,
    231, 279
Ming period (dynasty), 105, 111
Ming–Qing, 12, 111
mining, 54, 55, 56, 57, 67, 76, 144, 145,
    150, 167
Ministry of Education (MOEd), 27
minorities. *See* ethnicity
Mishan, 97
mobilization. *See* elites, entrepreneurs,
    intellectuals, political campaigns,
    United Front
"model civilized village", 167
modernization. *See also* bureaucracy; elites;
    entrepreneurs; Four Modernizations;
    industrialization
    bureaucratic rationalization, 223

colonialism, 87–95, 109
competing priorities, 111
discourses, 74, 124, 257, 258
economic and cultural elites, 79–82, 204
historical interpretations, 18, 45–50, 52,
    60, 61
integration of local communities,
    167–170
knowledge production, 8, 112, 152
migration and borderland, 143
mobilization, 257
northern Manchuria, 76, 77, 80
overseas connections, 194, 247, 254
Mongol. *See* ethnicity
Mongolia, 65, 259
monuments, 121, 189, 191
mosques. *See* religion
Mudanjiang, 167, 216, 238
Mulan County, 250
Muling River, 63
Muraviev, Nikolai, 66
museums, 26, 28, 42

Na Jie, 97
Nanjing Massacre Memorial Hall, 26
nationalism
    and local-regional identities, 28,
        144–152, 186–188, 237, 242, 245,
        251, 252–253
    and private enterprise, 66–74
    anti-imperialist, 30, 63–65
    anti-Japanese, 37
    anti-Russian, 1, 258
    borderland-centered, 4, 7, 75–109
    competing discourses, 45–50, 130–137,
        259–260
    education, 217, 229
    ethnicity, 11, 18, 41
    historiography, 26, 42, 118–119,
        125–127
    overseas Chinese, 196
    Party-centered, 43, 60–61, 201, 208
    political study sessions, 220–222
    state-sponsored, 175, 185
    united front, 7, 10, 115, 201, 203
"National unification" work groups
    ("National Reunification sub-
    committee"), 191, 192
native place. *See also* migration
neibu (internal), 9, 25, 200, 211, 212, 214,
    222, 224
Nenjiang, 101, 250
New York City (NYC), 196
newspapers, 24, 160, 195, 196, 214
Ni Yuande, 188

Niu Naiwen, 64, 89, 90, 215, 230, 231, 265
Northeast. *See Dongbei*
Northeast Allied Anti-Japanese Army, 85, 97, 149, 188, 189, 245, 279
Northeast Righteous and Brave Army, 85
nostalgia, 18, 78, 87, 88, 104, 140, 162, 191, 258, 260
People's Congress (National People's Congress), 30

objectivity (objectivism). *See also* bureaucracy
  discourses and philosophy, 23, 257
  historical inquiry, 90, 109–153, 176, 184–186, 187, 198, 213
  personnel recruitment, 20, 27
opium, 49, 52, 53, 76, 105, 144, 147, 148, 149, 228
"one country, two systems", 196
oral history. *See* all chapters
Oroqen. *See* ethnicity
overseas Chinese, 12, 27, 29, 35, 42, 113, 174, 186, 192, 193, 194, 195, 196, 213
Overseas Chinese Affairs Office, 226

Pan Enliang, 247, 262, 270
Party. *See* Chinese Communist Party
Party Academy, 243
Party history institutes, 2
Party History Office, 225
Party History Research Institute, 230, 235, 245
Party Secretary, 167
patriotism
  "political thought work," 121
  "seeking truth from facts," 126
  "spiritual civilization," 23
  anti-imperialist, 60, 64, 96, 97, 101
  commemorative sites, 246, 259
  competing meanings, 89
  education, 119, 238
  entrepreneurs, 52, 82
  historical re-evaluation, 26, 27, 131–133, 138, 187
  overseas Chinese, 197
  united front, 29, 124, 159–164, 173, 192, 200–222
Peace Preservation Army, 145, 150
peasant, 15, 37, 48, 122, 123, 124, 177
People's Daily (Renmin ribao), 213
People's Education Press, 27
People's Liberation Army (PLA), 146, 190

People's Political Consultative Conference (*Zhongguo renmin zhengzhi xieshang huiyi*). *See* all chapters
Perestroika, 101
Personnel Affairs Department, 175
pidgin, 75, 102
Pingyong University, 132
Pockmarked Wang, 65, 66, 262
policies. *See also* bureaucracy; Chinese Communist Party; ethnicity; governance; Maoism; People's Political Consultative Conference; political campaigns; United Front
  elites, 14
  intellectuals, 165
  Japanese and Manchukuo, 105, 148
  liberalization, 247
  private enterprise, 83–84
  promotion and enforcement of, 31, 167, 168–170
  restorative rehabilitation, 170–175
  retrenchment, 38
  Russian and Soviet, 67
  Taiwan, 189–198
  top-down and bottom-up processes, 22, 232–236, 241
Preservation Society, 142
professionalism. *See* bureaucracy
proletariat, 27
propaganda. *See* ideology
Propaganda Department, 191, 239
propaganda departments, 20
Protestantism. *See* religion
Pu Yi (Puyi), 39, 48
Public Security Bureau, 225, 228

Qilin Army, 146
Qing. *See also* evidential learning; Manchuria
  1898 reforms, 38
  artifacts, 86
  borderlands, 46, 53, 54, 143
  Boxer Rebellion, 117
  conflict with Russia, 75
  military, 139
Qingdao, 251
Qinghai (Amdo), 77, 212
Qiqihar, 87, 101, 179, 187, 188, 196, 197, 208, 238, 249, 251, 265
Qiulin Company, 72
Qu Puchen, 81, 268
Qu Yuan, 26, 273
qunxue, 201

radicalism, 32
radio, 24, 76, 89, 226
railroads. *See also* Chinese Eastern Railroad;
    imperialism; Jing-Feng railway; South
    Manchuria Railroad
Raohe, 16, 17, 48, 49, 52, 53, 96, 97, 105,
    107, 116, 121, 122, 125, 126, 174,
    175, 182, 183, 188, 207, 208, 209,
    210, 217, 225, 228, 229, 240, 241,
    242, 243, 245, 246, 247, 248, 250,
    261, 265, 266, 267, 269, 270, 271
reactionaries. *See* counter-revolutionaries
reconciliation, 3, 6, 7, 8, 9, 10, 13, 14, 16,
    17, 19, 24, 29, 33, 78, 85, 113, 143,
    153, 154, 155, 156, 157, 158, 173,
    193, 198, 199, 221, 225, 234, 255,
    256, 258, 259
Rectification Campaign. *See* campaigns
"redness", 43, 110, 115, 116
reeducation. *See* education
refugees. *See* migration
rehabilitation
    "dark" past, 52
    "middle peasant," 123
    affective community, 154–199
    historical figures, 26, 106, 131, 143
    persecuted elites, 14
    private enterprise, 64, 79–84
religion
    colonialism, 89
    ethnic minorities, 75, 108
    modernization and development,
        169
    revival and rehabilitation, 151, 170
    united front, 35, 42, 60, 213, 231,
        234
Republican period, 42, 55, 59
revolution
    1911 nationalist, 208, 213
    and colonialism, 77
    and market liberalization, 53–60
    and objective inquiry, 152
    and Russia, 90–95
    and United Front, 7, 53, 64, 85, 86, 87,
        90, 91, 94, 95, 96, 99, 100, 118, 125,
        132, 134, 135, 137, 159–161, 192,
        204, 208, 216, 230
    counter-revolutionaries, 26, 39, 40, 41,
        80, 84, 199, 234
    criteria for Party members and cadres, 20
    education and indoctrination, 216, 221
    narratives and interpretations, 4, 9, 10,
        47, 48, 111, 121, 124, 131–138, 142,
        151, 221, 232, 257

nationalist reinterpretation, 64, 84–87,
    95–101, 108, 118, 187–189, 208,
    253
Party ideology and identity, 37
Party's role, 40
pre-revolutionary, 34, 41
re-education, 177, 181
regional identities, 242
revolutionaries, 48
women, 228
Rong Mengyuan, 63, 116, 117, 138, 178,
    207, 208, 266
ruble. *See* currency
Russia. *See also* Chinese Eastern Railroad;
    colonialism; Harbin; Heilongjiang;
    imperialism; Manchuria; nationalism;
    policies; revolution
    anti-Russian resistance, 41, 46, 60, 64,
        66–74, 78, 79, 85, 96–101
    border issues, 54, 143, 190,
        222
    colonialism, 11, 49, 75–76, 87–95,
        199
    cross-cultural interactions, 101–104
    ethnic identities, 107–109
    re-evaluations of historical influence, 1,
        81, 114, 130–137, 258, 259

scar literature, 15, 28
schools. *See* education
science and technology
    "historical science," 110–153, 185,
        255–257
    as historical topic, 12, 42
    conferences, 227
    discourse, 23
    inspection and education, 167–170
    investigative research, 202
    political priorities, 34–36
    United Front, 5, 18, 86, 162, 246
"seeking truth from facts" (*shishi qiushi*), 12,
    13, 18, 25, 26, 109, 111, 113, 114,
    116, 117, 118, 119, 120, 122, 125,
    126, 127, 129, 140, 141, 142, 153,
    154, 158, 222, 235, 255, 256
Self-Strengthening, 54
sent-down youth, 52, 53
shamanism. *See* religion
Shandong Province, 1, 54, 62, 63, 70, 72,
    80, 81, 85, 90, 103, 128, 150, 151,
    273
Shanghai, 29, 36, 57, 58, 87, 89, 103, 196,
    262, 274, 275
Shanxi, 196, 208, 237, 251

Shen Meijuan, 36, 39, 41, 160, 162, 187, 195, 196, 266
Shen Zui, 39, 187, 195, 266
Shenyang, 75, 93, 132, 134
Shuangfagong, 134, 135
Shuanghesheng (Golden Rooster brand), 58, 59, 62, 197
Siberia, 54, 66, 67, 134, 261
Sichuan, 117, 182, 208
Singapore, 24, 175, 176, 272, 274, 279
Sino-Japanese War (Second Sino-Japanese War), 119
Sino-Vietnamese borderland, 87
Sixty-Four Villages East of the River (*jiangdong liushisi tun*), 1, 66, 67
Slovakia, 156
social science, 25, 99, 213, 231, 255
socialism
    education, 32
    gender, 92
    interpretations and applications, 30, 36–38
    mobilization for, 5, 20–21, 185, 200, 216, 220, 222, 230, 233, 242
    post-Mao re-evaluation, 3, 10, 18, 22–23, 47, 53–64, 74, 85–87, 90, 91, 95, 100, 108, 114, 119–125, 127, 131–137, 143, 151, 159–161, 187, 211
Solons, 11
Song (dynasty/period), 216
Songhua River, 16, 93, 133, 134, 188
Songjiang Hotel, 84
South Africa, 13, 14, 155, 156, 157, 180, 274
Southeast Asia, 65, 176, 274
Soviet Union. *See* Russia
speaking bitterness (*suku*), 9, 123, 177, 204
specialization. *See* bureaucracy
spiritual civilization, 22, 23, 97, 104, 105, 220, 233
standardization. *See* bureaucracy
State Council, 20
State Education Commission, 27
strikes, 64
subjectivity, 14, 23, 50
Suiling, 243, 270
Sun Changming, 83
Sun Weiben, 236
supply and marketing cooperatives, 174, 183
suzhi (human quality), 124, 257

Taian County, 247
Taiping Rebellion, 118, 185
Taiping Valley, 54, 55

Taiwan, 28, 91, 190, 191, 192, 193, 194, 196, 197, 198, 215, 221, 226, 247, 252, 271, 275
Tangshan, 93
Tangyuan County, 97, 217, 245, 250, 251
Taylor, Charles, 114
temples. *See* religion
textbooks, 26, 27, 28, 60
theater, 195, 214
Three Northeast Provinces (*Dongbei sansheng*), 17, 93, 252. *See also* Heilongjiang; Jilin; Liaoning; Manchuria
three first-hands, 156, 235, 256
Three People's Principles Youth League, 142
Three Self-Patriotic Movement, 170
Tiananmen Incident (Tiananmen Square Incident), 135
Tianbai Incident, 187
Tianfengyong, 81, 269
Tianfengyuan, 91, 94
Tianjin, 68, 93, 171, 244, 253
Tianxingfu flour mill, 61
Tibet, 77, 273
Tong Zhenyu, 138, 139, 178, 179, 180, 186, 266
Tonghe County, 250
Tongji company, 61
Tongjiang, 16, 58, 85, 86, 97, 106, 107, 261, 268, 270
Tongyongli, 70
towering wall literature, 157
trade. *See* commerce
transitional justice
    affective community and historical rehabilitation, 154–199
    truth and reconciliation, 13–16
treaties
    Aigun Treaty (Aihun Treaty), 66
    unequal treaties, 67, 88
truth and reconciliation. *See* transitional justice
TV (TV programming), 24, 26, 214, 216, 226
TVE (town and village enterprise), 220
two civilizations. *See* spiritual civilization

U.S., 193, 195
Uighur, 10, 77, 259
Unit 731, 100
united front (*tongyi zhanxian*). *See also* bureaucracy; education; elites; entrepreneurs; governance; intellectuals; nationalism; patriotism; People's

Political Consultative Conference; political campaigns; religion; revolution; science and technology
United Front Bureau, 41, 163
United States, 65
Ussuri (River), 11, 96, 134, 145, 229

vagrants, 202, 203
Vladivostok, 134

Wang Binzhang, 197
Wang Hui, 114
Wang Jinsheng, 84
Wang Lin, 104
Wang Mingkui, 88, 115, 215, 222, 241, 250, 267
Wang Mingxuan, 145
Wang Ruiyi, 54, 55, 56, 57, 58, 59, 144, 145, 146, 149, 267
Wang Shijie, 29
Wang Shusen, 65
Wang Weixing, 82
Wang Xingkun, 169, 170, 172, 173, 174, 236, 267
warlords, 131
Weber, Max, 223
Wen Zhongkui, 159, 267
wenshizhe (literature, history, philosophy), 216
West, the, 12, 23, 36, 54, 68, 73, 93, 111, 113, 185
Witte, Sergei, 49, 75
Women's Federation, 35
World War Two, 28, 29, 50, 158, 278
wounded literature, 157
Wu Baixiang, 61, 63, 64, 79, 164, 238, 267
Wu Peifu, 91, 92
Wuhan, 218
WW1 (World War One), 89

Xian Incident, 131
Xiao Hong, 140, 141, 142, 243
Xing Jinghuan, 51, 52, 90, 91, 92, 93, 95, 122, 124, 133, 135, 248, 249, 267
Xinhua news, 195
Xinjiang, 11, 65, 259, 272
Xu Rilu, 97
Xu Zhanhai, 165, 172, 173, 193, 194, 217, 218, 220, 267, 268
Xuantong, 122

yamen, 163
Yan Fu, 111, 114, 201
Yan Juqian, 249

Yanan Marxist Academy, 182
Yang Chao, 182
Yang Chengwu, 41, 42, 214, 221, 222, 232, 268
Yang Jingren, 233
Yang Jingyu, 191
Yantai, 145
Ye County, 70
Yellow Peril, 94, 277
Yellow Russia, 94
Yichun County, 144
Yifahe, 62, 264
yiku sitian (recalling bitterness and reflecting on sweetness), 9, 204
Yilan County, 250
Yili, 65
Yin Xingwen, 66, 69, 184, 268
Yonghezhan, 70
You Zhixian, 106, 268
Yuhuatai Martyrs Memorial Park, 26
Yunnan, 11, 77, 78, 110, 176, 259, 276

Zhang Fushan, 132, 133, 137, 138, 139, 140, 268
Zhang Jiazhou, 189
Zhang Jinsi, 188, 189
Zhang Jitai, 47, 134, 170, 171, 267, 268
Zhang Minghe, 82, 83, 165
Zhang Ruilin, 167, 168, 246, 266
Zhang Tingge, 59, 61, 62, 64, 79, 197, 264
Zhang Tong, 39, 41, 132, 213, 251, 269
Zhang Wenda, 164
Zhang Zhenbang, 52, 53, 96, 107, 116, 121, 124, 125, 126, 129, 207, 208, 210, 217, 225, 229, 230, 240, 241, 245, 246, 266, 269
Zhang Zuolin, 91, 131, 139
Zhangqiu, 80
Zhao Shangzhi, 149
Zhao Tian, 249
Zhao Yiman, 61
Zhao Yiya Incident, 23
Zhejiang, 196, 251
Zhenbao Island, 226
Zheng Chenggong, 190
Zhenyuan Company, 55
Zhi-Feng War, 91
Zhou Enlai, 3, 29, 30, 31, 33, 38, 39, 40, 41, 42, 48, 160, 162, 265, 269
Zhou Jimin, 82
Zhu Qinglan, 196, 251

Studies of the Weatherhead East Asian Institute
Columbia University

Selected Titles

(Complete list at: http://weai.columbia.edu/publications/studies-weai/)

Thought Crime: Ideology and State Power in Interwar Japan, by Max Ward. Duke University Press, 2019.

Statebuilding by Imposition: Resistance and Control in Colonial Taiwan and the Philippines, by Reo Matsuzaki. Cornell University Press, 2019.

Nation-Empire: Ideology and Rural Youth Mobilization in Japan and Its Colonies, by Sayaka Chatani. Cornell University Press, 2019.

The Invention of Madness: State, Society, and the Insane in Modern China, by Emily Baum. University of Chicago Press, 2018.

Fixing Landscape: A Techno-Poetic History of China's Three Gorges, by Corey Byrnes. Columbia University Press, 2018.

Japan's Imperial Underworlds: Intimate Encounters at the Borders of Empire, by David Ambaras. Cambridge University Press, 2018.

Heroes and Toilers: Work As Life in Postwar North Korea, 1953–1961, by Cheehyung Harrison Kim. Columbia University Press, 2018.

Electrified Voices: How the Telephone, Phonograph, and Radio Shaped Modern Japan, 1868–1945, by Kerim Yasar. Columbia University Press, 2018.

Making Two Vietnams: War and Youth Identities, 1965–1975, by Olga Dror. Cambridge University Press, 2018.

Engineering Asia: Technology, Colonial Development, and the Cold War Order. Edited by Hiromi Mizuno, Aaron S. Moore, and John DiMoia. Bloomsbury, 2018.

A Misunderstood Friendship: Mao Zedong, Kim Il-sung, and Sino–North Korean Relations, 1949–1976, by Zhihua Shen and Yafeng Xia. Columbia University Press, 2018.

Raising China's Revolutionaries: Modernizing Childhood for Cosmopolitan Nationalists and Liberated Comrades, by Margaret Mih Tillman. Columbia University Press, 2018.

Buddhas and Ancestors: Religion and Wealth in Fourteenth-Century Korea, by Juhn Y. Ahn. University of Washington Press, 2018.

Idly Scribbling Rhymers: Poetry, Print, and Community in Nineteenth Century Japan, by Robert Tuck. Columbia University Press, 2018.

Japan's Occupation of Java in the Second World War: A Transnational History, by Ethan Mark. Bloomsbury, 2018.

China's War on Smuggling: Law, Economic Life, and the Making of the Modern State, 1842–1965, by Philip Thai. Columbia University Press, 2018.

Forging the Golden Urn: The Qing Empire and the Politics of Reincarnation in Tibet, by Max Oidtmann. Columbia University Press, 2018.

The Battle for Fortune: State-Led Development, Personhood, and Power among Tibetans in China, by Charlene Makley. Cornell University Press, 2018.

Aesthetic Life: Beauty and Art in Modern Japan, by Miya Elise Mizuta Lippit. Harvard University Asia Center, 2018.

Where the Party Rules: The Rank and File of China's Communist State, by Daniel Koss. Cambridge University Press, 2018.

Resurrecting Nagasaki: Reconstruction and the Formation of Atomic Narratives, by Chad R. Diehl. Cornell University Press, 2018.

China's Philological Turn: Scholars, Textualism, and the Dao in the Eighteenth Century, by Ori Sela. Columbia University Press, 2018.

Making Time: Astronomical Time Measurement in Tokugawa Japan, by Yulia Frumer. University of Chicago Press, 2018.

Mobilizing without the Masses: Control and Contention in China, by Diana Fu. Cambridge University Press, 2018.

Post-Fascist Japan: Political Culture in Kamakura after the Second World War, by Laura Hein. Bloomsbury, 2018.

China's Conservative Revolution: The Quest for a New Order, 1927–1949, by Brian Tsui. Cambridge University Press, 2018.

Promiscuous Media: Film and Visual Culture in Imperial Japan, 1926–1945, by Hikari Hori. Cornell University Press, 2018.

The End of Japanese Cinema: Industrial Genres, National Times, and Media Ecologies, by Alexander Zahlten. Duke University Press, 2017.

The Chinese Typewriter: A History, by Thomas S. Mullaney. The MIT Press, 2017.

Forgotten Disease: Illnesses Transformed in Chinese Medicine, by Hilary A. Smith. Stanford University Press, 2017.

Borrowing Together: Microfinance and Cultivating Social Ties, by Becky Yang Hsu. Cambridge University Press, 2017.

Food of Sinful Demons: Meat, Vegetarianism, and the Limits of Buddhism in Tibet, by Geoffrey Barstow. Columbia University Press, 2017.

Youth for Nation: Culture and Protest in Cold War South Korea, by Charles R. Kim. University of Hawaii Press, 2017.

Socialist Cosmopolitanism: The Chinese Literary Universe, 1945–1965, by Nicolai Volland. Columbia University Press, 2017.

The Social Life of Inkstones: Artisans and Scholars in Early Qing China, by Dorothy Ko. University of Washington Press, 2017.

Darwin, Dharma, and the Divine: Evolutionary Theory and Religion in Modern Japan, by G. Clinton Godart. University of Hawaii Press, 2017.

Dictators and Their Secret Police: Coercive Institutions and State Violence, by Sheena Chestnut Greitens. Cambridge University Press, 2016.

The Cultural Revolution on Trial: Mao and the Gang of Four, by Alexander C. Cook. Cambridge University Press, 2016.

Inheritance of Loss: China, Japan, and the Political Economy of Redemption after Empire, by Yukiko Koga. University of Chicago Press, 2016.

Homecomings: The Belated Return of Japan's Lost Soldiers, by Yoshikuni Igarashi. Columbia University Press, 2016.

Samurai to Soldier: Remaking Military Service in Nineteenth-Century Japan, by D. Colin Jaundrill. Cornell University Press, 2016.

The Red Guard Generation and Political Activism in China, by Guobin Yang. Columbia University Press, 2016.

Accidental Activists: Victim Movements and Government Accountability in Japan and South Korea, by Celeste L. Arrington. Cornell University Press, 2016.

Ming China and Vietnam: Negotiating Borders in Early Modern Asia, by Kathlene Baldanza. Cambridge University Press, 2016.